Boulez, Music and Philosophy

While acknowledging that Pierre Boulez is not a philosopher, and that he is wary of the potential misuse of philosophy with regard to music, this study investigates a series of philosophically charged terms and concepts which he uses in discussion of his music. Campbell examines significant encounters which link Boulez to the work of a number of important philosophers and thinkers, including Adorno, Lévi-Strauss, Eco and Deleuze. Relating Boulez's music and ideas to broader currents of thought, the book illuminates a number of affinities linking music and philosophy, and also literature and visual art. These connections facilitate enhanced understanding of post-war modernist music and Boulez's distinctive approach to composition. Drawing on a wide range of previously unpublished documentary sources and providing musical analysis of a number of key scores, the book traces the changing musical, philosophical and intellectual currents which inform Boulez's work.

EDWARD CAMPBELL is a lecturer in the Music Department of the School of Education at the University of Aberdeen, where he coordinates the music education programmes and teaches courses in aesthetics, contemporary music, music education and visual culture. He is also a participant in the university's Centre for Modern Thought.

Music in the Twentieth Century

GENERAL EDITOR Arnold Whittall

This series offers a wide perspective on music and musical life in the twentieth century. Books included range from historical and biographical studies concentrating particularly on the context and circumstances in which composers were writing, to analytical and critical studies concerned with the nature of musical language and questions of compositional process. The importance given to context will also be reflected in studies dealing with, for example, the patronage, publishing and promotion of new music, and in accounts of the musical life of particular countries.

Titles in the series

Jonathan Cross
The Stravinsky Legacy

Michael Nyman
Experimental Music: Cage and Beyond

Jennifer Doctor
The BBC and Ultra-Modern Music, 1922–1936

Robert Adlington
The Music of Harrison Birtwistle

Keith Potter
Four Musical Minimalists: La Monte Young, Terry Riley, Steve Reich, Philip Glass

Carlo Caballero
Fauré and French Musical Aesthetics

Peter Burt
The Music of Toru Takemitsu

David Clarke
The Music and Thought of Michael Tippett: Modern Times and Metaphysics

M. J. Grant
Serial Music, Serial Aesthetics: Compositional Theory in Post-War Europe

Philip Rupprecht
Britten's Musical Language

Mark Carroll
Music and Ideology in Cold War Europe

Adrian Thomas
Polish Music since Szymanowski

J. P. E. Harper-Scott
Edward Elgar, Modernist

Yayoi Uno Everett
The Music of Louis Andriessen

Boulez, Music and Philosophy

Edward Campbell

CAMBRIDGE
UNIVERSITY PRESS

CAMBRIDGE UNIVERSITY PRESS

Cambridge, New York, Melbourne, Madrid, Cape Town, Singapore,
São Paulo, Delhi, Dubai, Tokyo, Mexico City

Cambridge University Press
The Edinburgh Building, Cambridge CB2 8RU, UK

Published in the United States of America by Cambridge University Press, New York

www.cambridge.org
Information on this title: www.cambridge.org/9780521862424

First published 2010

Printed in the United Kingdom at the University Press, Cambridge

A catalogue record for this publication is available from the British Library

Library of Congress Cataloguing in Publication data
Campbell, Edward C.
Boulez, music and philosophy / Edward Campbell.
    p.   cm. – (Music in the twentieth century ; 27)
ISBN 978-0-521-86242-4 (hardback)
1. Boulez, Pierre, 1925– Criticism and interpretation.   2. Music – 20th century – Philosophy
and aesthetics.   3. Music and philosophy.   I. Title.   II. Series.
ML410.B773C38   2010
780.92 – dc22   2010019221

ISBN 978-0-521-86242-4 Hardback

To my mother and my late father,
who first introduced me to music

Contents

Figures

Music examples

Tables

Acknowledgements

I am especially grateful to Arnold Whittall who saw a place for this study in the series *Music in the Twentieth Century*, and who throughout has provided invaluable help, responding to the text at each stage of its formation. I cannot thank him enough. Robert Piencikowski has been unstintingly generous and helpful in responding to my queries, sharing a great number of insights with me, allowing me to work from his transcriptions of Boulez's correspondence, and offering his comments on an early draft of the text. A great deal of material in Chapters 7–10 is a reworking of material which first appeared in my Ph.D. dissertation at the University of Edinburgh in 2000. In this regard I'd like to thank Professor Peter Nelson and Professor Raymond Monelle, who were my supervisors. Thanks to Adrian Wilding who read through some early drafts of Chapters 3 and 4 and who offered some very helpful suggestions. Thanks also to Pascal Decroupet, Peter O'Hagan, Pascale Criton and Michael Schwarz who responded to enquiries I made of them.

I am grateful to Pierre Boulez who has been generous in responding to a number of questions at different points in the project and who has kindly given permission for me to cite from his correspondence. Thanks also to his secretary Klaus-Peter Altekruse who generously facilitated these exchanges. Thanks to Professor Gilbert Amy who gave permission, on behalf of L'Association Pierre Souvtchinsky, for the publication of extracts from Souvtchinsky's correspondence.

A number of short trips were made in the course of this research. Thanks are due to the following: the staff of the Paul Sacher Stiftung in Basel, most especially to Robert Piencikowski, Michèle Noirjean-Linder, Evelyne Diendorf and Johanna Blask; the staff of Les Archives et Musée de la Littérature in Brussels, especially Jean Danhaive and Catherine Daems; the staff of the Bibliothèque nationale in Paris, especially Elizabeth Vilatte. Thanks are due to the British Academy for a small grant which made some of these trips possible.

Thanks to Aygün Lausch, Angelika Glatz and Ronald Kornfeil of Universal Edition, as well as Suzie Clement from the University of Aberdeen School of Education for the work they did on the examples and tables. I am grateful to the College of Arts and Social Sciences at the University of Aberdeen for the award of a small grant which contributed towards the cost of producing some of the musical examples and illustrations.

Published English translations of texts have been used where available, unless otherwise noted. All other translations, for example of correspondence and texts from French and German language books, are by the author, unless otherwise noted. I'd like to thank Gill Leach, Nick Nesbitt, Gitta Vernon and Frauke Jurgensen for occasional advice in translating French and German language texts.

I am grateful to Vicki Cooper, Becky Jones, Mary Worthington, Emma Walker and Rosina Di Marzo from Cambridge University Press who have been solicitous and supportive in helping me to complete this book. Thanks also to Penny Souster, who originally commissioned the project.

Finally I'd like to thank my family and friends, especially my partner Gill and my son Michael for their support and the many sacrifices they have made over the years that I have been working on this study.

Every effort has been made to contact all of the holders of copyright where this pertains and to seek permission from all institutions where research was undertaken. I gratefully acknowledge the permission given by the publishers and institutions for reproductions and examples, as detailed in the lists of music examples and figures.

Abbreviations

AML   Les Archives et Musée de la Littérature, Brussels
BN   Bibliothèque nationale, Paris
PSS   Paul Sacher Stiftung, Basel

1 Preparing the ground

Music and philosophy

Music and philosophy have been linked throughout the history of Western thought from the ancient Greeks onwards, and the history of musical aesthetics offers a rich panoply of creative encounters between sounding art and philosophical reflection. From the ambivalence of Plato's *Republic*, every period of music history has produced, together with the music of its time, a number of distinctive aesthetic concerns which have been pivotal for the creation and reception of its artworks. So it is that we can define a period in music history, at least in part, by the aesthetic issues surrounding the art of musical composition. From the time of the ancient Greeks to the Renaissance and beyond philosophers and musicians argued the relative merits of a rhetorical, language-based model for music as opposed to a mathematical paradigm. At different moments, questions of representation, musical expression, organicism, formalism, to cite only a few key terms, have assumed critical importance as composers have attempted to create a music for their time and as philosophers, musicians and theorists of less certain designation have striven to discuss new music conceptually and to define the issues which surround it.

The very word 'aesthetics', however, is rather slippery and difficult to pin down since aesthetic writings derive from more than one source. While aesthetics proper is a branch of philosophy, and many philosophers have produced aesthetic theories, we also speak of practising artists, writers and musicians as working on aesthetics when they attempt to articulate and conceptualise the aspirations and values within their creative practice. While philosophical aesthetics often attempts to produce a theory of art, albeit there are many radically different theories, practising artists and composers tend more to discuss the particular issues surrounding the production and reception of their works. While we can recognise significant aesthetic elements in the writings of ancient philosophers such as Plato and Aristotle, modern philosophers such as Kant, Schelling, Hegel and Schopenhauer have produced much more systematic reflections, which attribute to music greater or lesser importance in relation to the other arts, and within their overall visions of the world. Furthermore, there are clear divisions within philosophical aesthetics itself, and today we can choose from a wide range of positions, from Adorno's dialectical aesthetic theory, Gadamer's hermeneutic aesthetics, Merleau-Ponty's phenomenological aesthetics or even Scruton's approach from within the analytical tradition of philosophy, to name only a few.

Arising out of this spectrum of positions is the obvious problem that while philosophical aesthetics may be strong on philosophy, its practitioners are often less credible when tackling questions pertaining to specifics within the individual arts. So it is that not many writers have been equally competent in the fields of both music and philosophy, more commonly being either composers and/or music theorists or philosophers. The aesthetic theories of Kant, Schelling and Hegel, for example, all fall short in relation to music and it has more often been the case that their ideas have been applied later, with varying degrees of success, by lesser thinkers with greater musical understanding. The musical formalism which arose in the second half of the nineteenth century, and of which Eduard Hanslick is the best remembered exponent, is a case in point, having its roots in Kant's Third Critique, which found aesthetic form to be the most distinctive element within an artwork. Indeed, philosophers with acute musical sensibility and understanding have been rare, and Schopenhauer and Nietzsche in the nineteenth century as well as Adorno in the twentieth stand out as keen exceptions, with the second- and third-named also pursuing musical composition. The constellation linking Wagner with Schopenhauer and Nietzsche is particularly interesting in this regard and it provides a rare example in the history of musical aesthetics in which philosophers and composers may be said to have reached a high level of mutual understanding. In the normal run of things success is generally mixed when composers attempt to discuss their work from aesthetic or philosophical points of view, though this phenomenon has become more common among late twentieth-century or early twenty-first-century composers. While this may result, at least in part, from changes in educational practices, it may also reflect developing perspectives with regard to the nature of music.

Within musical modernism, composition is often accepted as a form of thinking which is intimately related to wider currents of thought, including philosophy. In a tradition of thought which may be traced to Schelling's philosophy of identity, and in particular to the work he produced between 1800 and 1804, a number of twentieth-century philosophers have articulated a range of views which, in common, recognise in art/music and philosophy two dependent and complementary elements. For Adorno, the analysis of new music should be fertile in producing philosophical insight just as philosophical reflection is intrinsically linked to the very condition of contemporary music.[1] In the work of Boulez and others, he acknowledges a necessary relationship linking reflective aesthetics with artistic technique, and philosophy and art are recognised as existing in a relation of mutuality whereby one serves to articulate aspects of thought which forever remain beyond what the other can capture. In this way philosophy ponders the truth content of art while art itself articulates those moments which evade philosophical expression. Adorno goes so far as to suggest that the composer needs a certain philosophical competence to enable her/him to work through the inevitable problems which arise in composition. However, he is also conscious of the danger whereby a composer or theorist may artificially inject into an artwork a dose of philosophy which can only remain extraneous to its working.[2] In a similar way, Umberto Eco considers certain works of modern art, including the music of the post-war avant-garde, to be 'epistemological metaphors', in that their structures present us with possible ways of knowing. For Lyotard, the preoccupation with space and time within avant-garde music, taken together with the frequent musical examples used to illustrate modern philosophies of time, clearly demonstrates the relationship of mutual support in which both activities are engaged.[3] Finally, the rhizomatic image of thought conceptualised by Deleuze and Guattari, in opposition to the more traditional, arborescent image of Western thought, is similarly fleshed out in musical terms, and they contrast the arborescent, tonal system of Western music with a kind of 'generalised chromaticism' in which all of the sound components, namely duration, intensity, timbre and attack, are placed in 'continuous variation' and through which music becomes 'a superlinear system, a rhizome instead of a tree'.[4] While John Cage is credited with having first produced such music, Boulez's metaphor of composition as the weed-like proliferation of musical material provides justification for Deleuze and Guattari to describe it also as rhizomatic.[5]

While it is clear that these writers differ from one another in significant ways, they nevertheless provide a philosophical basis for the present study in their common conviction that artworks and aesthetic reflection exist in a relationship which can be mutually illuminating. The fact that they have all also attempted, to greater or lesser degrees, to discuss Boulez's work philosophically or to use his concepts in new contexts lends further support to the view that his music and writings merit such consideration.

---

[1] Adorno 2002, 148. [2] Adorno 1997, 341. [3] Lyotard, in Samuel 1986, 16–17.
[4] Deleuze and Guattari 1988, 95. [5] Deleuze and Guattari 1988, 519.

Boulez and philosophy

Having provided a brief introduction to the relationship linking music and
philosophy both historically and in the thought of some more recent figures,
it must now be stated unequivocally that Pierre Boulez is not a philosopher.
While he acknowledges having read works by Descartes, Rousseau, Nietzsche, Foucault, Deleuze, Derrida and others, it would be foolish to attempt
to argue that he is in any sense a philosopher. From his early writings in the
late 1940s, he has drawn upon a wide range of literary and artistic figures
whose work has been absorbed into his own aesthetic, and whose ideas
are much more likely to be cited by him than any philosopher. The poets
René Char and Stéphane Mallarmé, as well as the artist Paul Klee, have
been particularly important for him, but they take their place among a large
number of creative figures whose influence he acknowledges. While Boulez's
published writings and interviews are fairly voluminous, explicit references
to philosophers are rare. While there are occasional, and not always significant, references to Descartes, Rousseau, Nietzsche, Husserl, Sartre and
Deleuze, such moments are often aphoristic and do not usually result in
any kind of sustained exploration which could be described as genuinely
philosophical.

Boulez has addressed the relationship between music and philosophy on
several occasions in his writings, though not always in the most favourable
of terms. He warns against the arbitrary connections which historians and
aestheticians can all so easily make,[6] while at the same time acknowledging
'some equivalence' between contemporary music and certain aspects of
modern mathematics and philosophy.[7] He is wary of the high turnover
of philosophical ideas and of any suggestion that music is dependent on
philosophy.[8] Recognising that philosophy may be used surrogately to divert
attention from a lack of musical meaning, he states that music 'cannot
undertake the task of expounding rational ideas', and that it will be untrue
to its own nature if it attempts to deal in concepts which are completely
foreign to it. Having said this, he concedes that music can qualify our
ideas.[9] He theorises that each historical period is marked by 'general lines
of force' which extend beyond the musical sphere and which characterise
important intellectual movements.[10] While he does not refer specifically
to philosophy in this regard, it undoubtedly forms a significant part of
the cultural constellation which he has in mind. At the same time, it is
important to note that this is not a question of merely applying philosophical
concepts to musical composition or of musical compositions acting simply

---

[6] Boulez 1971a, 14.   [7] Boulez 1991, 143.   [8] Boulez 1986, 74.
[9] Boulez 1986, 81.   [10] Boulez 1986, 121.

as conduits for philosophical concepts. Boulez has retained this ambivalence towards philosophy, in relation to music, right up to his Collège de France lectures (1976–95) and beyond. When questioned closely on philosophical matters he generally declares his lack of philosophical expertise, and he has spoken, for example, of his inability to keep up with Adorno when the philosopher embarked on more abstract discussion of aesthetic issues.

The lecture 'Nécessité d'une orientation esthétique' (1963) marks a moment when Boulez addressed the question of aesthetics more directly than at any other time. He begins with a frank acknowledgement of the grave suspicion harboured by the musicians of the serial generation towards the words 'aesthetic' and 'poetic' which led them to reject 'all aesthetic speculation as dangerous and pointless', while favouring the development solely of musical technique. While he suggests that this may be due to a 'lack of "culture"', to a legitimate reaction against 'precarious' philosophy and to a certain coyness on the part of composers in the face of more philosophically literate opinion, it may be that he believes there to be some validity in all of these charges.[11] It is clear from the round table discussions, in which he participated with Pousseur and Berio at Darmstadt in 1963, that aesthetic questions had finally arrived on the agenda. Recognising that his previous Darmstadt courses had focused on technical matters, he was now keen to redress the imbalance, and he expresses the desire that serial music be connected to wider aesthetic reflection and that it no longer be thought that the aesthetic work has been accomplished once the technical compositional problems have been solved.[12] While he perceives the technical and the aesthetic as enjoying a degree of independence from one another, they cannot be completely separated, and technical problems may in fact arise out of aesthetic considerations.[13]

While it has become almost commonplace to think of Boulez's work in relation to literature and visual art,[14] the present enquiry is based on the conviction that, despite his ambivalence, philosophical considerations are also significant in facilitating understanding of his music and ideas. To say so is not to make the present study dependent upon the extent to which he does or does not perceive philosophy to be integral to his compositional work, and it does not rely on the presence or absence of explicit philosophical citations.[15]

---

[11] Boulez 1986, 63.   [12] Nattiez 2005b, 26–7.   [13] Nattiez 2005b, 29–30.

[14] Stacey contextualises Boulez among 'the painters, poets and musicians who were influential in the formation of his language and style' (1987, p. viii). Samuel (1986) explores Boulez's links with Mallarmé, Proust, Joyce, Kafka, Klee, Eastern music and a number of Western composers.

[15] While François Nicolas minimises the place of philosophical thought in Boulez's aesthetic (www. entretemps.asso.fr/Nicolas/IM/), the present study is in agreement with André Souris, for whom the relationship linking music and philosophy is independent of any 'voluntary application of theories' by composers (Souris 2000, 23).

This study is predicated rather upon two factors, which when taken together make the rather compelling case that Boulez's music and writings are implicated at a number of levels with philosophical currents in a way that merits exploration. These are, in short, the existence of a series of philosophically charged terms and concepts which he uses in discussion of his music. These terms, as will become apparent, are not culled from any one organic philosophical system, but rather reflect a range of encounters which he has had with a spectrum of philosophical viewpoints and personalities. Indeed, he has made significant contact with, or at least his music has facilitated a notable response from, some of the most influential figures and philosophical currents from the second half of the twentieth century. While Boulez may not be steeped in particular aspects of philosophy and his philosophical knowledge may be basic or heavily mediated by others, significant currents and concepts are nevertheless clearly present within his writing and shape his thinking.

Creative encounters

When Boulez's career to date is considered from the point of view of philosophical ideas, five discrete moments suggest themselves as worthy of investigation. In Chapter 2 we will explore the development of the new music within the context of those movements which marked Parisian intellectual life during his formative years, and the influence in particular of Pierre Souvtchinsky, Boris de Schloezer, André Schaeffner and André Souris, four figures from an older generation, none of whom were professional philosophers, who were important in shaping his ideas. A number of related concerns can be identified which connect Boulez to some kind of dialectical philosophy. He uses the term 'dialectic' regularly in his writings, there are clear signs of negational thinking, particularly in his earlier works, and he employs a large collection of binary oppositions with which he conceptualises his practice throughout his career. He writes frequently of music having an evolutionary development and of a sense of historical necessity. This cluster of dialectical concerns will be considered in Chapter 3, as we explore their place within his aesthetic and how they may have been integrated within it from a number of musical and non-musical sources. Chapter 4 will then look to the specifics of Boulez's relationship with Adorno, whom he met at Darmstadt. Whatever practical problems Adorno experienced with the music of the post-war generation, he was, at least in theory, better qualified than anyone to think about new music in philosophical terms and to tease out its historical significance from a dialectical viewpoint. The development of serial thinking will be traced stage by stage as it unfolded in the contemporaneous writings of the serial composer and the dialectical philosopher, highlighting possible areas of influence, convergence and disagreement.

After this lengthy exploration of dialectical thinking we will shift in Chapter 5 to a brief consideration of a very different philosophical orientation, namely the tendency towards axiomatic, deductive thinking and the fascination with mathematics which is evident within Boulez's thought at the time of his 1960 Darmstadt lectures. Within these lectures he cites explicitly from the deductive axiomatics of Louis Rougier, from Léon Brillouin and indirectly from the mathematician Moritz Pasch. Deductive terminology has remained a standard part of Boulez's vocabulary since this time, but he has also, at times, been dismissed as an overly intellectual, blackboard composer and the accusation is made that his approach is somehow indecently mathematical, a charge which will be examined within this chapter.

Chapter 6 will consider Boulez and serialism in relation to the structuralism which came to dominate French thought in the late 1950s and 1960s. After identifying a series of concerns, for example with codes and structures, which, at least superficially, would seem to indicate some kind of commonality of interest between serialism and structuralism, the critiques of serialism produced by Ruwet and Lévi-Strauss, as well as the responses published by Eco and Pousseur, will be reviewed and evaluated. While Boulez does not respond on his own behalf in this debate, he is clearly a central figure as it is Boulezian serialism which mostly forms the basis for the discussion, and consequently, it is the epistemological and metaphysical nature of Boulezian serialism which is in question.

Structuralism was superseded in French thought after 1968 by a number of post-structuralisms which rejected codes along with traditional dialectics and posited instead the supremacy of difference over identity. Chapter 7 will briefly consider Boulez's relationship with the work of Foucault and Lyotard before providing a fuller reflection on certain aspects of Deleuze's philosophy which connect with Boulez in a number of ways. Boulez got to know Deleuze after his return to France in 1976 and it will be argued that some of the philosopher's concepts can be fruitful in understanding his ideas and music. It will also be shown how Deleuze, together with Guattari, adopted a number of Boulez's concepts which they integrated into their philosophy for their own purposes.

The final three chapters explore the working out of two key philosophical ideas in practice within Boulez's compositions, and mark a shift in emphasis from primarily philosophical/aesthetic discussion to the musical analysis of a number of scores. Chapters 8 and 9 consider Boulez's musical development from the point of view of the dialectic of identity and difference or more specifically of Deleuzian difference, a reading which Boulez implicitly offers in his Collège de France lectures, where his music is theorised at a number of levels in terms of the concept of the virtual. Chapter 10 will then look to the dialectic of the continuous and the discontinuous as it is manifested in the dialectically opposing musical spaces and times which Boulez theorised in his Darmstadt lectures, and which are significant elements within many of his compositions.

It would be false to suggest that each of these moments exists unilaterally in complete detachment from the others and, as Boulez's career progresses, aspects from all of these moments are found as integrated elements within his discourse. In the Collège de France lectures, for example, references to dialectics and deduction are found together with mentions of codes, difference, repetition and identity.

We will consider the nature of the relationships linking Boulez with each of these intellectual currents and their key representatives, their impact upon Boulez's work and the responses of some of these thinkers to his music and writings, as well as critically evaluating the legitimacy and significance of such connections. In practical terms, we will consider the historical facticity of Boulez's involvement with these philosophical ideas, drawing, where possible, upon whatever source material exists in terms of published texts, interviews and correspondence. We will proceed from there to consider the key issues linking composer, philosophers and ideas, through a patient detailing of the principal arguments which, as will become apparent, involve Boulez to varying degrees, before discussing and evaluating the issues which unite and divide them. An attempt will be made to identify the sources whereby such ideas have entered into Boulez's vocabulary. At times this will involve viewing his ideas in relation to individual thinkers, philosophical traditions, other composers and creative artists as we attempt to form genealogies of influence. For example, the notion of binary oppositions will be traced from Boulez through a number of figures with whom he was familiar, either personally or through their writings, in this case, Souvtchinsky, Schloezer, Breton and Adorno, back to the German Idealist philosophers for whom such oppositions were crucially important. It is not claimed, however, that Boulez has been fully aware of this genealogy of influence.

It is clear that Boulez does not, for the most part, refer directly to the traditions of thought or to the figures with whom he is linked in this study and, while he does not always acknowledge that he is engaging with their ideas, the contention, nevertheless, is that he is implicated with their discourses, albeit rather anonymously at times. He draws upon dialectical, deductive, structuralist and post-structuralist ideas without ever submitting his chosen concepts to close scrutiny beyond the clearly prescribed musical purposes for which he commissions them. In the cases of Adorno and Lévi-Strauss he appears as a central figure within debates without becoming personally involved. While his early writings are undoubtedly polemical, it is not clear that he intended to become embroiled in the serious debates which arose from his citation of certain authors, as his application of their ideas or his borrowing of their terminologies was subjected to serious scrutiny. At times it is left to other, more willing respondents to take up the challenge and to subject the arguments of his critics to the kind of consideration which he consistently fails to provide for himself.

It may be that his fault is primarily one of omission as he rather casually adopts concepts and ideas without providing a clear interpretative frame-work. As noted already, in certain interviews he carefully avoids commenting upon the writings of philosophers and thinkers on the grounds that he is unqualified to do so. Despite such reserve, he draws upon terms such as *deduction, dialectic, code, language*, the *virtual* and *difference* without clearly defining their use or providing the kinds of references or context which would enable their less ambiguous interpretation. Consequently, it will be of interest to attempt to clarify Boulez's use of these and other key terms, to establish how consistent his usage is and what musicological and philosoph-ical sense these terms have within his lexicon, finally to discern whatever difference these terms and relationships make to his music.

The connections linking Boulez with Adorno, Lévi-Strauss, Eco and Deleuze are largely unexplored in the literature, and there has been little mention of the role of early influences, such as Souvtchinsky, Schloezer, Schaeffner and Souris, certainly in English language studies. No study to date has explored these connections systematically, though some authors have considered certain aspects of them.[16]

To consider Boulez's ideas in relation to one of these intellectual currents would be difficult enough. To consider them in relation to several systems of thought, which cannot be easily mapped onto a common framework, complicates matters even further. That we cannot easily relate the dialectics of Adorno, Leibowitz and others, the axiomatics of Rougier, the structural-ism of Lévi-Strauss and Eco as well as the post-structuralism of Deleuze and Guattari to one another indicates the difficulty in making sense of them within the context of Boulez's music and writings. In attempting to do so, the goal is not to smooth over differences and inconsistencies, but rather to present the complexities of Boulez's evolving aesthetic positions as faithfully as possible within the contexts in which they first developed.

---

[16]　See Stoïanova (1978), Savage (1989) and Sweeney-Turner (1994).

2 Early influences and movements

Elders, colleagues and roads not taken

The key moments of Boulez's musical education in Paris in the mid-1940s are well known: that he came to the capital in the autumn of 1943 to become a musician; that he studied counterpoint with Honegger's wife, Andrée Vaurabourg, until 1945; that he was a member of Messiaen's harmony class in 1944–5, graduating with a first prize in harmony; that he attended classes with René Leibowitz in 1945–6 in which the elder composer conducted detailed analyses of works by the Second Viennese composers; that he broke with Leibowitz in 1946 and, finally, that he worked with the Renaud-Barrault theatre company as musical director between 1946 and 1956. It is the story of a deeply determined young musician who mastered his craft in a surprisingly short time to develop into a composer capable of producing works like his First Sonata for piano and his *Sonatine* for flute and piano when he was still only twenty-one years of age. Alongside the influence of his teachers, we can note the names of those composers who helped shape his trajectory, with Messiaen, Schoenberg, Webern, Stravinsky, Debussy and Varèse taking pride of place among his elders, while composers of the younger generation such as Cage and Stockhausen also contributed to his evolution as a unique creative voice. In a similar way, we can list a range of non-musical aesthetic influences with whom the young Boulez engaged, with the poets René Char and Stéphane Mallarmé and, to a lesser extent, Henri Michaux, as well as the artist Paul Klee, being the most important.

While this account covers some key moments in Boulez's early development, it gives no real indication of the wider intellectual life enjoyed in post-war Paris, or of the main currents of thought which shaped attitudes. The period from 1945 to 1960 in French philosophy is characterised as that of the 'three H's', in other words, of Hegel, Husserl and Heidegger, three German philosophers whose work was of central importance for French thinkers.[1] The surrealist movement, which had developed as a reaction to Dadaism in 1924, had succeeded in reintroducing Hegel to a French audience, as well as in promoting a greater interest in German philosophy in France. In addition to this initial impulse, the lectures of Kojève and Hyppolite in the 1930s

---

[1] Descombes 1980, 3–4.

introduced an entire generation of French intellectuals to Hegel and made of dialectical philosophy a pole around which other philosophies of the time gravitated. The existentialism of Sartre, Camus and others provided a philosophy of commitment which was welcomed by a nation striving to make the most of its new-found liberty. Taken together with Marxist philosophies of history as well as Merleau-Ponty's phenomenology, to name only some of the most significant currents, we begin to form an idea of the prevailing intellectual milieu.

While Sartre assumed a central position in French intellectual life in the years immediately following the Second World War, his philosophy, a blend of existentialism and Marxism, does not seem to have been of special interest to Boulez, though it would be surprising if it were completely absent from his thinking. It is interesting to note that Leibowitz wrote on musical matters for Sartre's journal *Les Temps Modernes* and that the two men were friends.[2] His bitter dispute with Leibowitz notwithstanding, it is inconceivable that Boulez could have found much common ground with Sartre in terms of the purposes or functioning of art. Socialist realism was believed by Sartre to be tenable on the grounds that it worked towards the establishment of an egalitarian society.[3] Furthermore, according to Sartre, the potential for commitment within avant-garde music was endangered by the elite nature of the audience it gathered, who were overwhelmingly bourgeois and not at all disposed to political change.[4] While Boulez's writings, in contrast, are striking in their avoidance of party politics, he has on a number of occasions described his own attitude as 'Marxist-Leninist'.[5]

In contrast with his musical formation, Boulez's initiation into the world of ideas was not facilitated by direct contact with the most important philosophers of his time, but must be traced instead to a small but significant number of distinguished, if less well-known, individuals who had varying degrees of influence on the development of his ideas and the mode of their expression. In these years, at the end of the 1940s and the beginning of the 1950s, Boulez's Parisian apartment became a meeting place for his rebellious artist friends, Armand Gatti, Bernard Saby, Michel Fano, Michel Philippot, Jean Barraqué and André Hodeir. This younger group were joined from time to time by Pierre Souvtchinsky, Boris de Schloezer and André Schaeffner, significant figures on the Parisian music scene from an older generation.[6] In addition to this trio of influence we can add the name of André Souris, a Belgian musician of many talents, who first encountered

---

[2] Leibowitz was a friend of Sartre, Merleau-Ponty and Lévi-Strauss and he attempted to apply Sartre's notion of committed art to music. In 'The Current Impact of Berg' (1948) Boulez criticises both Leibowitz and *Les Temps Modernes* (1991, 185).
[3] Carroll 2003, 49.   [4] Carroll 2003, 134–5.   [5] Jameux 1991, 158.   [6] Aguila 1992, 49.

and befriended Boulez in 1947. Since these figures are of particular consequence for Boulez's early aesthetic development, in what follows we will consider their relationships with Boulez as well as with one another in an attempt to map out a cartography of influence.

Pierre Souvtchinsky

Since the place of Pierre Souvtchinsky (1892–1985) within the history of twentieth-century music has only recently begun to receive the attention it deserves, it is perhaps necessary to introduce this rather mysterious man before proceeding to consider his relationship with Boulez. By the time he met Boulez, Souvtchinsky had amassed a wealth of experience in the domain of new music. As a young man in St Petersburg, the city of his birth, he assumed a position at the heart of musical and cultural life in the years immediately before the revolution, as he co-founded the reviews *Le Contemporain musical* and *Melos* between 1914 and 1917, as well as organising concerts of contemporary music where, amongst others, works by Prokofiev, Scriabin, Stravinsky and Wyschnegradsky were performed.[7] Having left St Petersburg in 1918, he spent time in Kiev, Sofia and Berlin before arriving in Paris in 1925 where he was to spend the rest of his life.[8] While he had been a friend of Prokofiev from their student days together and a proponent of his music, the focus of his interest shifted to Stravinsky after they met again in Berlin in 1922, an encounter which developed into a lifelong friendship, albeit not always a smooth one.[9]

As with his earlier years in St Petersburg, Souvtchinsky cultivated an amazingly wide range of friends and acquaintances from diverse Parisian cultural and intellectual milieux, including a number of figures who subsequently assumed not inconsiderable importance for Boulez. He had been in contact with Boris de Schloezer from the early 1920s, had met and collaborated with Antonin Artaud on his play *Les Cenci* in 1935, and corresponded with André Schaeffner from 1938.[10] In more formal terms, his philosophy is difficult to define on account of its multiple sources, which include Hegel, Marx, aspects of Heidegger, Bernard Groethuysen[11] and a number of Russian philosophers including Herzen, Rozanov, Chestov and

---

[7] Langlois 2004, 20–2.   [8] Langlois 2004, 24–53.

[9] Souvtchinsky and Stravinsky first met in 1910 (Langlois 2004, 19). Stravinsky described him as 'one of [his] oldest living friends' (Stravinsky 1972, 48) and Craft referred to him as 'the closest friend, champion, and unsparing critic of both I.S. and Boulez' (Craft 1972, 61). Prokofiev makes a number of favourable references to Souvtchinsky in his diaries.

[10] Langlois 2004, 64–5.

[11] Langlois 2004, 63. Groethuysen (1880–1946) was a German philosopher and a historian of French ideas.

Berdyaev.[12] His wealth of experience and breadth of knowledge notwithstanding, Souvtchinsky displayed a profound reticence throughout his life which kept him firmly in the background despite his intense and high-profile engagements with Stravinsky and Boulez. Hence the one book which he authored himself, *Un siècle de musique russe*, was written in the mid-1940s but not published until 2004.

Boulez and Souvtchinsky have given conflicting accounts with regard to their first meeting, with Souvtchinsky stating that he first met the young composer at the home of René Leibowitz in 1948, where he formed the opinion that Boulez was exceptional on the basis of his involvement in discussion. Boulez, in contrast, dates their first meeting to '1946–1947, certainly before 1948', not at Leibowitz's home, but at a conference-symposium at which he [Boulez] had spoken, and he recalls that Souvtchinsky approached him at the end of the event with a view to talking further about the issues under consideration. He also recalls meeting Souvtchinsky again at the première of Messiaen's *Harawi*.[13] While Langlois, building on Boulez's recollection, identifies the first of these occasions as a conference on Debussy at the Paris Conservatoire which took place at the beginning of 1946,[14] the première of *Harawi* occurred later that year on 24 June. The impressively large number of important contacts which Boulez made through Souvtchinsky in a very short space of time, personalities who rapidly became figures of real significance for him, suggests that the two had known one another from an early date.[15] While the first extant written communication between them, which undoubtedly followed their first meetings, dates from October 1947,[16] a letter to Stravinsky in December 1946 seems to confirm the likelihood that they had made contact by this time. Souvtchinsky writes of the emergence in Paris of:

> a youthful school of 'atonalists' which, with all its heresies, has unfortunately attracted a very talented circle of youngsters. I've got into a 'love–hate' relationship with this group, since I find that when it comes to culture these musical 'Trotskyites' are very interesting. The group has broken with Messiaen and is, of course, much more interesting than he is.[17]

---

[12] Craft 1972, 14.

[13] Aguila 1992, 42–3. In a more recent interview with Claude Samuel, Boulez states that he first met Souvtchinsky in 1945 or 1946 (Samuel 2006, 4).

[14] Langlois 2004, 74–5.

[15] Souvtchinsky introduced Suzanne Tézenas, André Schaeffner, Gilbert Rouget, Paule Thévenin and Boris de Schloezer to Boulez in 1947 (Langlois 2004, 77).

[16] Letter from Boulez to Souvtchinsky, postmark dated 21 October 1947 (BN). The Bibliothèque nationale in Paris holds over 100 letters from Boulez to Souvtchinsky and a small number of Souvtchinsky's letters to Boulez. A number of Souvtchinsky's letters are held in the Paul Sacher Stiftung in Basel. The correspondence dates from 1947 to 1984.

[17] Letter dated 22 December 1946 (PSS), cited in Walsh 2006, 200.

That Souvtchinsky and Stravinsky had been close friends since 1922 can be seen, for example, from the role Souvtchinsky is now known to have played in the planning of the composer's *Poetics*, the series of six lectures which Stravinsky delivered at Harvard University in the academic year 1939–1940.[18] Despite this, a certain coldness came between them in the years after the Second World War, an emotional as well as geographical distance which was only bridged in December 1956 when they met again in Paris.[19] In the intervening period, Boulez, it may be said, took the place of Stravinsky in Souvtchinsky's life since, at the time of their meeting, Stravinsky was living in Los Angeles and was no longer well disposed towards Souvtchinsky. His enthusiasm for the post-war generation irritated Stravinsky, who recognised that support for dodecaphony was tantamount to rejection of his music. It seems that Souvtchinsky had come to believe at this point that Stravinsky's moment had passed and that it was the start of an exciting new era in musical history. Boulez, it appears, satisfied a peculiar need within Souvtchinsky, namely a desire to identify a particular individual as a man of genius who would take events forward to the next stage of development.[20] In Stravinsky's absence, Boulez became Souvtchinsky's new project as he introduced him to a wealth of useful contacts in Parisian society and brought philosophical and aesthetic depth to the relationship, as well as a wide knowledge of things intellectual and artistic, which Boulez at that time lacked.

While it has hitherto been difficult to present a clear picture of their relationship or to assess the precise extent of Souvtchinsky's influence, their correspondence signals his importance in Boulez's life from the late 1940s until the early 1960s and undermines Boulez's retrospective evaluation which tends to minimise his role.[21] Souvtchinsky's remembrance, that he and Boulez were at one time in telephone contact almost every evening, is to some extent supported by Boulez's letters. He tells Souvtchinsky about many important events, significant encounters and the content of his other correspondence. He shares his ideas with him, seeks his counsel, invokes him as a mediator at times and sends him his articles as well as copies of distinctly polemical letters to various third parties such as Ernest Ansermet, Henri Barraud and André Malraux, for his opinion. Souvtchinsky was central in

---

[18] Souvtchinsky's planning for Stravinsky's *Poetics* will be considered in Chapter 3.
[19] Craft 1972, 48.
[20] If Boulez seemed to replace Stravinsky in this role, his position would later be taken by the younger French composer Gilbert Amy.
[21] Souvtchinsky's archives have been dispersed and many of his writings are still unpublished (Dufour 2004, 22). After his death, an association was set up by some of those who were close to him, including Boulez, in order to perpetuate his memory through reassembling his documents and the publication of his writings (Langlois 2004, 13–14). Humbertclaude's anthology seems to have been prompted by a suggestion made by Boulez (Souvtchinsky 1990, 299).

the founding of the Petit Marigny and Domaine Musical concerts which Boulez organised in Paris beginning from 1953 and he was also the general editor of a series of publications entitled *Domaine Musical*. The uncertainty of Souvtchinsky's stance in relation to the younger generation, which he described as a 'love–hate' relationship in his letter to Stravinsky, is perhaps glimpsed in a letter from 1948 in which Boulez invites him to his apartment for a private audition of his Second Sonata and other works, in the hope that he will have a better chance to grasp its 'meaning', and with a view to refuting his objections.[22]

Looking back in 1963, Boulez refers to Souvtchinsky as his 'most faithful and longstanding friend' and he recalls the numerous conversations they had when he lived in Paris.[23] Souvtchinsky, in turn, at the time of the Malraux affair in 1966, conveys to Boulez in intimate terms exactly what he means to him and what he takes to be his unique value for new music. He writes of the poor state of music in France between the two world wars as 'sick, lamentable, demoralised and demoralising' in order to press home the decisive, transformative role which he believes Boulez to have played in turning the situation around and the debt which he is consequently owed.[24] Despite such mutual appreciation, which is undoubtedly personal as well as professional, it is clear that the relationship was more complex, that it was compromised in the late 1950s by Souvtchinsky's renewed relationship with Stravinsky as well as by Boulez's relocation in Baden-Baden, the new concentration of his work in Germany and the shift in his activity from composing to conducting. While it will be argued here that Souvtchinsky is significant for Boulez's intellectual development in clearly identifiable ways, Boulez's recollection is that his ideas 'were already formed' and that while Souvtchinsky was 'an extremely intelligent and perceptive conversationalist', he does not believe that he directed him in any significant way.[25] While there are no references to Souvtchinsky in Boulez's early articles as gathered in *Stocktakings*, there are only three references in *Orientations*, and none in the Darmstadt lectures or the later Collège de France lectures.

While the relationship clearly waned in the mid-1960s, Souvtchinsky's correspondence with Stravinsky from 1958 onwards, in other words after the renewal of their relationship, reveals the extent to which the worm was already in the bud.[26] Stravinsky was furious with the disastrous performance of his *Threni* in Paris in 1958, for which Boulez was blamed. In addition

[22] Undated. The postmark is dated 21 January 1948 (BN).
[23] Undated. Provisional editorial date 16 April 1963 (BN).
[24] Undated. Provisional editorial date 10 October 1966 (BN).   [25] Aguila 1992, 44.
[26] The frequency of Boulez's letters to Souvtchinsky tails off at the end of the 1960s and there are only three written communications from Boulez from 1972 onwards.

to this, Souvtchinsky seemed intent on causing trouble when he wrote
to Stravinsky informing him of Goléa's claim in the recently published
Rencontres avec Pierre Boulez that Stravinsky's presence at the Domaine
Musical had been primarily a 'publicity coup' on Boulez's part.[27] While
Souvtchinsky claimed that he had consequently broken off all relations with
Boulez, this was untrue. Nevertheless, Souvtchinsky was clearly concerned
at this time with the growing attention Boulez was giving to his conducting
career as well as his increasing presence in Germany. In further letters from
1959 Souvtchinsky states baldly that 'relations with [Boulez] have become
extremely difficult: he talks only about himself and his plans'.[28]

After several further letters to Stravinsky that summer, in which Souvtchinsky continued to write about Boulez in unfavourable terms,[29] he
counsels his composer friend: 'don't trust him any more and I'm sure that,
having embarked on a course of the most banal careerism, he will go on
climbing regardless of the consequences and without remorse . . . Just don't
trust him!'[30] Despite such unequivocal attacks, Souvtchinsky was somehow
able to write to Boulez the following day in the most ingratiating of terms:

> Thank you for your letter, to which the word 'magnificent' applies a thousand
> times more than to mine. I thank you for it with all my heart, for it's true:
> there was 'something' of a break between us which is repaired, for me at any
> rate, in the friendship and admiration that I have for you and which will
> remain one of the 'essential' bases for what I call my 'existence'.[31]

While Boulez has written of Souvtchinsky's role as primarily that of an
'intermediary',[32] Jacques Derrida, with whom Souvtchinsky enjoyed 'very
friendly contact',[33] described him as a 'philosophical amateur, in the best
sense of the term'.[34] It is clear that Souvtchinsky was fully aware of the
derived nature of his thought from a letter to Boulez in which he refers to
his own reflections as the 'ramblings of a philosophical hobo [*clochard*]'.[35]
Consequently, his importance for Boulez, like several other members of

---

[27] Letter from Souvtchinsky to Stravinsky, dated 19 December 1958 (PSS), cited in Walsh 2006,
390–2; Goléa 1982, 195–6.

[28] Letter from Souvtchinsky to Stravinsky, dated 26 June 1959 (PSS), cited in Walsh 2006, 405.

[29] Letters dated 6 June, 26 June, 28 July 1959 (PSS). Walsh 2006, 410.

[30] Letter dated 22 August 1959 (PSS), cited in Walsh 2006, 410–11.

[31] Letter dated 23 August 1959 (PSS), cited in Walsh 2006, 411.   [32] Boulez 2005a, 655.

[33] Letter from Souvtchinsky to Boulez, dated 13 April 1973 (PSS). There is one letter from Derrida
to Souvtchinsky, dated 22 February 1973 (BN). In a drafted letter dated 27 February 1972 which
was presumably sent to Derrida, Souvtchinsky writes: 'I do not know – I avow it – where your
thought is situated, what your fundamental coordinates are, but it is in our time, the strongest
and most seductive that I know' (BN).

[34] Langlois 2004, 63.

[35] Letter dated 29 April 1963 (PSS). In a previous, undated letter (dated 16 April 1963 by the
provisional editor) Boulez had written that 'it is the day of the silly clots [cloches], in principle;
and not the day of the hobos of thought' (BN).

this group of influential figures, is not predicated on the basis of any out-standing philosophical originality but rather on his role as a mediator of ideas.

Boris de Schloezer, phenomenology and gestalt theory

While Boulez showed little formal interest in musical phenomenology, he was nevertheless influenced by the phenomenologically orientated musicologist Boris de Schloezer (1881–1969), whom he met through Souvtchinsky in 1947.[36] Like Souvtchinsky, Schloezer was a marginal figure in terms of the Russian émigré intellectual community in Paris, but nevertheless an important one for Boulez. Born in Vitebsk, he completed a doctorate in sociology in Brussels before working as an author and critic in both St Petersburg and Moscow on his return to Russia, and publishing in 1923 a study on the music of Scriabin, who was also his brother-in-law. Having left Russia, he arrived in France in 1921 and lived there until his death in 1969. During this time he wrote one of the first books on Stravinsky (1929) in addition to producing a number of studies on and translations of some of the great masters of Russian literature including Gogol, Tolstoy, Dostoyevsky and his friend, the philosopher Lev Chestov. Contact between Schloezer and Souvtchinsky, which pre-dates their arrival in France, was broken in the early 1920s on account of Schloezer's criticisms of the Eurasian movement, to which Souvtchinsky at that time belonged, and it was not renewed until after the Second World War.[37] It is interesting to note that while Schloezer criticised Souvtchinsky's 1939 article on Stravinsky as 'badly written',[38] when contact was re-established between them from the late 1940s, he was fulsome in his praise of Souvtchinsky's more recent writing.[39]

While Schloezer was one of the group who visited Boulez's apartment in the late 1940s and early 1950s it seems that, unlike Souvtchinsky, he did not correspond with him and there are only rare references to him, for example, in Boulez's correspondence with Souvtchinsky. Despite writing in 1948 of Schloezer's kindness to him[40] it is clear that Boulez was much closer to Souvtchinsky, and in two undated letters, presumably from 1956,

---

[36] Boulez draws upon Schloezer's books on Stravinsky (1929) and Bach (1947) in the article 'Bach's Moment' (1951) (1991, 3, 5–6).

[37] There are fifteen extant letters from Schloezer to Souvtchinsky. The first two letters date from 1921 after which there is a gap until 1948. The last letters which are dated were written in 1956 (BN). See Kohler 2003, 165–8.

[38] Letter from Schloezer to Leibowitz, dated 25 July 1939 (PSS).

[39] Letters from Schloezer to Souvtchinsky, dated 13 January 1950; 10 February 1950 and 30 September 1953 (BN).

[40] The postmark on the letter is dated 16 January 1948 (BN).

he expresses regret that Schloezer's article on *Le Marteau sans maître* was published in *La Nouvelle Revue Française* before Souvtchinsky's.[41] Nevertheless, that Boulez contributed to this prestigious journal between 1954 and 1957 was due to Schloezer, who was its music critic. Perhaps more significantly, he was instrumental in the development of Boulez's ideas.[42] André Boucourechliev commended him as the sole defender of the post-war generation of composers in *La Nouvelle Revue Française*, and he praised his *Introduction à J.-S. Bach* (1947) on the basis that it was the first attempt to speak to composers 'of the musical phenomenon as they conceived it and lived it themselves'.[43] Despite the impact which the book had upon Boulez and his generation, Souvtchinsky and Schaeffner, both of whom had been sent copies, failed to respond to the author's undisguised desire for critical feedback, and his disappointment is tangible.[44]

In his *Introduction à J.-S. Bach*, Schloezer considers the nature of a musical work, how it is constituted, what listening and understanding involve, and whether the work is capable of expression, before going on to study aspects of the music of J. S. Bach. His approach is to question everything he has previously learned in order to 'rethink the musical fact', a task he first set himself in 1927.[45] In doing so, he insists unambiguously on 'the cognitive value of music', since art opens up to us things which cannot otherwise be apprehended.[46] Its title notwithstanding, Schloezer's book is not primarily a study of J. S. Bach but rather a treatise on aesthetics. It is a musical phenomenology, which attempts to come close to the musical work, considering it at the levels of the graphic signs in the score, the performance of the score, the sound vibrations which are produced in the performance as well as the auditory impression which this makes on the listener and the states of consciousness which are consequently elicited. Schloezer concludes that the work has no objective reality, that it does not exist beyond the fact of its performance and that any musical text is only ever a 'virtuality'.[47] He is equally careful in rejecting musical subjectivism. Furthermore, he defines the work in the proto-structuralist terminology of musical signifiers and signifieds which, however, unlike spoken language, have only immanent meaning.[48] Consistent with the view he had held even at the time of his early monograph on Scriabin (1923), Schloezer argues that

---

[41] Undated. The provisional editor's suggested date for both letters is 1956 (BN). See Schloezer (1956, 930–2) for his review of the performance of *Le Marteau sans maître*; Souvtchinsky's review appeared a month later (1956, 1107–9).

[42] Piencikowski 1991, p. xxi.   [43] Boucourechliev 1981, 17, 19.

[44] Letter to Souvtchinsky, dated 10 February 1950 (BN).

[45] Schloezer 1947, 17. His earlier study 'A la recherche de la réalité musicale' appeared in four instalments in *La Revue Musicale* in 1928.

[46] Schloezer 1947, 11, 66.   [47] Schloezer 1947, 19.   [48] Schloezer 1947, 17–27.

all the musical elements or parameters form a musical whole and cannot properly be viewed in isolation from one another without distortion. While he agrees with Bergson and the gestalt theoreticians that the musical event is not purely subjective and that it has an 'immanent sense', he parts company with them in the conviction that it is necessary for each listener to decode the objective facts of the work in a personal act of synthesis in which the work is reconstituted by the intellect.[49]

Careful consideration of Schloezer's *Introduction* reveals a number of concepts and ideas which seem to indicate the immediacy of his influence upon Boulez, and not least of which is the distinction which he makes between organisation and composition.[50] The emphasis which he places on the concept of musical form, to which the second part of the study is devoted, is striking, with sections on rhythm, harmony and melody. His repeated references to the musical moment in terms of intensity, duration, pitch and timbre, which he dubs 'systems of relations', impress with their modernity.[51] Musical form is described as a hierarchy of systems[52] and he writes of open and closed musical systems, albeit not in the celebrated sense of the late 1950s.[53] He theorises a continuum of harmonic possibilities in which the laying out of homophony, polyphony and heterophony brings to mind the later taxonomy of Boulez's Darmstadt lectures.[54] His use of a range of concepts including that of the sound complex,[55] the field complex,[56] athematicism,[57] sound space[58] and the virtual work,[59] as well as a tendency to conceptualise in terms of binary oppositions and to think of music in both evolutionary and dialectical terms, shows something of the conceptual vocabulary which Boulez would have found in his work. While it would be wrong to read back into these terms meanings which they only developed later, it is nevertheless significant that Schloezer provides a range of terms which are later taken up by Boulez and his colleagues in their efforts to theorise a new music of which Schloezer could have had no conception.

Despite the absence of correspondence directly between them, a number of references to Boulez in Schloezer's letters to Souris provide a glimpse of the significant contact they shared in the late 1940s and early 1950s. He tells Souris in November 1947 of the 'excellent terms' on which Souvtchinsky finds himself with Boulez, or rather 'Boulaize', and that Souvtchinsky has proposed the young composer to write an article (*note*) for *Polyphonie* in his

---

[49] Schloezer 1947, 26, 39, 82–3. Schloezer quotes at length from Paul Guillaume's *La Psychologie de la forme* (Schloezer 1947, 40). The necessity of 'intellectual effort' on the part of the listener is already present in Schloezer in 1928 (1928c, 249).

[50] Schloezer 1947, 108–9; Boulez 1991, 6, 16, 156.   [51] Schloezer 1947, 111.

[52] Schloezer 1947, 75.   [53] Schloezer 1947, 79.   [54] Schloezer 1947, 196.

[55] Schloezer 1947, 166.   [56] Schloezer 1947, 180.   [57] Schloezer 1947, 215.

[58] Schloezer 1947, 167–71.   [59] Schloezer 1947, 302.

place. If Souris is in agreement with this then Schloezer is willing to inform Boulez of what is required.[60] A few months later, with the appearance of the second cahier of *Polyphonie*, Schloezer reports that he is unimpressed by the aggressive tone of Boulez's article 'Proposals' and by its failure to 'renew our rhythmic conceptions'. While acknowledging the possibility that his judgement may be unfair, he nevertheless confesses that Boulez's Artaudian depiction of music as 'collective hysteria and magic' is absolutely strange and even repugnant to him. He recognises, however, that he is almost in complete agreement with Boulez's judgements on Berg,[61] and he expresses a much higher opinion of the article 'Trajectories' in 1950 which he describes as 'excellent'.[62] Commenting on a joint visit to his home by 'Boulaize' and Cage in June 1949, Cage is described as a 'charming boy' but also as 'more of a theoretician and inventor than a creator',[63] and we learn that on another visit there in 1950, Boulez met the Belgian group of serial composers.[64]

Schloezer's relationship with serialism was, however, not unambiguous and his undoubted support, in the form of articles and reviews of the Domaine Musical concerts, was tempered with a number of serious reservations which developed over the 1950s. In his 1955 article 'Retour à Descartes' he took issue with the analytical tendency of Boulez, Fano and Barraqué to dissolve the musical work into its specific elements. For Schloezer, such an approach is a 'truncated' one which fails to engage with 'musical reality'. To dissect a work into its component parts, as Boulez does in his rhythmic analysis of Stravinsky's *Rite of Spring*, is to deal with abstractions and not with the 'thing itself' which is the musical event in all of its dimensions. While he describes Boulez's analysis as 'remarkable', he believes it to be ultimately unsuccessful in clarifying the rhythmic structures of the piece since it fails to take melodic and harmonic structures into account.[65] He is similarly ambivalent in his review of the Parisian performance of *Le Marteau* in 1956 in which, while generally praising the work, he admits to having some reservations.[66]

The correspondence which René Leibowitz initiated with Schloezer in 1936, and which continued until 1951, provides some insights into the relationship between music and ideas in France at that time, as well as into how Leibowitz came to the point of interpreting Schoenberg's musical

---

[60] Letter dated 22 November 1947 (AML). Boulez responded with the article 'The Current Impact of Berg (the Fortnight of Austrian Music in Paris)', which was published in *Polyphonie*, 2 (1948), 104–8.

[61] Letter dated 6 April 1948 (AML).   [62] Letter dated 16 February 1950 (AML).

[63] Letter dated 26 June 1949 (AML).   [64] Letter dated 3 January 1950 (AML).

[65] Schloezer 1955, 1084–6. Schloezer had previously expressed his reservations concerning Boulez's analytical approach to the *Rite of Spring* in a letter to Souvtchinsky, dated 30 September 1953 (BN).

[66] Schloezer 1956, 931.

innovations in philosophical terms. Schloezer's letters from between 1936 and 1940 are of particular interest. He refers to conversations he has had with Leibowitz on the subject of 'musical reality',[67] and he acknowledges how much he has benefited from their 'incessant contact'.[68] However, in a letter from October 1939, Schloezer makes some rather surprising remarks to Leibowitz, recommending, on the question of history, that he should read the work of the German philosopher Wilhelm Dilthey as well as Raymond Aron's *L'Introduction à la philosophie de l'histoire*. What is surprising is that Schloezer chides Leibowitz for his self-confessed failure to take ideas seriously, and for the suspicion under which he seems to have viewed any kind of abstraction. Schloezer attempts to make Leibowitz see that ideas and artworks are intimately related and that a work evinces an entire view of the world.[69] His comments in a letter from August 1940 are perhaps even more surprising in that, while noting Leibowitz's 'long silence', he remarks that his suspicion of ideas seems to have disappeared. He recalls that Leibowitz had written to him at the beginning of the war that music alone gave him 'the impression of the "real", of something "concrete"'.[70] The aesthetic transformation to which these letters testify is confirmed by Leibowitz himself in a chapter on Sartre, Husserl and phenomenology, which he includes in his unpublished 'Confessions', as well as in his correspondence with Michel Leiris, and a number of philosophers including Hegel, Husserl, Heidegger, Scheler, Sartre and Camus are named.[71]

Fuelled by such aesthetic engagements, Leibowitz, like Schloezer, makes a number of significant references to phenomenology in the books which he wrote in the late 1940s.[72] Interpreting the paraphernalia of tonality in terms of the individual subject and as the content of consciousness, Leibowitz suggests that in developing composition with twelve tones, concepts like 'tonality, scale, consonance [and] dissonance' cease to matter for Schoenberg, while more general concepts like 'themes, motives [and] chords' are no longer treated as 'fixed givens'. In doing so, Schoenberg is said to have placed '*the musical world "between parentheses"*', in other words he has performed a phenomenological reduction,[73] and Leibowitz claims in another context that the composer's approach is faithfully captured by Husserl's phrase 'Zu den Sachen selbst'.[74] Boulez, who had turned decisively away from Leibowitz, treated his one-time teacher's philosophical speculations

---

[67] Letter dated 15 October 1936 (PSS).   [68] Letter dated 20 October 1937 (PSS).
[69] Letter dated 21 October 1939 (PSS).   [70] Letter dated 4 August 1940 (PSS).
[71] Meine 2000, 69.   [72] Leibowitz 1949a and 1949b.
[73] Leibowitz 1949b, 101. While Husserl's philosophy was of the greatest importance for Leibowitz, his knowledge of it was mediated through the writings of Sartre and Camus (Meine 2000, 35, 72). He thanks Sartre for his help in formulating the philosophical elements within his reflections (1949b, 104).
[74] Leibowitz 1949b, 14.

with scorn, and in the article on Berg which he produced for *Polyphonie*, he alludes to Leibowitz's work when he states that his own approach to the topic will be 'much less pseudo-philosophical'.[75] Indeed, in a letter to André Souris in 1947, he writes of 'the badly digested philosophy with which [Leibowitz] surrounds himself.'[76]

In contrast to Boulez's dismissive response, Schloezer described *Schoenberg et son École*, in a letter to its author, as 'a beautiful and important book', albeit being careful to state that he is not always in agreement with it.[77] He was more ambivalent in his opinion of *L'Artiste et sa conscience*, which he praises in a letter to Leibowitz despite acknowledging its failure to resolve the doubts articulated by Sartre in his preface,[78] and it seems that his most honest appraisal was reserved for Souris to whom he described the book as a 'model of confusion'.[79] While Souvtchinsky, who had received a copy of Leibowitz's *Introduction à la musique de douze sons* from its author, described it in the only letter he ever wrote to Leibowitz as 'remarkable', his true view may not have been quite so straightforward.[80]

Following this thread into Boulez's own generation, it is clear that while Jean Barraqué (1954) notes the possibility of producing a phenomenological history of music,[81] philosophical references within his work are scattered and are never developed with any rigour. A more serious attempt to discuss the new music in phenomenological terms is made by Pousseur, who returns to the topic in several of his writings between 1954 and 1959. Unlike Boulez, Pousseur is willing to engage in brief moments of philosophical reflection drawing, for example, on Heidegger's ontology in which consciousness discovers itself already within the world as inextricably part of it, so that it is inconceivable that the subject should conceptualise itself in isolation from it.

Pousseur theorises the artwork in terms of this combinatory reality as 'a certain manner of existing' rather than as the representation of an external object or as the expression of an interior state.[82] In a similar way, while perception becomes a major concern for Boulez, he does not frame the question in phenomenological terms, as Pousseur does. Pousseur suggests that we should look to 'immediate perception and its "contents"' in order to draw whatever conclusions we can from it, a process he compares with

---

[75] Boulez 1991, 183.
[76] Dated 17 December 1947 by Souris (AML) (Wangermée 1995, 275). See also the letter from 6 November 1947 (AML).
[77] Letter dated 16 April 1947 (PSS). Schloezer was more critical in reviewing the work (Meine 2000, 203–4).
[78] Letter dated 5 December 1950 (PSS).   [79] Letter dated 17 November 1950 (AML).
[80] While the date on Souvtchinsky's letter is incomplete (22 December), the year will have been 1949, since Leibowitz's book was published in November of that year.
[81] Barraqué 2001, 69.   [82] Pousseur 1954, 110.

a 'return to the thing itself', in other words a phenomenological reduction. Nevertheless, he acknowledges that there is no primordial state of episte-mological or ontological purity as we cannot escape the cultural precon-ditions of our perceptions. Positing the existence of a dialectical process linking our most immediate consciousness of the world and its cultural determination,[83] the centrality which he gives to perception in appreci-ation of the aesthetic object leaves him loathe to relinquish the notion of immediate consciousness, and he states that 'maximum energy' must be expended on the discovery of such a phenomenological theory.[84] He rejects 'the immediacy of formal organisation' posited by the Gestaltists, supporting Schloezer in his conviction that the listener must be capable of making an 'intellectual synthesis', a reconstruction of the sound material in order to make sense of it as music. While Leibowitz wrote of Schoenberg's phenomenological reduction, for Pousseur it is Webern who has placed 'the traditional domain entirely between parentheses'. Unlike Boulez, Pousseur is explicit in drawing attention to his philosophical references. He calls on the Gestaltists Karl Koffka, Wolfgang Köhler and Kurt Gottschaldt to provide a more substantial intellectual basis for his reflections as well as on the work of Paul Guillaume, who first introduced gestalt theory, albeit in 'vulgarised' form, to a French audience with his *La Psychologie de la forme* (1937).[85]

In contrast with Pousseur, Boulez's writings yield only a small number of references to gestalt theory. While he warns in 1954 against 'superficial comparisons' linking serial music with gestalt theory and phenomenology,[86] there is one short citation (a footnote) from Paul Guillaume in the Darm-stadt lectures,[87] and he writes in 1970 of using a gestalt approach to analysis.[88] It may be that he discovered Guillaume's text through André Souris, but he will certainly also have read Pousseur's articles with their gestalt reflections from 1957. References to gestalt are a little more common in the later Collège de France lectures by which time, of course, the issue of perception has become much more important.[89]

André Schaeffner

The final member of the triumvirate of visitors to Boulez's apartment is the musicologist and ethnologist André Schaeffner (1895–1984) whom he

---

[83] Pousseur 2004, 99–100.
[84] Pousseur 2004, 199–202, 231–4, 124–6. These references date from 1957 and 1959.
[85] Wangermée 1995, 218–19.   [86] Boulez 1991, 143.
[87] Boulez 1971a, 32. The quotation from Paul Guillaume simply states that 'a form is something *other* or *greater* than the sum of its parts'.
[88] Boulez 1986, 117.
[89] Robert Piencikowski describes Boulez as 'a Gestaltist' (Conversation with the author, 17 October 2005).

also met through Souvtchinsky in 1947. While Schaeffner's wife, the distinguished ethnologist Denise Paulme-Schaeffner, described her husband, who had studied with Marcel Mauss and Romain Rolland, as a 'musician by formation, aesthetician by taste, ethnologist by professional choice',[90] he described himself as a historian of ideas.[91] Working from 1928 at the museum of the Trocadero in Paris, which later became the Musée de l'Homme, he founded the department of musical ethnology there and in the course of his work he made a number of significant ethnomusicological trips between 1931 and 1954.[92] His influence upon Boulez can be seen from their correspondence with one another between 1954 and 1970, and it is clear that he helped to refine some of the young composer's judgements, with Boulez for example, undertaking certain revisions to his article 'Trajectories' (1949) in response to criticisms made by Schaeffner in the article 'Variations Schoenberg' (1951).[93]

Boulez recalls Schaeffner's interest in and knowledge of African civilisations and music as well as his profound erudition with regard to instruments from all ages, and he recognises that Schaeffner's outlook was one which offered freedom from a rigidly European outlook.[94] Schaeffner stimulated and supported Boulez's interest in non-European music, allowing him to hear many tape recordings which he had made on his ethnomusicological expeditions and which were not commercially available.[95] Schaeffner had an undoubted influence on Boulez's knowledge and choice of African, Latin American and Asiatic instruments for his own compositions.[96] Like Souvtchinsky and Schloezer, Schaeffner had a strong connection with Stravinsky, having written one of the first books on the composer in 1931. He helped direct Boulez's reading of works such as Schoenberg's *Pierrot Lunaire* and Debussy's *Pelléas et Mélisande* and it may be that he facilitated the renewed appreciation of Debussy's modernism that we find in Boulez's article 'Corruption in the Censers' (1956).[97] Schaeffner and Boulez shared a poor opinion of Leibowitz and in 'Halifax RG587' (1946), in particular, he offers a scathing critique. For Schaeffner, Leibowitz's reading of history is a travesty in that it is incomplete, exaggerated and inaccurate, and he attacks his lack of 'musicological erudition', his tunnel vision which excludes everything which is not German or Viennese, and his 'obsession' with thematicism and athematicism.[98]

---

[90] Paulme-Schaeffner 1998, 13.   [91] Draft letter to Souris, dated 5 February 1967 (PSS).
[92] Schaeffner made six trips to West Africa in 1931, 1935, 1945–6, 1948–9 and 1954, visiting Mali, Guinea and the Ivory Coast (Rouget and Lesure 1982, 6–7; Paulme-Schaeffner 1982, 365).
[93] Piencikowski 1998, 14.   [94] Boulez and Schaeffner 1998, 10–11.   [95] Aguila 1992, 44.
[96] Tugny 1998, 21.   [97] Piencikowski 1998, 14.
[98] Schaeffner 1998, 229–39. Leibowitz's response to Schaeffner was originally published in the same volume (Contrepoints 5, Décembre 1946, 65–6).

French nationalism aside, given the extent of Schaeffner's erudition, it is easy to see why he found Leibowitz's writing wanting. His own work combines great historical precision along with impressive breadth of knowledge, drawing freely upon the entire history of Western music while subverting Western biases and orthodoxies as he integrates the realms of popular music, jazz, Eastern and African music within a basically unified musical vision. So it is that he writes with equal care and concern of his three great loves, namely Stravinsky, Debussy and Poulenc, of popular and folk music, of Eastern and Western music and of jazz. James Clifford, who considers his work in relation to surrealism, suggests that surrealist interest in the exotic is concordant with ethnography, for example in their shared rejection of any division of culture into high and low forms,[99] a tendency emphatically not shared by Boulez. Perhaps even more importantly, ethnography and surrealism may both be said to reinvent and reorganise reality.[100] For Schaeffner, aesthetic phenomena must be studied in the context of the societies in which they are manifested. He promotes music as it is performed in distinction to music as it is mediated by a score, and he is concerned with the conditions of composition and performance including the nature of instruments, musical practice and social contexts.

Souvtchinsky recalls that he was first introduced to Schaeffner in 1924 by Stravinsky and that their relationship endured until Schaeffner's death in 1980.[101] Consideration of Schaeffner's letters to Souvtchinsky reveals the deep intellectual culture which both men shared as they discussed Stravinsky's latest works or the philosophy of Nietzsche. That he could refer in 1959 to recently published extracts on Nietzsche by Heidegger and Deleuze as by far the best recent contributions to have been made on the German philosopher is an indicator of his philosophical awareness.[102] His correspondence with both Souvtchinsky and Souris also reveals something of his ambivalent interest in the structuralism of the 1960s with references to his friends Michel Leiris and Claude Lévi-Strauss as well as to Nicolas Ruwet.[103] While these are not the topics which he discussed in his correspondence with Boulez, it is inconceivable that these broader cultural concerns could have been completely absent from their relationship.

---

[99] Clifford 1982, 45; 49.   [100] Clifford 1982, 56.

[101] Souvtchinsky 1982, 390. Schaeffner corresponded with Souvtchinsky between 1938 and 1965 with a final letter dating from just before his death in 1980 (BN and PSS).

[102] Letter dated 15 October 1959 (BN). Deleuze's 'Sens et valeurs' and Heidegger's 'Le mot de Nietzsche "Dieu est mort"' appeared in the periodical *Arguments*, 15 (1959).

[103] There are fifteen letters from Schaeffner to Souris dating between 1947–8 and 1963–70 (AML).

André Souris, gestalt theory and encounters with surrealism

While the Belgian musician André Souris (1899–1970) lived in Brussels and was therefore not part of that small group of elders which frequented Boulez's Parisian apartment in the late 1940s and early 1950s, he was nevertheless a key figure in Boulez's early development.[104] Contemptuous of specialisation, he had performed a wide range of musical roles including that of composer, conductor and musicologist and he directed the first four numbers of the periodical *Polyphonie* between 1947 and 1949. Souris became part of the Belgian surrealist circle on its formation in 1925 and he remained within it until he was excluded from it formally in 1936. His presence as a musician at the centre of the Belgian group, along with that of Paul Hooreman, marks it off from its Parisian counterpart, whose members did not ascribe much importance to music. While the poet and theorist Paul Nougé, who was at the centre of the group and who had a profound influence on Souris, acknowledged the possibility of surrealist music,[105] André Breton, the self-appointed leader of the Parisian surrealists, was completely closed to such a prospect.[106] Souris maintained that music is not in contradiction with surrealism but is the medium that best embodies it. In addition to his involvement with surrealism, he nurtured a lively interest in ideas and he was a keen student of gestalt theory, existentialism, structuralism and post-Saussurean linguistics.[107] Prior to the Second World War he favoured Stravinsky's musical aesthetic but from 1945 onwards he also became a defender of dodecaphony under the influence of Leibowitz, whom he first met that year. Indeed, he and Leibowitz sustained a lengthy correspondence between 1946 and 1951 until the relationship collapsed on account of Souris's connection with Boulez.[108]

While Souris was familiar with Schloezer's pre-war writings in *La Nouvelle Revue Française*, they only met for the first time in 1947 and an intellectual bond quickly developed between them to which, it is clear from their correspondence, Schloezer brought aesthetic and philosophical depth, while Souris contributed a more detailed, technical knowledge of a wide range of music.[109] From this time, Schloezer introduced Souris into a range of Parisian artistic and intellectual circles. Schloezer's interest in the comprehension and perception of musical form purely on its own terms was

---

[104] See Wangermée 1995 and Souris 2000.

[105] Wangermée 1995, 124. Nougé and the artist René Magritte were the two most influential figures within the Belgian surrealist group.

[106] Wangermée 1995, 131–3. Breton recognised within himself a complete absence of musical understanding.

[107] Wangermée 2000, 8.   [108] Wangermée 1995, 252; 267–89.   [109] Wangermée 1995, 237.

shared by Souris, who drew, however, more on gestalt theory which he had discovered in 1941 through Guillaume's *La Psychologie de la forme*.[110] Nevertheless, it seems that Souris's acceptance of gestalt theory was tempered somewhat by his reading of Schloezer's book on Bach.[111] Schloezer certainly valued his opinion especially since, in distinction to most other musicians, he had a 'philosophical formation'.[112]

It was Schloezer who brought Boulez to Souris's attention and, on the basis of his remarks, Souris programmed the first performance of Boulez's *Sonatine* for flute and piano in Brussels in 1947. Indeed, he later described the work as the 'touchstone' of his affection for Boulez.[113] After meeting in Brussels in April 1947, they forged a real intellectual and musical connection, meeting frequently in Paris in the late 1940s and early 1950s and corresponding regularly between 1947 and 1953.[114] Robert Wangermée, who was on the scene at the time, judges that Souris valued Boulez's 'critical intelligence, quickness of mind', his 'intransigence' as well as his 'creative capacities', and that he was fascinated by him. Boulez, in turn, was taken with Souris's 'musical, literary and philosophical culture, his open-mindedness... his receptiveness, his rejection of conformism, his taste for everything audacious'.[115] In his capacity as editor of *Polyphonie* Souris achieved another first in inviting Boulez to contribute to its second number, which was dedicated to the topic of musical rhythm. Boulez, in fact, made two contributions to this number which appeared in 1948, namely the articles 'Proposals' and 'The Current Impact of Berg'. Souris warned Leibowitz of the criticisms Boulez had made of him in 'Proposals', and he describes the younger man as a 'little savage' who is 'full of a sort of anonymous rage', but nevertheless otherwise 'likeable', and he justifies his decision to give him the opportunity to express himself.[116]

While Souris became a proponent of serialism and a supportive figure for Boulez, Pousseur and other members of the younger generation, he nevertheless remained on the margins and, perhaps surprisingly, he did

---

[110] Wangermée 1995, 218.

[111] Wangermée 1995, 341. Souris was less appreciative of Schloezer's later *Problèmes de la musique moderne* which he wrote with his niece, Marina Scriabine, since it seemed to be too close to the position held by Ruwet. A lively correspondence ensued between them (Wangermée 1995, 331–2).

[112] Letter from Schloezer to Souris, dated 8 February 1948 (AML).

[113] Letter from Souris to Boulez, dated 27 June 1953 (PSS). Souris was later pleased to note that the published version of the work (1954) included a cut which he had proposed to Boulez on the recommendation of the pianist Marcelle Mercenier, who suggested that it would improve its formal balance (Wangermée 1995, 258–9; Souris 2000, 180–2).

[114] Thirty letters, one card and one telegram from Boulez are held in the Archives et Musée de la Littérature in Brussels. Two surviving letters from Souris are held in the Paul Sacher Stiftung in Basel.

[115] Wangermée 1995, 273–4, 284.   [116] Undated letter from Souris (PSS).

not write much about the new music. In the article 'Les sources sensibles de la musique sérielle' (1955), while noting the 'chaotic', 'monstrous' and unforeseen results produced by numerous serial composers, he recognises that if Boulez and Stockhausen had been able to produce a number of very good compositions by serial means they had done so precisely through the quality of their musical intuition which had taken them beyond automatism.[117]

In addition to his musical qualities, Boulez was interested in Souris's position within the Belgian surrealist circle,[118] and in his letters he mentions a number of important writers and painters who were either current or former members of the movement, including Breton, Aragon, Char and Artaud as well as some less significant names. According to Wangermée, Boulez was 'seduced by the surrealist tone' of the short text which Souris wrote in homage for Schoenberg's seventy-fifth birthday in 1947.[119] However, the fact of their agreement in locating Schoenberg's true value in the future possibilities offered by his work rather than in its actual attainment no doubt also facilitated Boulez's appreciation.

Boulez's relationship with surrealism is rather intriguing in its ambivalence and it may best be described as constellatory. It consists of a number of engagements with writers and artists who were, at some point in their careers, important members of the surrealist movement or who were, alternatively, in correspondence with figures who had close affinities with the movement while not themselves being members. While surrealism was and is primarily an artistic movement rather than a discrete philosophy, several of its most prominent proponents and adherents nevertheless provide clear philosophical underpinnings for their work. Despite the undoubted interest in surrealism in Boulez's early letters to Souris, it is equally clear that he was never an uncritical reader or viewer. He describes the second surrealist exhibition, which was held in Paris in 1947, and which heralded André Breton's return from the United States, as a 'great fiasco' on the grounds of its fundamentally retrogressive nature and the whole enterprise is dismissed as 'agaga, adada'.[120] In 2005 he again indicted the exhibition as encapsulating a lazy aesthetic marked by simplicity, nostalgia and 'useless folklore', and as a betrayal of the experience of the war years.[121]

---

[117] Souris 2000, 207–8.
[118] The letter from Boulez to Souris is undated but pertains to before 21 January 1947 (AML). See Wangermée 1995, 273.
[119] Souris 2000, 178–80. Letter from Boulez to Souris dated 'le 17' (AML). Wangermée specifies the date as 17 February 1947 (1995, 273).
[120] Letter from Boulez to Souris dated 'le 17' (AML).
[121] Le Monde 8 February 2005, cited in Olivier 2005, 81.

To take another example, Boulez responded with great hostility to Souris in 1952 when he read in a letter from Michel Fano that Souris and the Belgian group of serial composers were using the term 'La Révolution sérielle', that he had referred to all of the Parisian serial composers (Boulez, Fano, Barraqué and Philippot) as the Parisian 'group', and that the implication was there that this collective could together oppose the forthcoming international conference on contemporary music which was to take place in Rome in 1954 (La Musica nel XX Secolo).[122] Boulez's letters to Souvtchinsky and Souris show that he was angry to the point of accusing Souris of having fallen into old ways and he dismissed the surrealist reference as 'bizarre', as 'faded' and as a throwback to the 1920s. With equal fervour he rejected any notion that he belonged to a Parisian 'group' of composers or that he could ever subscribe to any surrealist-style group manifesto. He tells Souvtchinsky that should Souris persist in this way he would withdraw from him, leaving the 'group' 'to play the committees of public safety for café-concerto' and the entire affair is dismissed as 'twaddle' and as 'a veritable quarrel over a village loo'.[123] Souris, who resolutely rejected all of the charges while expressing some confusion at the seemingly disproportionate intensity of Boulez's anger, was bemused by the prominence of surrealism in Boulez's attack to the extent that it seemed to 'obsess' him in a way which he described as 'curious'.[124]

While Souris was clearly responding to the strange intensity of Boulez's rejection of certain aspects of surrealist practice, this alone does not explain his remark sufficiently. There is no doubt that Boulez was repelled by the nostalgic and retrogressive implications of allying serialism with a twenty-five-year-old surrealism, and that he was horrified by the prospect of participating in a group manifesto is not a surprise. As his correspondence with Souvtchinsky shows time and again, he prefers where possible to be in complete control and to act alone. Later attempts to portray him as part of a Darmstadt group of composers were also rejected by him and were so at the time. However, all of this, despite the intensity of its expression, does not satisfactorily account for the existence of so much curiosity on Boulez's part in reading surrealist texts and in discussing painting which, while not itself surrealist, was closely related to the movement. Consequently, it is important that we now consider a number of Boulez's creative encounters which would seem to relate him at some level or other to surrealism.

---

[122] Undated letter from Boulez to Souris. Dated 8 December 1952 by an unknown hand (AML).
[123] Undated letter from Boulez to Souvtchinsky. Provisional editorial date 8 December 1952 (BN).
[124] Letter from Souris to Boulez, dated 18 December 1952 (PSS and AML).

The poetry of René Char

The poet René Char (1907–88), who first aligned himself with the Parisian surrealists in 1929, was an important member of the group until 1934 when he began to distance himself from it. While his departure coincides with his discovery of a more elementary poetic language, his later poetry is also marked by his contact with surrealism, for example in its employment of juxtaposed images.[125] Boulez first read Char's poetry in 1946 and they first met in 1947, corresponding with one another from 1948 to 1976, though the bulk of their communication dates from between 1948 and 1957.[126] In a letter which seems to date from 1947, Boulez tells Souris that Char has 'made contact' with his music and he is clearly pleased that they have communicated with one another in what he describes as 'a more elementary way than through words'.[127] He recalls that he was drawn to 'an internal violence' which he discerned in the concentration of Char's expression, a trait which is found in a number of surrealist writers.[128] The collection *Le Marteau sans maître* (1934), from which Boulez selected three short poems for his composition of the same name, is often described as Char's surrealist masterpiece, and we can pose the question of the extent to which Boulez's composition may itself reflect elements of the surreal.[129] His *Le Soleil des eaux* (1948–65) and *Le Visage nuptial* (1946–89) are likewise based on Char's poetry, and he also planned in 1948 to set the collection 'A la santé du serpent' from Char's collection *Le Poème pulvérisé* (1945–7), but he did not complete the project.[130] Surrealist violence appears in the expression marking 'pulverise the sound' ('pulvériser le son') towards the end of the final movement of the Second Sonata for piano, and it also seems to underlie Boulez's comment in a letter to Stockhausen that music needs to *pulverise* 'unitary time'.[131] While creative communication with Char ends in the late 1950s and follows the shift in Boulez's poetic preferences to Mallarmé, a letter to Souvtchinsky in 1963 spells out the uncompromising change in Boulez's view. He claims that he has been disappointed by Char who is dismissed on the grounds that he is 'incapable of basing his poetry other than on sensation, and that his relation with Heraclitus, or the pre-Socratics, was

---

[125] Dupouy 1987, 46, 239; Worton 1992, 17.
[126] There are seventy-two letters in the Boulez–Char correspondence in the Paul Sacher Stiftung. I am grateful to Robert Piencikowski who made his transcription of these letters available to me.
[127] Undated letter from Boulez to Souris (AML).   [128] Boulez 1976, 43–5.
[129] For Hirsbrunner, the aesthetic of *Le Marteau sans maître* owes more to the tradition of *L'art pour l'art* than to surrealism (1985, 86, 97–8).
[130] See Boulez's letter to Char, dated 31 August 1948 (PSS) and letters from Boulez to Cage, dated November 1949 and 3, 11 and 12 January 1950 (Piencikowski 2002, 78, 91).
[131] Letter dated circa end of December 1954 (PSS).

only superficial, masking a cockeyed humanism and a purely erotic communication with the human "mystery"', which Boulez rejects as 'pathetically too little'.[132] It was, of course, at the time of his engagement with surrealism that Char first began to read the pre-Socratics, whose importance is also clear for Breton and the other surrealists including Souris.[133] The mutual admiration between Char and Martin Heidegger and their common fascination for the pre-Socratics clearly undermines Boulez's judgement since Heidegger found no fault with Char's understanding from the time of their first meeting in 1955 until his death in 1976. Indeed, for Heidegger, Char was the most important French thinker, more significant even than Sartre.[134] While Souvtchinsky, in a letter from 1968, perhaps rather nostalgically but also with conviction, reiterates his assessment of Char's worth as a great poet of dramatic and philosophical value whose interaction could still be of creative worth to Boulez, the moment had already passed and Boulez had moved on.[135]

André Breton and surrealism

The 'General Considerations' within Boulez's Darmstadt lectures of 1960 contain a number of references to the surrealists and their forebears including Alfred Jarry and Jacques Vaché, two figures whose work was revered by the Parisian surrealists. There are also citations from André Breton's *Second Surrealist Manifesto* (1930) and from a revolutionary paper delivered by Louis Aragon in 1920, as well as some extracts from his *Traité du style* (1928). The polemical energy of these proto-surrealist and surrealist texts contrasts keenly with the axiomatic-deductive rigour which informs so much of Boulez's lectures. While he does not explicitly name the composers who are the objects of his polemic, the references to surrealism must be understood against the background of Cage's successful visit to Darmstadt in 1958 and its influence on European composers such as Kagel, Bussotti and Stockhausen at the 1959 summer school. The explicit intention of Boulez's text seems to be to employ a range of surrealist references in order to discredit the new Cage-influenced aesthetic on the basis that it canonises the random gesture, tokenism, anti-art, nihilism and the banal, and consequently it is dismissed, albeit anonymously, as a naively belated Dadaism.

---

[132] Undated. Provisional editorial date 16 April 1963 (BN).
[133] Souris includes the pre-Socratic philosophers Heraclitus and Empedocles in an undated list of his 'planetary companions' (2000, 367).
[134] Worton 1996, 139.
[135] Letter dated 23 April 1968 (BN). From an earlier letter to Boulez dated 9 August 1959, it is clear that Souvtchinsky did not share his estimation of Mallarmé (PSS).

While this passage seems to condemn the surrealist writers who are quoted along with the Cage-inspired musical experimentalism which is the manifest object of Boulez's attack, this is not unambiguously the case. Without wishing to deny the starkness of the moments which he selects from these writers as exemplars of Dadaistic emptiness and excess, he could undoubtedly have made his point by citing from artists and writers whose work was much more anarchic and random. References to Jarry occur occasionally in Boulez's writings, always with humour, and it is difficult to make a strong comparison of the work of Breton and Aragon across their output with that of Cage. It may be that Boulez is facing off the challenge from Cage by flexing some surrealist muscles of his own, celebrating the vitality of surrealist language while reminding his opponents of surrealism's intrinsic Frenchness. Having moved to Baden-Baden shortly before the delivery of these lectures, Boulez was frequently criticised at this time and beyond for having capitulated to Germany and for having betrayed his homeland in doing so. The opening sections of the Darmstadt lectures show that Boulez is rooted aesthetically, if not musically, in French soil and the vast majority of his aesthetic references are to French writers.

That Boulez has selected for attention certain aspects of surrealist theory and practice which were not to his taste is obvious, but it is less clear that we can distil the sum and substance of his thoughts on surrealism from them alone. It is tempting to find here a reprise of the mutual antipathy between the surrealists and Erik Satie in the 1920s. The habitual lack of interest exhibited by the surrealists for matters musical did not inhibit their opposition to Satie, who was seen as a musical Dadaist, while the musical joker himself expressed hostility towards the Parisian surrealists in several texts.[136] Given Cage's affinity with Satie and the anti-Dada opposition which he received from Breton and Aragon, Boulez, according to this reading, ends up rather perversely on the surrealist side of the equation. While this reading may well be a little extreme, it at least has the merit of highlighting the elusiveness of Boulez's relationship with surrealism.

For Piencikowski, Boulez's attraction to Char and Mallarmé is to be understood in opposition to the surrealism of Aragon and Breton, and while he acknowledges Boulez's praise of surrealist vitality, this is to be interpreted as essentially ironic in nature. He hypothesises that the ambivalence in Boulez's relationship with surrealism is the result of a certain pliability which the composer allows himself within the context of a rigorous approach to aesthetic decision-making, a reading which coheres well with

---

[136] Wangermée 1995, 64, 104; Volta 1989, 173–87. Breton acknowledged in 1955 that Satie was an 'exceptional being' (Volta 1989, 186–7).

the Darmstadt lectures in which it is stated from the outset that the framework for action is determined by the dialectic of freedom and necessity.[137] In 'Corruption in the Censers' (1956), for example, having posited Debussy–Cézanne–Mallarmé as an 'axis' at 'the root of all modernism', Boulez notes that symbolism was superseded successively by the poet Guillaume Apollinaire and by the 'surrealist revolution'. Nevertheless, with the *bon mot* 'the surrealist lightning-for-the-weak-kneed trembles before the flashes of the "Coup de dés"', he compares Aragon's poem *Feu de joie* unfavourably as representative of surrealism in relation to Mallarmé's great work.[138]

Despite dismissing Breton's most recent poetry in 1949 as 'appallingly stupid',[139] Boulez has at times been drawn to his mode of expression. The title ... *explosante-fixe* ..., for example, is taken from a phrase in Breton's *L'Amour fou* (1937).[140] While Peyser wrongly attributes this title to another of Breton's books, namely *Nadja* (1928), she may have been confused by Boulez who, it seems, misquoted the phrase to her, conflating the famous last line of *Nadja:* 'Beauty will be CONVULSIVE or will not be at all' and the correct phrase from *L'Amour fou* which reads: 'Convulsive beauty will be veiled-erotic, fixed-explosive, magic-circumstantial, or it will not be.' More interesting is Boulez's recollection that the line stayed with him 'independently floating'.[141] Its interest relates less to the accuracy of Boulez's memory of why he chose it, more to the notion that it embedded itself within his consciousness in a rather isolated way. While we have no reason to question the integrity of his recollection, it is nevertheless mildly ironic that Boulez should perceive himself as having lifted the line so casually from a book which forces us repeatedly to question the possibility and meaning of chance and coincidence, and from an author who was rather in awe of the mysterious connectedness and strange correspondences which he perceived as quietly linking seemingly disparate relationships and events in quite inexplicable ways.

It is true, as Piencikowski notes, that Boulez is taken by Breton's turn of phrase, albeit describing him in 1954 as a 'distinguished old joker'.[142] Breton's phrase 'the infrangible kernel of darkness', for example, is cited by Boulez in 1964 in connection with the mysterious workings at the core of every creative personality, and it crops up again later in his Collège de France lectures.[143] While it would be foolish to make too clear a link between Boulez

---

[137] Piencikowski 2002, 50–1.   [138] Boulez 1991, 20.
[139] Letter from Boulez to Souris, dated 'February '49' (AML).
[140] Breton 1987, 19.   [141] Peyser 1977, 238.
[142] The phrase 'to reverse the poetic steam' is taken from Breton's *Ode à Charles Fourier* (1947) (Boulez 1991, 15). See Piencikowski 2002, 50–1.
[143] Boulez 1986, 83; 2005b, 92.

and Breton on the basis of a few choice quotes, the early interest in surrealism which Boulez revealed to Souris gives some grounds at least for openness to the possibility that its influence goes beyond occasional citation. While Boulez's aesthetic concerns seem far removed from certain key surrealist interests such as automatic writing, dream analysis, the communication between waking and dream life, differences in sexual practices, communism and the writing of group manifestoes, to name but a few, he is clearly closer to Breton's surrealism in his negational thinking and use of binary oppositions, his early aggressiveness and his interest in non-European cultures. While Breton was not alone in having these qualities and interests, and no causal relationship is suggested, we can simply note these intersections and pass on.[144] Whatever Boulez's view, Souris told Pousseur in 1953 that Surrealism continued to be of importance to him and, as Wangermée reveals, it was Breton's Second Manifesto which was the principal focus for his enduring interest. Indeed, he had defended the serial composers in an exchange of letters with René Magritte in 1953, in which he had queried the artist's capacity to make any kind of adequate judgement on Boulez's music.[145]

Artaud and Klee

Boulez's trajectory also brought him close to the work of Antonin Artaud, who animated the surrealist group between 1924 and 1926 until Breton characteristically decided that he was leading the group astray and diverting its energies. Boulez attended a public reading given by Artaud in Paris in July 1947,[146] it seems that he was present at his funeral in 1948,[147] and his early writings contain two significant references to him. In 'Proposals' (1948), Boulez called for a music which is 'collective hysteria and magic, violently modern – along the lines of Antonin Artaud', while ten years later, in 'Sound and Word' (1958), he identified the organisation of delirium, which he again specifically relates to Artaud, as an imperative for 'effective art'.[148] It is interesting to note that between these two citations, in an undated letter to Souvtchinsky from South America, which presumably emanates from his 1954 tour there, Boulez, having witnessed a macumba in Brazil with its hysterical states, had come to the paradoxical conclusion that hysteria is a purely passive state and that Artaud was on completely the wrong

---

[144] Schaeffner and Messiaen, for example, neither of whom were surrealists, are more immediate sources for Boulez's ethnomusicological interests.

[145] Wangermée 1995, 315–17.

[146] The reading took place at the Galerie Loeb in Paris (Boulez 1991, 43).

[147] Undated letter from Boulez to Souris (AML).

[148] Boulez 1991, 54; 43. References to delirium can be found in Artaud's *Le Théâtre et son double* (2005, 39; 46).

track. It is Mallarmé's 'Un coup de dés' with its absence of hysteria which now contains the 'true magic'.[149] Nevertheless, Boulez's abandoned project *Marges* (1962), a work for percussion, was to have had texts by Artaud, Rimbaud and Michaux. The Artaud text 'Tutuguri' or 'the rite of the black sun', which Boulez describes as 'very beautiful', pertains to a peyote rite of the Tarahumaras.[150] His knowledge of Artaud's oeuvre goes well beyond these particular texts and he was in an excellent position to get to know his work on account of his close friendship with Paule Thévenin (1923–93) who, after meeting the writer in 1946, had become close to him and the typist of his texts.[151]

Boulez's interest in the work of the artists Paul Klee, Joan Miró and André Masson are further instances of his fascination with figures who were on the margins of surrealism. While Klee and Miró were not surrealists, their works made a deep impression on the movement and were displayed, for example, at the first collective surrealist exhibition in 1925 along with many other artists including Masson. Boulez recalls that he first met Masson, Miró, and several other significant artists through Suzanne Tezénas.[152] Interestingly, Boulez and Miró featured together in an exhibition of their work entitled 'Joan Miró: Grafik, Pierre Boulez: Handschriften und Partituren' which formed part of the 1958 Donaueschingen Festival.[153] In a 1959 letter Miró, who shared Boulez's admiration for Mallarmé and especially for 'Un coup de dés', thanked the composer for sending him a copy of the score of one of his *Improvisation[s] sur Mallarmé*. He described the malleability (*plastique*) of the score as 'extraordinary' and his admiration for Boulez's use of different colours led him to request to see the manuscript on their next meeting.[154] Masson, a member of the surrealist group from 1924 until around 1930, worked with Boulez on productions for the Renaud-Barrault theatre company, devising scenic and costume design, as well as providing the sets for Barrault's production of Berg's *Wozzeck* in 1963 which Boulez conducted.[155]

---

[149] Undated letter to Souvtchinsky (BN).   [150] Boulez and Schaeffner 1998, 53.

[151] Artaud entrusted Thévenin in 1948 with the task of overseeing the publication of his work and she consequently spent much of her life editing his *Œuvres complètes*. Through Thévenin, whom he met around 1948, Boulez had access to unpublished texts by Artaud which he recalls discussing with her. See Boulez's tribute to Paule Thévenin in *Le Monde*, 12 May 2005.

[152] Samuel 2006, 5.

[153] The exhibition was organised by the Gesellschaft der Freunde junger Kunst, Baden-Baden and took place from 17 to 19 October 1958 at the Donaueschingen Stadthalle. Miró also provided a drawing for the programme booklet for Boulez's 'Musica Viva' concert at Munich in October 1960, which was later reproduced in the journal *Melos* (Heft 6 (June 1969), 249). I am grateful to Robert Piencikowski for this information.

[154] Letter dated 11 August 1959. There are three letters from Miró to Boulez (PSS).

[155] Robert Piencikowski has listed those painters, including Masson, whose work illustrated the Domaine Musical concerts (1991, p. xvi).

Concluding remarks

In this chapter we have attempted to reconstruct a history of musico-philosophical influence which was of great importance within French musical life in Boulez's formative years but which is almost unknown outside France today. While none of these figures is the equal of Adorno in philosophical terms and do not present the kind of sustained critique of twentieth-century and post-war music which we find in the Frankfurt philosopher, they have unquestionable interest in their own right, quite apart from the significant influence which they brought to bear upon Boulez. Their place in Boulez's development has been less well documented, and we do not, for example, find the same timely tributes in memory of Souvtchinsky, Schaeffner, Schloezer or Souris as those that he produced in the 1960s and early 1970s for Steinecke, Varèse, Scherchen, Désormière, Rosbaud, Adorno, Strobel and Maderna.[156] Boucourechliev, not Boulez, was the sole composer to honour Schloezer posthumously at a memorial evening in Paris in 1979.[157] While Schaeffner's widow told Souvtchinsky in 1980 that Boulez and Lévi-Strauss were the first to give their support to a projected volume of writings which she was planning in her late husband's honour,[158] no contribution by Boulez actually appeared, an omission which was only remedied by the *Avant-propos* provided by the composer for the publication of their correspondence in 1998.[159] In a similar way it was only with the posthumous publication of Souvtchinsky's *Un Siècle de musique russe* in 2004 that Boulez produced an appreciation of his old friend.[160] While Boulez recorded his debt to Souris in a letter to Schaeffner at the time of Souris's death, it is not something which has been the subject of sustained public reflection on Boulez's part.[161] The absence of memorial pieces should not, however, blind us to the importance of these figures in the composer's development. In introducing them within this chapter we are far from having exhausted their contribution, as will be seen for example in Chapter 3, which considers the place of dialectical thinking within Boulez's work.

[156] Boulez 1986, 495–524.   [157] Boucourechliev 1981, 17.
[158] Letter from Denise Paulme-Schaeffner to Souvtchinsky, dated 24 November 1980 (BN).
[159] Boulez and Schaeffner 1998, 9–10.   [160] Boulez 2005a, 654–6.
[161] Letter dated 27 February 1970. Cited in Boulez and Schaeffner 1998, 120–1.

3 Dialectic, negation and binary oppositions

The logic of musical development

Inherent within musical modernism is the conviction that music is not a static phenomenon defined by timeless truths and classical principles, but rather something which is intrinsically historical and developmental. While belief in musical progress or in the principle of innovation is not new or unique to modernism, such values are particularly important within modernist aesthetic stances. So it is, to take only some well-known examples, that Schoenberg is celebrated for having produced first post-tonal and then twelve-tone works which transcended the tonal system and embodied the apotheosis of chromaticism. In a similar way, the move beyond metrical rhythm accomplished by Stravinsky, the shift from dynamic forms to more static momentary sounds in Webern, the equalisation of parameters in Boulez, as well as the swallowing up of musical pitch in the more all-encompassing pitch/noise spectra of Stockhausen's electronic music, all signify the destruction of accepted musical norms which had previously constituted seemingly secure boundaries.[1]

While such radical changes have been rare in the history of Western music, slower, more progressive transformation, it seems, is more often the normal means whereby a given aesthetic movement, compositional technique, musical system, style or genre is replaced by another. The question of musical progress, which may be seen as one of musical logic, became a pressing concern at the time of the Enlightenment along with an interest in the kinds of historical processes which could produce such changes.[2] While belief in progress lies behind a number of significant eighteenth-century histories of music including those of Burney, Hawkins and Forkel, the aftermath of the French Revolution and subsequent Restoration fostered a more sceptical attitude towards the concept. Where Hegelian dialectical philosophy in the early nineteenth century and Darwinian evolution in the mid-century provided stronger bases for progressive modes of thought, it is clear that, from the late nineteenth century onwards, belief in progress as well as its outright rejection have at various times coexisted or have replaced one another in line with shifts in intellectual preferences. In the mid-twentieth century,

---

[1] Dahlhaus 1983, 68.   [2] See Sadie and Tyrrell 2001, vol. 11, pp. 546–58.

for example, Karl Popper provided one of the most robust refutations of historicism, which he dismissed as a mere tissue of speculations,[3] while application of the work of Thomas Kuhn may allow the hypothesis that music, like science, does not progress in a linear manner but rather through periodic revolutions which Kuhn refers to as paradigm shifts.[4]

The mechanisms of musical change may be theorised philosophically in a variety of ways, and it may be stated more specifically of Boulez that his work features a number of concepts which derive from a dialectical tradition of thought which, while it can be traced back to ancient Greek philosophy, is today most often associated with the tradition of German Idealism as embodied at its height in the philosophies of Kant, Schiller, Schelling and Hegel. Dialectical thinking undoubtedly has a significant place within Boulez's thought, but the specific sources for his interest are far from clear, hitherto mostly unexplored and, as we might expect, generally unacknowledged. That German Idealist philosophy is not explicitly cited within his writings should not be surprising to us as Boulez is after all a composer not a philosopher. Nevertheless, his frequent references to a number of dialectical relationships within music, his apparent concern with dialectical logic as expressed at various times in terms of negation and of synthesis, his habit of discussing the historical development of music in terms of its necessity or as the product of evolutionary or revolutionary processes, together with an almost all-pervasive tendency to think of the interior logic of composition as functioning through the operation of numerous binary or dialectical oppositions, all provide grist for the dialectical mill and a number of avenues for exploration. Consequently, the present chapter will consider each of these aspects of potentially dialectical thinking in Boulez's writing and composition. In doing so we will attempt to present a coherent account of his understanding of each concept while endeavouring to show how his ideas are related to those of a number of his musical and non-musical mentors and contemporaries. While this work will be to some extent genealogical, the intention is not to minimise the distinctiveness of Boulez's contribution but rather to enrich it by exploring the creative context within which it was conceived as well as showing how it relates to the dialectical tradition of thought.

Musical logic as negation

That Boulez and his fellow serial composers conceived their early innovations as embodying a fundamentally negational logic seems to have been

---

[3] Popper 1957.   [4] Kuhn 1962.

accepted without contention by supporters and opponents alike. Denis de Rougemont, for example, stated in 1954 that the serial composers appeared to be much more animated by the opposition they faced than by any intrinsic pleasure in their discoveries. These discoveries were made in self-conscious opposition to their opponents, while the composers themselves seemed to be primarily concerned with their incorporation within an evolutionary history which they declared to be 'necessary' by some unacknowledged form of Hegelian logic.[5] What for Rougemont was something of questionable rationale and intent was perceived very differently by Heinz-Klaus Metzger, who interpreted the undeniably negational aspect of serial composition as the genuine working out of a dialectical process. For Metzger, who praises the 'quasi-systematic consistency' which he finds in the works of Boulez, Stockhausen and Pousseur, the greatness of these works cannot be understood in purely immanent terms and has to be explained dialectically as deriving from the way in which these composers have '"compose[d] out" their historical positional value'. In doing so he believes that they have 'an exclusive claim to be the legitimate tradition'.[6] Rather than become entangled in the rights and wrongs of Rougemont's rather sceptical and disapproving judgement or Metzger's more apodictic claim, the fact of their convergence on the negational intent of serial composition is interesting in its own right and provides critical and historical grounding for the present enquiry.

Negation takes a number of forms within Boulez's work. It is glimpsed in the *Sonatine* (1946) to the extent that it is self-consciously written against the grain of early twentieth-century French chamber music, with its athematic transitions which separate the four notional movements. Boulez articulated his desire that the piece should produce an 'impression of shock, of violence' and he was delighted that the first performance in Brussels had caused a stir.[7] Negation is found in the exploding of traditional musical forms in the Second Sonata for piano (1948) where he has spoken in emphatic language of trying to 'destroy the first-movement sonata form, to disintegrate slow movement form by the use of the trope, and repetitive scherzo form by the use of variation form, and finally, in the fourth movement, to demolish fugal and canonic form'.[8] The works of the early 1950s, *Polyphonie X* and *Structures I* unleash the negational impulse with unprecedented vigour in confounding the kinds of relationships which had formerly linked the separate musical parameters within a unified whole. Furthermore, the very

---

[5] Rougemont 1954, 51. Boulez's opposition to Leibowitz, his temporary rejection of Messiaen and his epitaph for Schoenberg (is dead) are well-known examples.
[6] Metzger 1961, 24.
[7] These comments are found in two undated letters to Souris (AML).   [8] Boulez 1976, 41–2.

notion of the composer's subjectivity is negated in the algorithmical processes of *Structures Ia*. While *Le Marteau sans maître* marks a return to
freedom amidst the organisational complexity, negation here pertains to
the rejection of Western instrumental ensembles and timbres, and there
may also be an element of negation in the aleatoric aspects of the works
beginning with the Third Sonata for piano which at least weaken the concept
of closed musical forms.

   This negational impulse applies also to Boulez's musical theorising.
Recalling their first meeting in 1951, Pousseur acknowledges Boulez's
centrality in the formulation of serial principles, which were designed to
prevent all sense of tonal gravitation.[9] In the Darmstadt lectures of the
early 1960s, while setting out some basic principles for serial composition, Boulez stresses the importance of avoiding any kind of intervallic
relationship which conveys the conventional associations of tonality. He
writes of the need to avoid octaves, melodic and harmonic triads, indeed
'all intervals, or combinations of intervals, which have a tendency to
reinstate a functional principle of identity – of structural identification'.
Among such forbidden intervallic relationships, he includes intervals with a
strong gravitational pull and, in general, combinations with already 'established function[s]'.[10] Beyond musical syntax, negation also plays its part
in the concept of athematicism, which when viewed as the non-repetition
of figures and themes may be understood dialectically as the antithesis
of thematicism. In a similar way the concepts of smooth space and
smooth time may form dialectical antitheses to striated space and striated
time.

   Boulez was not alone in pursuing the path of negation, and consideration
of the writings of Pousseur and Stockhausen shows the extent to which it
was also central to their compositional programmes. In the article 'Situation
actuelle du métier de compositeur' (1954) Stockhausen, who formulated
and applied similarly negational principles within his early compositions,
relishes the almost unprecedented freedom which composers of his generation have at their disposal and, in language which clearly evokes the urban
challenges facing post-war architects and builders, he states boldly that 'the
"towns are rased" and one can recommence at the beginning, without taking
account of the ruins'.[11] In this view, composition, while acknowledging the
inevitable historical resonances within sounds, is to proceed by 'avoiding as
much as possible', and he notes elsewhere the deliberate attempt to avoid all
figurative repetition in the music which had been written since 1951,[12] an

---

[9] Peyser 1977, 73–4.   [10] Boulez 1971a, 49–50.   [11] Stockhausen 1954, 131.
[12] Stockhausen 1989, 41.

aspiration which was taken even further with the new electronic possibilities which enabled him to avoid all recognisable sounds.[13]

Negation was not, however, new or unique to the post-war generation. Indeed, comparison of Boulez's writings with those of Schoenberg reveals a number of close similarities in this regard. While Schoenberg does not himself suggest that his music is in any way dialectically negational, and it is precisely the 'negative quality' of the term 'atonality' which makes it unacceptable to him,[14] he does at times theorise new music in terms of the negative, speaking, for example, of the renunciation of a tonal centre in his second-period works.[15] He recommends that octave doubling be avoided since it would only emphasise the root in a quasi-tonic sense.[16] The task of composition between 1922 and 1930 is termed an involuntary duty which had to be accomplished in order to further musical progress,[17] and he describes the principles of this new music as presenting themselves

> even more negatively than the strictest rules of the strictest old counterpoint. There should be avoided: chromaticism, expressive melodies, Wagnerian harmonies, romanticism, private biographical hints, subjectivity, functional harmonic progressions, illustrations, leitmotives, concurrence with the mood or action of the scene and characteristic declamation of the text in opera, songs and choruses. In other words, all that was good in the preceding period should not occur now.[18]

In twelve-tone composition consonances such as major and minor triads as well as what he refers to as the 'simpler dissonances' of diminished triads and seventh chords, in other words the stock-in-trade of tonal harmony, are to be avoided as much as possible. For the new harmonic means to be explored fully the old orthodoxies must be excluded, at least temporarily. However, while some future reconciliation of the old and the new is possible, he believes that they are unlikely to meld harmoniously.[19]

It was Adorno, who, in the course of a number of essays, first developed an unambivalently dialectical account of Schoenberg's work and he presents his musical revolution as a 'rational execution, by the most advanced consciousness, of the historic compulsion to purify its material of the corruption of the decayed organic'.[20] Schoenberg's aesthetic radicalism is said to be legitimated by 'the tradition it negates', a tradition which it has both embraced and confronted in that he is simultaneously its heir and the instrument of its

---

[13] Stockhausen 1989, 58.   [14] Schoenberg 1975, 210–11.   [15] Schoenberg 1975, 86.
[16] Schoenberg 1975, 219.   [17] Schoenberg 1975, 53.   [18] Schoenberg 1975, 120.
[19] Schoenberg 1975, 207.
[20] See Adorno's 'On the Twelve-Tone Technique' (1929) and 'Reaction and Progress' (1930) (cited in Wiggershaus 1994, 90). See also his 'Arnold Schoenberg (1874–1951)' from 1953 (Adorno 1983, 147–72).

inevitable negation. In the *Philosophy of New Music* (1949), Adorno writes of the negative meaning of advanced music, which

> has no other alternative than to insist on its own rigidification without concession to that 'human factor' that it sees through, whatever attraction its allure still casts, as a mask for inhumanity. The truth of this music appears to reside in the organised absence of any meaning, by which it repudiates any meaning of organised society – of which it wants to know nothing – rather than in being capable on its own of any positive meaning. Under present conditions, music is constrained to determinate negation.[21]

Metzger acknowledges that his celebrated disagreement with Adorno in the late 1950s was primarily concerned with the extent to which negation within the new music was abstract or dialectical.[22] Following Adorno, he directs attention to the negational element immanent within musical terminology and within concepts themselves. The concept of atonality is viewed as a dialectical negation of tonality. The minor ninths and major sevenths of Webern's late works avoid all remaining tonal tendencies and, in this avoidance, dialectically posit what they self-consciously evade.[23]

That Boulez's music was understood by some writers almost from the start as negational is supported by Fred Goldbeck's remark that Boulez, following Webern, has taken even further 'the "syntax of avoidance" of the Schoenbergians'.[24] While negation was clearly a central element within Boulez's approach to composition, at least from 1946, it is only with the lecture 'Nécessité d'une orientation esthétique' in 1963 that he provides a sustained aesthetic reflection on this aspect of his practice. He scrutinises the nature of the negation which has been undertaken in post-war music and he questions whether or not creativity can begin with refusal, or whether destruction is necessary before reconstruction can begin.[25] He challenges the success of such destruction and wonders if it has not been naive and presumptuous to wish to build 'on ruins or on a tabula rasa'.[26] He considers the possibility that behind such doubt lies 'a pure appetite for annihilation' which is not completely hidden by its rationality. Furthermore, the very necessity for such doubt seems to be far from evident in many compositions. As in the article 'Alea', Boulez next focuses on the return to musical subjectivism, which he believes to be no more successful than the previous

---

[21] Adorno 2006, 19–20.   [22] Metzger 1961, 24.

[23] For Adorno, the negational value within Webern's work is to be located in the brevity of his forms which deny the possibility of temporal extension (1966, 12). Pousseur suggests that Webern, in his late works, uses the serial system dialectically, 'going beyond thematic methods without abandoning them' (1972, 97), that is *'going beyond some essentially negative positions of modern art'* (134).

[24] Goldbeck 1950, 292.   [25] Boulez 1995, 555.   [26] Boulez 1995, 556.

asceticism. All of this leads him to conclude that the adoption of one-sided extremes does not make clear why a method based on doubt should be applied in the first place as a basis for knowledge.[27] While negation challenges musical tradition, this is not a denial of its truth. Doubt is primarily an attempt to expose the ingenuity and artifice within musical elements which have come to be accepted as natural. This should not be translated into terms of 'disrespect and destruction' with regard to tradition.

Boulez reiterates his conviction that it is necessary to reject all inherited notions and to begin from a *tabula rasa* in order to reconstruct musical concepts on the basis of a new set of assumptions.[28] This, he believes, will open up aesthetic choice. He reflects that he and his generation inherited a musical situation which contained acute, inherent contradictions, which they countered through the attempted annihilation of subjective and accidental elements within composition. While he seems to accept that composers embarked upon this path without sufficient awareness of the risks which it entailed, and he acknowledges the correctness of certain criticisms from 'intelligent, if not well-disposed' commentators, he is, paradoxically, equally unequivocal in stating that composers had already anticipated most of these objections. He affirms that the fundamental idea within his own project was 'to eliminate . . . absolutely all trace of heritage' in terms of 'figures, phrases, developments, form' and so on, a stage which was to be followed by a gradual recuperation of these elements in a completely new synthesis which would not be corrupted by foreign elements such as 'stylistic reminiscences'.

Despite the problems produced by the early serial experiments, Boulez maintains that composers must continue to proceed by way of doubt, while distancing himself from any attempt to provide a philosophical basis for such a stance on the grounds that such undertakings have lacked rigour.[29] However he also acknowledges that his own justification is equally open to attack on the grounds that it based doubt upon 'the power of numbers, and on an almost "mystical" quality of the experience of emptiness!' While he locates 'productive doubt' within 'the interaction of rationality and affectivity' instead of in their separation, the challenge is to avoid needless destruction and to question the necessity of negation at every stage.[30]

In 'Nécessité', Boulez rarely uses the term 'negation', preferring to speak of 'doubt', a terminological choice which reflects the rereading of Descartes which he had undertaken in preparation for the lectures.[31] While it is clear that his thinking at this time was directly informed by this reading, it is nevertheless the case that the big picture of musical development, which

[27] Boulez 1995, 557–8.   [28] Boulez 1995, 561–4.
[29] Boulez 1995, 572–3.   [30] Boulez 1995, 574–9.
[31] He told Stockhausen this in an undated letter. The postmark is dated 20[?] December 1959.

emerges from his writings, is one which for all its Cartesian doubt is strongly dialectical, albeit in a mostly undefined way. Without wishing to suggest that there is anything deeply Hegelian in what Boulez is doing, it is interesting to note that Hegel, in his *Phenomenology*, distinguishes the dialectical project from the conventional understanding of doubt. This is characterised as a 'shilly-shallying about this or that presumed truth, followed by a return to that truth again, after the doubt has been appropriately dispelled – so that at the end of the process the matter is taken to be what it was in the first place'. Dialectical doubt, in contrast, is identified as 'the conscious insight into the untruth of phenomenal knowledge, for which the supreme reality is what is in truth only the unrealized Notion'.[32] It is, therefore, a radicalised doubt which seeks to push Descartes further since, in Hegel's view, the conclusions at the end of Descartes' *Meditations* ultimately fail to overcome the radical doubts which were proposed at the outset of the enquiry. In the case of Boulez and his fellow composers, the existence of a number of radical musical works is evidence enough that the musical doubt which they enacted did not leave things as they were before. It is also interesting that Boulez cites Souvtchinsky within this essay but omits to name Adorno, whom he presumably has in mind at certain points. Perhaps more surprisingly, in discussion with Berio and Pousseur that same year, he broadened the basis for fundamental doubt, suggesting that it is rooted also in a number of contemporary philosophers, of whom only the German phenomenologist Edmund Husserl is named.[33]

In the lecture 'Where are We Now?' (1968), Boulez characterises the music of the late 1940s and 1950s as the establishment of a new musical language, based on negation. While acknowledging the sometimes 'exaggeratedly strict' nature of integral serialism, this is understood to have been a necessary stage since:

> in order to forge a language strict disciplines are necessary and so is a knowledge of the *via negativa*, the phenomenon of negation. If you do not negate, if you do not make a clean sweep of all that you have inherited from the past, if you do not question that heritage and adopt an attitude of fundamental doubt towards all accepted values, well!, you will never get any further.[34]

Despite the negational thrust of Boulez's early activity, he was paradoxically of the opinion from as early as 1952 that after a phase of 'destructive experiment' which began around 1910, in which both tonality and regular metre were abolished, his own task was to unite the disparate achievements

---

[32] Hegel 1977, 49–50.   [33] Nattiez 2005b, 28.   [34] Boulez 1986, 446.

of his predecessors.[35] In Darmstadt in 1963 he drew attention to the importance of a positive dialectical gesture which is the necessary consequence and corollary of negation.[36] This synthetic impulse is much surer in 1968 when he states unequivocally with the passing of the negational stage that it is now time for a new phase which will take the form of a 'necessary synthesis' of musical, scientific, sociological and economic endeavours.[37] In 'Technology and the Composer' (1977), he reiterates the necessity of going beyond negation in the formation of a new musical language.[38] Despite such talk of dialectical 'synthesis', Pousseur is correct in identifying Boulez, of all the post-war generation, as the one who remained the most enduringly connected to the 'grammatical formulations' which were developed in the 1950s, still finding within them new possibilities for development, the 'undeniable efficacy' of which Pousseur continued to acknowledge.[39]

While Boulez spoke of a period of 'synthesis' around 1968 (and possibly 1963), some of his colleagues had already rejected the approaches of the 1950s as simplistic, and Pousseur felt the need, from as early as 1960, to go beyond the antitheses which had been the focus of their work for around twelve years, and which had marked composition from the beginning of the century.[40] Recognising that a degree of reintegration had already taken place in recent composition at the morphological level in the form of reference points, he suggested at Darmstadt in 1963 that certain harmonic means which had previously been excluded from practice should now be readmitted.[41] He describes this elsewhere as a 'progressive *refusal of refusal*'[42] and as its supersession to 'a higher level of synthesis'.[43] Boulez disagreed, warning that such intervals can only be admitted under precisely controlled stylistic conditions since they do not exist alone but rather within *Gestalten* which are pregnant with signification.[44]

While Pousseur and Boulez both used the dialectical term 'synthesis' to encapsulate the new music which they now envisaged, they had diverged significantly from one another in terms of aesthetics. They saw each other very rarely after the early 1960s and their correspondence, which had been regular and musically significant in the 1950s, became infrequent after

---

[35] Boulez 1991, 114–15. In 'Tendencies in Recent Music' (1953/7), he implies that while previous efforts had been expended on 'destruction', the next stage of technical development is to be a more 'constructive' one (Boulez 1991, 177).

[36] Nattiez 2005b, 43.

[37] Boulez 1986, 462–63. The conceptualisation of the dialectic in terms of 'thesis, antithesis (negation) and synthesis' is a misrepresentation of Hegel (Mueller 1996, 301) but may, nevertheless, be the model which Boulez, Pousseur and others had in mind.

[38] Boulez 1986, 493.

[39] Pousseur 1997, 165. Pousseur returns to the negational nature of 1950s generalised serialism several times in his writings (Pousseur 1997, 128–9, 195).

[40] Pousseur 1997, 191.   [41] Nattiez 2005b, 25–6.   [42] Pousseur 1997, 232.

[43] Pousseur 1997, 128.   [44] Nattiez 2005b, 46–7.

1964, although there was still communication until the beginning of the 1970s. The divergence in their aesthetic approaches is glimpsed in a letter from Boulez in 1963 in which the popular music, which clearly interests Pousseur, is scathingly termed 'folklore'. It is dismissed as 'completely dead' while any attempt to revive it is 'a pure illusion', a judgement which Boulez seeks to justify on the basis that the current stage of musical development has struck a 'definitive blow' against those 'local particulars' which remain, by which he seems to refer to the remnants of folk/popular/national styles which pre-date the formation of what he takes to be some new international musical currency.[45] In a similar vein, Pousseur cites a letter he received from Boulez in 1971, which he interprets as Boulez's opposition to his attempt to 'conciliate old and new, black and white, while he [Boulez] preferred to burn everything'.[46]

If the present study were concerned with the truth of the dialectic, the discrepancy in synthetic outcomes reached by Boulez and Pousseur would prompt us to question how it can be that these two composers can have accepted the same (or very similar) negational, antithetical positions in the 1950s only then to arrive at very different notions of what the resultant moment of synthesis should be. Without wishing to make inflated philosophical claims, it is interesting to note that such a multiform possibility is arguably consistent with even Hegel's position. As noted earlier, the idea of synthesis is a rather widespread simplification of the more properly termed *Aufhebung*, which entails a simultaneous cancelling and preserving of contradictory phenomena. The Hegel scholar Michael Forster, for example, presents a provisional account of the workings of the Hegelian *Aufhebung*, in which he suggests that 'Hegel thinks that for each pair of mutually implying contrary categories, there will be one and one only new category that can be said to unify them in a way that in a sense preserves while in a sense abolish[ing] them, thereby avoiding their self-contradictoriness'. If this were indeed the case, then the radically different moments of 'synthesis' reached by Boulez and Pousseur would be a serious obstacle to the workings of any kind of Hegelian dialectic in the development of serial and post-serial music. However, this turns out not to be the case since Hegel 'in fact believes that there will generally be *more* than one known new category that stands in this relation to a given pair of mutually implying contrary categories'.[47] This more open-ended reading is given a rather different spin by the more

---

[45] Letter from Boulez to Pousseur, dated 20 April 1963 (PSS).

[46] Cited in Peyser 1977, 241. The voluminous correspondence between Boulez and Pousseur is held at the Paul Sacher Stiftung in Basel.

[47] Forster 1993, 146–7. Forster suggests, for example, that the antithetical relations of *Being* and *Nothing* find a point of unity, not only in *Becoming*, as Hegel expounded in his *Logic* (§88)(1830), but also in *Beginning*.

Deleuzian Catherine Malabou who states that multiplicity in Hegel 'is not systematically and violently reduced to a unity'.[48] Consequently, the discrepancy between the musics of synthesis which were produced in the 1960s would in no way be problematic, in principle, for a broadly Hegelian understanding of what Boulez and Pousseur were doing. Such readings would also seem to be at odds with Metzger's judgement that Boulez, Stockhausen and Pousseur have 'an exclusive dialectical claim to be the legitimate tradition' since these more open-ended views can allow that if music does progress through the operation of a principle of negation, then any particular stance may only be one of a number of alternatively equal and valid positions.

The philosophy of history

Negation is not an isolated phenomenon in Boulez's early aesthetic and it forms part of a musical consciousness which perceives itself significantly, though not exclusively, in inherently historical terms. That the philosophy of history which is articulated within his writings is not original to him is less important than the insight it provides into his understanding of the workings of serial composition. It is perhaps surprising to discover the extent to which a number of variations on the theme of the philosophy of history was central in the mid-twentieth century to the musical schemas theorised by French-speaking writers such as Leibowitz, Souvtchinsky, Wyschnegradsky and Ansermet.

The 'Prolegomena to Contemporary Music' which opens Leibowitz's *Schoenberg and his School* (1947) presents a reading of Western musical history which is focused upon the developing concept of polyphony. In this context Leibowitz theorises a form of dialectic in which any polyphonic musical system is said to carry within itself 'the seeds of its own destruction'.[49] So it is that the epochs of modality, tonality and chromaticism, which Leibowitz identifies as having most significance in the history of Western music, are diagnosed as containing within themselves a '*destructive element*' which, while facilitating their development, also results in their inevitable annihilation,[50] and after which Schoenberg's twelve-tone technique then appears as 'a synthesis of all preceding techniques'.[51] From this clearly historicist perspective, which looks to Webern for support,[52] the supersession of tonality is thus merely an unavoidable moment in the evolution of musical language in which twelve-tone technique is hailed as the principal musical advance of the age.

---

[48] Malabou 1996, 134.   [49] Leibowitz 1949a, 7.   [50] Leibowitz 1949a, 23.
[51] Leibowitz 1949a, 103.   [52] Leibowitz 1949b, 35.

While Leibowitz's interest in aesthetic issues was traced in Chapter 2 to his contact with Schloezer, his particular concern for dialectical philosophy should be interpreted within the context of a renewed interest in Hegel, the dialectic and the philosophy of history which first appeared in France around 1924 in the work of André Breton and the Surrealists,[53] but which really took off in the 1930s through the efforts of the philosophers Alexandre Kojève and Jean Hyppolite, who were instrumental in the shift from primarily Bergsonian and Neo-Kantian models of thought.[54] While both taught highly influential courses on Hegel's *Phenomenology*, Kojève's lectures, which he delivered at the École Pratique des Hautes Études between 1933 and 1939, were attended by a significant number of important figures who, in turn, became proponents of dialectical thinking. So powerful was their combined impact that Hegelianism continued to flourish in France until the 1960s when a new generation of philosophers vehemently rejected the dialectic, turning instead to Nietzsche. While Leibowitz did not experience Kojève's lectures for himself, he belonged after the Second World War to a group of artists and philosophers who had, and his relationships with Bataille, Sartre, Merleau-Ponty and Queneau certainly provided him with opportunities for exposure to discussion of Hegel's *Phenomenology* as well as to the work of Husserl and Heidegger. Queneau, furthermore, was the editor of Kojève's Hegel lectures and therefore in an excellent position to keep Leibowitz well informed. Of course, the extent to which this possibility became actuality is unknown.[55]

Of even greater musical import is the fact that Leibowitz's dialectical account of the development of twelve-tone music did not take shape independently of Adorno and, presumably as part of his new aesthetic orientation, he wrote to the philosopher in 1946 requesting that he forward details of his 'music theoretical work'.[56] In contrast with the dismissive attitude displayed by Schaeffner and Boulez, the tone of Adorno's letters is unremittingly positive and supportive as he praises Leibowitz as 'a musician of the highest rank'.[57] His compositions are acclaimed as representing 'the highest level of composition which can be found today in general',[58] and Adorno

---

[53] Breton and his fellow surrealists interpreted the dialectic in their own idiosyncratic ways, as they attempted to go beyond the contradictory antinomies of Western thinking. See Breton 1963, 76–7.

[54] Eribon 1991, 15–23; Macey 1993, 31–3.

[55] While Ulrich Mosch suggests that the directness of this link is a matter of speculation (2004, 176), Sabine Meine is more confident that Kojève's ideas will have filtered through to Leibowitz through his contact with these figures (2000, 72). Schloezer described Kojève's book as the clearest and strongest thing which he had read on Hegel (Letter to Souris, dated July 1947 by Souris).

[56] Adorno responded with a list of his writings. Letter dated 3 May 1946 (PSS). The correspondence between Adorno and Leibowitz was conducted between 1946 and 1965.

[57] Letter from Adorno to Helene Berg, dated 23 November 1949 (PSS).

[58] Letter from Adorno to Leibowitz, dated 24 November 1948 (PSS).

even offers support for his musicological prose, suggesting that he should write a book on twelve-tone technique.[59] The extent of Adorno's importance for Leibowitz, in turn, may perhaps be judged from a letter to the philosopher in 1963 in which he writes: 'I somehow knew that I had found my entire way through you.'[60]

While Boulez often gives the impression that he is far removed from Leibowitz's views, there are undoubtedly points of convergence and it may be that their relationship was more complicated than it appears.[61] Despite their common dismissal of all contemporary composers who do not share the twelve-tone imperative, Boulez rejects the teleological tendency within Leibowitz's account, positing instead that discontinuity within musical evolution is as significant as continuity, a point which, as we will see, stems from Souvtchinsky. Furthermore, 'necessary' developments are not predictable in advance but are instead justified after the event. While Schloezer makes a number of criticisms of *Schoenberg and his School*, Leibowitz's thesis nevertheless appears to him as 'otherwise well grounded on the whole'.[62] He praises its thesis of a dialectical development which roots the Second Viennese composers within the German tradition while also criticising its absolute view of the compositional technique of the Second Viennese composers. For Schloezer, Leibowitz's reading of history is far too simplified an account, ignoring anything which does not fit neatly into its evolutionary scheme. Of course, Schaeffner, as we have seen, had made some of these same criticisms with greater force and less sympathy a year earlier in the article 'Halifax RG587', in which he rejects the almost exclusively Germanic nature of Leibowitz's musical historicism.[63] While Souris, who had been on friendly terms with Leibowitz from 1945, was generally supportive, he nevertheless distanced himself in 1951 from his unilateral view of musical progress as the unswerving expansion of musical complexity.[64] Leibowitz, we may note, was undoubtedly correct in attributing this shift to the influence of Boulez.[65]

While Boulez is critical of Leibowitz's historicism, it is difficult to avoid a certain historicism within his own thought, particularly in his early statements where he writes of 'the "necessary" work',[66] of 'the felt necessity, of our time',[67] or of serialism as 'a logical consequence of history – or

[59] Letter from Adorno to Leibowitz, dated 24 December 1949 (PSS).
[60] Letter dated 6 October 1963 (cited in Meine 2000, 31). Meine provides a full discussion of Leibowitz's philosophical engagements including his 'dialogue with Adorno' (Meine 2000, 182–4, 208–10). Adorno found Leibowitz's account 'too apologetic and uncritical' (Meine 2000, 208).
[61] See Mosch 2004, 183 ff.; Meine 2000, 213.   [62] Cited in Meine 2000, 202–3.
[63] Schaeffner 1998, 229–39.   [64] Souris 2000, 185–6.   [65] Wangermée 1995, 289.
[66] Boulez 1991, 13.   [67] Boulez 1991, 115.

historically logical'.[68] His writings are replete with statements which continually seek to forge a particular conception of musical history. This is perhaps most clearly the case in the entry on *Counterpoint* which he contributed to the *Encyclopédie Fasquelle de la musique* in 1958, in which he telescopes the history of Western music into three evolutionary phases, namely of monody, of polyphony (from counterpoint to harmony) and a new third phase which he describes as 'a kind of "polyphony of polyphonies"; that is, a phase where one has recourse to a *distribution* of intervals, and no longer a straight superimposition'.[69] Without wishing to overstate their similarity, it is difficult not to compare Boulez's scheme with the earlier tripartite model formulated by Leibowitz.

Before considering the particularities of Boulez's position further it may be helpful to look briefly at the philosophy of history which was formulated by the Russian émigré composer and music theorist Ivan Wyschnegradsky (1893–1979). In his *Une philosophie dialectique de l'art musical* (1936) or *Le Loi de la pansonorité* (1953) he presented a dialectical scheme of music history in which he theorised the development of Western music as occurring in three stages, each of which is transitory and preparatory. Accordingly, medieval modality is replaced dialectically by tonality, which is itself replaced by a number of supratonal forms (atonality, metatonality, ultratonality or microtonality) which find their consummation in what he called pansonority.[70]

The dialectic which Wyschnegradsky theorises obeys its own developmental laws which, despite their apparent illogicality in the sense that progress is not universally linear, nevertheless result in the system of pansonority which is described as 'the end of music'.[71] In this scheme, each stage in music's historical development contains within itself 'the germs of its own destruction' but, while negation is involved in each transition, it is not a sufficient explanation as each new stage also encapsulates a positive aspect which is irreducible to the preceding stages.[72] The system of pansonority which is theorised as the quasi-Hegelian end-point of musical development cannot therefore be reduced to merely the negation of a previous musical system, and it is posited instead on the basis of a 'new constructive

---

[68] Boulez 1991, 214.   [69] Boulez 1991, 232.

[70] Wyschnegradsky 2005, 14; Jedrzejewski 2005, 8. The content of the three periods is not identical in the 1936 and the 1953 versions of Wyschnegradsky's study. It is also interesting to note that in the 1840s, the Belgian musicologist François-Joseph Fétis (1784–1871) theorised the development of harmony in four discrete stages. The *ordre unitonique* relates to modal music, the *ordre transitonique* to the advent of tonal modulation, the *ordre pluritonique* to the advanced system of modulation which he believed was personified in Mozart, and the *ordre omnitonique* where modulation is so chromatic that tonality is threatened (Sadie and Tyrrell 2001, vol. 8, p. 747).

[71] Wyschnegradsky 1996, 101; 104.   [72] Wyschnegradsky 1996, 60.

principle' centred on the concept of musical spatiality.[73] Seen in this light, musical history becomes the gradual opening up of universal musical space in terms of all its dimensions. Wyschnegradsky spells out this dialectic of continuity and discontinuity as taking place within the framework of what is now believed to be a mistaken conception of the Hegelian dialectic as the succession of thesis, antithesis and synthesis.[74]

While there is a certain interest in the tripartite historical schemes which Leibowitz, Wyschnegradsky and Boulez produced, we cannot simply reduce Boulez's historical divisions to the work of his two elders. Leibowitz and Wyschnegradsky find in a particular musical system, dodecaphony for the former and pansonority for the latter, a point in musical evolution which in quasi-Hegelian terms could be construed as constituting the end of music. While Schoenberg imagined that he had constructed a musical system which would keep composers busy for a hundred years, it is not clear that Leibowitz foresees a time when dodecaphony will be dialectically overcome in its turn. It is even more certain that for Wyschnegradsky the attainment of pan-sonority, when musical space will be opened up to the greatest extent that human perception will allow, will mark the end of music's historical development. It is not so clear that the third stage in Boulez's tripartite scheme, the polyphony of polyphonies, is to be understood in such a definitive, consummatory manner.

Evolution, revolution and necessity

While the evolutionary model of musical progress is one which was adopted by a number of mid-century composers and theorists including Leibowitz, Schloezer, Schaeffner and Wyschnegradsky, its frequent use alongside that of revolution in Boulez's writings from the late 1940s right up to the present is indicative of the kind of development he believes to be operative in musical history. While Debussy is credited with having accomplished 'a radical, if not always spectacular revolution',[75] and the music of the Second Viennese composers is described in both revolutionary and evolutionary terms,[76] the uneasy coexistence of innovation and tradition in Schoenberg is dismissed as a revolutionary pretence which is undermined by his care for tradition.[77] Schoenberg was in fact extremely solicitous that his music and theory should be considered in an evolutionary rather than a revolutionary perspective

---

[73] Wyschnegradsky 1996, 71.
[74] Wyschnegradsky 1996, 253. The dialectic of continuity and discontinuity is central to Wyschne-gradsky's theory from its early formulation in 1927 to its later versions in 1936 and 1953.
[75] Boulez 1991, 276.   [76] Boulez 1991, 201, 231–2, 287, 297.
[77] Boulez 2005a, 378; 2005b, 534.

and it was important to him that he had been true to his predecessors and that his techniques were rooted in the past.[78] In fact his concern to disseminate this image of his project led him after the First World War to downplay those aspects of his work which he had previously been content to think of as revolutionary and to portray them within a more evolutionary historical model.[79]

Given Schoenberg's preferences, it is interesting to note that references to evolution far outnumber those to revolution in all of Boulez's writings.[80] They appear as early as 1949 in 'Trajectories' where he writes of the evolution of musical technique,[81] while in 'Bach's Moment' (1951), he thinks of dodecaphony as obeying a discontinuous, evolutionary dialectic.[82] In the articles from the late 1940s and 1950s he writes of the evolution of rhythm and sound materials,[83] of musical morphology, and of systems and procedures.[84] In the early 1960s he states that music's condition is one of 'permanent revolution'[85] and that 'history is divided into periods of evolution and periods of mutation, or, in other words, periods of conquest and periods of stabilisation'.[86] There are numerous references to musical evolution in the Collège de France lectures where, to take only a few examples, he sees it at work with regard to technology, instruments, style, musical thought, formal structures, expression, counterpoint and harmony, timbre, the Idea, musical parameters as well as musical *écriture*. Evolutions are now divided into those which are 'slow and continuous' and those which are 'abrupt and discontinuous', while composers are equally categorised as either inscribing themselves 'within a continuous evolution' or, alternatively, as being almost unconcerned with evolutionary continuity.[87]

For Boulez, serialism is legitimated on the basis of its 'historic necessity' as it responds to conflicts within twelve-tone and neo-classical composition. In 'Possibly ...' (1952), he refers to its opponents as detractors on the basis that they absolutely refuse to acknowledge it as a natural historical outcome, preferring to view it as the result of more random efforts.[88] They are berated for holding an anti-historical position. Of course, it is also within this article that Boulez, following Leibowitz, declares that 'any musician who has not experienced – I do not say understood, but truly experienced – the necessity of dodecaphonic language is USELESS. For his entire work brings him up short of the needs of his time.'[89] The question of the historical or ahistorical

---

[78] Schoenberg 1975, 50–1, 76.   [79] Auner 2003, 165.
[80] A number of references to evolution and dialectic can also be found in Pousseur's writings from the 1950s and early 1960s.
[81] Boulez 1991, 204.   [82] Boulez 1991, 13.   [83] Boulez 1991, 108.   [84] Boulez 1991, 142–3.
[85] Boulez 1986, 71.   [86] Boulez 1986, 35.   [87] Boulez 2005b, 549.   [88] Boulez 1991, 113.
[89] In *Introduction à la musique de douze sons* Leibowitz writes of Schoenberg's music as the ' "guide" for every truly contemporary [actuel] musician' (Leibowitz 1949b, 13).

nature of serialism was not so easily settled, however, and in 'Aesthetics and the Fetishists' (1961), Boulez again refers to the 'refusal to accept history and the historical perspective' as a criticism which has been made against him.[90] Calling upon Adorno for support, he reflects that a composer must draw out the consequences which are implicit in the language which has been inherited, and he postulates the existence of 'a dialectical relationship between history and the individual' in which history provides a challenge for the individual while the individual is charged with reconfiguring history in some kind of irreversible way. Caught up in this dialectic, it is consequently impossible for the composer to be independent of his time.

Boulez's reflection, however, seems rather tame in comparison with another passage from Adorno, this time from his 1934 article 'The Dialectical Composer', which Boulez does not refer to. Here, while acknowledging that the dialectic of the composer and the musical material is not new to twentieth-century music, Adorno formulates the insight that what is really special about Schoenberg and what sets him apart from the rest is the way in which the 'dialectical relationship between artist and material...achieved its Hegelian "self-consciousness"' in his music.[91] In articulating the other dialectical pole within the closely related opposition of composer and historical material, it is not, however, Adorno, but rather Souvtchinsky who Boulez calls upon and it is clear that it is Souvtchinsky's philosophy of history which he takes up as his own. While there is no reason to believe that Boulez was aware of the sources from which Souvtchinsky's philosophy is drawn, it is of interest for the present study to explore them to some extent, and to consider how such ideas have been transmitted through Souvtchinsky to assume a capital place in Boulez's musical world-view.

Souvtchinsky's philosophy of history stems from a tradition of Russian thought which arose in the 1850s out of the influence of German Idealism (Schelling in the 1830s, Hegel in the 1840s) and German historicism, mediated through a great number of other minds such as Alexander Herzen (1812–70) in the nineteenth century and Nicolas Berdyaev (1874–1948) in the twentieth. In those writings in which Souvtchinsky considers pre- and post-revolutionary Russian history, while assessing present possibilities, a clear historicism emerges in which words such as 'inescapable' and 'predetermined' are used freely alongside equally charged phrases which tell of Russia's 'specific historic mission' and of its historical hour.[92] Of course it is

---

[90] Boulez 1986, 39–40.   [91] Adorno 2002, 207.

[92] Souvtchinsky 1990, 33, 51–4. Souvtchinsky draws upon a nineteenth-century tradition in Russian thought which looks to Hegel's concept of the 'world-historical individual'. These are exceptional figures who have the ability to rise above the restricted horizon of their time to discern the direction in which history is moving (Beiser 2005, 269). The notion of 'a

as a central figure in the Eurasian movement in the 1920s that Souvtchinsky spent his energy in theorising Russia's post-revolutionary political, religious and cultural future in dialectical terms. Drawing on the philosophers Vladimir Solovev and Nicolai Fedorov, he envisaged aesthetic experience as playing a central part in the reconfiguration of society for which it would be necessary to forge a new conception of art and creativity,[93] and in the article 'Deux Renaissances' (1926) he analysed the cultural renaissance in Russian society in the 1890s to support the Eurasian thesis that yet another cultural renaissance could spring up in post-revolutionary Russia.[94]

When Souvtchinsky left politics behind with the demise of the Eurasian movement in 1928–9, he devoted himself once again to cultural-philosophical and more specifically musical concerns, while retaining important aspects of this philosophy of history. In 'À propos d'un retard' (1954), in which he considers the concept of musical evolution, he contrasts two distinctive views of history which he summarises as 'process' and 'fact'. The first is 'a *dynamic* process, like a torrent, like an uninterrupted chain of causal relations, where each link, each moment is determined and "explained" by the preceding, while preparing the following'. This is contrasted with the view that history can be understood 'as a discontinuous sequence of events, of facts, each having a precise aspect, limited in space and time, *static*, so to speak'. For Souvtchinsky, these two distinct conceptions have equal justification and are united and fulfilled in 'a single, ontological conception of history'. While they are 'indivisible' they are nevertheless 'clearly distinguishable'.[95] It is evident that none of this is original to Souvtchinsky and it forms part of a distinctive tradition of Russian thought which is much more fully theorised for example by Berdyaev.[96]

In 'Aesthetics and the Fetishists' (1961), Boulez draws explicitly upon Souvtchinsky's historical conception as formulated in 'À propos d'un retard', citing him as follows:

> Even if we allow due importance to the role played in the development of genius by social and technical evolution, if we view the phenomenon of 'culture' as a dialectical process that is apparently continuous, and if we recognise to the full the importance of the milieu and the age as both

world-historical mission' is found in Herzen and Berdyaev and for the latter 'the Russians cannot exist without a messianic hope' (1950, 169). Schloezer's opposition to the Eurasian idea of a Russian cultural mission and its messianism led to a break with Souvtchinsky in the early 1920s which was not repaired until after the Second World War (Kohler 2003, 175, 166).

[93] Glebov 2006, 213–15.   [94] Souvtchinsky 1990, 72–9.   [95] Souvtchinsky 1954, 121–3.

[96] Berdyaev states that 'there is no such thing in the history of mankind as a continual progress upward in a straight line' (1933, 57) and that 'the path of man throughout the ages is not a continuous, unbroken development. On the contrary, it is characterised by the eruption of irrational forces: it is a trial of man's freedom, undetermined, ambiguous and unpredictable' (1950, 216–17).

determining the creative formation of one generation and acting as a stimulus to the formation of the type and mentality of the next, it is still essential to recognise that, despite all such 'preparation', the appearance of a great creative artist is always something unexpected, something unpredictable.[97]

In 'À propos d'un retard', which was written at a moment of serial self-examination, while commending the ability and courage of Boulez's generation of composers, Souvtchinsky acknowledges that serialism had often neglected to establish a hierarchy of musical values. However, in overtly messianic terms, reminiscent of his hopes for post-revolutionary Russia, he lauds Boulez, who is not named, as the 'predestined musician' who can enable 'a new generation to take definitive consciousness of itself, of its historic value' in order to overcome the setback (*retard*) which music has suffered.[98] In 'Ceux du Domaine Musical' (1963), he further terms Boulez a 'grand créateur' and judges that the number and quality of his musical gifts set him apart from the other members of his generation.[99] Finally, in 'Deso Aura sa Legende' (1965), he writes of the early serial moment in 1946–50 as 'a movement of "revolt"' to which he imputes 'historic significance'. The serial composers are now judged to have affirmed their 'historic necessity' and to have attained a balance between music's aesthetic and technical dimensions, a fact which he relates explicitly to Boulez's Darmstadt lectures.[100]

In the 'Interior Duologue', which serves as an introduction to the Darmstadt lectures (1960), Boulez grapples in a more flippant way with the same dialectical opposition of freedom and discipline, each of which, he believes, can only be found within the other. He ponders the related dialectical dilemma between the 'ineluctable necessity of language' or of the 'unbreakable laws of evolution', on the one hand, and 'the exceptional personality' on the other. Once again he theorises this evolution in Souvtchinskian terms as something which, while moving forward in an unambiguous direction, is subject to all kinds of breaks, delays, reverses and oblique moves. However, he perhaps reveals signs of anxiety in his concern that concentration upon the undoubted importance of the milieu may in fact reduce the role of the composer to no more than its expression.[101] While he wishes, at least in theory, to acknowledge the necessary engagement of composer and milieu, he is never far from tipping over into a more subjectivist position which clearly favours the particular over the general, the individual composer over the milieu. On the other hand, while he seems intent on limiting the

[97] Souvtchinsky 1954, 124; cited in Boulez 1986, 40. See also Souvtchinsky 1990, 99–100.
[98] Souvtchinsky 1954, 126–7.   [99] Souvtchinsky 1990, 253–5.
[100] Souvtchinsky 1990, 172–3.   [101] Boulez 1971a, 14–15.

importance which is to be attributed to the milieu in the act of composition, he is more open to the elusive qualities within the completed work which, if it is a great work, will have untold potential of which even the composer will be unaware.[102] In this notion of the great artwork or the great musical composition as the one which combines the conscious and the unconscious, the intended and the unintended, the rational and the irrational, we can place Boulez, beyond Souvtchinsky, within a tradition of thought which goes back to Schelling's *System of Transcendental Idealism* and to the threshold of dialectical thinking itself.

Dialectical thinking

References to 'dialectic' occur regularly in Boulez's writings and interviews from around 1949. In 'Bach's Moment' (1951), while dodecaphony is presented as the positive result of a musical dialectic,[103] neo-classicism is rejected on the same basis.[104] Despite subscribing to an evolutionary and dialectical reading of dodecaphonic development, he rejects any attempt to forge a new collective language as an illusion, and even Webern must be negated, or to use Boulez's term, dismembered.[105] When in 'Possibly ...' (1952), he refers to the series as a natural historical outcome and to its *de facto* historical development as embodying 'the felt necessity, of our time', this, for Boulez, involves an attempt to forge a dialectic linking morphology, syntax and rhetoric.[106]

Such references are not exclusive to Boulez and they can also be found from around 1954 in the writings of several composers with whom he was at that time closely involved. For Jean Barraqué (1928–73) the dialectical thinking which the series engenders is the apex of musical thought, clearly above morphological and syntactical considerations,[107] and, like Boulez, he attributes it solely to Webern. Echoing both Leibowitz and Boulez, he declares that 'those who have not admitted or assimilated serial thought are condemned to silence'.[108] The only published volume of the journal *Domaine Musical*, which appeared in 1954, provides further evidence of dialectical thinking in essays by Michel Philippot (1925–96) and Michel Fano (b. 1929), both of whom were close to Boulez at this time and who often shared his point of view.[109] Philippot, who had studied with Leibowitz, expresses interest in the logical basis for the musical work and he finds, like

---

[102] Boulez 1971a, 18.   [103] Boulez 1991, 1.   [104] Boulez 1991, 13.
[105] Boulez 1991, 3, 13.   [106] Boulez 1991, 113–19.   [107] Barraqué 2001, 72.
[108] Barraqué 2001, 76. Barraqué made this statement in 1954, two years after Boulez's 'Possibly ...' (1952).
[109] Wangermée 1995, 307.

Leibowitz, Boulez and Barraqué, a historical and dialectical justification for the serial principle.[110]

That Leibowitz was not the sole source of all things dialectical in French musical life in the late 1940s and early 1950s is clear from the work of Souvtchinsky and Schloezer. There are a few dialectical references in the extracts from Souvtchinsky's *Un siècle de musique russe* which appeared in *Contrepoints* in 1946 and 1949. Both writers contributed articles to a 1954 volume of the *Cahiers de la Compagnie Renaud Barrault*, which considered the new music within its historical locus. While there are a number of references to dialectical processes in Schloezer's *Introduction à J.-S. Bach* (1947), including the claim that music is in effect 'self-movement, dialectical process',[111] he was more circumspect by 1955. Despite describing serialism as enabling 'a dialectical organisation of the different musical parameters' he has become suspicious of the ubiquity and indiscriminate use of the term 'dialectic' and he fears that we may be being knowingly or unknowingly hoodwinked.[112] In 'Musique contemporaine, musique moderne' (1954) musical modernism is identified as being 'against, particularly against the art of its contemporaries'. Furthermore, modern composers are said to 'clearly take account of what they deny and why they deny it, they know what they want to accomplish and why it must be accomplished'.[113] In this instance, he defends modernist composers against charges of intellectualism and the abuse of theory. Despite such a sympathetic reading of avant-garde intentions and practice, for Schloezer, the old musical system is not dialectically overcome, but rather dissolves out of its inability to resolve musical difficulties and contradictions. Furthermore, he does not share the conviction of 'Boulez and his friends' for whom the serial technique 'is the only one capable of ordering the vast sound world'. This viewpoint is reiterated in *Problèmes de la musique moderne* (1959), where dodecaphony is valued as only one of several equally valid currents within contemporary music, which has contributed a number of significant works without constituting 'a decisive stage' in musical development.[114] In a passage which may echo Leibowitz, but which goes beyond the horizon of the Polish composer, he writes of the unviability of the Schoenbergian dodecaphonic system since it also, it now seems, 'contained the germ of its own overcoming'. Schloezer does not, however, reveal what this germ is or how exactly it will effect this overcoming.

---

[110] Philippot 1954, 34–6.   [111] Schloezer 1947, 154.

[112] Schloezer 1955, 1087. In 1963 Schloezer refers to the dialectic as a 'magic wand' which is employed to go beyond contradiction, whereby, instead of merely 'clarifying the present in the light of the past', we also 'clarify the past in the light of the present' (1963, 245).

[113] Schloezer 1954b, 514–15.   [114] Schloezer and Scriabine 1959, 139–40.

Table 3.1. *Boulez's dialectical oppositions*

'Proposals' (1948)	Fixed/Mobile Static/Dynamic	Rational/Irrational values Regular/Irregular rhythm
'Possibly …' (1952)	Mobile/Immobile register Regular/Irregular tempo	Mobile/Immobile series Sensibility/Intelligibility
'Current Investigations' (1954)	Strict global organisation/ 　(Free) temporary 　structure	
'At the Edge of Fertile Land' (1955)	Continuity/Discontinuity	
'Alea' (1957)	Composition/Chance Definite/Indefinite structure Amorphous/Directional 　structure Divergent/Convergent 　structure Homogeneous/Non- 　homogeneous sound 　space	Mobile elements/Fixed structures Strict/Interpretative Strict/Free performance
Darmstadt lectures (1960; 1961)	Global/Partial structures Strict/Free writing Fixed/Mobile tempo Smooth/Striated space Automatism/Choice Static/Dynamic structure	Form/Morphology Structure/Material Fixed/Mobile distribution Pulsed/Amorphous time Rational/Irrational Immanence/Transcendence
'Poetry – Centre and Absence – Music' (1962)	Music/Language	
Collège de France lectures (1976–95)	Repetition/Difference Analogy/Difference Virtual/Real Smooth/Striated time Thematic/Athematic Similarity/Contrast Order/Chaos Order/Disorder Law/Accident Closed/Open form	Formal/Instantaneous Formal/Informal [*informel*] Obligatory [*obligé*]/Free *écriture* System/Idea Chance/Necessity Foreseeable/Unforeseeable Continuous/Discontinuous Evolution/Rupture Complete/Incomplete Whole/Fragment

Dialectical oppositions: a genealogy

The dialectic which emerges within Boulez's work is marked out by a large number of binary or dialectical oppositions, a habit of mind and working practice which is found from as early as 1947. In a letter to Souris he provides a full account of the contents of the article 'Proposals' in which he lays out a range of rhythmic possibilities in terms of binary oppositions while considering the prospect that one might pass from one pole of an opposition to the other or that an opposition may be transformed or deformed.[115] While similar pairs are found in early writings such as 'Possibly ...' (1952) and 'Current Investigations' (1954), there is a clear proliferation of oppositions in 'Alea' (1957), they are central to the Darmstadt lectures of 1960, and their number is increased significantly in the later Collège de France lectures. While Table 3.1 does not provide an exhaustive list of the oppositions which Boulez uses, it includes those with perhaps the greatest dialectical potential. They operate at every level from that of the individual parameter to that of form, and they enable the composer to mark out a field of possibilities in which every alternative in one area is combined with all of the others.[116]

While Boulez's dialectical oppositions may derive from a number of sources, there is a strong likelihood that Souvtchinsky and, to a lesser extent, Schloezer were decisive influences upon him in this regard. It is in the preparatory work which Souvtchinsky did for Stravinsky's *Poetics* (1939–40) that we find the clearest evidence of his taste for oppositional thinking.[117] While Roland-Manuel[118] worked on a number of drafts for the lectures, as well as on the final text, the discovery of a four-page manuscript in Souvtchinsky's hand suggests that Stravinsky's preparatory notes were in fact based closely upon Souvtchinsky's outline plan. Where Craft states that Stravinsky characteristically presents the arguments within his notes in the form of 'dialectical distinctions',[119] we can now say that this form stems most likely from Souvtchinsky.[120]

---

[115] Letter to Souris, dated 6 November 1947 (AML).

[116] For Nattiez, the positing of binary oppositions is 'the fundamental characteristic of Boulez's thinking' and he notes that it operates in the form of binary organisation, binary forms, doubles, mirrors and dialogues (1986, 27–8). A number of oppositions are also found in Pousseur's writings between 1957 and 1966 (2004, 78, 95, 107, 128, 134, 190).

[117] For the genesis of Stravinsky's *Poetics* see Craft 1992, 82–103; Stravinsky 2000, 11–55; Walsh 2006, 91–7 and especially Dufour 2003, 373–92; 2006, 213–44.

[118] Roland Alexis Manuel Lévy (1891–1966) was a musicologist and a composer.

[119] Craft 1992, 86.

[120] Soumagnac writes of the close working relationship between Stravinsky, Souvtchinsky and Roland-Manuel in the production of the *Poetics*, which unfolded as the fruit of 'numerous conversations' between them. Describing Souvtchinsky as the 'éminence grise' of the trio, whose judgement was important throughout the undertaking, she acknowledges that he contributed more specifically 'to establishing the general plan, partly inspired the second lesson and completely conceived the fifth' (Stravinsky 2000, 25–6). Dufour, who presented Souvtchinsky's

Table 3.2. *Binary oppositions in Stravinsky's* Poetics of Music

Stravinsky's notes	Souvtchinsky's notes
Contrast/Similarity	Contrast/Similarity
Active/Passive	–
Pure/Descriptive	–
Planned/Unexpected	Planned/Unexpected
Order/Disorder	Order/ –
Necessity/Freedom	Necessity/Freedom
Continuous/Discontinuous	Continuous/Discontinuous
Determinate/Indeterminate	Determinate/Indeterminate
Submissive/Unsubmissive	Imposing/Submissive
Presence/Absence	–

Source: Dufour 2006, 222–7; 216–18.

Table 3.2 shows that Stravinsky's notes include a wide range of oppositions, which it now seems clear are mostly drawn directly from Souvtchinsky's plan. It is evident that Souvtchinsky had already expounded a number
of these same oppositions in articles written over many years.[121] The overt
similarity and high degree of overlap between Souvtchinsky's binary oppositions and those of Boulez is striking and leads inescapably to the hypothesis
that he influenced the young composer in this regard.

While Boulez would also have encountered a number of significant binary
oppositions in Schloezer's *Introduction à J.-S. Bach*, such thinking is not so
prominent in his later writing (see Table 3.3). While it is difficult to be
comprehensive in detailing just which binaries are used by each writer,
Table 3.3 suggests that while Schloezer and Souvtchinsky share a number
of binaries which Boulez also uses, there are also a number of oppositions
which are distinctive to each of them.

It is clear that the dialectical oppositions which are found in Souvtchinsky and Schloezer and many of those used by Boulez are found in the
tradition of German Idealism. Kant, in his *Critique of Pure Reason* (1781/7),
presents four antinomies, that is four pairs of antithetical propositions which
arise because of the difficulty which reason encounters when it attempts

> sketch material for the first time, suggests that the genesis of the *Poetics* had three main stages:
> the production of Souvtchinsky's plan, its adoption by Stravinsky, and its transformation
> into a final text by Roland-Manuel. Stravinsky seems to have copied, reorganised, expanded,
> replaced, reformulated, modified and augmented Souvtchinsky's ideas (Dufour 2004, 17–23;
> 2006, 213–44).

[121] Souvtchinsky 1990, 246; 1946, 23, 27, 28, 31; 1956, 1107; 2004, 208.

to 'think the whole'.[122] So it is, to take only the first three antinomies, in skeletal form, that there are good reasons to accept both sides of the oppositions of (1) finite and infinite (time); limited and unlimited (space); (2) the simple and the composite, and (3) freedom and necessity.[123] Such antinomies are not true contradictions but rather what Kant describes as dialectical oppositions. Following Kant, Schiller, in *On the Aesthetic Education of Man* (1795), produced a large number of antithetical oppositions, and this expanded set was in turn drawn upon by Schelling and Hegel. Oppositional thinking is of clear importance in the works which constitute Schelling's philosophy of identity such as his *System of Transcendental Idealism* (1800), the *Philosophy of Art* (1802–3) and *Bruno* (1802), as well as being the inspiration for Hegel's dialectic. While Hegel produces a number of dialectical oppositions in his *Phenomenology of Spirit* (1807), this is significantly expanded for example in his *Logic* (1830) and important oppositions are also to be found in his *Aesthetics*. In his *Logic* (1830) Hegel considers the decisive importance of Kant's antinomies while acknowledging that the principle is not restricted to the four which Kant had identified since they 'appear in all objects of every kind, in all conceptions, notions, and Ideas'.[124]

The list of dialectical oppositions which is culled from these philosophers and which is shown in Table 3.3 is not exhaustive since it seeks only to demonstrate something of the range and commonality of oppositions in German Idealist philosophy. As Adorno tells us, such concepts and ideas can never be attributed exclusively to any one figure since their articulation has often involved a number of thinkers; nor can their interpretation be routinely narrowed to their specific meaning within the work of any one philosopher or philosophical system.[125] Table 3.3 shows nevertheless that there is significant agreement in the dialectical oppositions shared by Boulez with Souvtchinsky and Schloezer, Kant, Schiller, Schelling and Hegel, as well as with Adorno, whose position will be considered in Chapter 4.

As has already been acknowledged, dialectical oppositions from the German Idealist tradition were most likely transmitted to Souvtchinsky through the mediation of a number of Russian philosophers with whom he was familiar. They are found for example in Alexander Herzen who, along

---

[122] Allison in Honderich 1995, 436. Boulez uses the term 'antinomy' in his Darmstadt lectures and in the Collège de France lectures.
[123] Kant 1929, 396, 402, 409.   [124] Hegel 1975, 77–8.
[125] Adorno 1993, 60. For Dastur, it is Hölderlin who in 1795, before Schelling or Hegel, considers 'the genetic unity of opposites' which goes back to Heraclitus and which, 'rediscovered by German mysticism, led Nicholas of Cusa to the idea of a *coincidentia oppositorum*' (2000, 61–2).

Table 3.3. *Binary oppositions in selected writers from the German Idealists to Boulez*

Boulez	Souvtchinsky	Schloezer	Herzen [H], Berdyaev [B], Chestov [C]	Adorno	Kant [K], Schiller [S], Schelling [Sch], Hegel [H]
Similarity/Contrast	Contrast/Similarity	Regularity/Diversity	Diversity/Unity [H]	Similarity/Contrast	Identity/Opposition [Sch]
Repetition/Difference		Identity/Diversity	Identity/Identity	Identity/Non-identity	Identity/Difference [K, H]
Analogy/Difference		Difference/Resemblance	Contradiction[C]	Identity/Return	Unity/Diversity [S]
					Unity/Variety [S]
Real/Virtual	Imaginary/Defined		Potentiality/Actuality [H]	Thematic/Athematic	Actual/Ideal [S]
Thematic/Athematic					Ideal/Real [Sch]
					Possibility/Actuality [Sch, S]
Strict/Free	Determinate/Indeterminate			Strict/Free	Form/Formlessness [Sch]
Strict/Interpretative		Active/Passive	Active/Passive [B]	Freedom/Organisation	Limited/Unlimited [K]
Fixed/Mobile	Imposing/Submissive		Freedom/Necessity [H, C, B]	Constructive/Mimetic	Limitable/Illimitable [Sch]
Composition/Chance	Imaginary/Defined		Finite/Infinite [H, B]		Finite/Infinite [K, Sch, S, H]
Definite/Indefinite	Freedom/Necessity		Determinate/Indeterminate [H, B]		Freedom/Necessity [K, Sch, S, H]
Choice/Automatism					Compulsion/Freedom [S]
Free/Obligatory					Passive/Active [S]
Chance/Necessity					
Closed/Open		Closed/Open			
Continuous/Discontinuous	Continuous/Discontinuous	Continuity/Discontinuity	Indivisible/Divisible [H]		Continuous/Discrete [H]
Smooth/Striated					
Evolution/Rupture					

Global/Partial Immanence/ Transcendence Whole/Fragment Complete/Incomplete	General/Particular [Stravinsky]	Unity/Multiplicity One/Many	Universal/Particular [H, C, B] Unity/Multiplicity [H, B]	Universal/Particular General/Particular Part/Whole Fragment/Totality	Universal/Particular [K, Sch, H] Whole/Parts [K, S, Sch] Fragment/Whole [S] Simple/Composite [K]
Sensibility/Intelligence Rational/Irrational	Sensibility/Intelligence	Rational/Irrational			Sensibility/Understanding [K] Sensuous/Formal [S] Reason/Senses [S] Impulse/Reason [S] Thought/Sense [S] Conscious/Unconscious [Sch] Rational/Sensible [H]
Order/Disorder Order/Chaos Law/Accident	Order/Disorder [Stravinsky]		Order/Chaos [C]	Order/Chaos	
Foreseeable/ Unforeseeable Formal/Instantaneous	Intentional/Unexpected				
Static/Dynamic	Fixed/Inert	Static/Dynamic	Static/Dynamic [B] Eternal /Transient [H] Permanent/Changing [C] Eternal/Temporal [C, B]	Static/Dynamic	Motion/Rest [Sch, S]

with an entire generation of Russian thinkers, was influenced by Schiller and Schelling. They feature in the work of Lev Chestov (1866–1938) and Nicolas Berdyaev, who like Souvtchinsky and Schloezer were émigré intellectuals living in Paris. Chestov and Berdyaev influenced Souvtchinsky and were closely associated with Schloezer.

Berdyaev acknowledges that a concern with fundamental antitheses was one of the most important aspects of his philosophy,[126] and recognising like Kant that such antinomies can never be reconciled in the phenomenal world, he theorises an 'ultimate unity in which all contradictions and antinomies are resolved', which he conceives in terms of Nicholas of Cusa's *coincidentia oppositorum*.[127] Like Berdyaev, Souvtchinsky's notes for Stravinsky's *Poetics* refer explicitly to Cusa's *coincidentia oppositorum* and it may be that this reference can help us to appreciate how Souvtchinsky understood the operation of his dialectical oppositions. For Cusa, who speculated on the fact of the mutually exclusive differences, distinctions and oppositions which mark all finite beings, it seemed that such opposed elements could only be reconciled beyond the apprehension of human rationality in an ideal, Absolute term, that is in infinite Being, which he terms the coincidence of opposites.

While a number of commentators have discovered flashes of the modern in Cusa's work, and it has been suggested that it anticipates, amongst other things, the philosophy of Hegel, indeed all of German Idealism, this view is no longer widely held by scholars in the field.[128] For Jasper Hopkins, his writings incorporate a number of ideas that 'were developed by his Modern successors, without his having directly influenced most of those successors through his own writings, of which they had scarcely any first-hand knowledge'.[129] With this caveat in place we can draw attention to Schelling's philosophy of identity, in which the Absolute is similarly viewed as 'the vanishing point of all differences'.[130] While Cusa's ideas of the Absolute and of the resolution of differences have prompted some writers to make comparisons with Hegel, Cusa maintains that reason in the sense of the understanding (*Verstand*) cannot subsume the Absolute,

---

[126] Berdyaev 1950, 86, 96.

[127] Berdyaev 1938, 68, 117–18. Nicholas of Cusa (1401–64).

[128] Jasper Hopkins argues that a number of significant commentators, writing between 1880 and the 1960s, are mistaken in linking Cusa with German Idealism and with other elements of modern philosophy (Hopkins 2002, 2, 15–16). Cusa 'does not anticipate' the German Idealists, he is cited nowhere by Hegel (Hopkins 2002, 13–14), and as Emerich Coreth has stated, his 'direct influence on Modern thought is small; an immediate common-bond is scarcely confirmable' (cited in Hopkins 2002, 14).

[129] Hopkins 2002, 14.   [130] Coplestone 1990, 318–19.

a position which is rejected by Hegel, for whom dialectical logic can penetrate the identity of opposites. This suggests that Souvtchinsky's dialectical oppositions are closer to Schelling than Hegel since, in Schelling's philosophy of identity, each member of each oppositional pair is united in an Absolute Identity which is the ground of all being and which is originary and primary, 'prior to any distinction of opposites from one another'.[131]

Interestingly, in the 1936 version of his book, Wyschnegradsky compares musical pansonority with the concept of 'the Absolute' and he explicitly equates it with Cusa's *coincidentia oppositorum* as that point where all of music's dualisms are united and annulled.[132] While Hegel and Marx both feature in Wyschnegradsky's account, it would seem that in terms of the workings of his dialectical oppositions, like Souvtchinsky his conception is closer to Schelling.

In conclusion

Several of the concepts which have been discussed in this chapter also feature in some of those writers whose work has had the greatest impact on Boulez. Char and Mallarmé, for example, both operate at times by negation and Mallarmé includes the concepts of the Absolute and of necessity. Binary oppositions, which do not reach any moment of synthesis or *Aufhebung*, are important for Char. Likewise Breton, whose relationship with Boulez is less clear-cut, shares with the composer a strongly negational impulse. His oppositions do not result in any orthodox Hegelian *Aufhebung* but rather in the juxtaposition of antinomies which ultimately, in the manner of Cusa, Schelling, Souvtchinsky and Wyschnegradsky, are fused and resolved within some kind of 'mental Absolute' which he terms the *point suprême*.[133] While these connections are clearly of interest, it is difficult to establish the extent of their importance for Boulez. Indeed, in a letter to the artist René Magritte, who had no understanding or appreciation of serial music, Souris stated curiously that in Boulez and the serial composers 'there is no longer any trace in their minds of the old dualist thinking which surrealism, with its bourgeois intellectual habits, relentlessly attempted to resolve in vain', and most distinctively by means of Breton's 'famous *point*'.[134] Magritte

---

[131] Vater (in Schelling 1984, 23–4).   [132] Wyschnegradsky 2005, 163–8.
[133] Breton 1963, 76; 1969, 153–4.
[134] Letter to Magritte, dated 25 March 1953. Cited in Wangermée 1995, 315. Wangermée notes Souris's attachment to Breton's concept of the 'point' (Wangermée 1995, 316–17).

responded that the young composers were therefore as 'unlike dualists as metronomes'.[135]

As for more specific interpretation of Boulez's oppositions, it is clear that the concept of the dialectic is rather variable and there is no one agreed understanding against which individual stances can be measured. Kojève's reading of Hegel, for example, was a very personal one which did not meet with universal agreement and the term 'dialectic' did not have a uniform meaning among those French thinkers who followed him in the 1930s and 1940s. For Descombes it 'became such a lofty concept that it would have been offensive to request a definition. For thirty years it was almost the God of negative theology – beyond formulation, it could only be approached through the explanation of what it was not.'[136] It is perhaps not surprising in this climate that composers such as Leibowitz and Boulez, with no professional philosophical training, made dialectical statements which are under-theorised, and sometimes misconceived, factors which make detailed and consistent evaluations of their positions somewhat problematic. In tracing a quasi-genealogy of binary oppositions the intention is simply to show the rootedness of the ideas upon which Boulez is drawing, whether knowingly or unknowingly.

Boulez's oppositions, as transmitted through Souvtchinsky, may owe more to Schelling than to Hegel, since they do not seek (Schelling would say they are incapable of) definitive resolution. While Schelling's oppositions are united in the Absolute, this moment, unlike that of Hegel, is not a further stage in a progressive, historical, dialectical movement. It is that point where, for example, subject and object are held inextricably together. The positing of dialectical oppositions is perhaps Boulez's way of attempting to capture the musical whole within which each pair of inseparable polar opposites forms a distinct moment. Taken as a whole, the being of music is made, however incompletely, philosophically determinable, through the positing of such dialectical distinctions. Each pair of oppositions marks out a territory, posits a new musical parameter within which the musical moment can be conceived and constructed. In addition, we can detect fundamentally Schellingian impulses in Boulez's sense of 'the interlocking roles of sensibility and intelligibility in all creative work'[137] as well as in his awareness that his analysis of Stravinsky's *Rite of Spring* 'may perhaps be accused of exaggerating the arithmetical relationships and paying too little attention to the unconscious'.[138] As for his sense of musical history,

---

[135] Letter to Souris, dated 26 March 1953. Cited in Wangermée 1995, 315.
[136] Descombes 1980, 10.   [137] Boulez 1991, 138.   [138] Boulez 1991, 107.

which again draws upon Souvtchinsky, it is unclear whether this owes more to Hegel, to Schelling or to some less determinable cultural mediation of ideas. We may say that Boulez's early negational stance is broadly Hegelian, albeit filtered through the efforts of Schoenberg, Leibowitz and numerous commentators. However, as we shall see in Adorno's critique, there is more to negation than simply the rejection of the previous aesthetic.

4 Boulez, Adorno and serial critique

Introduction

Theodor Wiesengrund Adorno has a special place in the history of Western music in being a philosopher of profound originality and insight, as well as a composer of merit who had studied with Alban Berg, participating in the life of the Schoenberg circle in Vienna from 1925. His writings on music are inherently philosophical and his engagement with music's actuality is marked by the integration of technical knowledge and of a penetrating critical analysis of the significance of modern music from a dialectical perspective. While Souvtchinsky, Schaeffner, Souris and Schloezer all played their part in the development of Boulez's ideas, none of them aspired to what Adorno attempted, namely to provide a genuine philosophy of new music. On his return from exile in America in 1949, in addition to the great number of articles, lectures and books which he produced, he became involved in a variety of innovative projects in West Germany including the Darmstadt summer courses, as well as contributing to more than 160 radio broadcasts on a number of subjects, including music, between 1950 and 1969.[1]

It seems likely that Boulez and Adorno first met in 1955 at Darmstadt where they attended a number of summer courses in the 1950s and 1960s.[2] Boulez recalls that their first conversation took place when they both sat by chance at the same table in a café after a concert.[3] Despite some linguistic difficulties in that Boulez's spoken German was as poor as Adorno's French, it seems that they somehow or other had a fairly detailed discussion on the topic of Stockhausen. Whatever difficulties Adorno experienced with the music of the post-war generation, it is clear that he had a high

---

[1] Leppert, in Adorno 2002, 17.

[2] Adorno 2003, 246–7. Boulez attended the Darmstadt International Summer Courses on New Music in 1952, 1955, 1956, 1959, 1960, 1961, 1962, 1963 and 1965, lecturing there in the 1960s. Adorno participated in nine Darmstadt summer courses, in 1950, 1951, 1954–7, 1961, 1965 and 1966, directing courses, lecturing, participating in discussions and teaching composition.

[3] The principal texts in which Boulez discusses Adorno are the following: an homage written at the time of Adorno's death in 1969 (1986, 517–18); an article 'L'Informulé', which Boulez wrote in 1985 (2005a, 663–70); some comments in a 1988 interview (Menger 1990, 6–9); 'Le Labyrinthe Adorno', a text which Boulez read in 1992 on receipt of the Adorno prize (2005a, 660–63) and three short responses which he contributed in 2003 to a dossier on Adorno in *Libération* (1 August 2003).

opinion of Boulez's intelligence, his musicality and his leadership qualities. Adorno's public and private writings from the 1950s are sprinkled
with brief comments in which, while articulating certain musical reserves,
there is undoubted respect for the younger man. While he warned his
pianist friend Eduard Steuermann in 1954 that many of the talented and
interesting people he would meet in Darmstadt would be under Boulez's
'questionable influence',[4] there is a hint of surprise in a later letter from
1955, again to Steuermann, where he now observes that Boulez is someone
you can talk to, and he recalls having had a long discussion with him at
Darmstadt along with Stockhausen and Metzger who are less flatteringly
described respectively as the 'unfortunate' and the 'little'. Clearly unimpressed by Stockhausen's talk of sine-tones, he is happier with Boulez, who
discusses music in musical terms and who is prepared to discuss compositions in detail. Boulez is hailed consequently as 'a highly gifted person
and a real musician', who in consequence of his position as 'the pope of
this church' displays 'a certain independence in the manner of the Marxist
dictum'.[5]

Boulez, for his part, was certainly aware of Adorno by 1954 to the extent
that he and Stockhausen wrote to him to request an article for a review
which they were planning,[6] but this aside, the older man does not seem
to have featured significantly in Boulez's life for the rest of the 1950s and,
consequently, the bulk of what may be said about his early relationship
with Adorno, or even his opinion of him, is culled from remarks made
retrospectively. Boulez recalls, for example, that Adorno's writings were
mostly closed to him in 1953–4 since they had not yet been translated into
French and were exclusively available to German-speaking musicians such
as Stockhausen. At some moments he gives the impression of being rather
niggardly in his appreciation when he grants, for example, that Adorno
'gave two or three important lectures' at Darmstadt or in his assessment
that he and his young colleagues had a greater influence on Adorno than
the philosopher had upon them.[7]

He recalls the severe doubts which Adorno harboured concerning the
music of the post-war generation, while noting that he and Stockhausen
were exempted from his criticism of the lack of craft in many contemporary
works. On the other hand, Adorno's attachment to Berg and Schoenberg,

---

[4] Letter to Steuermann, dated 14 April 1954. Cited in Adorno 2003, 246.
[5] Letter to Steuermann, dated 14 October 1955. Cited in Adorno 2003, 247–8.
[6] In a letter to Souvtchinsky (postmark dated 20 August 1954) Boulez relates that he and Stock-
    hausen have written to Adorno to request an article from him (BN). In letters to Stockhausen
    (dated 16 October 1954 and 23 October 1954) Boulez notes that he has had no response from
    Adorno (PSS). No article by Adorno appeared.
[7] Menger 1990, 7, 9.

amongst other things, led the younger generation, with some justification, to regard him as somewhat passé. While he was at first known at Darmstadt only as a composer, Boulez dismisses him as a rather 'second-rate' one, and as 'a representative of a generation that had not known how to go beyond its predecessors'.[8] Hence, Boulez recalls that their respect was for the man and much less so for what he stood for.[9] Goeyvaerts and Stockhausen, for example, remember Adorno's difficulties in the face of Goeyvaerts's Sonata for two pianos at Darmstadt in 1951. When he unsuccessfully attempted to approach the composition using the traditional categories of motives, antecedents and consequents, Stockhausen responded to him, 'Professor, you are looking for a chicken in an abstract painting.'[10] While Darmstadt archivist Wilhelm Schlüter notes that Adorno's response to Goeyvaerts's piece was one of complete incomprehension,[11] Walther Friedländer reported more generally that Adorno's efforts in his 1951 composition course in fact 'dampened the optimism of the young'.[12]

On a more positive note, Boulez has at times been more openly appreciative of Adorno's professional qualities. He states in a letter to Schaeffner in 1968 that his writings along with those of Adorno were the only ones of value to him.[13] In the homage which he wrote after the philosopher's death in 1969, he values the necessarily inexplicable aspect of what fascinated him and the subtlety and ultimately unresolvable nature of his personality and of the questions which he explored.[14] In the text which he read on receipt of the Theodor Adorno prize in 1992, he acknowledges that he was 'very intimidated' by the complexity of Adorno's thought and language and by the strength of his connection to the Second Viennese composers. While they met several times over the years in Darmstadt, Frankfurt and in Baden-Baden, corresponded between 1965 and 1969[15] and conducted two extended radio conversations,[16] Boulez estimates that the relationship was

---

[8] Adorno's musical compositions date from between 1918 and 1946, and most were composed in the 1920s and 1930s.

[9] Menger 1990, 9.   [10] Stockhausen 1989, 35–6; Kurtz 1992, 35–6.   [11] Boivin 1995, 111.

[12] Borio and Danuser 1997, vol. 3, p. 408. Adorno returns to this incident or others like it several times throughout his writings in the 1950s and 1960s (1998, 282; 2002, 172–3; 657–8; 1999, 159–60). Goeyvaerts provides his own account of this incident (Delaere 1994, 44).

[13] Letter dated 17 November 1968 (Boulez and Schaeffner 1998, 104).

[14] Boulez 1986, 517–18.   [15] Their correspondence is held at the Paul Sacher Stiftung.

[16] Boulez and Adorno conducted the conversation 'Gespräche über den Pierrot Lunaire' for North German Radio on 26–7 November 1965 (Adorno and Boulez 2001, 73–94). A second discussion 'Avant-garde und Métier' is discussed briefly in a letter from Adorno (dated 1 November 1966) and in Boulez's reply (dated 11 November 1966) (PSS). Michael Schwarz of the Walter Benjamin Archive at the Akademie der Künste in Berlin reveals that this discussion took place on North German Radio on 6 January 1968 (e-mail to the author, 9 February 2009). After Adorno's death, his widow wrote in a letter to Boulez, that her husband referred often to this discussion as 'one of the best' (dated 12 November 1970), to which Boulez acknowledged in return that he too had a good memory of it (dated 22 December 1970) (PSS).

'primarily intellectual'.[17] The correspondence between them is rather disappointing and is mostly restricted to practical matters. While Adorno, for example, praises Boulez's performance of *Wozzeck*, Boulez in turn expresses his admiration for the agility of Adorno's thought.[18] He remembers how at Baden-Baden they discussed questions of chance, determinism and style and that he was greatly intimidated by Adorno's formidable intellect. While he was happy to disagree with him in matters of 'musical pragmatics' he felt much less confident when the philosopher's speculations shifted from specifics to more general considerations and he acknowledges that while he admired Adorno's acuity, it was almost impossible 'to measure up to him'.[19]

While Chapter 3 attempted to trace a number of dialectical threads, primarily within the French language culture of Boulez's early years, the present chapter looks to map out the critique of serial music which is found in the writings of Boulez and Adorno from around 1952 to 1969. Adorno is at once both philosopher and musicologist and no attempt will be made to separate these functions within his writing. His critique of serial music is unambiguously philosophical and it challenges Boulez and his colleagues really to consider the philosophical import of serialism and more specifically the nature of the negation which is undertaken within their works. That Adorno, as Boulez suggested, may have shown greater interest in the new generation of composers than was ever truly reciprocated does nothing to reduce the force of his critique and it is to that which we now turn.

The ageing of the new music

Following its publication in 1949, Adorno's *Philosophy of New Music* was received with great interest in Europe as a significant philosophy of musical history, as a comprehensive application of dialectical thinking to musical composition and as a source of theoretical legitimation for post-war serial music.[20] Despite the impact which it is generally believed to have had upon composers and contemporary music enthusiasts of the post-war generation, with some figures reputedly learning German in order to read it for themselves, the interpretative difficulties which it presented should not be underestimated. The fact that the theory of musical material which it embodies had been worked out over twenty years before its reception by the post-war avant-garde makes clear that it could never let itself be recuperated uncritically in order to provide convenient legitimation of post-war serial

---

[17] Peyser 1977, 241.   [18] Letter dated 22 May 1966 (PSS).   [19] Boulez 2005a, 662.
[20] Wiggershaus 1994, 512; Metzger 1960, 63; Paddison 1993, 265.

practices. If many of the core ideas which it contains were developed in the twenty years prior to its appearance, the later critique of serial composition which Adorno formulated in the 1950s and early 1960s emanated, in a similar way, from this key work and from those same concerns.

To follow Adorno's critique of serialism, it is essential to understand that it is a consistent part of a much more expansive philosophy of musical material which begins with his reading of Beethoven's late works. The episodic and fragmentary nature of Beethoven's late style is for Adorno a manifestation of negational thinking (in the Hegelian sense), and the beginning of a thought which is found again, according to the *Philosophy of New Music*, in Schoenberg and the Second Viennese composers. The consequent criticism which Adorno makes of the post-war avant-garde centres upon what he perceives to be its failure in the face of the negative power of this line in musical thinking. It is a line of thought which is progressively theorised in a number of articles from the 1950s and 1960s and which has two main moments, the first chronicling the critique of generalised serialism, and the second offering a potential way forward. The first is stated most clearly in the lecture 'The Ageing of the New Music' which Adorno delivered in 1954 at the Stuttgart Week of New Music, while the second is found in 'Vers une musique informelle', a Darmstadt lecture from 1961.

The specific origins of Adorno's earliest critique of the new music, as expressed in his writings from the early 1950s, are far from clear. Without hoping to recover the precise sequence of events which prompted him to focus this critique upon the new music, it is evident that the incident with Goeyvaerts and Stockhausen at Darmstadt in 1951 was uncongenial to him. While he does not reveal which serial compositions he was familiar with at the time, we must accept that he had heard some between 1951 and 1954, including works by Boulez, who is named as the central figure within his critique at its outset. Of course, the publication of Boulez's polemical article 'Schoenberg is Dead' (1952) would have been sufficient in itself to stimulate his engagement.

In the article 'Schoenberg is Dead', Boulez criticises Schoenberg's work for its lack of ambition, taking issue with the alliance of a variation principle and strict or academic counterpoint in some of the atonal works.[21] The twelve-tone works are similarly taken to task for their 'ultra-thematicisation', in which the notions of the theme and the series become confused.[22] Their use of pre-classical and classical forms creates a serious division between structures and language, and such borrowings merely result in displaced romantic 'clichés' and 'stereotypes'.[23] The return of 'tonal functions' in

[21] Boulez 1991, 210.   [22] Boulez 1991, 212.   [23] Boulez 1991, 212–13.

Schoenberg's American period is written off as an incoherent absurdity and the 'one-sided' investigation of pitch to the neglect of the other musical parameters prompts the general conclusion that his music lacks 'intrinsic unity'.

While Adorno's article 'The Relationship of Philosophy and Music' (1953) is not an explicit reply to Boulez's critique, it is difficult not to conclude that it contains his response, at least in part. For Adorno, who was not himself uncritical of aspects of Schoenberg's practice,[24] Schoenbergian rationalisation, far from lacking in ambition, as Boulez suggests, allows rhythmic, and a degree of melodic, freedom, which facilitates expressiveness and protects subjectivity. It is contrasted favourably with the total serialism of the younger generation, who are termed 'zealots of objectivism', with Boulez's music singled out as an example. For Adorno, it 'sounds as if it were composed only of dissociated individual sounds', as if it 'has been cleansed of all language', and 'it leaves behind an impression of abstruseness'.[25]

The notes for the introductory lecture of his 1954 Darmstadt seminar on 'New Music and Interpretation' testify to Adorno's hostility to what he called 'the hermetic isolation of the new music'.[26] That Adorno, Eduard Steuermann and Rudolf Kolisch conducted this lecture series in self-conscious opposition to the team of younger composers as represented by Boulez, Klebe and Maderna is supported by a letter to Kolisch in which Adorno writes of the younger composers as 'the twelve-tone brutes' who were working 'in the style of Boulez'.[27]

While we should not indiscriminately lump Adorno together with Steuermann, Kolisch and the other defenders of the older generation, such remarks nevertheless bring to light the gulf which separated two generations of musicians, one which saw the immediate imperative for the new music in the dissemination of the Schoenbergian heritage, and the other which took the new possibilities found in Webern, in preference to Schoenberg, for its standard. Adorno had harboured serious misgivings towards Webern's composition from the mid-1920s[28] and when he came to articulate his critique of post-war serialism with full force in 'The Ageing of the New Music' in 1954, he openly stated his concern that the younger generation were in fact intensifying these same dangers.

---

[24] In a letter to Berg (dated 6 September 1927) he expressed the view that Schoenberg's use of the twelve-tone technique was mechanical, with its rhythmic monotony, 'incessant complementarities' and melodic arbitrariness (Adorno and Berg 2005, 110).
[25] Adorno 2002, 156–7.
[26] Cited in Rolf Tiedemann's 'Nur ein Gast in der Tafelrunde' which considers the nature of Adorno's position at Darmstadt (1996, 150).
[27] Letter dated 4 June 1954 (Tiedemann 1996, 151).
[28] Letter from Adorno to Berg, dated 28 June 1926 (Adorno and Berg 2005, 60).

In 'The Ageing of the New Music', Adorno is critical of what he takes to be a decline in 'inner tension' and 'formative power' within the new music.[29] While he recognises that it has a certain technical purity, homogeneity and rigour, this leads all the same to works which are 'technocratic'; the musical material is levelled and neutralised with the result that its expressive power and subjective dimension are lost.[30] The relationship between musical content and form is ruptured to the extent that composers now mistake the 'preparation of tones' for composition itself, and in doing so they produce merely abstract negation.[31] In making this judgement, Adorno invokes the Hegelian distinction of negations which are dialectical and negations which are merely abstract as a means of questioning the nature of the negation which is operational within new music. Put simply, while abstract negation occurs where one of any two dialectical terms annihilates the other, with the result that nothing is achieved, negation is only truly dialectical where 'the overcome-entity . . . survives the fact of being overcome'.[32]

Already in the *Philosophy of New Music* Adorno had expressed concern that Schoenberg's later twelve-tone music was in danger of falling into a self-alienating abstractness.[33] In 'The Ageing' and several later articles it seems that this threat has been actualised in the music of some of the serial generation, but Boulez is ultimately exempted from this charge. To be truly dialectical, serialism cannot disregard the existence of tonality but must rather negate it, since in avoiding its formal and tonal aspects it 'preserves them within itself through the very process of exclusion'.[34] Serial innovation consequently depends upon the critique of tradition which it embodies rather than in simply the composer's decision to do something differently from the past.[35]

In 'The Ageing' Adorno traces this tendency which leads to abstract negation to Webern's late works, with their putative fusion of traditional forms and twelve-tone technique, and while he judges the results to be not musically unsuccessful, they nevertheless come close to reducing the musical material to the level of formal processes and to the unfolding of rows.[36] While these criticisms are not directed explicitly or implicitly at Boulez he is, nevertheless, identified by Adorno as being at the head of that group of composers who have developed along Webernian lines, and who aim to eliminate all '"compositional freedom" . . . every vestige of traditional musical idiom' and 'every subjective impulse', through extending

---

[29] Adorno 1988, 96.   [30] Adorno 1988, 100.   [31] Adorno 1988, 102.
[32] Kojève 1980, 15; Hegel 1977, 111–19.   [33] Adorno 2006, 92.   [34] Adorno 1999, 160.
[35] Adorno 1998, 260.   [36] Adorno 1988, 100–3.

the serial principle to all of the compositional parameters.[37] While the aim of this project is a completely 'integral rationalisation' of materials, Adorno recognises its paradoxical arbitrariness and suggests that it results in merely a 'semblance of objectivity' since the system, despite its rigidity, inevitably gives rise to many unforeseen relationships. Furthermore, 'the total rationalisation of music' is said to stem from an aversion to musical expression which he correctly relates to the equation of expression with Romanticism and *art nouveau*. Any such equation is false and results only in works which are without musical meaning.[38] Extreme musical systemisation is ultimately a reflection of an identity thinking which excludes anything which lies outside itself or which cannot be integrated within an oppositional relationship.[39] Indeed, where construction becomes everything, there is no composition and 'music regresses to the pre-musical, the pre-artistic tone'.[40]

In the French and English versions of the lecture which appeared in 1956, Adorno refers to Boulez's article 'Current Investigations' (1954), in which the composer faces with equal candour the difficulties presented by generalised serialism.[41] He concludes that 'Boulez intends to free his ultra-constructivist aesthetic from the deadly rigidity which threatens it, without however making any concession as regards the necessity of maintaining a strict discipline'. While Boulez, it seems, is absolved from blame, Adorno sets his sights on those serial composers who are judged not to have attained such standards.[42]

If Boulez did not respond in print to Adorno's article,[43] Heinz-Klaus Metzger did so on several occasions; with the article 'Just Who Is Growing

---

[37] Adorno refers to Boulez as 'a highly cultured and exceptionally gifted musician, with the highest sense of form and with a power that is communicated even where he disavows subjectivity altogether' (Adorno 1988, 102).

[38] Adorno 1988, 106–7.

[39] Adorno 1988, 114–15. Adorno alludes here to the opposition of identity and non-identity which is central within his thought. In *Negative Dialectics* (1966) he states that Hegel's dialectic was unsuccessful in attempting 'to use philosophical concepts for coping with all that is heterogeneous to those concepts'. Adorno recognises, in contrast, 'that objects do not go into their concepts without leaving a remainder . . . the concept does not exhaust the thing conceived' (1973, 4–5). He is concerned with what the concept 'fails to cover, what its abstractionist mechanism eliminates' (p. 8) and he seeks to reorient 'conceptuality, to give it a turn towards non-identity' (p. 12).

[40] Adorno 1988, 110.

[41] Adorno's lecture was originally delivered in Stuttgart in April 1954 (Adorno 1972, 8), but it was not published until May 1955 when it appeared in *Der Monat*. The definitive German text which was published in *Dissonanzen* in 1956 does not contain the reference to Boulez's 'Current Investigations' which is found in the French and English versions from 1956. This English version which was translated from the French, and which appeared in *The Score* (December 1956, 18–29), is described by Robert Hullot-Kentor and Frederic Will as 'a peculiar, abbreviated and completely confabulated paraphrase' (Adorno 1988, 95).

[42] Adorno 1956, 26–7.

[43] While Boulez (1992) acknowledges that he 'had trouble deciphering' 'The Ageing of the New Music' (2005a, 661), presumably in the original German, it also appeared in French translation in *Preuves* in February 1956 (pp. 24–34).

Old?' (1958/60) in which he suggested that it was not new music but rather Adorno himself who was ageing,[44] in a radio conversation with Adorno in 1957, and in a further article which seems to date from 1958. While we cannot presume that Metzger speaks for Boulez, he develops the argument significantly, if rather defensively in places, and highlights several serious shortcomings in Adorno's critique.

Metzger imputes a number of errors to Adorno which are attributed in part to a failure to consult the necessary primary and secondary sources.[45] In opposition to Adorno, he defends Webern, and the experiments undertaken by Boulez, Stockhausen and Pousseur, on the grounds that they are the only composers to have seriously taken up the challenge of new music and the contradictions, acknowledged by Adorno himself, to be inherent within Schoenberg's work.[46] In doing so, Metzger turns Adorno's own historical analysis back against him. On the question of integral rationalisation, while acknowledging certain problems with the system employed in Messiaen's *Mode de valeurs et d'intensités* (1949), he exposes Adorno's failure to recognise that while such a system may be used to organise the parameters in a senseless way, it does not preclude their meaningful arrangement. Boulez's *Structures Ia*, in contrast to Messiaen's piece, is consequently judged as being 'on the right road' and Adorno is reproved for having failed to notice the difference between them.[47]

Metzger challenges Adorno's tendency to generalise, his disregard for the significant differences in the approaches of individual composers, and his failure to note a single concrete musical example by way of evidence. Furthermore, he can find no leading contemporary composer who sanctions the unfolding of blind processes which is, after all, the substance of Adorno's attack.[48] On the question of expression, he cites the note to Boulez's Second Sonata for piano to show that, far from attempting to exorcise expression, the composer was simply seeking to avoid any kind of hyper-romanticism. As for the claim that serial compositions can only be explained in terms of systems, Goeyvaerts's unfortunate experience in 1951 is identified as the origin of this remark, thus simultaneously absolving Boulez and Stockhausen while damning Goeyvaerts.[49]

---

[44] Metzger broadcast the lecture 'Das Altern der Philosophie der neuen Musik' on 23 October 1957 and it was then published in *Die Reihe* (1958/60). Adorno and Metzger debated the issue in a radio conversation entitled 'Jüngste Musik – Fortschritt oder *Rücksbildung*?' which was transmitted on 19 February 1958. The essay 'Zur Verdeutlichung einer Polemik und ihres Gegenstandes' was written around 1958. All three texts can be found in Metzger 1980, 61–112.

[45] Metzger 1960, 66.   [46] Metzger 1960, 69–70.   [47] Metzger 1960, 70–1.

[48] Metzger 1960, 74.

[49] Metzger 1960, 78–9. Metzger's analysis of the situation, which exempts 'the élite' from Adorno's criticism, is accepted, for example, by Ligeti and appears in articles from 1958 and 1966 (2001, 135, 157). Ligeti had of course offered his own criticisms of *Structures Ia* in *Die Reihe* 4 in 1958.

In conversation with Metzger in 1957, Adorno explained any confusion in his critique with the defence that the most important serial works such as Boulez's *Le Marteau sans maître* and Stockhausen's *Gesang der Jünglinge* and *Zeitmasse* were either not yet composed or were at least unavailable to him when he first wrote 'The Ageing'.[50] In his introduction to the second printing of *Dissonanzen* in 1958 he explicitly exempts works such as *Le Marteau* and Stockhausen's *Zeitmasse* from its critique.[51] This defence clearly outraged Metzger who in a further article, apparently from 1958, dismantled it, laying out exactly which compositions Adorno could have heard in the early 1950s, with details of times and places of performances as well as the availability of key scores.[52] Augmenting Metzger's inventory and taking only Boulez's compositions into account, the Second Sonata for piano was published in 1950, the First Sonata for piano in 1951, the *Sonatine* for flute and piano in 1954, and most significantly of all, a first (unauthorised) version of *Le Marteau* was printed in the autumn of 1954, six months before the first publication of 'The Ageing'. In terms of performances, Adorno could have heard the performance of a short piece entitled *Séquence* on the Westdeutschen Rundfunk in 1952, the first book of *Structures* on the radio in November 1953 or at Darmstadt in 1955.[53] It is possible that he heard a tape recording of the 1951 Donaueschingen performance of *Polyphonie X* which had been produced by Südwestfunk.[54] The Second Sonata for piano was performed at Darmstadt in 1954. Movements Ia, Ib and II of the *Livre pour quatuor* were performed at Donaueschingen in 1955. *Le Marteau*, which had its première in Baden-Baden in June 1955, was heard in Darmstadt in 1956 while the *Sonatine* was played there in both 1956 and 1957.

Generalised serialism reassessed

Whatever the specifics of Adorno's experience, it is clear that the systemic rigour of early serialism, epitomised by *Structures Ia*, was only a brief moment in Boulez's development, which he abandoned fairly quickly as he attempted to reintroduce elements of freedom into his composition. Despite the clear rejection of automatic composition and of completely controlled generalised serialism, in almost simultaneous writings from Boulez and Adorno, we do not know whether or not, or the extent to which, Adorno's lecture may have influenced Boulez's development. In his 1985

---

[50] Metzger 1980, 99, 95.   [51] Adorno 1972, 8.   [52] Metzger 1980, 108–9.
[53] Jameux 1991, 52.
[54] The tape was played at Darmstadt in 1953 but Adorno was not present (Borio and Danuser 1997, vol. 3, p. 562).

article, 'L'Informulé', which was published in a special volume of *La Revue d'esthétique* dedicated to Adorno, Boulez provides no explicit or implicit reference to 'The Ageing of the New Music' or to any part Adorno may have played in the change of musical direction undertaken in the mid-1950s, and signalled in 'Current Investigations'. Instead, he skips from a brief recognition of the influence of Adorno's *Philosophy of New Music* to an equally concise discussion of the lecture 'Vers une musique informelle' which he presented at Darmstadt in 1961. Given his silence on the matter, we can only turn to the self-critique provided in 'Current Investigations' and to some of Boulez's later statements in which he elaborates upon his earlier judgements.[55]

Boulez had already accepted the problems with 'extreme automatism' by November 1954 while also recognising that a composer can exploit the 'creative tension' which results from the interaction of subjectivity and technique. In 'Current Investigations' he writes:

> Webern only organized pitch; we organize rhythm, timbre, dynamics; everything is grist to this monstrous all-purpose mill, and we had better abandon it quickly if we are not to be condemned to deafness. One soon realizes that composition and organization cannot be confused without falling into a maniacal inanity, undreamt of by Webern himself.[56]

With some irony, he notes that while composers have sought to learn from the example of the best possible model, namely Webern, and while they have been justified in pursuing a negational stance, their efforts have nevertheless risked falling into 'sterile mannerism'. It is a judgement which converges with Adorno's conviction that negation alone is not enough to produce music. Having said that, while Boulez accepted in retrospect that there had for a short time been an overemphasis upon technique, which he recognises within his own work, this still seemed to be justifiable on the basis that it was impossible to do otherwise.

As Deliège correctly notes, 'Current Investigations' marked a change of direction for composition which seemed to many composers to nullify their research, their experiments and their compositions.[57] For Boulez, however, this change was justified against the background of what he refers to as the serial academicism and number fetishism which characterised the time. He says:

---

[55] While Boulez's 'Current Investigations' appeared in the November 1954 edition of *La Nouvelle Revue Française*, Adorno's lecture, as already noted, was originally delivered in April 1954, but not published until May 1955.
[56] Boulez 1991, 16.   [57] Boulez 1976, 63.

I reacted pretty violently against this kind of thing, and I was quite right to
do so since it was a completely sterile cul-de-sac. Some of the concerts at
Darmstadt in 1953/54 were of quite lunatic sterility and academicism, and
above all became totally uninteresting. One could sense the disparity between
what was written and what was heard: there was no sonic imagination, but
simply an accumulation of numerical transcriptions quite devoid of any
aesthetic character.[58]

In terms of the relationship between the critiques presented in Adorno's
'Ageing' and Boulez's 'Current Investigations', opinion is divided and
the following views have been expressed: (i) Boulez's critique anticipates Adorno's;[59] (ii) the critiques are simultaneous and in parallel;[60] and
(iii) that despite their almost simultaneous appearance, Adorno's critique
may have exercised some influence upon that of Boulez. Williams, who proposes this third possibility, suggests that Boulez accepted Adorno's argument
that extreme automatism, whatever its source, endangers subjectivity, and
that his subsequent integration of technique and subjectivity, as well as his
increasing interest in aesthetics, may be attributable, at least in part, to the
philosopher's critique.[61]

It is clear, however, that Boulez considered his own critique to have been
independent and prior to that of Adorno. In the lecture 'Nécessité d'une
orientation esthétique' (1963), while evaluating the experience of *Structures
Ia* and total serialism, he states that he was 'probably the first to denounce
the vanity of the experience'.[62] This view is supported by a letter which
he wrote to Pousseur around October 1952, and in which he registers his
reaction on hearing the recording of *Polyphonie X*. Boulez tells Pousseur
that the experience has made him reflect on his work of the previous two
years:

I fear I let myself go a little too much, presently, in terms of virtuosity of
pointillist technique, without referring, strictly speaking, to overall
compositional sensibility. In other words, the details are not fully integrated
within a perceptible whole. This is perhaps the most serious fault with which
I reproach myself: by limiting myself to analysis and variation, I am falling
into greyness and automatic processes. . . . There are some passages where the
synthesis of language and sensibility appears striking to me, and others where
the musical 'construct' [*faire*] is not at the level I would have liked to express,
or conversely the musical 'construct' [*faire*] becomes independent and
undoes what I wanted to express. In both cases, I am unable to make the two
coincide.[63]

---

[58] Boulez 1976, 64. Boulez did not visit Darmstadt in either 1953 or 1954.
[59] Grant 2001, 67.   [60] Leppert, in Adorno 2002, 16.   [61] Williams 1997, 50–1.
[62] Boulez 1995, 572.   [63] Letter cited by Decroupet in Borio and Danuser 1997, vol. 1, p. 319.

It is undoubtedly the case, then, that between 1952 and 1954, with or without Adorno's contribution, Boulez had already moved decisively away from any kind of 'automatic activity' and its resultant 'greyness'. Despite being agreed on the general point that there were difficulties with the current state of serial composition, including a loss of subjectivity, Adorno approached the matter in a markedly different way from Boulez. For Adorno, for whom artworks are inherently critical, the ageing of the new music signified the loss of this critical quality, and he interpreted the emphasis on the objective and upon the rational which he discovered in these early works within the framework of the dialectic of enlightenment which he had theorised together with Horkheimer ten years before.[64] To the extent that this is the case, his concerns are far removed from those of Boulez, who at this point is completely focused upon technical compositional problems, pure and simple, irrespective of their putative societal function or critical significance.

Serial critique: 1955–1957

Adorno's name does not appear anywhere in Boulez's writings between 1948 and 1962, either before or after 'The Ageing of the New Music'. Nor is he cited in Boulez's Darmstadt lectures. Adorno, in contrast, continues to acknowledge Boulez and in 'Neue Musik heute' (1955) he addresses the anti-Schoenbergianism inherent within new music, which he describes as a 'kind of rebellion against the father figure'.[65] Adorno now seems to accord a certain validity to Boulez's criticism of Schoenberg's duality and he accepts that the Viennese composer did not deal with the contradiction arising from the alliance of twelve-tone processes and traditional forms, since he simply 'made music' with his rows. This anomaly, which Adorno recognises as 'the gap between the elements of musical language [dem Musiksprachlichen] and the rows', is one which Webern, in distinction to Schoenberg, is credited with trying to close in most of his works from the Op. 21 Symphony onwards, though at a cost.

In a line of thought which develops in a similar way to 'The Ageing', Adorno cites Boulez, Stockhausen, Maderna and Nono as key exponents of this development who, in their 'objective construction', 'expulsion of the subject' and 'allergy to expression', have produced a music which is indifferent to its own sound. It is said to be robotic and only distantly related to musical language, having its roots instead in the science of cybernetics and

---

[64] Their book *Dialectic of Enlightenment* was published in 1944 and revised in 1947.
[65] Adorno 1984, 131–3.

in 'industrial automation'. For Adorno, quoting Halldór Laxness, 'our ears died in Buchenwald' and the possibility of absolutely constructed music is perhaps the inevitable corollary of the mechanistic horrors of the Holocaust. However, while music can embody such horrors, he believes that even 'the strongest compositional powers' will produce a glimmer of our former human freedom. Consequently, he can state that a composer of Boulez's eminence can move beyond these ascetic limitations to write 'valid music'.

It may be that Adorno wished to clarify, or even modify, the implications of 'The Ageing of the New Music' in relation to Boulez. Consequently, in 'Music, Language and Composition' (1956), he insists that Boulez has managed to avoid falling prey to serial dogmatism, a position which is supported by the composer's reliance upon both Debussy and Webern.[66] Furthermore, Boulez's refiguration of musical structure in line with the immanent demands of his musical material, it is said, can also change the syntactical nature of music as 'even the subtlest small articulations would be the result of tiny differentiations within the series, along with equally fine differentiations of the various forms of the series itself'.[67]

Despite such a positive appraisal, which as Metzger correctly observed was not based on detailed musical analysis, Adorno now theorises the problem of serial composition with even greater philosophical rigour than in 'The Ageing'. Combining themes from his earlier essays, he judges that much new music

> has absented itself, with modish phrases, from the dialectical effort and
> merely rebelled reactively against the linguistic element . . . It was thought
> that simply by uprooting [the similarity to language] it would be possible
> to regain what had been lost, without accepting the challenge of actually
> salvaging that best element from the irrevocable state of both consciousness
> and material. Composers fell into a state of what Hegel would have termed
> abstract negation, a technique of consciously induced primitivism, of mere
> omission. Through an ascetic taboo against everything that was linguistic in
> music, they hoped to be able to grasp pure musicality in itself – a musical
> ontology, so to speak – as the residue, as if whatever was left over was the
> truth. Or, looked at in a different way, they repressed the nineteenth century
> instead of transcending it.[68]

For Adorno, this rejection of music's quasi-linguistic nature is at root an ahistorical impulse. Again, contrasting the serial composers unfavourably with Schoenberg, he highlights those traditional elements within the Viennese composer's practice which enabled understanding of his music in a

---

[66] Boulez's lecture 'Claude Debussy et Anton Webern' was given at Darmstadt in 1955.
[67] Adorno 2002, 124–5.   [68] Adorno 2002, 119–20.

quasi-linguistic way. The younger serial composers are berated, in contrast, for attempting to eliminate the linguistic element within music, for deceiving themselves into thinking that it is possible to begin again with a *tabula rasa*, and for replacing the traditional guarantors of musical coherence with mathematical relationships which they equate with objectivity. This objectivism, however, leads not to new-found freedom but rather to musical reification and to the production of music which is both meaningless and irrelevant. If, therefore, music cannot escape its similarity to language, nor can it settle for merely 'the abstract negation of its similarity to language'.[69]

A change in Adorno's attitude to the younger generation of composers is perceptible between 1956 and 1957 and is perhaps attributable to developments in compositional practice among the young, to changing attitudes towards Schoenberg, and to a decisive shift in the balance of power at Darmstadt, where the younger generation assumed control in 1957. In a letter to Wolfgang Steinecke, in the context of his 1956 Darmstadt lecture series on 'Schoenberg's Counterpoint', he welcomes the fact that Schoenberg's music and aesthetic have begun to make an impact upon the thinking of the younger generation.[70] In the lecture 'Criteria of New Music', which he gave at Darmstadt in 1957, he no longer compares serial works unfavourably with Schoenberg's compositions, setting out instead to establish musical criteria with which to judge their success or failure.[71]

Several brief passages in 'Criteria of New Music' give the impression that Adorno wishes to correct or at least modify positions taken in 'The Ageing'. For example, he now estimates that the younger generation of composers are just as gifted as the generation from forty years before, perhaps even more so, and he accepts that the new musical material is simply not imbued with the qualities of tension and of subjectivity which marked musical material formerly.[72] Furthermore, he has grasped that it is not possible to conceptualise this music in terms of antecedents and consequents, and he perhaps softens his criticisms of the non-expressivity of new music on the basis of its markings.[73] Nevertheless, Boulez's *Le Marteau sans maître* and his Second Sonata for piano are cited as examples of a form of pointillism which experiments with 'extreme, unconnected possibilities', and he finds that the 'primitiveness' which this engenders is 'only justified as a critical exercise, an extreme mode of demolition and estrangement'. Despite this concern, *Le Marteau* is also commended for its textural density, its timbral richness and the power of its detailed characterisation, and he is unconcerned with

---

[69] Adorno 2002, 121–2.
[70] Letter dated 18 June 1956, cited in Borio and Danuser 1997, vol. 1, p. 193.
[71] Tiedemann detects 'a certain irony' in this change in Adorno's position (1996, 152).
[72] Adorno 1999, 179.   [73] Adorno 1999, 162.

whether this 'looser organisation' was intended by Boulez or whether it was merely the result of greater structural flexibility.[74]

Having found something within the new music to which he can relate perceptually, Adorno has moved to the second moment of his critique of serialism. It is a significant shift in his thinking, as the unfavourable Schoenbergian parallels are now replaced by a more forward-looking appraisal of the next stage within music's dialectical process. In 'Music and Technique' (1958), he recommends that the gestures within a composition be highlighted by means of, for example, 'tone colour or rhythm'[75] and structural instrumentation, in the sense of controlling timbres. 'Mode of orchestration' is consequently offered as a means of articulating all of the structural elements within a composition.[76]

'Vers une musique informelle'

Several of Adorno's articles from 1959 to 1961 show that he continued to believe his earlier misgivings on generalised serialism to have been basically correct. While he acknowledges that new music has clearly moved on from the pointillist, Webern-inspired compositions of the early 1950s, he nevertheless persists in relating serial composition to progressive rationalisation.[77] However, he now strikes a more conciliatory tone and, echoing his rather resigned acceptance of Schoenberg's twelve-tone music in the *Philosophy of New Music*, he suggests that the employment of 'administrative methods' is the only way to be heard in an 'administered world'.[78] He is willing to grant that at its best the new serial music equals the Second Viennese composers and he lists a select number of compositions by the younger generation which have impressed him. *Le Marteau sans maître* is reckoned to be 'a modern *Pierrot Lunaire*, forty years younger',[79] in which he correctly diagnoses a switch to the individual pole of the dialectic.[80] While Stockhausen's *Zeitmasse*, *Gruppen*, *Kontakte* and *Carré*, Boulez's Second and Third Sonatas for piano and his *Sonatine* for flute and piano, as well as Cage's Piano Concerto, have all impressed him, he is, nevertheless, troubled by his inability to 'reconstruct them' aurally to his satisfaction.[81]

It is apparent that, in Adorno's eyes, Stockhausen has now replaced Boulez as the nominal head of the post-war generation and, while there are a number of significant references to Boulez, these are outnumbered

[74] Adorno 1999, 170–1. Stockhausen's *Gesang der Jünglinge* is also praised on account of its contrasting 'characters'.
[75] Adorno 1999, 209.   [76] Adorno 1999, 212.   [77] Adorno 1998, 217.
[78] Adorno 1998, 222.   [79] Adorno 1998, 219.   [80] Adorno 1998, 220.
[81] Adorno 1998, 270–1.

by references to his German colleague. Despite this, there are indications that Adorno's position has drawn closer to Boulez in some respects. He writes: 'Up to now every composer who has insisted on his own integrity and refused to compose in any other way than that suggested by his own spontaneous reactions, or who has rebelled against the constraints of the principles of construction, has failed miserably in his attempt to break fresh ground.'[82] It is not difficult to find in this passage an echo of Boulez's phrase concerning the uselessness of composers who had not experienced the imperative of dodecaphonic or serial composition. Furthermore, it is possible that the change which Adorno acknowledges in his 'reservations about Webern' may also have been stimulated by his ongoing assimilation of serial composition and theory.[83] What is beyond doubt is that he is conscious that both he and Boulez have shifted ground since the mid-1950s.

Adorno now argues the case for the development of more extended musical forms, while noting that the serial composers themselves had begun to doubt the power of the series to achieve this aim,[84] and his critique consequently switches emphasis from the identification of serial deficiencies to shaping the future direction of new music. In 'Vers une musique informelle' (1961), he draws on Metzger's notion of an *a-serial* music which will constitute the next stage in music's development from a dialectical perspective.[85] While he is confident enough to predict that this a-serial music, which he terms *musique informelle*,[86] will overtake both serial and indeterminate music, he is unable to say exactly what form this will take since any simple definition he could give would be a merely positivist reduction, and so he instead limits his contribution to the attempt to discern the contours of the concept. It is to be

> a type of music which has discarded all forms which are external or abstract or which confront it in an inflexible way. At the same time, although such music should be completely free of anything irreducibly alien to itself or superimposed on it, it should nevertheless constitute itself in an objectively compelling way, in the musical substance itself, and not in terms of external laws.[87]

Musique informelle is not simply to recuperate traditional musical categories, but is to produce new, alternative ones, more suited to new musical means.[88] The notion of the traditional 'theme', for example, is no longer to

---

[82] Adorno 1998, 277.   [83] Adorno 1998, 289.   [84] Adorno 1998, 181–2.
[85] Adorno 1998, 272.
[86] Because of the lack of a direct English equivalent to the term, the original French *musique informelle* is generally used.
[87] Adorno 1998, 272.   [88] Adorno 1998, 282.

be restricted to the melodic order and can now be expanded to include a much wider set of possibilities. Adorno in this case provides as an example the 'theme-like force' of the opening bars of *Le Marteau sans maître*. He similarly suggests that *musique informelle* should avoid any juxtaposition of sections, which should instead be 'placed in a dynamic relationship, comparable to the relationship of subordinate clauses and main clause in grammar', and he again draws upon Boulez's work with its 'so-called parentheses' as an example of what he has in mind.[89]

The concept of *musique informelle*, which has its origins in Schoenberg's Op. 11 no. 3, his *Erwartung*, Op. 17, and Webern's Opp. 7–11,[90] is an attempt to resume the project of free atonality in a post-serial context, and it is not insignificant that these are precisely the works by Schoenberg and Webern which also made the most marked impression upon Boulez. However, while Boulez and Adorno share a lasting attachment to the works of Schoenberg's atonal period, as well as a less favourable estimation of his dodecaphonic compositions, the bases for the negative judgements which they make with regard to his twelve-note works are not the same.[91] Despite this, in 'Vienna' (1960), Adorno still takes Boulez and his generation to task for failing to acknowledge their debt to Schoenberg. While Boulez's 'Schoenberg is dead' is not named, there is no doubt that Adorno again has it in mind and he interprets the rejection of Schoenberg as a conflict between a father and his sons. Identifying Leibowitz as 'a pupil of Webern's', he emphasises that 'Boulez was not just Messiaen's pupil; he was Leibowitz's too, and thus a direct descendant of the Viennese tradition'. It is a historical position which, according to Adorno, Boulez reveals 'in his attitude to Webern'.[92] In this passage Adorno simultaneously calls the post-serial composers to account for their failure to acknowledge fully their patrimony, while equally furnishing them with the kind of genealogy which could legitimate their project within a historicist view of the development of musical composition.

Adorno's concerns with twelve-tone technique are obviously more philosophical in nature than those of Boulez. In bypassing dodecaphony to focus attention upon early atonality, he is building upon the critique within the *Philosophy of New Music* where he is ambivalent towards Schoenberg's twelve-tone music in the belief that it fails to fulfil its own potential in falling back upon aspects of tonality.[93] Despite such serious misgivings, Schoenberg retains Adorno's support since it is beyond the powers of any

---

[89] Adorno 1998, 311–14. In 'Nécessité d'une orientation esthétique' Boulez writes of *Structures Ia* as putting musical language 'between parentheses' (1995, 565).
[90] Paddison 1993, 182.
[91] For Boulez's early writings on Schoenberg see Boulez 1991, 11, 197–200, 209–14 and 278–92.
[92] Adorno 1998, 217–18.   [93] Adorno 2006, 73.

single composer to overcome 'the contradiction between unchained art and enchained society' and since the best which can be achieved is the production of an emancipated art which opposes and undermines this society.[94] Schoenberg's music is, therefore, to be understood as 'an image of the world against which it rebels', since it replicates its total repression without subscribing to its ideology.[95] Even the Hegelian notion of abstract negation is present in this early critique, as Adorno identifies a 'growing indifference' within the musical material which is analogous to the alienation of the musical subject.[96] Consequently:

> if it is to hope to make it through the winter, music must emancipate itself
> as well from twelve-tone technique. This emancipation, however, is not to
> be accomplished by a return to the irrationality that preceded it and that
> is now thwarted at every turn by the postulates of exact composition that
> twelve-tone technique itself cultivated; rather, it is to be accomplished
> through the absorption of twelve-tone technique by free composition and
> of its rules by the critical ear. Only from twelve-tone technique can music
> learn to remain master of itself, but only if it does not become its slave.[97]

While it is striking that this passage from the early 1940s subjects Schoenberg's twelve-tone technique to many of the most important criticisms which appear again in the 1950s in the face of serialism, Adorno had already identified in 1928 that the greater imaginative freedom of construction in *Erwartung* would prove much more fruitful for the future of new music than any resort to past musical forms or to a mechanistic application of twelve-tone technique.[98] It seems that the direction which Adorno sets out in the *Philosophy of New Music* is not really so different from that offered twenty years later in 'Vers une musique informelle'. Both analyses prescribe the recapture of the spirit which animated the early post-tonal works of Schoenberg and Webern with their greater freedom. It is a point of view which is reiterated in the *Aesthetic Theory* where Adorno again floats the possibility that Schoenberg's twelve-tone system may have fallen short of the standard achieved with free atonality.[99]

In 'Vers une musique informelle', it is now Cage and his followers, in place of Schoenberg or the serial composers, who are suspected of producing merely abstract negation in the purported freedom and immediacy which they presume in their relationship to musical material.[100] Abstract negation is not, however, the only logical problem with which Adorno is concerned at this point and he offers a series of perceptive comments on some of the

[94] Adorno 2006, 82.   [95] Adorno 2006, 88.   [96] Adorno 2006, 92.
[97] Adorno 2006, 89.   [98] Letter to Berg, dated 14 May 1928 (Adorno and Berg 2005, 119–20).
[99] Adorno 1997, 216.   [100] Adorno 1998, 315.

putative logical systems by which music may be thought to operate. It will be a mark of *musique informelle* that it will abolish the current 'deformation of rationalism', replacing it with a 'true rationality',[101] which will predictably be dialectical, and he illustrates the point with a citation from Stockhausen's '... how time passes ...' (1957) in which the German composer asks: '"should he not" (the composer, that is) "accept the contradiction and resolve to compose from out of the dialectical relationship, since it frequently appears more fruitful to start from a contradiction than from the definition $2 + 2 = 4$ "'.[102] Even so, Adorno cannot give Stockhausen's dialectic his unalloyed approval since he finds aspects of the context in which the statement is couched 'difficult'. Nevertheless, this is obviously preferable to the following:

> The virtually total organisation, in which every feature serves the whole and the whole on its side is constituted as the sum of the parts, points to an ideal which cannot be that of a work of art – that is to say, the ideal of a self-contained thing in itself. It comes increasingly to appear to be something which it can never become, precisely because of its axiomatic character as semblance [*Schein*].[103]

It is possible that Adorno has in mind here Boulez's espousal of Rougier's axiomatic deductivism, which the composer had integrated one year before 'Vers une musique informelle' in his own Darmstadt lectures, and which will be discussed in Chapter 5 of the present study. Whatever the accuracy of these observations, Adorno encapsulates his disagreement with the various non-dialectical, philosophical currents which have been invoked in the service of serialism in the prospect that future generations may be 'astonished at music's failure to rejoice in its own freedom and at its short-sighted commitment to ideas that were disastrous philosophically, as well as in other respects'.[104]

From *musique informelle* to signals and envelopes

We have seen how Adorno envisaged *musique informelle* as revivifying musical functions which were previously served by concepts such as the theme, not through their restoration, but rather through their replacement. Boulez expresses a seeming distaste for the term in the Darmstadt lectures where as part of a scathing summary of the successive phases of post-war music up to 1960 he writes that 'we can already foresee the year of the informal

---

[101] Adorno 1998, 318–19.   [102] Adorno 1998, 288.   [103] Adorno 1998, 306.
[104] Adorno 1998, 293.

[*l'informel*]; that word will have a great career!'[105] With this in mind, while Daniel Charles reads the lengthy chapter on technique in *Boulez on Music Today* as being aimed precisely against the spread of this new 'epidemic', he cannot avoid the possibility that Boulez, perhaps despite himself, ultimately furthers the cause of *musique informelle* with his theories of variable musical times and spaces.[106] He suggests that the lectures in fact place serial composers 'at the threshold . . . of the informal', as understood by Adorno, since Boulez acknowledges the limited nature of all systems and the inevitability of accidents which will subvert the system.

Certainly, while successive waves of new music have aged, been modified and, indeed, superseded, the concept of *musique informelle* has survived and continues to challenge composers and theoreticians. Its comparative conceptual emptiness and utopian qualities, precisely those aspects which Dahlhaus found problematic, are simultaneously its enduring strength.[107] It is interesting to compare Boulez's early response to the concept with a later reflection in 'L'Informulé' (1985), in which, while acknowledging its inconclusiveness, he now seems to commend it, albeit indirectly, in praising Adorno as an 'extremely attentive and intelligent listener' who guarded against any 'divorce between intention and perception'.[108] This point may in fact delineate the principal importance of *musique informelle* for Boulez.[109] Deliège, for example, notes the much greater attention which he gives to perceptibility from the time of *Structures II* and *Éclat* onwards,[110] a shift which Nattiez conceptualises semiotically as the reconnection of the poietic and esthesic levels, a goal which perhaps reaches its point of consummation with *Répons*.[111]

It may be that the decisive shift in Boulez's thinking and the beginnings of the attempt to reintegrate intention and perception are rooted, at least in part, in response to Adorno's articulation of the aporia. Those elements within Boulez's practice which Charles relates to *musique informelle*, namely the play of contrasting musical spaces and temporalities, comprise two of the most important means through which Boulez increasingly shapes his

---

[105] Charles 1965, 153. The published English translation of this passage misses out on this allusion, translating 'l'année de l'informel' of the original (Boulez 1963, 17) as 'the "formless" year' (Boulez 1971a, 21).

[106] Charles 1965, 152–5. It seems that Adorno discussed some of the ideas which were later included in 'Vers une musique informelle' in a prior conversation with Boulez and Ligeti at Darmstadt (Burde 1993, 140). The term also appears in Adorno's article 'Zum Stand des Komponierens in Deutschland' (1960) with reference to the road to freedom not taken by the compromising Henze (Adorno 1984, 138).

[107] Dahlhaus 1987, 159–60.   [108] Boulez 2005a, 669.

[109] While Adorno connects the concept of *musique informelle* with Boulez's work at various points, several authors relate it to Ligeti's compositions.

[110] Deliège 1988, 199.   [111] Nattiez 1993b, 204.

later music. Nevertheless, with or without Adorno's *musique informelle*, it is undoubtedly the case that composers had embarked upon a more perceptually aware approach from the mid-1950s. Pousseur, for example, wrote of an emerging awareness of perceptual criteria in works such as *Zeitmasse* and *Le Marteau sans maître*, which he compares favourably with the earlier completely pointillist works in which he notes a discrepancy between what is produced and what is perceived. The existence of what he refers to as 'transitional works' such as Boulez's *Structures Ib* or Stockhausen's *Kontrapunkte*, indicates increasing awareness of 'certain regularities of perception' which composers integrated within their works and which facilitated better musical communication where the desired effect is produced perceptibly without any consequent loss of freedom.[112]

It is a reading which is supported by Boulez's texts from the 1950s. While in 'Possibly ...' (1952) he was still concerned primarily with combining all of the musical parameters within an 'integrated rhetoric', between 1952 and 1954, as has already been noted, he began to accord much greater importance to the question of musical perception. In 'Current Investigations' (1954) he considers how serial developments and transformations can be made more perceptible, thus avoiding the monotony which he recognised to be the de facto perceptual effect of much over-determined serial music. Drawing upon acoustics he considers that a composition could have a form analogous to 'the "formants" of a timbre', a scheme which would enable him to provide perceptual coherence without depending upon the formal concepts of the past.[113] In 'Alea' (1957), he moves tentatively towards the concepts of 'signal' and 'envelope' albeit without the clarity of his later writings, and tempo and timbre are described as '"enveloping" phenomena' and as 'signals and common reference points'.[114] In 'Form' (1960), formants have now become the sole providers of 'points' or 'areas' of reference which facilitate the perceptible articulation of form, and he stresses the importance of determining pitch registers and the density of events within local structures'.[115]

By the time of his Collège de France lectures Boulez is in possession of a fully developed musical vocabulary which is focused on musical perception and which includes the terms 'signal', 'envelope', 'aura' and 'satellite'.[116] Taken from the fields of acoustics and psychoacoustics, Boulez transforms these terms so that where an envelope is defined in acoustics as 'the

---

[112] Pousseur 1964, 92.   [113] Boulez 1991, 17–18.   [114] Boulez 1991, 34–6.
[115] Boulez 1986, 93–5.
[116] Nattiez notes the resemblance of Boulez's terms such as the 'envelope', the 'signal' and the 'aura' to Schaeffer's concepts of the 'allure', the 'accident' or 'impulsion' and the 'resonance' (1993b, 204).

amplitude of a wave as a function of time',[117] it now becomes the contour which is traced by a work's dominant parameter. It involves fixing the parameters in such a way that one parameter is given primacy over the others in order to form the contour of a section of a work. This envelope creates a shape, a profile which enables any number of complex sound events to be unified within perception, at least at a simple, initial level of understanding. In this way it directs the listener through a work or through a section of a work. A signal, in contrast, is a recognisable gesture which is placed as a kind of marker within a piece and which sets out structure and offers points of orientation. Perception is consequently said to operate on two levels, with envelopes and signals providing an initial path through the work at what Nattiez calls the macrostructural level, which is to be followed by a more detailed reading at the microstructural level.[118]

Boulez's compositions, at least from the early 1980s, are often articulated with the help of spatial signals and envelopes which provide fixed reference points and thereby facilitate enhanced perception. The contrast of smooth and striated pitch spaces, the deliberate manipulation of pitch register, the employment of polar notes, the active utilisation of the exterior performance space and the structured variation of timbres are all utilised in order to provide clues for the memory as the listener perceives the form of a work through the simple recognition and placing of such objects in musical space. This principle is easily illustrated in the case of pitch register. In the 1980s, Boulez spoke of the increasing importance of register within his later music, comparing the lack of registral control in his Second Sonata for piano with the carefully controlled registers within *Répons*.[119] Indeed, in the Collège de France lectures, he reinterprets his earlier compositions in terms of these new analytical concepts, considering for example the *Sonatine* for flute and piano in terms of its rhythm, density and register which are now described as distinctive envelopes in the athematic transitions which link the four continuous sections of the work.[120] In other works temporality is similarly employed as an envelope, opposing the twin temporalities of pulsed and unpulsed time as an effective means of articulating form and of playing with perception.

In the Collège de France lectures, which are replete with references to signals and envelopes,[121] Boulez now attributes his use of the notion of the signal primarily to Berg and then to Webern, but he makes no reference to the possibility that Adorno or Stockhausen may have had any influence in this regard.[122] Only brief references are made to *musique informelle* in

---

[117] Goldman 2001, 62.   [118] Nattiez 1993b, 202.   [119] Gable 1985–6, 111.
[120] Boulez 2005b, 292–6.   [121] Boulez 2005b, 312–15, 415–18.
[122] Boulez finds envelopes in Berg, Webern, Debussy, Bartók and Carter.

these lectures and where they appear he makes clear that he is not using *l'informel* 'in Adorno's sense of the term'.[123] Nor does Boulez acknowledge the potential influence of Stockhausen's concept of group composition from which both Adorno's *musique informelle* and his own signals and envelopes may have benefited. Indeed, the more general acceptance of this kind of group/envelope thinking is also demonstrated by Schloezer and Scriabine who recognised in 1959 that serial works can only be perceptible when the composer limits the number of elements and permutations in use at any particular moment. Clearly echoing the emerging group/envelope thinking, they suggest that dynamism can be maintained if one parameter is stable while the others are varied.[124]

Despite such incipient commonality in the late 1950s, it is clear from Adorno's *Philosophy of New Music* that, prior to the development of the generalised series or of pointillism, he had already recognised the problem of articulating form with the observation that it would be necessary to do so through the provision of 'drastic contrasts of register, of dynamics, of scoring, of timbre', that is of 'ever-more-striking qualities'.[125] While he described this measure at the time as crude, it is difficult not to read the passage as a precursor to the more fully developed parametric approach conceptualised later by Stockhausen's groups, Boulez's signals and envelopes, as well as his own *musique informelle*.

Late Adorno: 1964–1969

In 'Difficulties' (1964), Adorno reconsiders some of the issues previously tackled in 'The Ageing' and in 'Vers une musique informelle'. While Boulez and Stockhausen were still committed to serialism, he retained his misgivings about the 'total determination', 'progressive rationalisation' and reification which he believed were implicit to it and on this basis he reasserts that the ageing of new music was taking place, and that 'the best' of his Darmstadt colleagues, who were unhappy with this view in 1954, now seemed to be mostly in agreement with it.[126] Boulez is, presumably, counted among their number.[127] While *musique informelle* or a-serialism remains the goal towards which new music should be working, he is as unable as before to define it with any degree of precision other than to say that it could serve to relate the wealth of integral serialist detail to the composed whole. The lecture on 'Form' which he gave at Darmstadt in 1965 is dedicated to

---

[123] Boulez 2005b, 335, 398, 403–4.   [124] Schloezer and Scriabine 1959, 166, 163.
[125] Adorno 2006, 62.   [126] Adorno 2002, 656–9.
[127] Boulez reprises the criticisms of serial practice, which he first formulated in 'Current Investigations', notably in his Darmstadt lectures (1971a, 25; 1986, 66).

Boulez, perhaps in reciprocation for the composer's earlier contribution to a *Festschrift* for the philosopher.[128] Here, once again, the by now familiar themes of failed objectivity and the means of music's renewal are considered from the point of view of form, and he suggests that the introduction of a new kind of formal fantasy, in which structure would be articulated by means of parametric 'characters', would avoid the arbitrariness resulting from over- and deficient construction.[129]

In the posthumously published *Aesthetic Theory* Boulez is commended for his aesthetic turn, and Adorno specifies that his aesthetic is not a normative or traditional one, but rather a 'historicophilosophical theory of art'. Drawing upon Boulez's 'Nécessité d'une orientation esthétique', he states that his notion of an aesthetic orientation pertains to

> the critical self-awareness of the artist . . . Boulez's central point is that he had been puzzled by the current opinion of avant-garde artists, who believe that annotated instructions for the employment of technical procedures already amount to an artwork; on the contrary, the only criterion – according to Boulez – is what the artist does, not how and with whatever advanced means he intended to make it. Boulez too, realizes, with regard to the contemporary artistic process, that insight into the historical situation – through which the antithetical relation to tradition is mediated – converges with binding implications for production. The dogmatic separation of craft and aesthetics, which Schoenberg decreed out of a then justified critique of a praxis-alien aesthetics, a separation that was self-evident to the artists of his generation as well as to those of the Bauhaus, is disavowed by Boulez in the name of craft and *métier*.[130]

Adorno clearly finds within Boulez's aesthetic turn an attitude towards composition which is ultimately harmonious with the criticisms of serialism which they had both produced in 1954. Where early serialism had privileged technical means, Adorno finds vindication in Boulez's revised formulation in which the artwork cannot be reduced to this aspect alone. However, Adorno now expresses a degree of aesthetic commonality with Boulez which goes well beyond this. He imputes to him an acceptance of the importance of the historical situation, and of some kind of mediation which operates between tradition and production, and which is linked to Boulez's notion of *métier*. Rejection of history was a criticism which was levelled at 1950s serialism in its seeming attempt to begin again with a musical *tabula rasa*,

---

[128] Boulez's Darmstadt lecture 'Nécessité d'une orientation esthétique' (1963) was published in French in the *Festschrift* for Adorno's sixtieth birthday.
[129] Adorno 1966, 19–21.   [130] Adorno 1997, 342.

and against Boulez in the light of his connections with French structuralism in the 1960s.

History and *métier*

The question of the relationship, dialectical or otherwise, between the individual composer and the historical legacy, which was discussed in Chapter 3, is clarified to an extent by Boulez with the renewed concept of *métier* which becomes a point of convergence with Adorno, as the composer seeks to reconnect system, technique and objectivity with history and subjectivity. In 'Alea' (1957), he opposes chance-based music on the grounds that it is inimical to craftsmanship (*artisanat*), and he rejects the quest for absolute compositional objectivity in the conviction that arbitrariness flourishes the more we try to avoid it. However, he is equally dissatisfied with composition which rejects objectivity and which merely cultivates the arbitrary. While the term *métier* is not used, Boulez describes its substance when he suggests that composition consists in the production of a 'framework of probabilities' from which the composer must choose on a solution by solution basis.[131] The term is used explicitly in a 1958 letter to Wolfgang Steinecke in which he proposes the composer's *métier* as an essential element in the course which he would like to present at Darmstadt, a goal which is presumably accomplished in the second part of the lecture 'Nécessité d'une orientation esthétique'.[132]

While Adorno is cognisant of the theoretical melding of expression and technique implied by Boulez's understanding of *métier*, he questions it in practice in the face of the rational and objective overdetermination still found in certain post-war works, a failing which has led to reliance on a 'speculative ear' to provide objectivity while avoiding arbitrariness.[133] He agrees with Boulez that *métier* is distinguished from the artisanal in its innovative quality, which involves breaking with tradition, but it is the nature of this break which concerns him. When he rejects the claim that originality can result from a *tabula rasa*, it seems that Boulez is spared from this charge since *Le Marteau* is considered to be a 'critique of the ideology of any absolute new beginning, of starting out with a clean slate'.[134] However in doing so, he seems to base his view more on what he believes Boulez to have done in *Le Marteau* than on what he wrote in 'Nécessité' where, with some reservations, the composer basically defends the strategy of beginning from

---

[131] Boulez 1991, 26–30.
[132] Letter dated 15 February 1958. Cited by Decroupet in Borio and Danuser 1997, vol. 1, p. 380.
[133] Adorno 1998, 317, 221, 258; 1966, 19–21.   [134] Adorno 1997, 43, 216.

a blank slate.[135] Adorno agrees that *métier* concerns the subjective powers of the artist in the face of musical material, not the objective demands posed by the material itself, and where specific musical material suggests a particular set of possibilities or problems, *métier* concerns the composer's wherewithal in developing or solving them. *Métier* must be rethought in the light of the nominalist artwork for which traditional technical supports are no longer available, and for which rules are not external to but, rather, completely immanent to the musical material.[136] This is central to Adorno's concept of musical composition and it excludes the possibility that a composer may proceed from a set of axioms to make all kinds of deductions, if the already mediated nature of these axioms and deductions is not acknowledged from the outset.

In Adorno's hands, Boulez's understanding of the normally unassuming concept of *métier* is given greater philosophical depth, and it may be that his reflections have found their way back into Boulez's later theory. In 'Idée, Réalisation, Métier' (1978), Boulez states that historical technique and compositional innovation are inextricably linked and that while their relative proportions may vary, *métier* consists in a 'permanent osmosis' between them.[137] While *métier* involves transgression, there are no universal solutions and composers must formulate their own provisional rules.[138] In negotiating a path from the musical Idea, that is the generative impulse, multiple deductions must be made at a number of levels and shifting hierarchies of materials and parameters have to be formulated so that the idea is deductively discovered and then proliferated.

Since deduction subsumes the particular under a universal concept, Adorno would have had difficulty supporting Boulez's conviction that deduction is the force to which the Idea is subjected, or that unity and homogeneity can be attained through the establishment of hierarchies which completely dominate the musical material.[139] Such notions suggest a relationship between subject and object in which, while the work is mastered, its subjective dimension is repressed by its objective pole.[140] For Boissière and Savage the purported dialectic of *Le Marteau*, for example, is undermined by Boulez's resort to deductive logic. Its quasi-dialectic between freedom and necessity or between innovation and historical tradition does not escape from a rationalist agenda in which its innovative features are

---

[135] Boulez 1995, 561–4.
[136] A nominalist view of the artwork is one which refuses all generalisation, focusing on the specific elements of each work, understood on its own terms.
[137] Boulez 2005b, 94.   [138] Boulez 2005b, 86–92, 106.   [139] Boulez 2005b, 53.
[140] Boissière 1999, 120.

also rationally programmed and, consequently, fail to produce the desired dialectical tension of rational and irrational forces.[141]

It may be that only detailed empirical study of Boulez's working methods can produce evidence capable of determining the actual relationship of freedom and system within particular compositions. Pascal Decroupet, who has studied the preparatory sketches for *Le Marteau*, concludes that the importance which is given to the systematic is not inimical to the exercise of freedom and that while the work's innovative, unexpected moments are consistent with the logic of the system, this does not imply that they are engendered in any mechanistic way.[142] Writing to Stockhausen in May 1953 Boulez makes clear that for him 'everything is not determined' and that 'it would be more satisfying . . . not to create a hierarchy before beginning, but rather to discover this hierarchy as one goes along within the work'. In a further letter from December 1954, he notes that 'the system has no existence in itself. It only exists through what it becomes, and what it becomes depends on each instant.'[143] He consequently recommends neither the abolition of formal schemes nor the one-sided acceptance of purely subjective composition. Despite important differences between them, Boulez again draws strangely close to Adorno in the Collège de France lectures in accepting that invention ultimately eludes theorisation in dualist terms and that the most one can do is to hold the twin dialectical poles, of which *métier* is composed, in an aporetic tension which can, at best, deliver only partial insight.[144]

Conclusion

In the 1960s Adorno became more involved with both Stockhausen and Boulez.[145] Despite corresponding regularly with him, Stockhausen nevertheless described him as an opponent,[146] and, understandably, neither composer could really engage with him on a fully philosophical basis. Boulez attributes his own early neglect of aesthetics, in part, to 'the fear of appearing inferior to intellectuals better armed for fighting',[147] and we can only speculate that Adorno is one of those whom he has in mind. In an analogous way, the extent to which Adorno really assimilated serial music is legitimately open to question, and he seems to have been torn between articulating the problems of serialism in philosophical terms and wanting to be able to

---

[141]   Savage 1989, 37–8, 59.   [142]   Decroupet 2003, 55–7.
[143]   Both letters are cited in Albèra 2003, 65–6.   [144]   Boulez 2005b, 105–6.
[145]   Adorno and Stockhausen conducted a radio conversation in April 1960 entitled 'Resistance to New Music'.
[146]   Letter dated 14 May 1960. Cited in Kurtz 1992, 106.   [147]   Boulez 1986, 63.

understand and accept the challenging music of a generation of composers who clearly fascinated him.

It is notable that, right up to the *Aesthetic Theory*, when Adorno refers favourably to compositions by Boulez, it is invariably to those same works, and principally *Le Marteau*, which he had identified already in 'Vers une musique informelle'. *Le Marteau* is the work in which he finds the greatest dialectical currency, and its positive reception contrasts starkly with a series of less appreciative remarks which he made in relation to other works. The first book of *Structures* is described disparagingly in a 1955 letter to Steuermann as 'en noir et noir' (in black and black).[148] A diary entry from 1961 records his impressions of *Pli selon pli*: 'Very long, much métier, magnificent sound, weak compositional substance. Only colour relationships. No line and polyphony. Thus yet another Boulez. Rather boring.'[149] In his *Introduction to the Sociology of Music* (1962) he notes that it had been referred to as 'L'après-midi d'un vibraphone',[150] while also comparing what he had heard of the *Livre pour quatuor* unfavourably with *Le Marteau*.[151]

Boulez most likely does not share Adorno's philosophy of mediation and its social implications for composition. Where his negations are defined in purely musical terms, for Adorno it is the nature of societal critique which is at stake, and affirmative thought, musical and non-musical, is false precisely because it pretends that the world is harmonious and that what is truly human can be perceived immediately. If the charge of abstract negation refers at all to Boulez, it can only be for the very brief experimental moment of total serialism, and he becomes Adorno's chief musical exemplar in the formulation of *musique informelle*. While the moment of negation passed for Boulez, the dialectic and its binary oppositions retain a central place in his thinking to the present, even though, as we shall see, he began to express himself successively in more structuralist and post-structuralist terms.

---

[148] Adorno 2003, 248.   [149] Adorno 2003, 255.   [150] Adorno 1976, 113.
[151] Adorno 1976, 99.

5   Deduction and the scientific model

Few people who come into contact with the music, writings, aesthetic or broader cultural influence of Pierre Boulez do so in a spirit of indifference. He is a decisive figure, who elicits extremes of support or dismissal from those who believe him to be either one of the most significant figures in post-war Western music or a false prophet who for a time led music into a sterile cul-de-sac. While proponents of the latter view have come to this conclusion for a number of reasons, one of the commonest criticisms, which is found from his earliest years as a composer, has been that he and his music are 'exclusively rational and logical',[1] and that his involvement with mathematical and scientific thinking defines his approach to its detriment. This judgement is not confined to Boulez, who is seen by some as simply a significant representative of a depoliticised, 'technocratic, positivistic, and rationalistic high modernism'.[2]

Suggestions of scientism or positivism are often traced to the details of Boulez's early education, to his school success in physics, chemistry and mathematics. His attainment of a scientific baccalauréat at the end of his schooling (1941), his completion of a hypotaupe[3] in Lyons (1941–2) and his subsequently enforced matriculation on a course in mathematical theory, which he attended until his departure for Paris in 1943, only adds further fuel to the flame.[4] It is not surprising, therefore, that Boulez later rejected all talk of 'mathematical talent' in the face of the charge that he was nothing more than an 'algebraic composer' and a 'blackboard musician'. That he was to address the theme 'Is Intellectualism in Music a defect?' at Royaument in 1951 is indicative of the mood of the time,[5] and he acknowledges in 'Possibly ...' (1952), that his theoretical speculations will be interpreted by many as nothing more than 'the glorification of intellectualism over instinct'.[6] Of course, this was not something new in French musical life and, to take only one example, the danger of intellectualism had been raised by

---

[1] Boulez 2005a, 47.   [2] Bernstein 2002, 210.
[3] A term used formerly for a preparatory course in science preceding entry to one of the 'grandes écoles'.
[4] Jameux 1991, 5–8; Nicolas 2005, 140, accessed 12 March 2008.
[5] Cited in a letter from Schloezer to Souris, dated 30 May 1951 (AML). This colloquium, which was titled 'La Musique et le Cœur', was directed by Schloezer and took place 5–15 June 1951. While Boulez attended, he can no longer recall whether or not he delivered this paper (e-mail to the author 13 May 2008).
[6] Boulez 1991, 133.

the philosopher Gabriel Marcel in 1927 in relation to the work of Boris de Schloezer.[7]

One source of this problem, in Boulez's case, is the terminology he uses to discuss compositional questions. While he acknowledged that his account of recent musical investigations ran 'the serious risk of being accused of intellectualism',[8] he defended the use of a scientifically based vocabulary and the misunderstanding which this could entail in 'Alea' (1957), on the grounds that it was a 'temporary risk', necessary for the clarification of newly emerging ideas.[9] The dense, scientifically laden prose in his treatment of musical technique in the Darmstadt lectures (1960), and their later, partial publication as *Boulez on Music Today*, did nothing to dispel such dangers. In these lectures he argues 'the absolute necessity for a logically organised *consciousness*',[10] while dismissing a certain 'mathematical' or '"para-scientific" – mania' with its 'illusion' of scientific, rational exactness and objectivity as 'a pious illusion'.[11] Concluding the lectures, Boulez states:

> Why all these analogies with mathematical method, you may well be asking. I have never established any direct relationship between music and mathematics, only simple relations of comparison. Because mathematics is the science with the most developed methodology at the present time, I have taken it as an example that may help us to fill the gaps in our present system. I have tried in some way to lay the foundations of a methodology of music which must be detached, as such, from the methodology of mathematics with which I have tried to establish an analogy.[12]

Despite the clarity of his stated intention, it remains the case that he attributes the fetishistic and regressive epigonism of certain contemporary trends to 'a profound lack of intellectualism', acknowledging the paradoxical nature of these words, given the more common judgement that contemporary music is 'hyper-intellectual'.[13]

The foundation of IRCAM in 1977, with its goal of uniting scientific research and musical creation, stands for some as further evidence of a mathematical-scientific cast of mind, while the cool, analytical clarity of his performances and recordings as an orchestral conductor have all too often been assimilated in the light of his statements that music is both an art and a science.

He was not alone in theorising new music in mathematical or scientific terms, and it is interesting to note, for example, that when Stockhausen

---

[7] Marcel 2005, 99.   [8] Boulez 1991, 138.   [9] Boulez 1991, 35.   [10] Boulez 1971a, 33.
[11] Boulez 1986, 73.   [12] Boulez 1986, 98.   [13] Boulez 1971a, 22.

writes to Boulez in 1953, using a number of terms which are culled from the scientific-mathematical domain,[14] Boulez is clearly confounded, and is forced to seek clarification and explanation.[15] While he acknowledges 'applying modulos' to duration, dynamics and pitches in his own music, he asks Stockhausen to explain the phrases: 'statistical composition', '"improvisation" between the different limits', 'statistical spaces', 'rotation in values', and how he applies 'logarithmic proportions' in terms of frequency and dynamics to time. Even after Stockhausen has provided explanations for several of the problematic terms in a further letter,[16] Boulez writes again, expressing his ongoing confusion, and he admits to finding Stockhausen's use of the word 'feld' (field) 'profoundly unclear'.[17]

Scientific language is also found in Pousseur's writings, for example, in 'L'Impossible Objet' (1954), in which classical music and tonality are linked with Newtonian mechanics and the law of universal gravitation, in order then to compare Webern's music with the uncertainty of quantum physics. He is careful, however, in clarifying that the arts are not simply practical applications of scientific theories. The role of mathematics in serial music is justified on the basis of the claim that it is 'the most universal language . . . the basis of all linguistic systems', and a guarantor of their comprehensibility. Consequently, it is held up as the ideal which other disciplines including music must draw close to in order to qualify as knowledge and as a means of communication.[18]

While Messiaen stated that the espousal of scientific modes of thinking was 'quite in keeping with our age . . . almost necessary and even inevitable',[19] Adorno had come to a different conclusion in 'The Ageing of the New Music', in the conviction that 'the aesthetic rationality of the materials neither reaches their mathematical ideal nor dominates reality: it remains the mimesis of scientific procedures, a kind of reflex to the supremacy of science'.[20] He understood such approaches as symptomatic of the erosion of individual freedom within post-war Europe, and at worst as representing 'a violent and external totality, hardly different from political totalitarianism'. Schloezer expressed concern in 1955 with the linguistic borrowings by Boulez, Fano and Barraqué from modern physics and mathematics, recommending that they look instead to the newly emerging structuralism of Lévi-Strauss, a conjunction which will be considered

---

[14] Date of letter estimated by Robert Piencikowski to be the beginning of November 1953 (PSS).
[15] Date of letter estimated by Robert Piencikowski to be mid-November 1953 (PSS).
[16] Letter dated 20 November 1953 (PSS).
[17] Date of letter estimated by Robert Piencikowski to be the end of November 1953 (PSS). Boulez uses the word 'field' twice in his early writings (Boulez 1991, 119, 151) and then much more freely in the Darmstadt lectures (Boulez 1971a).
[18] Pousseur 1954, 112–13.   [19] Samuel 1976, 122.   [20] Adorno 1988, 108–11.

in the next chapter.[21] Again in 1959, Schloezer and Scriabine highlighted the use of contemporary physics, mathematics, cybernetics, linguistics and phonology, which the younger generation of composers made by way of explanation and justification of their work.[22]

The philosophically rationalist aspect of the serial programme is undoubtedly self-conscious, and Boulez on a number of occasions invokes Descartes and his project of methodical doubt. In articles from 1954 we are told that everything about the musical work has been called into question, from its fundamental conception to its linguistic morphology, by means of a paradoxical kind of logic, which indispensably governs intuition and guarantees coherence.[23] Radical doubt, however, results not in doubt but in certainty, and in the establishment of a new hierarchy of musical values.[24] Writing to Stockhausen in 1959 about the preparation of his six forthcoming Darmstadt lectures on 'new musical methodology', he reveals that he is rereading Descartes,[25] and in the lecture 'Nécessité d'une orientation esthétique' he suggests that

> The logical way seems to be to start from the basis of all aesthetics – that
> famous philosophical 'doubt' which, if we apply it to the totality of any
> musical project, will provide a firm starting point and rid our minds of
> a number of existing handicaps. We will forget for the moment all the
> traditional concepts and reconstruct our ideas from basically new data,
> which will open up a hitherto unexplored field of aesthetic choice.[26]

Dissatisfied with the inconsistency and lack of rigour in current 'musical reasoning', Boulez articulates a desire to produce a more stringent musical thought.[27] Like Pousseur, it is in modern mathematical works that he finds the realised ideal of 'pure thought' and the combination of 'rigour' and 'freedom' which he desires for music, if only musicians could catch up with their mathematical counterparts. The strength of the necessity which is the basis for their speculations, as well as the success of their symbolic systems, which subsume older symbolic conceptions within a more expansive explanatory framework, is the object of his respect, and a foil for the poverty of current musical symbolic systems. In this way the trend for graphic scores, prevalent at that moment, is rejected on the basis that it amounts to 'a pure regression', with the alternative recommendation that

[21] Schloezer 1955, 1085.   [22] Schloezer and Scriabine 1959, 190.
[23] Boulez 1991, 141.   [24] Boulez 1995, 31.
[25] Date of letter estimated by Robert Piencikowski to be [20]? December 1959 (PSS).
[26] Boulez 1986, 79–80. It was suggested in Chapter 3 that the element of Cartesian doubt in Boulez's thought should be seen as operating within the context of a more radical dialectical negation. Daniel Charles accuses Boulez of producing 'pseudo-Cartesianism' in this essay (1965, 157).
[27] Date of letter estimated by Robert Piencikowski to be [20]? December 1959 (PSS).

the way forward for musical thought is to 'find more and more abstract symbols which engender networks of actions (and not a single action, as in the case of the classical)'. A degree of exposure to mathematical writers is stimulating a 'searing revision' of his thought, and his hope is that he can 'extract from them their mode of creation and of reasoning'. In a further letter from February 1960, the feebleness of musical thought is traced to its lack of a 'general and genetic process' as its basis.[28]

All of this made its way into the text of the Darmstadt lectures, where he reflects on the reckless nature of the early serial experiments from a logical and mathematical point of view, and on the relatively uncomplicated nature of the 'theory of permutations' which serialism employed.[29] There is a great gulf separating such activities from the rigorously structured theories of contemporary logic, mathematics or physics.[30] Nevertheless, it is in the accomplishment of the Darmstadt lectures, particularly the first two, which deal with musical technique, that he draws most explicitly upon the language of formal logic, in the concepts of the axiom and deduction. The notion of deduction had, however, been part of his conceptual paraphernalia from the time of his early writings.

Axiomatics

In employing an axiomatic, deductive method, Boulez is drawing on a tradition which goes back to the third century BC, to Euclid's geometrical axioms. Positing a number of simple principles or axioms as the most fundamental truths within his subject, Euclid used them to derive all other geometrical truths, by means of a series of logically compelling deductions. Plato, who was attracted to the notion of an axiomatic deductive system, considered the possibility that all human knowledge could be formulated within one axiomatic system, deduced logically from an initial set of truths.[31] Aristotle was equally impressed by the possibilities of axiomatisation, but he did not subscribe to Plato's utopian hope that the totality of knowledge could be deduced from one set of axioms. For Aristotle, each particular area of knowledge has to be developed and formulated as a separate axiomatic system,[32] and he raises a number of questions, concerning, for example, which statements should form the axioms within a given system. What conditions need a proposition satisfy to be counted as an

---

[28] Letter dated February 1960 (PSS).   [29] Boulez 1971a, 25.
[30] Boulez 1971a, 29.   [31] Barnes 2000, 39–40.
[32] Barnes 2000, 59. Aristotle poses such questions in his logical writings and in the works known as *Prior and Posterior Analytics* in particular (Barnes 2000, 46).

axiom, and what rules will determine how deductions are to be made from axioms?[33]

Boulez was not the first post-war composer to think specifically in terms of axioms. In the article 'Les Comptes d'Orphée', which appeared in *Contrepoints* in 1946, Virgil Thomson set out twenty axioms on the composer's *métier*.[34] These may be more accurately termed a series of wistful maxims on the inverse relationship between degree of financial security or affluence and the composer's independence of style. Consequently, they are not predicated as the basis for a greater theoretical or logical system. While Boulez will most likely have read this article, it is not the immediate stimulus for his own espousal of axiomatic thinking, which draws instead upon the work of the philosopher Louis Rougier (1889–1982).[35]

In a letter to Stockhausen from 1956, Boulez acknowledges that he had read 'a sensational article by Louis Rougier on "the new theory of knowledge" in the NRF', and he is keen to discover whether he has produced a book on the subject.[36] He is dazzled by Rougier's method, which begins with mathematical ideas before applying them to the more general sphere of logic. Still impressed, he writes several years later in the published version of the Darmstadt lectures:

> I could do no better than to quote these sentences by Louis Rougier on axiomatic method, which could serve as an epigraph to this series of studies: 'Axiomatic method allows the construction of purely formal theories which are both networks of relationships and tables of the deductions which have been made. Hence, a single form may apply to diverse material, to groups of differing objects, provided only that these objects respect the same relationships among themselves as those present among the undefined symbols of the theory.' I feel that such a statement is fundamental to contemporary musical thought; note especially the last clause.[37]

The musical examples, which are given in *Boulez on Music Today*, are handled, as Decroupet has noted, 'as a class of problems and not as an accumulation of individual cases'.[38] In an earlier study, *La Structure des théories déductives* (1921), which is not referred to by Boulez, Rougier argues that 'demonstration never consists in combining universal principles

---

[33] Barnes 2000, 46.   [34] Thomson 1946, 17–45.

[35] Rougier's philosophy, which was forgotten in France for many years, partly as a result of his compromised relationship to the wartime Vichy régime, has recently received a degree of attention. While his output is wide-ranging in scope, it is his work on logical axiomatics which is of explicit interest to Boulez. Out of step with the main trends in French philosophy in the first half of the century, he was a supporter of the positivist Vienna Circle and a friend of Moritz Schlick, one of its most important figures (Engel 2006, 9–15; Dosse 1997, vol. 1, p. 83).

[36] Date of letter estimated by Robert Piencikowski to be the end of August 1956 (PSS).

[37] Boulez 1971a, 30, 83.   [38] Decroupet, in Borio and Danuser 1997, vol. 1, p. 384.

syllogistically among themselves, but *in logically combining objects, applying these principles to these combinations*.[39] It entails a system without contradictory laws, and he recommends the application of analogy in the work of classification, since 'it suffices to recognise, in an individual case, the presence of the small number of characters which define a class, in order to apply it *ipso facto* to all the properties derived from this class'.[40]

For Boulez it is essential that a musical system should be built exclusively upon 'musical criteria', and he cites the geometrician Moritz Pasch (1843–1930),[41] for whom 'if geometry is to become a deductive science, its procedures of reasoning must be independent of the meaning of geometric concepts just as they are independent of diagrams; nothing but the relationships imposed upon these ideas by postulates and definitions should figure in deduction'.[42] Consequently, in determining his own methodology, Boulez states:

> It is important to choose a certain number of *basic concepts* having a direct relationship with the phenomenon of sound, and with that alone, and then to state postulates which must appear as simple logical relationships between these concepts, independent of the meaning attributed to them. Having established this, it must be added that this condition of *basic concepts* is not restrictive, for, as Rougier says: 'there is a limitless number of equivalent systems of concepts and propositions which can be used as starting points, without any one of them *imposing itself* by *natural right*'. 'Thus', he continues, 'reasoning must always be independent of the object involved'. The dangers which threaten us are clearly stated: in relying almost entirely on the 'concrete, empirical or intuitive meaning' of the concepts used as starting-points, we may be led into fundamental errors of conception. Choosing the basic ideas in terms of their own specifications and logical relationships seems to be the first reform urgently needed in the present disorder.[43]

Rougier is again invoked in support of the notion that what 'we call "laws of nature"' is 'purely anthropomorphic language, for the regularity and simplicity of these laws are only true in the initial evaluation, and frequently the laws degenerate and disappear on further examination'. The physicist

---

[39] Rougier 1921, p. xi.

[40] Rougier 1921, 27. In *Les Paralogismes du Rationalisme* (Rougier 1920), Rougier sets out to refute philosophical rationalism in the belief that it cannot establish the truth or necessity of whatever first (a priori) principles are chosen. In espousing self-evident first principles, rationalism transforms relative truths into absolute truths and 'hypothetical necessity into unconditional necessity' (p. 64). Instead, it may be said that 'the principles proper to the deductive sciences, being treated as propositional functions, are neither true nor false, neither apodictically necessary nor assertorically true: they are conventions' (p. 77).

[41] Pasch worked on the foundations of geometry. His *Vorlesungen über neuere Geometrie* (1882) is said to be the first rigorous treatise on geometry.

[42] Boulez 1971a, 30.   [43] Boulez 1971a, 31.

Léon Brillouin (1889–1969) is more emphatic in stating that 'it amounts to a confidence trick to speak of the *laws of nature* as if they existed independently of man. Nature is much too abundant for our minds to be able to embrace it. We isolate fragments, observe them, and devise representative *models* (simple enough to be useful).'

Boulez, like Rougier, is careful in stressing that the concepts, functions and relationships, which are to be deduced, are not to be confused with any musical reality, and that what we apprehend of the world is 'its structure, not its essence'. Just as we grasp the world 'in terms of relationships and functions, not of substances and accidents', so should we think of music.[44] Ultimately, what matters is that logical coherence is attained in purely musical terms, without recourse to the extra-musical, in that 'the concept of coherence' replaces 'the concept of evidence' and 'the concept of tautology' replaces that of necessity.[45] This proto-structuralist theme is reinforced with a citation from the French philosopher Roger Martin (1920–79), at the head of the Darmstadt lecture 'Time, Notation and Coding' (1960), in which he states that 'entities [are] studied exclusively by means of their relationship to each other'.[46] Daniel Charles suggests, however, that the coherence of the system, which is presented in *Boulez on Music Today*, may be 'metaphorical' or 'illusory', and that its genuine gains, far from being systematic, are really a series of partial, but nevertheless brilliant, 'intuitions'.[47]

In terms of assessing Boulez's engagement with the authors and ideas which he draws upon in *Boulez on Music Today*, we should note that all of the citations from Rougier are taken from an article published in *La Nouvelle Revue Française* entitled 'La nouvelle théorie de la connaissance'.[48] The citation from Pasch is also taken from Rougier, who used it both in his article and in a substantial volume on epistemology, *La Traité de la connaissance*, which he published in 1955.[49] The reference to Brillouin is taken from the article 'Science et imagination' which appeared in *La Nouvelle Revue Française* in 1961,[50] in other words, between the delivery of the lectures at Darmstadt and their publication in German in 1963. While it is not known for sure if Boulez read Rougier's treatise, any of his other philosophical books, or anything more substantial by Brillouin, it is clear that in the course of preparing his Darmstadt lectures, in both their oral and written formats, he drew fairly freely on the contributions which these, his

---

[44] Boulez 1971a, 32.   [45] Boulez 1971a, 129.   [46] Boulez 1986, 84.   [47] Charles 1965, 151.
[48] *La Nouvelle Revue Française*, 4/42 (June 1956), 999–1015.
[49] Rougier 1955, 335. The source of the citation from Pasch is his *Vorlesungen über neuere Geometrie* (Leipzig, 1882), 16.
[50] Brillouin 1961, 839–40. Boulez cites from this passage again in 'Aesthetics and the Fetishists' (1961) (1986, 41). François Nicolas first identified the source of this quotation (2005, 141).

fellow contributors, made to *La Nouvelle Revue Française*. We have no reason to doubt Deliège's remembrance that Boulez acknowledged not having got past the preface of presumably Rougier's treatise on epistemology,[51] and it is no more likely that his knowledge of Brillouin was any more profound.

François Nicolas is undoubtedly correct in noting the essentially illustrative character of Boulez's borrowings from these authors, whose work is used to provide some kind of ancillary scientific confirmation and support for his musical theorising.[52] Having established the essentially mistaken nature of Boulez's reputation as a composer who was immersed in and motivated by the study of mathematics or science, it is unclear why it is so questionable to Nicolas that Boulez should support his text in this way, and why he should be held to account for not having a more comprehensive knowledge of scientific, mathematical and philosophical problems. That the accounts provided by Rougier and Brillouin are much more nuanced than that of Boulez is neither cause for surprise nor grounds for disqualification of what is an essentially clear application of principle in Boulez's text.[53]

It may be helpful to view Boulez's appeal to Rougier, Pasch and Brillouin in the light of the perceived connection between the Bourbaki group of French mathematicians and the linguistic structuralism which swept French intellectual life in the late 1950s and early 1960s. Bourbaki attempted to extend the axiomatic method to the entire field of modern mathematics,[54] and, like Pasch's geometry, it wanted mathematics to be treated as something completely autonomous, without external input or interference.[55] The structuralism, which Bourbaki applied to the mathematical realm, formed a kind of parallel to that which Lévi-Strauss introduced into the human sciences, and both movements grew in status from just after the war until their peak around 1966.[56]

While Lévi-Strauss had used the services of the Bourbaki mathematician André Weil in the development of his 'elementary structures' in the 1940s,[57] of all the principal figures writing within the structuralist paradigm only Piaget drew attention explicitly to the Bourbaki circle and to its production of a structural method based on a number of axioms or 'parent structures'.[58] In a series of lectures from 1952, which were published under the title *Logic and Psychology*, he articulated his desire that axiomatic logic be applied to psychology, thus constructing a 'psycho-logic'.[59] That Piaget is an

[51] Cited in Nicolas (2005, 145).   [52] Nicolas 2005, 142.   [53] Nicolas 2005, 144.
[54] Bourbaki was the nom de plume for a collective of French mathematicians operating from 1939 until the 1970s (Aubin 1997, 298, 305; Dosse 1997, vol. I, pp. 82–3).
[55] Aubin 1997, 307.   [56] Aubin 1997, 311.   [57] Aubin 1997, 302, 308.
[58] Piaget 1971, 24; Aubin 1997, 323. Piaget judges that 'a critical account of structuralism must begin with a consideration of mathematical structures' (Piaget 1971, 17).
[59] Piaget 1953, 25.

exceptional case among the structuralists, who generally did not produce any worked-out relationship with mathematics,[60] did not prevent others from exploiting its validatory potential. Aubin notes the claims to scientificity which were made by the proponents of structuralism at two interdisciplinary conferences in 1959,[61] and there is no doubt that the Bourbaki conception of structure, as an axiomatic system, was readily assimilable as a form of scientific justification for linguistic structuralism.[62] While there was a dialogue between them, it was, in Aubin's judgement, 'unsustained' and generally 'rather superficial'.[63]

That Boulez's engagement with Rougier, Pasch, Brillouin and Martin may amount to no more than a few choice quotations from a small number of supportive articles should not surprise us, and it may well be the case that he, like many structuralists, sought some kind of mathematical legitimation. His letters to Stockhausen, however, demonstrate an unmistakable sincerity in the face of this discovery and provide compelling evidence of the impact which even a little exposure to these core ideas had upon him. While deduction is retained as an essential Boulezian concept, and appears frequently in the Collège de France lectures, the notion of the axiom disappears from his writings after the Darmstadt lectures. It seems that the late 1950s and the early 1960s was the time in Boulez's development for axioms. The quasi-mathematical and wholly logical conception which they embody is symptomatic of the stage which had been reached in the theoretical development of serial music. That it was not repeated is probably due, at least in part, to the change of emphasis in Boulez's activities after this time, and to the fact that he spent less energy in the articulation of his theoretical positions, preferring the interview to the article. Once achieved, it was no longer necessary to formulate new axioms, and there is no doubt that while his later music underwent some important changes, at a variety of levels, it remained faithful in principle to the key discoveries which had been made in his earlier work.

Deduction

Boulez writes of deduction with great regularity from his earliest articles right through to the Collège de France lectures from the mid-1970s, 1980s and 1990s. His method of expounding the morphology of serial theory is often deductive in nature, and tends to begin from what he considers to be first principles, which may be a definition of the series or some other theoretical aspect. This is the route which he takes, for example, in

---

[60] Aubin 1997, 309, 311.   [61] Aubin 1997, 315.   [62] Aubin 1997, 316.   [63] Aubin 1997, 333.

'Proposals' (1948),[64] 'Possibly ...' (1952),[65] and in the Darmstadt lectures. From this initial definition, he then proceeds to 'create a network of possibilities', working systematically through all of the possible permutations available to him.[66] This, as Decroupet notes, is usually achieved through the application of binary oppositions to the given concept, the terms of which are, in turn, divided into further binary oppositions, until he has mapped out as many possibilities as he can logically imagine.[67] In 'Tendencies in Recent Music' (1953/7), in an attempt to escape the tyranny of the number twelve, Boulez writes of the need to 'gather up our various investigations, generalize our discoveries, and expand the resources'.[68] The systematic laying out of deductive possibilities can be seen, at least initially, as an imaginative attempt to move away from the problematic situation in which total serialism found itself. He sums up the method of his first two Darmstadt lectures as one which proceeds 'from the elementary to the most general level' in 'an attempt to construct a coherent system by means of methodical investigation of the musical world, deducing multiple consequences from a certain number of rational points of departure'.[69]

The concepts of deduction and hierarchy are central to Boulez's definition of the series in the Darmstadt lectures, where he describes it as:

> the germ of a developing hierarchy . . . endowed with a greater or lesser selectivity, with a view to organising a FINITE ensemble of creative possibilities connected by predominant affinities, in relation to a given character; this ensemble of possibilities is deduced from an initial series by a FUNCTIONAL generative process . . . Consequently, all that is needed to set up this hierarchy is a necessary and sufficient premise which will ensure the total cohesion of the whole and the relationships between its successive parts.[70]

Schloezer had already, of course, presented the musical work as a hierarchy of systems in his *Introduction à J.-S. Bach*, and there is a strong likelihood that Boulez has been influenced by this argument.[71]

In Boulez's case, this definition of the series is applied by means of the deductive method to the parameters of pitch, duration, dynamics and timbre, as well as to a number of sub-components which are derived from the principal parameters, including, for example, both '*homogeneous* complexes of pitch, duration, dynamics and timbre' as well as '*combined* complexes of pitch/duration, pitch/dynamics' and so on.[72] The intention is to establish,

---

[64] Boulez 1991, 50.   [65] Boulez 1991, 115.   [66] Boulez 1991, 120.
[67] Decroupet, in Borio and Danuser 1997, vol. 1, p. 386.   [68] Boulez 1991, 177.
[69] Boulez 1971a, 142–3.   [70] Boulez 1971a, 35–6.   [71] Schloezer 1947, 75.
[72] Boulez 1971a, 36.

for each of these elements, 'a network of possibilities' which can then be divided into the following four, paired categories: (1) 'Absolute value'; (2) 'Relative value'; (3) 'Fixed density of generation', and (4) 'Mobile density of generation'.[73] In doing so, he announces that he has 'defined a perfectly constituted and logically based formal world' in which sound complexes are to be 'deduced from one another'.[74] The serial hierarchy is 'no longer based on the principle of identity by transposition, but, on the contrary, on localised and variable deductions',[75] and tables of deductive possibilities are set out for tempi,[76] timbral possibilities,[77] spatial possibilities,[78] 'the internal structure of a series',[79] pitch spaces[80] and musical time.[81] In this way, the initial definition of the series is the provisional axiom which Boulez uses as a starting point, and from which all of his deductions, relating to each of the musical parameters, are derived. While Boulez does not in fact set out a series of explicit axioms which can be identified unambiguously within his text, it would be possible to compile a list of principles which would seem to have a provisionally axiomatic status in the setting out of his system. Examples could include the ideas that 'sounds and noises must be treated as a *function* of the formal structures which employ them',[82] and that the twelve semitones do not have 'to remain strictly and immovably equal amongst themselves'.[83] Any such reconstruction would, however, be both artificial and arbitrary, and it may be that his principles are closer to maxims than axioms.

Deductive thinking is not diminished in importance in the Collège de France lectures. Leaving aside those statements which link deduction with the exercise of the composer's *métier*, and which were discussed in Chapter 4, the following points can be made. In Boulez's musical logic, one note is deduced from another, one line from another, one chord from another, one motif from another, one interval from another, and the vertical dimension can be deduced from that of the horizontal.[84] A musical work may be deduced in part from a preceding work, with regard to particular features, which were contained there in embryonic form.[85] Indeed, in Boulez's view of composition, the concepts of deduction, necessity and responsibility combine in the best musical works, and it is deduction which facilitates discovery of the musical idea and its necessary proliferation. Invention is consequently defined as 'profusion *in deduction*'.[86]

A distinction is made between 'superficial' deductions, which are repetitive or lacking in innovation, and 'unforeseeable' deductions which enrich

---

[73] Boulez 1971a, 38.   [74] Boulez 1971a, 39.   [75] Boulez 1971a, 42.   [76] Boulez 1971a, 51.
[77] Boulez 1971a, 65.   [78] Boulez 1971a, 68.   [79] Boulez 1971a, 76.   [80] Boulez 1971a, 87–8.
[81] Boulez 1971a, 93.   [82] Boulez 1971a, 43.   [83] Boulez 1971a, 45.   [84] Boulez 2005b, 88–9.
[85] Boulez 2005b, 106.   [86] Boulez 2005b, 91–3.

the initial idea. In this connection, deduction is particularly necessary where musical 'codes have been loosened' and frameworks relaxed, since the composer now has to deduce materials, forms and structures from initial ideas which consequently have even greater generative force than before. While deduction can be conscious or intuitive, the goal is to make 'idea and form' coincide,[87] in a situation where multiple, indeed unlimited deductions are possible, and in which no one option has hierarchical priority over any other,[88] a topic which will be explored in Chapters 7, 8 and 9 of the present study. Furthermore, deduction should not be equated solely with rationality, and there is the possibility that it can be 'highly illogical or irrational' and disruptive in effect.[89] While deductive possibilities can be selected directly by composer intervention, computer technology presents the option of non-directional deductions, in which a number of outcomes may be possible, depending on context.[90] If deductions were made independently with regard to each of the musical parameters at the moment of strict serialism, this was followed by an attempt to re-establish more perceptible deductive processes.[91]

While deduction should start out from 'fundamental ideas' and should enshrine a unified logic, the accidental must also be integrated in the shape of unforeseeable events.[92] Despite the importance of deduction in composition, there is a danger that it may be exaggerated in a way which does not accurately reflect the work's gestation,[93] and Boulez stresses that the creative process of a composition cannot be reconstituted by simply retracing the deductions which led to its completion.[94]

In the article 'Zur Situation des Metiers (Klangkomposition)' (1953) Stockhausen shows that he shared Boulez's taste for deduction, and he writes of the deduction of series from an original series and of the work having a 'necessary formal consistency [*Konsequenz*]'.[95] In 'Erfindung und Entdeckung' (1961), while discussing the question of musical form, he distinguishes between 'invented' and 'discovered' forms, and deduction is presented as constituting the investigative aspect of the process of invention in terms which are very close to those of Boulez in the Darmstadt lectures. The work of composition is presented as an exercise in deductive method,

---

[87] Boulez 2005b, 148.   [88] Boulez 2005b, 687.

[89] Boulez 2005b, 92–3. Deduction is at the heart of Boulez's late reading of Schoenberg (p. 367), who claimed that he could predict all of the deductions yielded by a particular theme at the moment of its invention (pp. 240–1). His twelve-tone work from around 1929 is described as 'a period of extreme deductive logic' (p. 665).

[90] Boulez 2005b, 152.   [91] Boulez 2005b, 283.   [92] Boulez 2005b, 332–3.

[93] Boulez 2005b, 664.   [94] Boulez 2005b, 351, 365.

[95] Stockhausen 1963a, 46. An incomplete translation of the article – 'Situation actuelle du métier de compositeur' – appeared in the periodical *Domaine Musical 1* which was produced under Boulez's direction (Stockhausen 1954, 128).

in which the composer 'derives a form, which should fulfil very specific conditions which he has set, from the axioms which are put in place for a specific work'.[96]

An interest in deduction is also found in Barraqué (1953), for whom 'a logical chain of deductions' links Wagnerian chromaticism with Schoenbergian atonality and serialism.[97] Pousseur (1975), citing Schoenberg's claim that his practice of deducing all of the material within a musical work from 'a single generating figure' derives from J. S. Bach, acknowledges that his own *Épreuves de Pierrot l'Hébreu* is deduced in this way.[98] However, in a text from 1988, he writes of the deductions which Boulez and Goeyvaerts made from 'Messiaen's teaching on *Mode de valeurs et d'intensités*' as a 'particularly totalitarian version of the idea of the "generalised series"'.[99] One reference which is absent from Boulez's account is not surprisingly that of Leibowitz, who in his *Introduction à la musique de douze sons* makes a significant number of references to deduction, including the deduction of an entire structure from a single cell,[100] of variation from an original form,[101] and of everything from 'an initial series of intervals'.[102] It may be that Boulez's interest in deductive terminology or process, in its simplest sense, has its origin in Leibowitz's classes and writings.

Conclusion

There is a significant rationalist streak in Boulez's musical thought, which is manifested, from his early works, in a logical-deductive approach to composition. It is primarily present in his more theoretical writings in his references to Descartes, Rougier, Pasch, and, more importantly, in his attempts to define key concepts and to make chains of deductions. It is nevertheless the case that Boulez's thought is not determinable purely in terms of this one thought stream, and consideration of his writings shows that they are equally marked by dialectical, structuralist and post-structuralist ideas.

These are traditions of thinking which do not comfortably coexist with one another. Hegel could write in his *Phenomenology* that 'current opinion has already come to view the scientific regime bequeathed by mathematics as quite *old-fashioned* – with its explanations, divisions, axioms, sets of theorems, its proofs, principles, deductions and conclusions from

---

[96] Stockhausen 1963a, 223; 1963b, 147–8. A French translation/version 'Invention et Découverte' was published in *La musique et ses problèmes contemporains* (1963b, 147–68).
[97] Barraqué 2001, 52.   [98] Pousseur 1997, 145. See for example Schoenberg 1975, 165–6.
[99] Pousseur 1997, 185.   [100] Leibowitz 1949b, 37.   [101] Leibowitz 1949b, 61.
[102] Leibowitz 1949b, 75.

them'.[103] Adorno argued forcefully against any resort to 'an abstract, mathematical necessity that imposes itself on the musical phenomenon from outside, without subjective mediation'.[104] He acknowledges that this 'desire to spin everything out of a common core' is one of a number of tendencies linking the Viennese composers and 'the [new] Serialists',[105] and he attacks the 'unity of a deductive system' on the grounds that it is 'predetermined down to the very last accent by the initial choice of material', and that it excludes 'every element of chance'.[106] While we will return to such problems as we explore the relationship between Boulez's thought, structuralism and post-structuralism, it is sufficient for the moment to recall the emphasis which the composer places on the unforeseeable, the intuitive, the irrational, the non-directional and the accidental in relation to deduction, all of which are clearly articulated in the Collège de France lectures.

[103] Hegel 1977, 28. Hegel rejected Spinoza's 'geometric method . . . of beginning with axioms and definitions and then rigorously reasoning from them' as 'a defunct remnant of the older rationalism' which Kant had overcome in his Transcendental Dialectic (Beiser 2005, 91).
[104] Adorno 1999, 204–5.   [105] Adorno 1998, 218.   [106] Adorno 1999, 203.

6 Serialism and structuralism

The late 1950s and early 1960s witnessed the transformation of the French philosophical and cultural landscape as Sartre's existential phenomenology with its emphasis on individual freedom came to stand for outdated values which no longer reflected the mood of the time. While the dialectic was still central to discussion after 1960, it had fallen from favour on the grounds that it embodied an identity logic which was now found wanting.[1] The return of the anthropologist Claude Lévi-Strauss from the United States had an impact on French intellectual and cultural life well beyond the limits of his own discipline and brought to fruition, on a grand scale, a methodological conception which had its roots ultimately in Ferdinand de Saussure's *Course in General Linguistics* and in the phonology of the Prague linguists Nikolai Trubetzkoy and Roman Jakobson.[2] Lévi-Strauss, who met Jakobson in New York in 1942, adopted his phonological model, applied it to anthropology and argued on that basis from the mid-1940s onwards that anthropology could learn directly from the linguistic model.[3]

Lévi-Strauss's work had a particularly significant impact upon the intellectual climate of the late 1950s, and he came to public attention in France in 1958 with the publication of his book *Structural Anthropology*, which found a readership well beyond its natural constituency and which became the manifesto for the entire structuralist movement. However, it was really with the appearance of *The Savage Mind* in 1962 that the structuralist vogue began, and that his work began to exert a deep influence on almost every branch of French cultural life.[4] The attraction of structuralism, for many, lay in its general nature, as its idiosyncratic exponents attempted to apply linguistic theory, stemming from Saussure, to a great number of non-linguistic areas of human activity. These, it was maintained, could be studied as systems of signs in which a structural analysis aimed 'to isolate the underlying set of laws by which these signs are combined into meanings'.[5] To take only some of the best-known examples, it motivated Jacques Lacan's

---

[1] Descombes 1980, 75.

[2] While the term 'structure' was only used three times in Saussure's *Course in General Linguistics* (1916), it and the term 'structuralism' were used more generally by Trubetzkoy and Jakobson (Dosse 1997, vol. 1, p. xxii). It seems that Jakobson coined the term 'structuralism' in 1929 (Aubin 1997, 310).

[3] Dosse 1997, vol. 1, p. 52.   [4] Lévi-Strauss and Eribon 1991, 71.   [5] Eagleton 1996, 84.

psychoanalysis, Roland Barthes's literary criticism, Louis Althusser's political theory as well as being associated with the *Nouveau Roman* as represented by Alain Robbe-Grillet, Michel Butor, Claude Simon and others.

While structuralism is not primarily a philosophy (Lévi-Strauss repeatedly claimed that it was a scientific method), it had an undoubted impact upon philosophy.[6] It entailed a radical shift from existential phenomenology and its concept of the human subject, the author or the composer, towards ahistorical structures which are said to exist within the human mind. Meaning is no longer to be located within the expressive human subject but rather within language since human subjectivity itself is constituted by and the consequence of signifying systems which precede it.

Structural analysis defines a set of relations in terms of their properties and thus establishes the basis of a structure which is taken to be only a model of the structure itself, as manifested through the model. Concerned primarily with the isomorphism of the fundamental structure and its individual manifestation, structuralism does not deal in any pure way with the actual structure of a particular thing but rather with 'the set, of which this thing may be considered as one *representation*, in comparison with other sets'.[7] Despite the diversity of the areas of enquiry in which the structuralist method was employed, it can nevertheless be said that its heterogeneous exponents shared 'a preoccupation with embodied relationships – whether political, literary, religious, historical, psychoanalytic, or ethnological' which they accepted as objectively given, as 'sharing or borrowing the structure of language, and reflecting the unconscious structure of mind'.[8]

A number of writers have posited a relationship between serialism and structuralism, and Boulez, in particular, has been cited as someone upon whom structuralism had a significant influence.[9] While many of the key issues regarding their connection have been discussed by Ruwet, Lévi-Strauss, Eco, Pousseur and others, this chapter attempts to explore the question of its validity and the extent of its specific legitimacy for Boulez. In doing so we must first explore those elements in Boulez's theory and practice which have suggested such connections, before considering in some detail the critical discussions which were conducted in a number

---

[6] Dosse 1997, vol. 2 p. 83. Descombes distinguishes between 'the method of *structural analysis*', the fusion of structuralism and semiology, and 'a philosophical "orientation"' engaged upon a critique of phenomenology and semiology (1980, 81).

[7] Descombes 1980, 85–7.   [8] Caws 1992, 293.

[9] For Dosse, Boulez's work displays the same 'science of structure' as is found in Barthes and Butor (Dosse 1997, vol. 1, p. 207; vol. 2, pp. 201–2). See also Breatnach 1996, 136–7; Peyser 1977, 152–3 and Dufourt 1993, 71, 73. The title of Boulez's *Structures* for two pianos (1951–2; 1956–61) may have stimulated the comparison.

of publications beginning with Ruwet's critique in 1959. Having compared and contrasted serialism and structuralism, we can then trace those concepts from the structuralist lexicon which have endured within Boulez's practice, before finally showing how the structuralist model was itself superseded by a post-structuralist thought which has also engendered comparisons with serialism.

The transition from the dialectical moment to that of structuralism did not require the complete negation of all that had gone on before and there are some clear points of contact. Despite falling out of favour, elements of the dialectic remain in Lévi-Strauss's work in a way which is not absolutely clear, and he describes how his 'common-sense Kantian[ism]' is the result of his reading of Marx and Hegel.[10] Binary oppositions for example, which featured prominently in Chapter 3 in the context of dialectical thought, were also important for a number of structuralist theorists including Saussure, Jakobson, Lévi-Strauss and Barthes. The replacement of dialectics by structuralism also instantiates a troubling paradox between the historical and the structural, or between temporal processes and atemporal structures, of which writers at the time were keenly conscious, and which surfaces also in relation to Boulez.

It is finally of interest to note a number of connections linking Souvtchinsky, Schaeffner and Schloezer with structuralism. Souvtchinsky and Trubetzkoy constituted two of the four founding members of the Eurasian movement at the beginning of the 1920s,[11] and it seems that Trubetzkoy stimulated a shift in focus for Souvtchinsky from music to reflection upon Russia's historical situation in the light of the revolution, an aspect of his thought which we have already noted.[12] It is less clear, however, what he thought of Trubetzkoy's work on phonology.[13]

Despite being on friendly terms with both Lévi-Strauss and Ruwet, Schaeffner seems to have been fairly ambivalent towards structuralism. While he recognised the significance of developments within linguistics, and attempted to keep up with the latest structuralist publications, these did not make a significant impact on him.[14] Nevertheless, his ethnomusicological work brought him close to Lévi-Strauss, and they both benefited enormously from the work of the anthropologist Marcel Mauss, with whom Schaeffner studied, and whom Lévi-Strauss credited highly as having prepared the way for his structural anthropology.[15]

---

[10] Lévi-Strauss and Eribon 1991, 108.   [11] Glebov 2006, 170.   [12] Walterskirchen 2006, 34.
[13] There are 131 letters from Trubetzkoy to Souvtchinsky dating from 1921 to 1928 (BN).
[14] Letters from Schaeffner to Souris, dated 26 March 1963 and 26 April 1966 (AML).
[15] Dosse 1997, vol. 1, pp. 26–30.

   While the main philosophical thrust of Schloezer's *Introduction à J. S. Bach* was concerned with phenomenology and gestalt theory, he states that he is more interested in the structure of something than in its genesis,[16] and that the psychological value of a musical composition does not depend upon the listener but rather arises from the 'structure of the sound system', which is an objective value.[17] The work is a 'complex system of mutually interpenetrating relations, a system where each sound and group of sounds is situated within a whole, assumes a precise function and acquires specific qualities from the fact of their multiple relations with all of the others'.[18] In 'Retour à Descartes' (1955), in criticising the post-war serial composers for their reliance on language taken from modern physics and mathematics, he advises that the study of a system's structure '"takes better account of its nature and properties than analysing it into its elements" (Lévi-Strauss)'.[19] In *Problèmes de la musique moderne* (1959), in harmony with his earlier statements, Schloezer and his niece Marina Scriabine judge that 'the musical "thing itself" is a certain sound structure which is simultaneously melodic, harmonic, rhythmic' and that these terms relate to three inseparable aspects of the same reality.[20] While his lifelong interest in artworks as objective structures is clear, and there are aspects of his thought which are concordant with the later structuralists, it is equally apparent that he is not a structuralist in this sense.[21] Nevertheless, it is also likely that the emphasis which he placed on structure played some part in shaping Boulez's view and perhaps even prompted him to consider the structuralism of Lévi-Strauss.

Form and content

Music plays an important role in the formulation and expression of Lévi-Strauss's ideas and it may, in part, have been this which attracted Boulez. Nevertheless, while Lévi-Strauss undoubtedly exercised some influence on his thinking in the early 1960s, the development of Boulez's ideas in relation to structuralism is unclear. It seems that the first reference to Lévi-Strauss is found in a Darmstadt lecture from 1960 where he writes:

> As the sociologist Lévi-Strauss affirms, on the subject of language proper, I am convinced that in music there is no opposition between form and content, between abstract on the one hand and concrete on the other. Form and content are of the same nature, subject to the same analytical jurisdiction. 'The content', Lévi-Strauss explains, 'draws its reality from

---

[16] Schloezer 1947, 84–5.   [17] Cited in Kohler 2003, 292.   [18] Schloezer 1947, 26.
[19] Schloezer 1955, 1085. He does not reveal the source of the citation from Lévi-Strauss.
[20] Schloezer and Scriabine 1959, 102.   [21] Picon 1981, 65.

its structure, and what we call form is the *structural disposition* of local structures, in other words of the content'. Also these structures must comply with the principles expounded above, concerning the logic of musical form.[22]

Daniel Charles fears that in adopting this Lévi-Straussian position Boulez is surrendering to a deductive logic of the kind which Adorno had already warned against,[23] and he is concerned with its 'historicism and relativism' which would reduce the history of music to 'the history of forms' or more generally to 'a mere history of the mind'. In other words, he indicts Boulez for theorising the musical work in terms of the kind of structural modelling which Lévi-Strauss had introduced into anthropology. Understood in this way, the musical work would relate primarily to mental structures within the subject, of which it would be only a token. While he acknowledges that Boulez's intention is to avoid formalism, and he refers to Boulez's rather self-conscious statement of the fact, he believes him to have been unsuccessful in this regard since the equation of form and content leads inevitably to this outcome. Ultimately, Charles considers Boulez to be mistaken in equating content with structure, and form with 'the structuring of the local structures', since such a step appears to stem from a 'naive' application of Lévi-Strauss and leads to the problematic claim that music is a language.[24]

The question of the relationship between content and form was clearly not a new one and while it is undeniable that Lévi-Strauss is de facto the thinker whom Boulez chooses to cite in making his point, it would be a mistake to imagine that he first discovered this insight from the ethnologist. It is difficult to ignore the evidence which suggests that his disposition towards Lévi-Strauss's view was facilitated by the work of a number of earlier writers whose positions share something with his own. Already in the nineteenth century, when the aesthetician Eduard Hanslick stated that in music form and content are inseparable, controversy ensued over the nature of their relationship, and in response to the suggestion that content could be reduced to form or that they are identical or indistinguishable.[25] When Mallarmé in his 'Crisis in Poetry' suggested that 'the inner structures of a book of verse must be inborn', he similarly rooted poetic content in poetic form in implying that the poem develops out of its own resources

---

[22] Boulez 1971a, 32. This quotation from Lévi-Strauss (1973, 158) also appears in the lecture 'Form' (1960) (Boulez 1986, 90) and 'Periform' (1965) (Boulez 1986, 104). See Piaget 1971, 112–13.

[23] Charles 1965, 150–1.

[24] For Boissière (1999), the equation of content and form, the definition of form as structure and the functionalist, self-referential codification of musical material into generalised serialism, results in an emptying of the work's 'historic dimension'. Dufourt criticises the construction of the serial language 'on the model of artificial languages or formal systems' (1991, 89).

[25] Hanslick 1986, 77–83; Lippman 1992, 298–301.

and that it is constituted by these 'inner structures'.[26] In his *Introduction à J. S. Bach*, Schloezer considered music as a limit case among the arts in which 'the signified is immanent to the signifier [signifiant]' and content is immanent to and identified with form.[27] Categorising music among closed artistic systems, the musical artwork is defined as 'an object in which unity is simultaneously form and sense; or again: an object in which form is identified with content'.[28] Souris, in the early 1940s, had come to the conclusion that the problem of musical form and content is resolved by gestalt theory since musical sense is immanent to the musical material and changes in form result in changed signification.[29] Interestingly, Boulez, like Souris, cites the gestalt writer Paul Guillaume in order to clarify the passage from Lévi-Strauss. Boulez writes: 'it must be clearly remembered that the term *structural disposition* is not meant to suggest a simple summation of these local structures. "A form", as Paul Guillaume states, "is something *other* or *greater* than the sum of its parts".'[30] Even Adorno, who thought of content and form as having an 'inseparable reciprocal relation',[31] but who did not equate or unify them as Boulez seems to, had charged early serialism in 'The Ageing of the New Music' with rupturing their relationship.

Structures, language and codes

Whatever the genealogy and development of the word 'structure' within post-war musical theory and composition, there can be no doubt that its use pre-dates the rise of the structuralist movement, and we have already encountered its importance for Schloezer. In '... Near and Far' (1954), Boulez seems to imply the existence of some kind of general structural commonality linking music with the other arts,[32] and in 'Sound and Word' (1958) he identifies structure as 'one of the words of our time', arguing that the connection of poetry and music is to be achieved structurally at every level beginning with that of morphology.[33] He perhaps comes closest to structuralism in his 1961 Darmstadt lecture 'Taste: "The Spectacles Worn by Reason"?' in which he questions:

---

[26] Cited in Jonathan Scott Lee 1996, 182–3.
[27] Schloezer 1947, 24–5. Schloezer had written in 1928 that 'musical content does not transcend form, but is immanent to it' (1928b, 51).
[28] Schloezer 1947, 80.   [29] Wangermée 1995, 220.
[30] Boulez 1971a, 32 (translation amended by the author); Guillaume 1979, 18.
[31] Letter from Adorno to Berg, dated 6 January 1926 (2005, 37).
[32] Boulez 1991, 143. A conference in Paris in April 1956, 'Notion of Structure and Structure of Knowledge', featured only one mention of Lévi-Strauss's name and no reference to Jakobson. This suggests that 'the notion of structure was then very commonly used and that in 1956, as opposed to 1959, it was up for anyone to grab' (Aubin 1997, 315).
[33] Boulez 1991, 40–1.

> Can it be that after all there are some constant factors in taste in addition
> to the many variables? The answer, I believe, is an unhesitating 'yes'. Any
> comparison of different literatures, and of means of expression in general,
> will reveal the fact that beneath very different appearances taste is
> characterised by a number of strongly marked constants. These depend
> primarily on reactions to human existence, shared by all human beings, and
> on similarities that exist between all forms of society. Whether it is a question
> of the individual or of society as a whole, the transcending element enables
> us to appreciate works of the remote or recent past that do indeed express
> that past, yet in some way or other transcend it.[34]

Similarly in 1963 he speaks of archetypes, of 'practically permanent conceptual gestures' which are to be found in almost every form of expression and
civilisation throughout the world, but which are not so easily identified in
practice.[35] He presents the view that 'mental structures' are always exteri-
orised by virtue of 'the same preferential circuits', and that a number of these
circuits, that is, 'primitive conceptual functions', lie at the root of geograph-
ically and historically diverse music right up to the present and constitute
the basis of all musical expression.[36] The clear focus here upon the artwork from the point of view of constants and variables brings Boulez close
to one of Lévi-Strauss's central concerns. In a similar way, Pousseur, who
is contemplating the possibility of reintegrating some previously occluded
harmonic elements into his musical syntax, conceives of this as a forward
movement in which the past is absorbed, and in which a language is constructed 'which is sufficiently general in order to reintegrate, among other
things, all the functions of the past'.[37]

Structuralism aside, Boris de Schloezer had in 1954 described the crisis
within new music as primarily one of language, drawing the conclusion
that only in dealing with it as such would some kind of satisfactory solution
be discovered.[38] Two years later Adorno, in the article 'Music, Language
and Composition' (1956), berated the serial composers for attempting to
eliminate the linguistic element within music, and for accepting merely
'the abstract negation of its similarity to language'.[39] In 'Nécessité d'une
orientation esthétique' (1963) and in many other places Boulez, like his
fellow serial composers, writes loosely and metaphorically of their musical developments in terms of linguistic advance, and he often considers
the new musical resources in terms of grammar, syntax and morphology.
While it is clear that this linguistic metaphor was widely used outside the
structuralist paradigm, it is also understandable that such fashionable discussion of music in linguistic terms would facilitate the supposition of a new

---

[34] Boulez 1986, 53.   [35] Nattiez 2005b, 32.   [36] Nattiez 2005b, 43–4.
[37] Nattiez 2005b, 33–4.   [38] Schloezer 1954a, 119–20.   [39] Adorno 2002, 122.

structuralist music in France concordant with structural anthropology and the rest.

In line with this common appeal to a linguistic base, Boulez, like Lévi-Strauss and the other structuralists, introduces the notion of the code into his theoretical speculations. While he writes in a number of places of the transmission of codes which are common to the sender and receiver, it is important to note that Schloezer had also conceived of music in this way.[40] In 'Aesthetics and the Fetishists' (1961/2), Boulez asserts that it does not make sense for a composer to 'conceive his "message" without a morphology – a formal scheme – capable of communicating it to the listener' and he dismisses the 'concept of an abstract "message"'.[41]

The notion of the code is treated more explicitly in the Darmstadt lecture 'Time, Notation and Coding' (1960) in which musical notation is described as a 'coded grid' which can be used in order to 'initiate an interaction between composer and performer', and he spells out this coded relationship as follows:

A   the *composer* originates a *structure* which he *ciphers*
B   he *ciphers* it in a coded *grid*
C   the interpreter *deciphers* this *coded* grid
D   according to this decoding he reconstitutes the *structure* that has been transmitted to him[42]

Boulez's four-stage version of the code recalls Jakobson's linguistic model which he had already expounded in 1958 as follows:

> The ADDRESSER sends a MESSAGE to the ADDRESSEE. To be operative the message requires a CONTEXT referred to . . . seizable by the addressee, and either verbal or capable of being verbalised; a CODE fully, or at least partially, common to the addresser and addressee (or in other words, to the encoder and decoder of the message); and, finally, a CONTACT, a physical channel and psychological connection between the addresser and the addressee, enabling both of them to enter and stay in communication.[43]

Jakobson schematised this in the following way:

CONTEXT
ADDRESSER MESSAGE ADDRESSEE
– – – – – – – –
CONTACT
CODE[44]

---

[40] Schloezer 1947, 42.   [41] Boulez 1986, 34–5.   [42] Boulez 1986, 87.
[43] Jakobson 1988, 35. In a letter dated 29 April 1963, Souvtchinsky asks Boulez whether he has had the opportunity to meet Roman Jakobson (PSS).
[44] Jakobson 1988, 35.

For Boulez, the terms 'structure' and 'coding' refer to '*overall* structure and *local* coding, since local structure and local coding are part of the same mental operation'. Local structures cannot be generated abstractly but need a code as a form of alphabet in which they can be transcribed, with more complex structures relying more heavily on the fact of coding.[45] Indeed, the history of notation can be conceptualised in terms of codes which have become ever finer as composers have sought to transmit their messages as precisely as possible. He conceives of two situations, one in which:

> composer and performer agree to 'play' with the coding; the performer consciously reproduces the messages intended by the composer; the coding is a complicity between the two. In the second case the composer knows that his coding cannot possibly be deciphered by the performer, whose reproduction of his message will therefore be defective. The performer, on the other hand, is simply faced with the problem of this deciphering and must try to transmit the message as faithfully as he can. In other words, the margin of error beyond which he is working must be made increasingly smaller, though it will always exist and can never be reduced to zero. In this last case . . . it is the sheer *difficulty* of deciphering the code that is the problem, the difficulty of performing extremely complicated rhythms or large and small intervals at the same set speed, etc.[46]

In discussion in 1970 Boulez reflected something of the structuralist interest, and more particularly Schloezer's interest, in relationality, in arguing that what is interesting about the analysis of complex musical phenomena is not the process by which the composer has arrived at formal structures or musical objects but rather analysis of 'the relationship of these formal structures and the relation which there can be between the expression of a form, for example, and the content of the composer's thought'.[47] Simply to reveal the series or musical principle underlying a musical work is ultimately pointless and it is more important to discover similarities within structures or the 'conjunctions' which may pertain from one form to another or from one structure to another.

While it would be easy to conclude from all of the foregoing that Boulez, if not a structuralist, at least had structuralist leanings, we must note a significant point of difference in the serial and structuralist projects which emerges already in 1960 in Boulez's reflections on 'Form'.[48] Since the serial interest in variations in musical form and in local structures necessarily entails the discovery of new forms through which local structures can be structured, it is, unlike structuralism, relative and it cannot settle for 'fixed,

---

[45] Boulez 1986, 87.   [46] Boulez 1986, 87–8.   [47] Boulez 1971b, 37–8.   [48] Boulez 1986, 90–1.

non-relative forms'. Drawing on the example of Mallarmé's figure of the *Operator* and its 'networks of possibilities', he posits the desirability of serial material and connections which are mobile and constantly evolving, and a syntax which is equally unfixed. The serial composer no longer has pre-existing general laws, abstract relationships, schemes or archetypes to follow and, in this new nominalist situation, the form of any particular work will be 'essentially and irreversibly linked to its "content"'. While the structures theorised by Lévi-Strauss are quasi-ontological in status,[49] it is clear that Boulez's local structures are not at all essentialist or ontological in nature, being rather functional, evolutionary and developmental. It is this more flexible notion of structure which brings Boulez much closer to the work of Umberto Eco and beyond to Deleuzian post-structuralism.

Tel Quel and the *Nouveau Roman*

Beyond this range of issues and use of terminology, the practicalities of publication also brought Boulez into structuralism's fashionable domain. In the early 1960s, two of his Darmstadt lectures were published in structuralist-based French literary reviews.[50] 'Taste: "The Spectacles worn by Reason"?' appeared in two issues of *Tel Quel* (1963) which was at that time an organ of the structuralist movement,[51] and 'Nécessité d'une orientation esthétique' was published in *Mercure de France* in 1964. Piencikowski, who correctly recognises that certain aspects of Boulez's terminology would have been regarded favourably in structuralist quarters, is nevertheless solicitous in the face of any attempt to confuse the composer's work with the at that time influential methodological paradigm.[52]

The *Tel Quel* group, which was initiated by writers and which aimed itself at an avant-garde audience, was interdisciplinary in nature. While Philippe Sollers declared in 1965/6 that Mallarmé was the origin of their engagement with literature and literary theory, Dosse later encapsulated the entire *Tel Quel* project within the poet's legacy in its experimental approach

---

[49] Ontology is that branch of philosophy which considers the ultimate nature of reality. To say that something exists ontologically is to give it objective status, to posit that it is truly real, for example, in forming the structures underlying our perceptions. Lévi-Strauss seems to make this kind of claim for structures.

[50] Piencikowski 1991, pp. xxvi–xxvii.

[51] *Tel Quel*, 14 (summer 1963); 15 (autumn 1963). The review was launched in 1960 with the intention of targeting an interdisciplinary, avant-garde, intellectual audience (Dosse 1997, vol. 1, pp. 276–8). While structuralism was an important influence between 1962 and 1967, the *Tel Quel* group shifted ideologically several times. The contemporary music journal *Musique en jeu* (1970–8) was clearly related to *Tel Quel* and it featured Roland Barthes, Jean-François Lyotard, Ivanka Stoïanova and Philippe Sollers among its contributors (Rey 1993, 46).

[52] Piencikowski 1991, pp. xxvi–xxvii.

to questions of literary genre and form.[53] Boulez shared with it an interest in
the literary or musical object and in the basic questions of literary/musical
language. In the summer 1968 edition of the review, he signed a seven-
point manifesto entitled 'La Révolution ici maintenant' ('The Revolution
is here now') which asserted the palpably theoretical nature of the group's
objectives. Just as *Tel Quel* professed a form of Marxist-Leninism in the late
1960s, Boulez around that time was also known to have declared himself on
occasions to be 'a 300% Marxist-Leninist',[54] despite showing little interest
in politics beyond its aesthetic dimensions. In a 1970 interview he stressed
his connection with *Tel Quel* as follows: 'Personally, I am very linked with
this group . . . I follow their works – I know them personally – I follow the
work of all of the group around the review *Tel Quel* with great attention'.[55]
While Ffrench, like Piencikowski, recognises that *Tel Quel* stood to benefit
in terms of prestige through association with avant-garde figures such as
Boulez and through the publication of his theoretical work,[56] it is not clear
that convenience and mutual benefit exhaust the relationship or disqualify
the genuine interest and curiosity which the group shared with Boulez.
For example the attempt by *Tel Quel* to hold structuralism and dialectical
materialism within a coherent view runs in parallel with Boulez's concern
for both structure and historical process.

As for the exponents of the *Nouveau Roman*, who were also associated
with structuralism, Boulez was interested solely in Michel Butor, whose
novel *L'Emploi du temps*, with its notion of 'the plan of an unknown town',
he used in order to illustrate the performer's route through the *Constellation*
formant of the Third Sonata for piano.[57] Of course, while Butor produced
the essay 'Mallarmé selon Boulez' in 1961,[58] he was much more closely
involved with Pousseur, with whom he collaborated for over forty years,
producing most notably the opera *Votre Faust* (1960–7). With the exception
of Butor, Boulez is critical of practically all of the representatives of the
Nouveau Roman who, compared with Joyce and Beckett, are dismissed as
'epigones and epicentres, epiphenomena, and épifaussesphanies!!!'[59]

Structuralist controversies 1: Ruwet and Pousseur

The first explicit pairing of structuralism and serialism occurred in
Nicolas Ruwet's 1959 article 'Contradictions du langage sériel'.[60] Appearing

---

[53] Dosse 1997, vol. 1, p. 344.   [54] Jameux 1991, 158.   [55] Boulez 1971b, 39.
[56] Ffrench 1995, 76–7.   [57] Boulez 1986, 151.   [58] Butor 1964, 95–109.
[59] Undated letter to Souvtchinsky, suggested date 1962 (BN).
[60] Ruwet had read Saussure, Trubetzkoy and Jakobson as well as attending the seminars of Émile
Benveniste, André Martinet, and Lévi-Strauss (Dosse 1997, vol. 2, pp. 3–5).

five years in advance of Lévi-Strauss's treatment of the subject, it is clear, nevertheless, that Ruwet drew upon Lévi-Strauss's work. As a former pupil of the Belgian composer Pierre Froidebise and a friend of Souris, Pousseur and Deliège,[61] he was concerned with what he took to be the gulf between avant-garde theory and practice, a problem which he identified as one of musical linguistics. While he agrees with the serial composers that 'the tonal system is dead', he charges that they have attempted to create a new musical language while ignoring the determining conditions necessary for the possibility of language.[62] If 'Boulez and his friends' have elsewhere been criticised for the systematic aspects of their work, Ruwet holds that they have not been systematic enough in their understanding of what it means for music to be a language.

For serial music to constitute a recognisable language, it must adhere to rules pertaining to communication systems. What distinguishes differentiated, articulated systems of communication as found in myths, rites and languages from undifferentiated kinds of communication such as shouts and looks, is the greater complexity of the former, which is achieved in part through the imposition of necessary limitations and exclusions. Ruwet is concerned that some serial theoreticians have not acknowledged this and Pousseur is charged, as an example, with neglecting to limit the new universe of sonic possibilities through the imposition of linguistic rules, and thus with reducing it to the realm of undifferentiated communication.

Concerning the notion of the linguistic code, Ruwet, following Trubetzkoy, holds that for an act of communication to take place, there must be a certain commonality of language between the sender and the receiver which is essentially 'general and constant'. This linguistic commonality, *langue*, is the condition of every unique act of communication, *parole*.[63] He suggests that the attempt to translate the notion of the linguistic code into serial terms is problematic since serialism seems to operate only at the level of *parole*, of individual utterance, and lacks the general and constant *langue* level necessary for codes to be communally understood. Boulez, according to Ruwet, confuses the two levels and reduces them both to that of *parole*, a criticism which is illustrated with the example of the traditional musical concept of the *chord* and the serial concept of the *sound block*. To prefer the concept of the sound block to that of the chord involves removing

---

[61] Wangermée 1995, 330. [62] Ruwet 1972, 25–6.

[63] Ruwet 1972, 27–9. For Saussure, *langue* is the abstract structure of language, which precedes all utterance, while *parole* is the individual utterance, formed from the abstract linguistic structure by the speaker. According to Leach, 'there is a close, but not exact equivalence' between the distinction of language (*langue*) and speech (*parole*) 'and the information theory distinction between *code* and *message*' (1970, 45–6).

something on the *langue* plane and replacing it with something which operates purely as *parole*.

Drawing upon Trubetzkoy's insight that 'only a limited number of phonological systems can be combined within the same grammatical structure',[64] Ruwet questions the viability of the generalised series which applies the serial principle to duration, attack and dynamic as well as pitch, and he suggests that serial composers have not sufficiently considered the degree of complexity involved in producing a successful communication system. They failed to take account of the *distinctive* or *phonological* oppositions which, according to Trubetzkoy, all linguistic systems depend upon, and he compares serial music with a language in which the system of phonological oppositions has very quickly broken down leaving behind the prospect of chaos.[65] The serial composer is consequently forced to tackle linguistic and stylistic problems simultaneously, a situation which Boulez attempts to legitimate through making certain parallels with Mallarmé's work, parallels which Ruwet rejects. Where it is possible to distinguish between two distinct levels of activity in language, namely between phonemes and morphemes, he finds only one level in music.

Like Adorno, Ruwet prefaces his study with an acknowledgement of the musical importance of Boulez's *Le Marteau sans maître* as well as Stockhausen's *Zeitmasse* and *Gruppen*, which he exempts from criticism without explaining how they can possibly be successful while lacking the criteria which he deems to be necessary for communication to take place.[66] He concludes, ultimately, that the 'structural possibilities' within serialism are limited and that they 'may already have been exhausted by Webern and some exceptional works such as *Le Marteau sans maître*'.[67]

Pousseur was the only serial composer to respond to his friend in print, and the first of his two significant contributions, 'Music, Form and Practice (an attempt to reconcile some contradictions)', appeared alongside Ruwet's article in the *Revue Belge de Musicologie*. Identifying the tonal language, not as something existent within nature, but rather as a product of 'bourgeois individualism',[68] he concludes that the serial 'quest for a new *grammar*' is justified if it is understood to be engaged in the definition of certain

---

[64] Ruwet 1972, 30.
[65] Ruwet 1972, 33–6. See Trubetzkoy's *Principles of Phonology* (1939) and Dosse 1997, vol. 1, p. 57. Meaningful linguistic utterances can be analysed into morphemes which are the basic linguistic units which concern meaning. Morphemes can similarly be analysed into phonemes, which are the basic units of material sound which are recognised as being different from one another, without reference to meaning. These are referred to by Lévi-Strauss as 'levels of articulation'. Fred Lerdahl theorised that serial works such as *Le Marteau sans maître* are problematic because they display an unfortunate gap between compositional grammar and listening grammar (Lerdahl 1992, 99–100).
[66] Ruwet 1972, 23, 36.   [67] Ruwet 1972, 40.   [68] Pousseur 1964, 79.

significance-providing constants, rather than in an attempt to fix language in a definitively sedimented way.[69] It was the serial composers themselves, not Ruwet, who first recognised the lack of differentiation within certain pointillist works, and it was these same composers who, having diagnosed the problem, attempted to move beyond it. In a brief but significant parenthesis, he locates the serial moment more precisely than its often vague opponents in the music which resulted from the initial pointillist experiments, and he makes clear that what Ruwet (and later, Lévi-Strauss, Eco and others) refer to as serialism is a development of Webern's work which went through a number of distinct phases, centring successively upon (1) *points/pointillism* and (2) *groups*. The group helped to restore something of the coherence which had been lost in the pointillist phase, since it concentrated on 'global qualities, common to all its elements' which distinguished it from other groups. Since groups were therefore more structured than points and could also be structured in relation to one another, group composition could be described as the 'structural method *par excellence*' and, in opposition to Ruwet, as a method whose possibilities seemed to be far from exhausted.

Anticipating Eco's later, much more detailed taxonomy of linguistic structures and codes, Pousseur charges that Ruwet's critique presumes that language (verbal and musical) has a consistency which is not in fact the case.[70] If verbal languages are in a constant state of modification and development, why should this not also be the case for music? Criticism of serialism, invoking the necessity of two linguistic levels, is also mistaken in so far as it presumes a certain consistency in language and music. Pousseur focuses alternatively, not on the structures common to utterances, but rather on what makes each speech-act unique, and on the fact that it is this which has made works such as *Le Marteau sans maître*, *Zeitmasse* and *Gruppen* successful. He also rejects any supposed opposition between a strictly coded musical language and completely undifferentiated sonic chaos as false since both elements, namely order and the loosening of order, are necessary if communication is to be vibrant and productive, and if order is not to be pursued fetishistically as some kind of ascetic ideal.

Structuralist controversies 2: Lévi-Strauss

While Lévi-Strauss first alludes to the question of serialism and structuralism in a published conversation with Georges Charbonnier in 1961,[71] it is in his introduction to *The Raw and the Cooked* (1964), that he presents

---

[69] Pousseur 1964, 82–3. [70] Pousseur 1964, 86, 88–9. [71] Charbonnier 1961, 146–9.

his fully worked-out concern that serial interest in structure has been superficially mistaken for the properly structuralist study of structures. Acknowledging the 'vigorous theoretical ambitions ... very strict methodology, and ... brilliant technical achievements' of serialism, his goal is nevertheless to look beyond the qualities it shares with structuralism, namely 'a resolutely intellectual approach, a bias in favour of systematic arrangements, and a mistrust of mechanistic or empirical solutions', in order to distinguish them as clearly as possible.[72]

Lévi-Strauss's critique, unlike that of Ruwet, is based on his conviction that all communication systems including those of mythology and music are based upon two levels of articulation, one natural and one cultural. He is satisfied that tonal music possesses both of these levels and that, while they are complicated by polytonality and atonality, they nevertheless remain intact.[73] Music is explained in terms of a code in which enjoyment or appreciation is the result of a balance between the fulfilment and frustration of expectation, as the 'transmitter and receiver' of the message play with a common code.

While claiming that colours in visual art perform the function of a first level of articulation on the grounds that they 'are present "naturally" in nature', he contends that 'there are no musical sounds in nature, except in a purely accidental and unstable way; there are only noises'.[74] It is this rather arbitrary premise, that musical sounds are entirely culturally produced, which allows him to theorise that within music the first level of articulation should be located in 'the hierarchical structure of the scale'.[75] While making clear that the intervallic relationships which characterise individual scales are not naturally determined, he nevertheless maintains that as with any phonological system, 'all modal or tonal (or even polytonal or atonal) systems depend on physical and physiological properties, selecting some from among the infinite number no doubt available, and exploiting the contrasts and combinations of which they are capable in order to evolve a code that serves to distinguish different meanings'. In other words, he has found confirmation within music of his premise that every empirical structure is a manifestation of an essential structure, or, in this case, that all scales, somehow or other, adhere to the relationships which, he believes, pertain within an essential scale, the existence of which he presupposes. The core of his disagreement with Boulez and the serial composers is encapsulated in Schoenberg's rule whereby pitches are to be organised purely by 'the total system of relations of the sounds with one another' since this definitively

---

[72] Lévi-Strauss 1970, 27. He also includes *musique concrète* within his critique.
[73] Lévi-Strauss 1970, 16–17.   [74] Lévi-Strauss 1970, 19.   [75] Lévi-Strauss 1970, 21–2.

prohibits any relationship between a given set of sounds, ordered in particular relationships, and the kind of Ur-structure or proto-scale which, for
Lévi-Strauss, is a sine qua non.

While acknowledging the sophistication of serial 'grammar and syntax',
he argues that it reduces the particularity of the individual tones and allows
only for their minimal organisation.[76] Boulez's conviction that serial music
has moved beyond preconceived scales, forms and structures is rejected as
an attempt to produce a sign system with only one level of articulation,
an outcome which would risk depriving listeners of the kind of general
structure necessary for 'the encoding and decoding of individual messages',
and which would leave them with the task of reproducing the creative act.
Lévi-Strauss suggests that the serial composer would respond by saying
that the second level of articulation had replaced the first, while an entirely
new level was introduced to replace the previous second level. He even
associates this level with Boulez's concept of the 'polyphony of polyphonies',
a move which he rejects since he does not believe the first level within a
language to be interchangeable, and its mobility is very limited. It is a rather
strange moment in Lévi-Strauss's argument, which poses the question:
has he merely speculated on a serial response to the perceived problem
of double articulation and then used Boulez's concept of the 'polyphony
of polyphonies' arbitrarily to serve as a candidate for the missing level?
If this is the case he has merely set up a straw man. Alternatively, is this
suggestion based on an otherwise unreported discussion with Boulez or
another serial composer or theorist, perhaps at that time keen to place
serialism within the fashionable orthodoxy of structuralism and double
articulation?

Lévi-Strauss concludes that serialism, lacking an essential ingredient, cannot be considered a language, and that the listener to a serial composition
will consequently be able to appreciate only fragmentary elements within
it. When, however, he enumerates a sense of timbre or a feeling for register
as examples of such fragmentary appreciation, we begin to understand the
gulf in listening priorities which separates him from the serial composers. It
becomes clear that his chief interest in engaging with serialism and *musique
concrète* in this way is actually to enact a pre-emptive strike upon them,
based on a desire to anticipate criticism of his own understanding of structuralism and the crucial place which he has given to music within it. Since
he maintains that 'music and mythology appeal to mental structures that
the different listeners have in common',[77] it is imperative that he attack two
significant musical movements which were also in the process of becoming

---

[76] Lévi-Strauss 1970, 23–4.   [77] Lévi-Strauss 1970, 26–7.

wider epistemological metaphors or models, at odds with his own world-view. He says as much in referring to the 'general structures that serialist doctrine rejects and whose existence it even denies', and in recognising that it 'sets itself up as a conscious product of the mind and an assertion of its liberty'.

It is suggested by some writers that non-theoretical reasons may be primarily responsible for Lévi-Strauss's anti-serial position. While Lévi-Strauss stated rather curiously in 1973 that his remarks were intended to be humorous, Nattiez proposed that his treatment of contemporary music may be based more upon 'tastes and intuitions' than upon rigorous critique. This view is to some extent supported by Lévi-Strauss's punning comment that while music after Stravinsky interested him, made him think and at times provided tones which he found pleasantly moving, it didn't 'speak' to him.[78]

Eco's response to Lévi-Strauss

Lévi-Strauss's unfavourable judgement on serialism was not challenged openly in print by the compositional community, with the exception once again of Pousseur, who addressed it in 1968.[79] Schaeffner, who expressed some concern for what Boulez would think about it, was ultimately perplexed at how best to deal with the errors in Lévi-Strauss's text without damaging the excellent relationship which both he and his wife enjoyed with the anthropologist.[80] That he did not comment on the matter in his correspondence with Boulez is perhaps noteworthy but not necessarily surprising, given his closeness to Lévi-Strauss; nor is any mention of the matter made in Boulez's correspondence with Souvtchinsky. Responses were, however, more forthcoming from the musicologists Deliège and Nattiez, while the most detailed replies came from the philosopher Raymond Court and, above all, Umberto Eco who formulated his critique over a number of years.[81] The discussion of Eco's position will consequently move freely between several sources.[82]

---

[78] Nattiez 1973a, 4; Lévi-Strauss and Eribon 1991, 180; Charbonnier 1961, 152.

[79] Pousseur 1970, 20–8.

[80] Letters from Schaeffner to Souvtchinsky, dated 8 October 1964 and 11 April 1965 (BN). While Schaeffner considered addressing Lévi-Strauss in print, there is no evidence that he did so. That Lévi-Strauss valued Schaeffner's work highly is clear from a letter dated 10 December 1980 in which he praises Schaeffner's newly published essays (PSS).

[81] Deliège 1967; 1992; 1995; 2001. Nattiez 1973a; 1973b; 1993b; 2008. Court 1971. Eco 1971; 1976; 1989.

[82] Eco's theories and viewpoints are in an almost permanent state of development and he often expands upon aspects of his previous work. He came into contact with several members of the musical avant-garde in the late 1950s. Eco and Berio became friends, and through Berio, he got to know Cage, Boulez and Pousseur.

In 'Series and Structure' (1989), while acknowledging that Lévi-Strauss's critique focuses on Boulez's poetics in particular, Eco suggests that the issue goes well beyond serial music and ultimately concerns his mistrust of all artistic forms which seem to challenge the traditional forms, which many had come to consider as archetypes and as given facts of nature. What is at stake for Lévi-Strauss is therefore not simply the consideration of two methodological systems but rather, two 'visions of the world'.[83]

Focusing upon Boulez's opposition of tonal thought, which is defined by the qualities of 'gravitation and attraction', and serial thought which envisages the perpetual expansion of material, he views the latter through the prismatic aesthetic of the *open work*, which he had first discovered through the music of Boulez, Stockhausen and Pousseur. While the topic of openness, which is at the root of the structuralism/serialism debate, forces us to consider whether the openly oriented series can be reconciled with the structuralist enterprise, it is clear that Eco does not ultimately intend to effect their complete theoretical separation.[84]

He exposes the linguistic ambiguity in the relationship with the help of Jean Pouillon's distinction of *pensée structurale* (which Lévi-Strauss uses), on the one hand, and *pensée structurelle*, on the other (which Lévi-Strauss does not use). For Pouillon, the adjective *structurel* refers to what analysis reveals about an object, while *structural* refers to 'the laws that uniformly govern the various occurrences of structured objects' within a number of systems. Consequently, it may be said that 'serial thought produces open-structured (*structurelles*) realities (even when these realities appear unstructured), whereas structuralist thought deals with structural (*structurales*) laws'.[85]

Agreeing that structuralism and serialism have been superficially linked, Eco goes on to spell out their key differences much more systematically than Lévi-Strauss. The fundamental premises of structuralist analysis are identified as (1) the necessity of a 'pre-established code shared by both the addresser and the addressee'; (2) the presence of two levels of articulation, communication being established when second-level units result from the combination of first-level units and (3) the notion that 'every code is based on a more elementary code', whereby all linguistic, cultural and more generally significatory communications lead to a prior code, an 'Ur code'.[86] In serial thought, in contrast: (1) the code is questioned by every message and

---

[83] Eco 1989, 217–18. Eco's reflections were published in French in 1971.
[84] Like Lévi-Strauss, Eco focuses solely on Boulez's conception of serialism. He does not really clarify the relationship between serialism and the open work, but instead presumes that the open work provides 'a poetics of serial thought'.
[85] Eco 1989, 218–19.   [86] Eco 1989, 220–1.

each work provides its own 'linguistic basis' and poetic justification which go beyond previous systems and boundaries which would attempt to limit it; (2) the series behaves as 'a field of possibilities', which yields multiple choices, and (3) new means of communication are produced through the identification and challenging of historical codes. It therefore involves the evolution of codes rather than a search for an 'original generative Code (the Structure)', and it aims to create the new, the perhaps unexpected, not to excavate the same timeless structures from everything. While the articulation of these differences adds clarity to the problems highlighted by Lévi-Strauss, Eco nevertheless seeks to find a middle way.

Despite acknowledging the necessity for two levels of articulation in linguistics, Eco disagrees with the criticism of serial music on the basis of a perceived lack of two such levels. He suggests that music is based instead on freer, more flexible articulatory systems,[87] and he attributes the presumption of two levels to 'a dangerous verbo-centric dogmatism', which was prevalent during the 1960s and which retained the prestige of 'language' exclusively for systems with double articulation.[88] More specifically, he disagrees with Lévi-Strauss's conviction that all language operates through double articulation, and that these levels cannot be altered in any way since their structure 'is based on deep natural structures of the human mind'. He posits instead, following Prieto (1966), the existence of systems with 'two articulations, systems with only the first articulation, systems with only the second articulation . . . systems without articulation' and systems with 'mobile articulation'.[89] In illustration of this principle of mobility, he cites Pierre Schaeffer's example of timbre which, in the case of *Klangfarben-melodie*, shifts from its previously subservient parametric status to being the central musical parameter. It is transformed from being 'the optional variant of a previous system' to assuming 'the function of a phoneme – that is, the function of a distinctive feature, of a significant opposition'.[90]

While he can envisage the existence of a matrix which lies behind all sign systems and their particular manifestations, he takes issue with the metaphysical nature of the Ur-Code, posited by Lévi-Strauss, as well as with its hasty identification with traditional tonality, as if this one system included music's total possibility within itself. Believing his judgement on serialism to be insufficiently comprehensive and premature in its conclusions, Eco tentatively posits an alternative middle way in which the series would no longer negate structure but would instead be the expression of a historical, self-questioning structure.[91] For this to happen it would be necessary to find an articulatory level that would facilitate understanding of '"serial

---

[87] Eco 1989, 225.   [88] Eco 1976, 228–9.   [89] Eco 1976, 231–3.   [90] Eco 1989, 225.
[91] Eco 1989, 232.

thought" in terms of "structural thought".[92] In contrast to Lévi-Strauss's preference for constants over variants, Eco proposes to give variants at least the same value and importance.[93] While serialism goes beyond structuralist constants, he still maintains that serial technique should be explained with the help of a structuralist methodology, but one which values the innovative as much as the traditional. No particular series can then be said to be the most basic structure since every structure will always be provisional and capable of being explained in terms of 'a more final basis'.

The 1989 version of Eco's text, which replaces the 1971 pairing of *constant* and *variation* with Lucien Sébag's opposition of 'original locus' and 'historical process',[94] grapples more overtly with the possibility of some kind of reconciliation between the hitherto antithetical values of structure and history or structure and process. He is nevertheless forced to conclude that this cannot succeed since, while '*historical rationality*' may produce a number of different 'events and readings', 'the very materiality of the historical process vanishes the moment everything is made to depend on the discovery of their original locus'.[95] He concludes that 'structure (stable and objective) and process (qua creation of continuously new structures) explode' and that 'what is left is no longer structurable'. Indeed, the paradox of reconciling fixed structures with historical processes leads him to the threshold of post-structuralism and to Deleuze's concepts of *virtuality* and *difference* which will be considered in Chapters 7, 8 and 9.

With regard to codes, the main point of disagreement with Lévi-Strauss seems to lie in Eco's conviction that codes need not necessarily be closed, but that they can also be open.[96] Considering the factors which would enable a listener to distinguish the work of one post-Webernian composer from another, he attempts an explanation based upon the concepts of expression and content:

> The artist discovers at the deeper level of the expression-continuum a new system of relations that the preceding segmentation of that continuum, giving rise to an expression form, had never made pertinent. These new pertinent features, along with their mode of organization, are so detectable and recognizable, that one becomes able to isolate the work of a given artist, and thus to distinguish, for instance . . . Boulez from Berio.[97]

---

[92] Eco 1989, 234.   [93] Eco 1971, 56.

[94] Lucien Sébag's *Marxism and Structuralism* (1964) attempted to reconcile structuralism and Marxism in the form of Lévi-Strauss, Lacan and Marx. While Lévi-Strauss definitively rejected the possibility of considering structure and process simultaneously, Lucien Goldman first countenanced it at a 1959 colloquium in Cerisy (Dosse 1997, vol. 1, pp. 173–6). Boulez also attempts to reconcile structure and process (1971b, 37).

[95] Eco 1989, 234–5.   [96] Eco 1984, 187.   [97] Eco 1976, 244.

Furthermore, if 'these forms convey a content' then 'an entire code is proposed as the work is established'. For Eco, a code may be an 'open matrix'
which permits 'infinite occurrences', and it is this opening up of possibilities
which led the post-structuralists in the late 1960s to reject the concept of
the code and to replace it with those of 'the "whirl," the difference, the
béance', which operate beyond the level of the code.[98] It is paradoxical that
while the code was introduced, at least in part, as a means of controlling
structures, the key concepts of ultimate codes and of an Ur-Code gave way
to that of 'the unshaped "origin"', which made codes unmanageable and
they were replaced altogether by the post-structuralists with the more fluid
concepts of 'drives, *désirs*, pulsions [and] drifts'.[99] Ultimately, Eco's reading
of the history of the code cannot be separated from his early reflections
on the open work. In a sense, the dialectic of open and closed forms, the
opposition of author and reader, or of composer, performer and listener, is
central to his creative development, in a way which mirrors Boulez's own
trajectory.

Pousseur and Court

Pousseur, in the 'response to Lévi-Strauss' which he formulated in 1968,
accepts with the benefit of almost ten years' reflection that his reply to Ruwet
was in some respects unsatisfactory.[100] Attempting to locate a first-level,
natural basis for serial music, he looks to Webern's idiosyncratic approach
to the twelve-tone series, which entails the fastidious selection of a pertinent
musical syntax from the myriad possibilities provided by nature. This, it
is claimed, enables him to build a strictly organised, indeed organic piece
of music, which hopefully fulfils Lévi-Strauss's articulatory requirements.
Webern's aesthetic, which embodied 'a new humility towards nature', a
position which was not, according to Pousseur, grasped at first by the post-
Webernian composers, coheres well within a structuralist perspective since it
seems to recognise that previous musical systems were merely codifications
or only one of many possibilities.

   Pousseur next exposes Lévi-Strauss's inconsistency in accepting colour
as a natural element within visual art while failing to recognise a com-
mensurate level within music. Since tonal scales are not natural, but rather

---

[98] Eco 1984, 187–8.
[99] Eco 1984, 168. Commenting on the events in Paris in May 1968, Dosse notes that 'beyond
      the overturned cars, it was codes that were targeted and crushed' (1997, vol. 2, p. 114). The
      structuralist movement was dismissed with the phrase 'structures don't go out into the streets'
      (cited in Lévi-Strauss and Eribon 1991, 92).
[100] Pousseur 1970, 21–2.

products of culture, he alternatively identifies music's first level of articulation as that of sound vibration. Acknowledging that culture develops
continually as it reveals 'new properties in nature',[101] he nevertheless draws
close to the emerging post-structuralism in noting that this is not 'a truly
actual nature' since 'its properties are virtual, potential, and have need of
culture to actualise themselves'.[102] He interprets Boulez as saying that the
serial composer has now to select from the 'totality of the possible' for
the expression of the individual work, and he suggests that the first level
within serial music pertains to 'an "unconscious" level or to a still more
general infra-consciousness, to what phenomenologists might call non- ...
"thematised" perception'.[103]

Raymond Court, who responds to Lévi-Strauss from a phenomenological perspective, contends that while aesthetic languages have two levels,
these are not identical to those found in verbal languages.[104] Arguing, like
Eco, for acceptance of a 'plurality of semantic universes',[105] he attempts
to theorise the working of the serial language in terms which can accom-
modate Lévi-Strauss's criterion of double articulation. He argues that the
structural originality within aesthetic languages consists in their possession
of two planes, both of which signify in a symbolic sense, in contrast to the
conceptual meaning of ordinary verbal language.[106] Poetic language, for
example, signifies 'beyond signification' and operates on the basis of breaking down typical significations in forming new ones. For Court, music,
unlike the other arts, has an *autonomous* first level which emerges immediately without reference to representation, and which plays variably on
the cusp of perceptual and linguistic structures while eluding any simple
reduction to one or other. Perceptually, it draws upon the entire realm of
sound or noise while simultaneously becoming incorporated into a rigorous, quasi-linguistic system.[107]

Court attempts to move beyond a false nature/culture opposition. We
are to de-condition ourselves by returning in an unprejudiced way to the
pre-musical realm of sound, bracketing phenomenologically the culturally
motivated grid provided by acoustics with its particular human concerns.
He recommends Pierre Schaeffer's phenomenologically based concept of
'reduced listening' and his careful distinction of 'the *characteristics* of sound
and the *values* which are defined by reciprocal differentiation within a
particular system'.[108] Applying all of this to serialism, he suggests that each
series is a 'primary *material*' marking out a unique space in which the

---

[101] Pousseur 1970, 24.   [102] Pousseur 1970, 22.   [103] Pousseur 1970, 25.
[104] Court 1971, 18.   [105] Court 1971, 16.   [106] Court 1971, 18.   [107] Court 1971, 23.
[108] Court 1971, 25–6.

particular structures of a work are formed. While this space is distinct and personalised for each work, it is possible to articulate two levels of operation with the help of Boulez's differentiation of '*organisation* and *composition*'. Organisation now refers to a first level in which 'sound is transmuted into musical value through its integration into a coherent system, while composition designates the second level, where the structures of the musical work itself are elaborated through modulation of the first'.[109]

Structuralist threads in late Boulez

In Pousseur's view, Boulez was to some extent responsible for Lévi-Strauss's mistaken point of view, and he can understand how some of his statements permitted the anthropologist to equate serial composition with the construction of 'arbitrary systems'.[110] His silence in the face of Lévi-Strauss's criticisms is attributed by Deliège to a fundamental scepticism towards the opposition of nature and culture, as well as to a sense that there was something precarious about theorising serialism in terms of codes,[111] an intuition which has found more systematic articulation and support in Eco's open codes and in post-structuralist *difference*.

It is not clear, however, that Boulez has not responded to Lévi-Strauss, and certain passages in his writings, which do not name the ethnologist, and which do not explicitly refer to double articulation, nevertheless seem to address the issue, even if they do not add anything particularly new to the debate. In 'Pensée européenne/Non-européenne?' (1984), Boulez considers the question of musical language and whether it is possible 'to recapture, pertinently, the elements or at least some elements of this language?' While, as with all languages, he acknowledges the necessity for rules in the construction of intervals and scales, he rejects the presumption whereby the hierarchy of musical intervals is often taken as being analogous to nature. In contrast, every intervallic hierarchy is recognised as being only one possible cultural selection taken from the 'brute matter' of sound itself, a position which does not seem so different from Court's reading of double articulation.[112] Likewise, in highlighting the tendency to homogeneity, standardisation and exclusivity in Western musical systems, and in questioning the practicality of the utopian desire for a universal musical language, it may be that Lévi-Strauss is one of Boulez's intended targets.[113]

---

[109] Court 1971, 28.   [110] Pousseur 1970, 16.
[111] Deliège 2001, 206. Jacques Derrida deconstructed Lévi-Strauss's nature/culture opposition in his 1966 lecture 'Structure, sign and play in the discourse of the human sciences'.
[112] Boulez 2005a, 592–3.   [113] Boulez 2005a, 603.

There are also a number of passages in the Collège de France lectures in which aspects of Lévi-Strauss's critique are alluded to rather anonymously. Boulez may have him in mind when he states that while music can draw upon any possible sound phenomenon, the indiscriminate acceptance of sound would destroy any possibility of producing a 'coherent and organic musical language'. Since all languages operate on the basis of the elimination of some possibilities and the selection of others, musical language must likewise eliminate certain options. Boulez, however, intends that his own organisational structures should open up possibilities rather than close them down. Like Eco, he acknowledges the paradoxical nature of an open structure while maintaining that 'it still deserves to be called a structure' since such a musical language consists of 'a sort of universality' in which expressive possibilities will be enlarged.[114]

On the question of the linguistic nature of the series, Boulez maintains that 'it rests only upon a single dimension' and that, since it is unsupported by the other 'linguistic elements' and by the kind of grammatical elements which pertain to themes, it is a case 'only of elementary morphology'.[115] In distinguishing between 'an elementary stage of écriture', which is sufficient for the invention of 'an isolated object', and the relations which are necessary for the constitution of a language, which, he tells us, 'are situated at another level', Boulez perhaps draws close to Lévi-Strauss's double articulation.[116]

While the notion of the code retains its place in the Collège de France lectures, since almost every score is said to have one,[117] and listening is 'totally dominated by linguistic codes',[118] which can be pre-existent, temporary or transitory, the loosening of codes, in the sense of formal structures, is now connected to what he refers to as the Idea.[119] In order to produce coherence beyond the workings of an existing common code, composers need to deduce their 'materials, forms [and] structures', from ever more specific initial ideas. He promotes the transgression of codes, the quest for new individual or collective codes, as well as the 'destruction, transformation or reconstruction' of older codes, in order to produce new meanings or suggest new directions. He postulates the evolution of Western music as increasingly reflecting the opposition 'between language and the individual, between collective means of communication and individual means of describing oneself'.[120] Early twentieth-century atonality is explained as the abolition of the general code of tonality and its replacement by a new code, which could be generalised while still depending on individual choice.

[114] Boulez 2005b, 116–17.   [115] Boulez 2005b, 222.   [116] Boulez 2005b, 443.
[117] Boulez 2005b, 54.   [118] Boulez 2005b, 422.   [119] Boulez 2005b, 90–4.
[120] Boulez 2005b, 114.

Schoenberg's later notion of a collective musical language with some kind of permanence is dismissed as an 'illusion' in favour of his less codified early atonal music,[121] and Boulez similarly expresses his preference for those of Webern's works which are less strictly coded in that they are formally 'much freer, more supple, more "progressive"'.[122]

The passage from 'the initial idea to the completion of the discourse' is structured and enlarged in accordance with codes, which establish and develop the Idea and extend form.[123] However, Boulez places the code and the Idea in a kind of dialectical relationship since the more the musical language has been based upon codes, the less it has needed the dominance of the Idea, and conversely, the Idea grows in potency as codes become weaker to the extent that it actually replaces them. In what follows, he shows that he has to some extent moved on to a more post-structuralist kind of thinking where it is no longer a question of simply coding and decoding meaning. The challenge is now to create a situation in which the musical components are reduced to a 'coded substrate', a term which suggests the molecular flux of Deleuzian philosophy. He acknowledges that musical codes change much more quickly than grammatical laws.[124] In the music of Schoenberg and Stravinsky, for example, he suggests that the notion of a system no longer pertains. The 'idea' is paramount and self-sufficient in 'establishing its own hierarchies [and] inventing its vocabulary', while at the same time following 'general norms... such as chromatic complementarity' in order to facilitate its progress.[125] However, while every work has a personal form which depends upon individual means, there is no question of starting out each time from scratch and 'some very general principles of écriture' are carried over from work to work, albeit applied differently each time.[126]

Conclusion

While Boulez was not a structuralist, in the sense that Lévi-Strauss, Barthes or Lacan were, the structuralist elements within his work are not insignificant, and Eco's critique affords the possibility that his thought can be accommodated within a more open structuralism. While his interest in structure is independent of structuralism, the references to Lévi-Strauss in his writings perhaps indicate a limited influence at a particular moment in his development. While it is tempting to read his appeal to linguistic terms such as morphology, syntax, codes and so on as providing evidence of a musical structuralism related somehow to the Saussurean model, the

[121] Boulez 2005b, 286.   [122] Boulez 2005b, 290.   [123] Boulez 2005b, 207–9.
[124] Boulez 2005b, 343.   [125] Boulez 2005b, 357.   [126] Boulez 2005b, 419–20.

evidence does not bear such an interpretation. While fleeting aspects of structuralist discourse appear in Boulez there are also significant differences. He undoubtedly shared something of the general preoccupation with structures which is found in a number of areas of thought in the 1950s, and Lévi-Strauss's structuralism was too pervasive not to have made some kind of impact upon him. His texts and interviews strongly suggest, however, that he picked up some aspects of structuralist discourse which were pragmatically useful to him in the elaboration of his practice and that, as structuralism waned and was superseded by post-structuralism, he likewise focused on those aspects of this new philosophy which could equally be useful and true to his impressively single-minded purpose.

7 Post-structuralist encounters

Structuralism proved to be an important but transitional moment in post-war French thought, and it was superseded before the end of the 1960s by what came to be called post-structuralism. As the appeal and practical value of structuralism waned after 1968, with the work of Derrida, Deleuze, Lyotard and others, its referential function within Boulez's writings similarly declined. While linguistic terminology and the concept of the code remained, Lévi-Strauss's place as an occasional theoretical source was taken, it seems, by the *Tel Quel* group, Derrida (one example) and Deleuze, to whom Boulez now alludes. Indeed, the reception of Boulez's work by Deleuze, and to a lesser extent by Lyotard, was much more welcoming than the critical reflections of Ruwet and Lévi-Strauss, and demonstrates the affinities between their projects. In this chapter we will consequently consider a number of connections linking Boulez with Barthes, Foucault, Lyotard and Guattari, but above all with Deleuze. While Barthes is a structuralist, a term from which Foucault eventually distanced himself, the others embody various aspects of the post-structuralist moment.

Deleuze acknowledges that it was in Eco's *The Open Work* that he discovered 'the revelation of "the absence of centre"' in contemporary art, which he described in *Difference and Repetition* (1968).[1] Attention shifted from structures and codes to fluxes and multiplicities and, as Dosse puts it, 'May '68 exploded the notion of a hermetic structure. The lock was picked and the point became a knot', with the result that openness, infinite transformation and the rejection of limits became the key ideas for the new post-structuralist models of thought.[2]

Foucault and the Collège de France

While Boulez and Foucault first met in 1951, they were not at that time friends, and Boulez says of those early days that while they 'saw each other', they 'intersected rather than met'.[3] It was from Barraqué, not Boulez, that Foucault first came to knowledge of the contemporary music scene and the two men had not seen each other for twenty years when Foucault approached Boulez to propose his nomination and election to the Collège

---

[1] Schiffer 1998, 167–8. [2] Dosse 1997, vol. 2, p. 132. [3] Eribon, 1991 64–5.

de France in 1975.[4] While they were never close friends, the existence of Foucault's article 'Pierre Boulez, Passing through the Screen' (1982),[5] as well as their 1983 dialogue 'Contemporary Music and the Public',[6] is evidence of the connection which developed between them in the late 1970s.

Michel Fano recalls that in the early 1950s Foucault was not really committed to contemporary music, preferring Bach,[7] and Foucault himself stated later that he had been merely 'a passerby held by affection, a certain perplexity, curiosity, the strange feeling of witnessing something [he] was incapable of being contemporaneous with'.[8] He attributed his difficulties with new music, at least in part, to the lack of an aesthetic discourse in terms of which it could have been discussed. While he recognised the importance of the transformations which had taken place in new music, he admitted in 1982 that he was incapable of discussing it, a point which Boulez later reiterated.[9]

At the colloquium *Le Temps musical*, which Boulez organised at IRCAM in February 1978, there were workshops and a debate in which Barthes, Deleuze and Foucault were all invited to participate. A massed gathering of over two thousand people assembled on the fifth and final evening for a discussion chaired by Boulez in which

> Barthes read 'a Taoist story' about a butcher whose intellectual concentration on the cow he was butchering meant that, ultimately, he saw before him simply 'the principle of dissection', whereas Foucault effectively refused to participate and contented himself with answering questions. Only Deleuze entered the public debate with any enthusiasm.[10]

Foucault, in his contribution, analysed the anomalous contrast in the philosophical and musical preferences of the Parisian intelligentsia, namely his colleagues and students who, while reading Nietzsche and Heidegger, listened to indifferent rock groups in preference to the challenging sounds emanating from IRCAM.

While he acknowledged his own difficulties in confronting contemporary music, he was equally conscious of the powerful effect which Boulez's ideas had upon him, and he described the encounter with Boulez as one of seeing 'the twentieth century from an unfamiliar angle – that of the long battle

---

[4] The possibility of a chair in musical research was forwarded by Foucault along with Roland Barthes and Emmanuel Le Roy Ladurie (Jameux 1991, 197–8; Nattiez 2005a, 14–15; Eribon 1991, 65).

[5] Foucault 1998, 241–4. While Nattiez interprets this article as a 'beautiful text which Foucault consecrated to [Boulez]' (2005a, 15), Eribon believes that it is really in honour of Barraqué who had been Foucault's lover in the early 1950s (1991, 66–7).

[6] Foucault and Boulez 1985, 6–12.   [7] Eribon 1991, 66.   [8] Foucault 1998, 241.

[9] Di Pietro 2001, 56–7.   [10] Macey 1993, 398–9.

around the "formal".[11] Indeed, he suggests that the music of Boulez and Barraqué helped him to escape from a dialectical world-view.[12]

In a short article in 1986, in which he recorded some of his memories of Foucault, Boulez noted that while he had read Foucault's books, he was unwilling to discuss questions pertaining to the scholar's domain.[13] Like Foucault, he acknowledges a certain 'proximity' and 'parallelism' in their thinking, in their efforts to renew thought through a reworking of the fundamentals of musical and philosophical language.

Lyotard and contemporary music

References to contemporary composers, including Boulez, appear at a number of points within Lyotard's writings.[14] In 'Plusieurs silences' (1972) he attempts to think music in terms of the body, an approach which he relates initially to Merleau-Ponty's *Phenomenology of Perception*, which goes beyond any Kantian location of the event purely within the mind.[15] He is dissatisfied, however, with the result which he judges is 'still much too phenomenological, too related to a subject of experience'.[16] In the anarchic *Libidinal Economy* (1974), he rejects any form of communication theory which is predicated on the basis of messages and codes, since signification 'is constituted by signs alone . . . carries on endlessly' and 'is always deferred'.[17] He draws on Adorno's observation, with regard to Schoenberg, that 'the material . . . in serialism does not count as such, but only as a relation between terms', or in other words, that 'the material is immediately annihilated', since 'where there is a message, there is no material'. This leads him to say of Boulez's serialism that 'there will be nothing but relations, not only between pitches, but also between intensities, timbres, durations. Dematerialisation', and it is clear that he understands this as being more akin to post-structuralist flux than to structuralist codes.

In 'La Réflexion Créatrice' (1986), which appeared in an anthology of dedications to Boulez on the occasion of his sixtieth birthday,[18] Lyotard recalls how a performance of Boulez's *Répons* reinforced for him the impossibility of defining musical forms conceptually, since 'something always exceeds understanding'. While understanding is undoubtedly involved in

---

[11] Foucault 1998, 242.   [12] Macey 1993, 53.   [13] Boulez 2005a, 672–4.

[14] The earliest musical references are mostly to John Cage. There is an essay on Berio's *Sequenza III*: '"A Few Words to Sing" Sequenza III' (1971), an essay 'Adorno come diavolo' (1972) which considers Adorno's negative dialectic in relation to Schoenberg, and an article 'Plusieurs silences' (1972) which focuses primarily on Schoenberg, Cage and Adorno with passing references to Kagel, Xenakis, Zappa and Hendrix.

[15] Lyotard 1972, 65.   [16] Lyotard 1972, 70.   [17] Lyotard 2004, 42–3.   [18] Lyotard 1986, 14–17.

the creation of musical forms, they are not reducible to it. Again, in *Post-modern Fables* (1993), *Répons*, as well as Cage's *Mureau*, is included in a range of artworks which exhibit 'some solitude, some retreat, some excess beyond all possible discourse', whether 'their material [is] language, timbre or colour'.[19] In 'La Réflexion Créatrice' Lyotard observes the close implication of philosophy and the arts, for example in the preoccupation with time within avant-garde music, and the fact that philosophers have so often used musical examples to expound their ideas of time. Indeed, more generally, it may be said that 'philosophy attempts . . . to dramatise the questions posed by the artist', and in Boulez's *Répons*, ... *explosante-fixe* ... and some of Cage's works, he believes that he discovers 'questions which are as fundamental as those of which philosophers speak', but within their own medium.[20]

In the article 'Obedience' (1986), which first appeared in the IRCAM journal *InHarmoniques*, Lyotard identifies two paths within contemporary music, which he designates as the 'intuitionist', which he associates with Cage, and the 'axiomatic', for which Boulez is given as the chief exemplar. While the former is conceptualised as an unweaving of sound, the latter entails the creation of 'more complex weaves, not so much rhetorical as cognitive, often called "structures", in which the various dimensions of sound are experimented with, with a view to being made "present" to sound feeling'.[21] Ultimately, however, Lyotard thinks that their apparent opposition is merely 'illusory', since both approaches operate in the service of enhanced listening. It is a conclusion which he returns to in the essay 'Music, Mutic' (1993), where Boulez and Cage are again cited as exponents of opposing tendencies. Boulez's approach is characterised here as 'multiplying the constraints on how [timbres] are put into phrases so as to give birth, as if by forceps, to the sonorous matter of the gesture not spontaneously given by the phrasing'.[22]

While Lyotard's remarks are interesting in their own right, and he clearly ventures a little further than Foucault into the musical domain, his work is ultimately of limited importance for the study of Boulez's music and ideas. Consequently, we turn now to Deleuze.

Deleuze and Boulez

It was after his return to Paris in 1977 that Boulez first came into contact with Deleuze, through the auspices of his nephew, who attended the

---

[19] Lyotard 1997, 206.   [20] Lyotard 1986, 16–17.
[21] Lyotard 1991, 176–7.   [22] Lyotard 1997, 219.

philosopher's seminar at Vincennes. Boulez recalls how Deleuze approached him with a view to participating in the IRCAM seminar on 'Time', which he [Boulez] was organising in 1978. 'Making Inaudible Forces Audible', the position paper which Deleuze delivered, and in which he primarily considers the concepts of pulsed and non-pulsed time, and how Boulez makes both temporalities audible,[23] was later described by the composer as 'a fantastic development'. Deleuze also contributed an essay 'Occupy without Counting: Boulez, Proust and Time' to Boulez's sixtieth-birthday anthology in 1986,[24] and the composer noted later that Deleuze's interest in his article on Wagner, 'Time Re-explored', was the starting point for the philosopher's reflections on musical time.[25] Recalling their subsequent relationship, Boulez says that 'later on, there was really a connection' between them.[26]

Boulez and Deleuze are also linked through a number of references in their writings. He refers to Deleuze's *Difference and Repetition* in a Collège de France lecture from 1980.[27] Not only does it become the starting point for a brief reflection in this lecture,[28] but it may also have helped Boulez towards his choice of topic for the courses in 1983–5, which are exclusively concerned with questions of thematicism, athematicism, identity and variation.[29] References to Boulez's ideas in the writings of Deleuze, both alone and together with Guattari, are more frequent, and Deleuze refers to several concepts used by Boulez in a number of works, but most significantly in *A Thousand Plateaus*, the second volume of their monumental *Capitalism and Schizophrenia*.[30]

Deleuze and Guattari create a philosophy which draws on the work of a great number of artists, writers and musicians, including Mallarmé, Joyce, Proust, Klee and Messiaen, whose activity has also significantly influenced the production of Boulez's thought. While Boulez is far from being the only composer whom they cite,[31] the breadth of musical reference and critical comment in *A Thousand Plateaus* should not obscure the connections which link their work with that of Boulez.

---

[23] Deleuze 2006, 156–60.   [24] Deleuze 1986, 98–100.   [25] Menger 1990, 9.

[26] Interview with the author, 28 August 1998.

[27] Boulez 2005b, 153. He also refers to 'repetition and difference' in an interview with Jonathan Cott (Boulez and Cott 1985, 148).

[28] Boulez 2005b, 153–7.   [29] Boulez 2005b, 205–336.

[30] References to Boulez can be found in: *Dialogues* (Deleuze and Parnet 1987, 94); *The Fold, Leibniz and the Baroque* (Deleuze 1993, 33, 82, 163–4 n. 37); *Foucault* (Deleuze 1988, 22) and *Negotiations* (Deleuze 1995, 155, 163, 202 n. 7a). Deleuze and Guattari together draw upon Boulez in *A Thousand Plateaus* (1988, 262, 267, 269, 477–8, 518 n. 22, 519 n. 8, 527 n. 39, 541 n. 36, 548 n. 14, 553–4 n. 20) and *What is Philosophy?* (1994, 195).

[31] *A Thousand Plateaus*, in particular, features a vast array of sources including references to a large number of composers.

Deleuze, Guattari and a new image of thought

Deleuze and Guattari do not formulate a fixed system of thought, and their collaborative studies continually coin new concepts, as they strive to articulate and rearticulate a new image of thought. This new image of thought is made up of concepts which are non-representational, fluid and molecular, and which form constantly shifting planes of immanence. It contrasts with the dominant image of traditional Western thought which is termed the plane of organisation (or of transcendence). While the plane of organisation attempts to fix entities, and to block all lines of flight or deterritorialisations which would result in their collapse, the plane of immanence strives to escape from the plane of organisation, as its fixed functions dissolve and are constructed ever differently in new combinations of concepts or assemblages.[32] It is posited that every great philosopher and creative innovator traces her/his own planes of immanence through such processes of deterritorialisation, in which concepts break down and are uprooted from their context, in order to be reassembled with other heterogeneous elements in new assemblages (reterritorialisation). For Deleuze and Guattari, historical developments in musical expression have likewise depended upon such deterritorialisations, as lines of flight escape from their musical assemblages to form new ones. Deterritorialisation is theorised in terms of Boulez's concept of the diagonal, in which the contribution of an original creator is conceptualised as a quasi-diagonal line, which passes between previously accepted horizontal and vertical coordinates, to mark out a philosophical or musical territory of its own.[33]

This new image of thought is also conceptualised with the vegetal model of the rhizome, and stands in opposition to the traditional image of thought, which is defined as arborescent.[34] In contrast with the hierarchically structured branches found within tree systems, a Deleuzo-Guattarian rhizome has lines which allow the connection of any of its points with any other,[35] and where arborescent systems have 'hierarchical modes of communication and preestablished paths, the rhizome is an acentred, nonhierarchical, nonsignifying system'.[36] While the Western tonal system is identified as embodying an arborescent image of thought, an alternative rhizomatic image is accomplished through what Deleuze and Guattari refer to as a 'generalised chromaticism', in which all of the 'sound components – durations, intensities, timbre, attacks' are placed 'in continuous variation', and through

---

[32] Deleuze and Guattari 1988, 270; Deleuze and Parnet 1987, 99.
[33] Deleuze and Guattari 1988, 296–7; 1994, 191; Deleuze 2006, 293.
[34] Deleuze and Guattari 1988, 15.   [35] Deleuze and Guattari 1988, 7–8.
[36] Deleuze and Guattari 1988, 21.

which 'music itself becomes a superlinear system, a rhizome instead of a tree'.[37]

Deleuze and Guattari believe that a number of modern musicians have produced an 'immanent sound plane' in opposition to the hitherto dominant transcendent plane of organisation,[38] and John Cage is nominated as the first to have 'deployed' such a plane, in which process and experimentation are affirmed in preference to the values of structure, genesis and interpretation. Boulez's music is likewise considered to be rhizomatic because it is like 'a seed which you plant in compost, and suddenly it begins to proliferate like a weed'.[39] His concepts of the smooth and the striated are understood as corresponding respectively to the planes of immanence and organisation since, while the striated concerns distinct, fixed things, organising, and producing 'order and succession', the smooth entails 'the continuous variation [and] continuous development of form'.[40]

In Deleuzo-Guattarian terms, Boulez's work, like that of every significant creative figure, comprises a heterogeneous assemblage of materials, drawn from a variety of different milieux, which they term a refrain, and in which musical sound is only one component among others, including the literary, artistic and philosophical.[41] The infinitesimal or molecular components of Boulez's refrain may consequently be found in aspects of the work of the composers, writers, artists and philosophers who have influenced him, as well as in his experience of music, musical instruments, ensembles, performance practice and so on. This is not to reduce an artwork to a number of previous artworks, or to play a game in which we merely identify the influences within a work. The concept of the diagonal/transversal is the mark of originality and uniqueness within each new work, which connects and assembles aspects of previous musical practice on a new plane through a new connective principle. Boulez's works, when viewed as Boulezian assemblages, are not reduced to aspects of Webern, Mallarmé, and others – they remain distinctively Boulezian. When we say that many of the forces which are found in one of Boulez's scores are reterritorialised lines of flight, which can be seen differently in Mallarmé, Klee and others, we do not reduce Boulez's work. We simply acknowledge that some of its forces now speak within music as they also speak within visual art, poetry or philosophy.

Some of Boulez's own statements can be understood in a way which is generally supportive of this Deleuzo-Guattarian reading. On his relationship with Joyce's work, and on the question of analysing works of art, he writes

---

[37] Deleuze and Guattari 1988, 95.   [38] Deleuze and Guattari 1988, 267.
[39] Deleuze and Guattari 1988, 519.   [40] Deleuze and Guattari 1988, 478.
[41] Deleuze and Guattari 1988, 323.

of extracting 'a new element from a model, to examine the possibilities of the model and to transform it'.[42] Speaking of Klee's use of musical terms such as 'rhythm, polyphony, harmony, sonority [*Klang*], intensity, dynamic, variations' and so on, Boulez says that it is not 'a simple "translation"', but rather 'an attempt to apply the riches of music to another mode of expression, to study and transpose its structures'.[43]

There is nothing of eclecticism in this approach and Boulez dissociates himself entirely from any heterogeneous synthesis of elements which would amount to a superficial linking of disparate materials. This is emphatically not Boulez's way. Instead, each significant composition, or even an entire compositional output, formulates a new assemblage[44] in which the composer's unique intention produces a novel synthesis of certain elements, leaving others aside. In a similar way, the genesis of the musical idea is explained by Boulez as 'the product of a certain combination of circumstances' and as the 'synthesis of a certain number of scattered and . . . *presupposed* givens'.[45]

Difference, repetition, the virtual and the actual

The image of thought which is formulated in the books which he produced with Guattari arises out of a philosophy of difference which Deleuze had already worked on in his independent studies, and most fully in *Difference and Repetition* (1968) and *The Logic of Sense* (1969). While his earlier essays explored the work of a series of anti-rationalist philosophers including Lucretius, Spinoza, Hume, Nietzsche and Bergson, the last two named are of particular importance in the development of the philosophy of difference. Bergson's philosophy, which Deleuze first drew upon in the mid-1950s, values 'internal difference', in contrast to the Platonic 'dialectic of alterity' or Hegelian contradiction,[46] which operate on the basis of two antithetical options, apparently oblivious to the diversity of intermediate positions made possible by a philosophy of difference.

This philosophy of difference found further support in the early 1960s in Nietzsche's critique of Enlightenment reason, which pinpoints Kant's failure to include the realm of values in his critical analysis, where he simply assumes the value of the True, the Good and the Beautiful. Nietzsche, in contrast,

---

[42] Samuel 1986, 107.   [43] Boulez 1989, 36.
[44] Boulez 2005b, 78. Boulez uses the word *agrégation* and not *agencement*, the term used by Deleuze and Guattari, which is translated here as 'assemblage'.
[45] Boulez 2005b, 144.
[46] Deleuze 2004, 38–40. Deleuze first formulates a Bergsonian philosophy of difference in two articles from 1956: 'Bergson, 1859–1941' (2004, 22–31) and 'Bergson's Conception of Difference' (2004, 32–51).

places a critique of values at the centre of his genealogical philosophy, as he attempts to trace their development to their origins. It is at this point that he discovers difference, and two alternative approaches to the generation of difference, namely affirmation and negation.[47]

The history of thought in Deleuze's Bergsonian-Nietzschean analysis is variably exemplified in the philosophies of Plato, Aristotle, Leibniz and Hegel as favouring identity over difference, a situation he sets out to reverse with the positing of a new image of thought. Drawing upon certain Nietzschean currents, Deleuze identifies Platonism as the origin of this dominant tradition, this representational thought, which suppresses or excludes difference in favour of 'identity, resemblance and similitude'.[48] Most philosophers 'had subordinated difference to identity or to the Same, to the Similar, to the Opposed or to the Analogous: they had introduced difference into the identity of the concept, they had put difference in the concept itself, thereby reaching a conceptual difference, but not a concept of difference'.[49]

For Plato, the authenticity of something is determined by the degree of identity it shares as a copy with its original, hence the inadequacy of simulacra which are judged to be merely imperfect copies of the only true realities, the Platonic Forms. Deleuze, in contrast, rejects the philosophy of identity within the theory of Forms, and seeks to overturn it through a philosophy of difference, which cannot be explained in terms of representation and identity. Accordingly, he denies 'the primacy of original over copy, of model over image', elevates simulacra and, thereby, places difference above sameness. For Deleuze, everything is a simulacrum since there are no absolute foundations or identities.[50] Despite setting out to overturn Platonism, he acknowledges that in doing so 'many Platonic characteristics' will be conserved,[51] and it is clear that he retains the basic structure of Plato's method, while replacing identity with pure difference.[52]

It is important to understand that difference, in the Deleuzian sense, is not difference *'from* or *within* something'.[53] Where traditional thought has tended to view difference from the standpoint of sameness and unity, Deleuzian difference conceives 'difference differentially'. Within the

47   Deleuze 1983, 89–91; 1994, 137; Bogue 1989, 16.
48   Patton 1994, 145. In a note to his *Nachlass*, Nietzsche refers to his philosophy as 'an "inverted" or "reversed" Platonism', and in the preface to *Beyond Good and Evil*, Platonism is dismissed as the 'dogmatist's error' (cited in Patton 1994, 143–4). Opposition to the Platonic concepts of 'the One, the Same, and the Whole' are found throughout Nietzsche's works (Bogue 1989, 28; Deleuze 1994, 68–9, 55–6, 127).
49   Deleuze 1994, p. xv, 32.
50   Deleuze 1994, 66, 128. Deleuze says that in the *Sophist* 'Plato discovers . . . that the simulacrum is not simply a false copy, but that it places in question the very notations of copy and model' (1990, 256).
51   Deleuze 1994, 59.   52   Williams 2003, 79–80.   53   Foucault 1977, 181–3.

framework of traditional identity-based thinking, 'global resemblances' are found within phenomena, which are then viewed in terms of 'differences and partial identities'. At the end of this thought process we are left with a range of likenesses and resemblances which can be classified in terms of their degree of identity or difference from the initial idea. While dialectics recaptures every difference in a future *Aufhebung* ('overcoming'), Deleuze desires to free difference, a liberation which can only be achieved 'through the invention of an acategorical thought'.[54] Such a mode of thought would no longer provide primordial unities within which differences and multiplicities can be categorised, and it is this acategorical thought or univocal being which prevents the categorisation of phenomena, and which enables difference to escape 'the domination of identity'.[55]

In aesthetic modernity, especially modernist art, literature and music, Deleuze finds a world which is defined in terms of difference and simulacra.[56] He writes of the 'permutating series' and 'circular structures' of modern art, which direct philosophy away from representation, since with representation, every unique viewpoint must have a corresponding 'autonomous work with its own self-sufficient sense'. He looks instead to works such as Mallarmé's *Livre* or Joyce's *Finnegans Wake*, which challenge and invert the notion of a model or pre-eminent position, as 'the identity of the object read really dissolves into divergent series defined by esoteric words, just as the identity of the reading subject is dissolved into the decentred circles of possible multiple readings'.[57]

Deleuze relates the concept of difference to that of repetition, which he also believes to have been subject to thinking in terms of 'the identical, the similar, the equal or the opposed'.[58] He posits a repetition, no longer subject to identity and sameness, but rather to difference and variation, and which, he suggests, is best exemplified in Nietzsche's notion of the eternal return. This is not the return of the same, in the sense of history repeating itself, the same thing occurring again and again in the same way, nor is it to be understood in its moral sense as an affirmation of life. It is a return of the same which is ever different,[59] and in which each return is a unique manifestation of a virtual, which is inexhaustible in its possibility, and which has no primary term.[60]

The concepts of the virtual and the actual were taken up by Deleuze from his reading of Bergson, who had introduced the opposition in *Time and Free Will* (1889) as a way of thinking the distinction between the continuous

---

[54] Foucault 1977, 186.   [55] Foucault 1977, 192.   [56] Deleuze 1990, 265; Patton 1994, 154.
[57] Deleuze 1994, 68–9, 56.   [58] Deleuze 1994, p. xv.   [59] Deleuze 1994, 13, 40–1, 115, 126.
[60] Deleuze 1994, 17.

and the discontinuous.[61] Bergson used the terms in a more developed way in *Matter and Memory* (1896), where he theorised that memory starts out

> from a 'virtual state' which we lead onwards, step by step, through a series of different *planes of consciousness*, up to the goal where it is materialized in an actual perception; that is to say, up to the point where it becomes a present, active state; in fine, up to that extreme plane of our consciousness against which our body stands out. In this virtual state pure memory consists.[62]

Again, Bergson reflects that 'the localizing of a recollection' does not 'consist in inserting it mechanically among other memories, but in describing, by an increasing expansion of the memory as a whole, a circle large enough to include this detail from the past. These planes, moreover, are not given as ready-made things superposed the one on the other. Rather they exist virtually.'[63] For Deleuze, Bergsonian virtuality involves the 'possible coexistence' of all of the degrees or nuances within something. It is also another way of describing the Bergsonian *durée* (duration).[64] In *Difference and Repetition*, where the virtual and the actual are discussed more comprehensively, he makes clear that the virtual is not opposed to the real, that it is fully real and 'completely determined', and that it must not be confused with the possible.[65] Indeed, the real includes the virtual, the actual and their 'reciprocal determination'.[66]

It is from this principle of the virtual that the eternal return operates, designating return, 'not of being and the same, but of becoming and difference', and the flux and multiplicity which it engenders results in the production of innumerable permutations of forces.[67] Recognising the aesthetic valency of the concept, Deleuze writes of artworks as 'immersed in a virtuality', a phrase which he exculpates from all vagueness in defining it as 'the completely determined structure formed by its [the work's] genetic differential elements, its "virtual" or "embryonic" elements'. Furthermore, these 'elements, varieties of relations and singular points coexist in the work or the object, in the virtual part of the work or object, without it being possible to designate a point of view privileged over others, a centre which would unify the other centres'.[68]

In terms of the present study, it may be that Deleuze's reading of Bergson and Nietzsche gives philosophic expression to something which, in its own

---

[61] Pearson suggests that Bergson has taken up the pairing of the continuous and the discontinuous (discrete) from the mathematician G. B. Riemann (1854) (Pearson 2002, 15).
[62] Bergson 2004, 319.   [63] Bergson 2004, 322.   [64] Deleuze 2004, 28, 44.
[65] Deleuze 1994, 209–11.   [66] Williams 2003, 164.   [67] Bogue 1989, 28–9.
[68] Deleuze 1994, 209.

way, informs the literary production of Mallarmé, Joyce, Artaud and Proust, as well as the geometry of Klee, and which is taken up, to some extent, in the music of Boulez. It would certainly seem that this is the view taken by Deleuze, and later shared by Guattari.

Deleuze explicitly applies his thinking of difference and repetition to Boulez's music and thought in the essay 'Boulez, Proust and Time' (1986), in which he views Western tonality as a musical system based essentially upon the principle of identity. While artistic and musical expression involve an enlarging of perception, this is dependent upon perception breaking free from identity.[69] Boulez's music is perceived as leading to 'a general rejection of any principle of identity' in its 'variations and distributions'. Nevertheless, Deleuze acknowledges that music such as this, based upon difference and variation rather than identity, can give rise to serious perceptual problems, since the listener may be faced with unceasing variation, and little in the way of reference points with which to orient the ear. He recognises that Boulez solves this problem through the introduction of fixed elements, by which he refers to Boulez's signals and envelopes.[70] Their function, according to Deleuze, is to articulate formal structure or to isolate 'a group of constitutive elements' in such a way that perception is enriched and memory can operate more successfully.

Like Boulez's music, Proust's *À la recherche du temps perdu* also operates through the use of fixed elements, but Deleuze is careful to reject any implication that this entails the restoration of any principle of identity. The fixed element 'is not defined by the identity of a repeated element, but by a *quality common* to elements that would not be repeated without it'. For example, the Proustian idea of a taste which is 'common to two moments', does not reveal identity lurking behind a façade of variation, but instead displays a variation which is 'individuation without identity'. It is precisely this new type of variation which is the locus of the enlarged perception facilitated by art, since it enables us to perceive difference, no longer tethered to a dominant principle of identity, but purely in itself. Using the example of the village of Combray, which is so prominent in the memory of the narrator throughout *À la recherche*, Deleuze tells us that for Proust, this 'taste, as a quality common to two moments, identifies Combray as always different from itself'. In other words, while Proust uses the village as a fixed point, as a familiar reference point throughout the work, its aspect is constantly varied with each appearance. Likewise, in music, 'the functional play of repetition and difference replaces the organic play of identity and variation'.[71] In this way, 'the fixed do not imply permanence', but rather enable us to perceive

[69] Deleuze 2006, 296.   [70] Deleuze 2006, 297.   [71] Deleuze 2006, 298.

'variation or dissemination', while Boulezian envelopes similarly produce not fixed identities but rather 'shifting relation[s]'.[72]

Even before the appearance of this reflection on Proust and time, Boulez recognised that Deleuze's philosophy of difference could be helpful in discussion of his work. In a 1985 interview, when explaining the reintroduction of more clearly perceptible elements in his music, he noted that Deleuze bases perception on repetition and difference. While it was necessary to have 'a certain form of repetition' to articulate form more clearly, this has nothing to do with predictable, literal repetition, and it is really a question of 'similar appearance'.[73] Boulez has also stated that he 'was very happy to discover' the links connecting Deleuze's concept of difference and his own work, and that when he first discovered it, he believed that it expressed his own thoughts exactly. He agreed wholeheartedly that Deleuze's terminology was felicitous for discussion of his music, and stated that their encounter had been based upon the concepts which they shared.[74]

In *The Fold: Leibniz and the Baroque* (1988), Deleuze developed his philosophy of difference further, in elucidating the concept of the fold, with illustrations from Klee and Boulez, who respectively produce multiple lines and heterophonies. Noting how Klee inflects a singular geometric point to produce a number of related curves,[75] Deleuze replaces the notion of the unique curve or the permanent object with Bernard Cache's idea of the *objectile*, which, in contrast to the singularity of the object or line, expresses the multiplicity of the *virtual line* or *virtual curve*.[76] For Deleuze, the coexistence of Klee's multiple lines are examples of what Leibniz called incompossibility, that is, the possible coexistence of ideas or notions which are mutually contradictory, and which cannot coexist within the same world, within a traditional world-view.[77] Deleuze and Boulez seem to be in agreement, however, in suggesting that for many modern philosophers and artists, 'divergences, incompossibilities, discords [and] dissonances' coexist 'in the same world'.[78] Chaos is defined here from a cosmological point of view, as 'the sum of all possibles' and, in relation to perception, as 'the sum of all possible perceptions'.[79] Deleuze draws a further parallel between the passage from the closed world of compossibles to the open world of divergent incompossibles and the progressive development of musical harmony.[80] The latter is traced through the emancipation of dissonance, the development of harmony, its eventual dissolution, to polytonality and to the

---

[72] Deleuze 1986, 100 (trans. EC).   [73] Boulez and Cott 1985, 148.
[74] Interview with the author, 28 August 1998.   [75] Deleuze 1993, 14–15.   [76] Deleuze 1993, 19.
[77] We may also think of Nicolas of Cusa's coincidence of opposites, which was discussed in Chapter 3.
[78] Deleuze 1993, 81–2.   [79] Deleuze 1993, 76–7.   [80] Deleuze 1993, 82.

incompossibility of Boulez's polyphony of polyphonies, or heterophonies. Modernist creators such as Mallarmé, Klee and Boulez turn away from the unilinearity of compossibles in favour of incompossibles, which affirm divergences and no longer suggest the traditional world of the familiar.[81]

Smooth and striated space

In *A Thousand Plateaus*, Deleuze and Guattari use Boulez's concepts of smooth and striated space to formulate a smooth space of thought. An entire plateau (chapter) of the book is devoted to the smooth and the striated, in which the Boulezian origins of the concepts are acknowledged, and a number of models of smoothness and of striation are explored within a range of contexts.[82] Boulez, they suggest, is

> concerned with the communication between the two kinds of space, their alternations and superpositions: how a 'strongly directed smooth space tends to meld with a striated space', how 'a striated space in which the statistical distribution of the pitches used is *in fact* equal tends to meld with a smooth space'; how the octave can be replaced by 'non-octave-forming scales' that reproduce themselves through a principle of spiraling; how 'texture' can be crafted in such a way as to lose fixed and homogeneous values, becoming a support for slips in tempo, displacements of intervals, and *son art* transformations comparable to the transformations of *op art*.[83]

For Deleuze and Guattari, Boulez makes these fundamentally different spacing types musically perceptible. He 'makes palpable or perceptible the difference between non-metric and metric multiplicities, directional and dimensional spaces. He renders them sonorous or musical.'[84] For Deleuze, 'it's not a matter of setting philosophy to music, or vice versa. Rather, it's once again one thing folding into another: "fold by fold", like Boulez and Mallarmé.'[85] Of course, this reflection is not musicological in intent, and primarily serves the authors' idiosyncratic purpose of articulating two distinct images of thought.

Smooth and striated time

As with pitch space, Boulez's twin temporalities are used to exemplify the Deleuzo-Guattarian image of thought, on the basis that they correspond to

---

[81] Boulez's interest in multiplicity can also be related to Artaud's radical fragmenting of language and Char's poetic of the labyrinth.
[82] Deleuze and Guattari 1988, 474–500.   [83] Deleuze and Guattari 1988, 478.
[84] Deleuze and Guattari 1988, 477.   [85] Deleuze 1995, 163.

the planes of consistency (immanence) and organisation (transcendence). Boulez's concepts of pulsed and non-pulsed time are related by them to *Chronos* and *Aion*, two distinct, yet complementary, conceptions of time which Deleuze discovered in Stoic philosophy, and which he had expounded in *The Logic of Sense*.[86]

Like Boulez, Deleuze conceptualises two distinct temporal modes, a measureless present which he refers to as *Aion*, and a variable and measured present termed *Chronos*. *Aion* is 'infinitely subdivisible' time, where 'each present is divided into past and future ad infinitum', and all measure is subverted.[87] *Chronos*, in contrast, is like an eternal present, which is always limited and capable of being taken up into a much larger present which includes the past and future within itself.[88] In *A Thousand Plateaus*, *Chronos* is said to correspond to Boulez's striated or pulsed time, while *Aion* putatively corresponds to smooth or non-pulsed time.[89] In the paper which he presented at the IRCAM colloquium on time in 1978, Boulez's non-pulsed time is related to Proust's 'time in its pure state',[90] an insight which is further expanded in the article 'Boulez, Proust and Time'. For Deleuze, Proust's *À la recherche du temps perdu*, like Boulez's music, contrasts a striated, pulsed time with a smooth, non-pulsed time, which 'only refers to chronometry in a global way'.[91] He defines non-pulsed time, in Boulezian terms, as occupying time without counting, and pulsed time as counting in order to occupy time,[92] and he is surely correct in suggesting that Boulez's distinction of the smooth and the striated is of less value as a division than as a continuum, since they can be alternated or superposed, a phenomenon we will meet, for example, in sections of *Répons*.

Once again, Deleuze and Guattari are writing primarily about the characteristics of a new image of thought, and Boulez's concepts are adopted because they are useful to them in its articulation. Nevertheless, while it is clear that they are not doing musicology or producing a musical aesthetic, and it would be a mistake to read their texts as such, something central to Boulez's music, the sensible opposition of smooth and striated, of pulsed and non-pulsed time, is recognised by Deleuze and Guattari as relating to their new image of thought. Deleuze understands Proust's *À la recherche* and Boulez's compositions as making time sensible.[93] While chronometry is easily perceived, the experience of 'time as a *force*, time itself, "a little time

---

[86] Deleuze draws upon Victor Goldschmidt's *Le Système stoïcien et l'idée de temps* (1953). In *The Logic of Sense* the spelling *Aion* is used, whereas in *A Thousand Plateaus* it has become *Aeon*. I have opted for the spelling *Aion* in general use.
[87] Deleuze 1990, 61–2, 163–4.   [88] Deleuze 1990, 150, 162.
[89] Deleuze and Guattari 1988, 262.
[90] www.le-terrier.net/deleuze/19ircam-78.htm (accessed 24 June 2008); Deleuze 2006, 157.
[91] Deleuze 2006, 294.   [92] Deleuze 2006, 292.   [93] Deleuze 2006, 298.

in its pure state"', is much more difficult to capture.[94] It is precisely this normally inaccessible aspect of time, its 'mute force', which Deleuze finds in Proust and Boulez.

It is not suggested that Boulez's temporalities are translations of or direct equivalences to Stoic philosophy, Proust's *À la recherche* or the new Deleuzo-Guattarian image of thought. Boulez's knowledge or ignorance of Stoic philosophy, and the nature of his connection with Proust, is not what is most significant here. What matters is the ultimately irreducible temporal experiences which they facilitate, and which link them. Indeed Boulez, who later had Deleuze's paper published, was interested in the philosopher's application of his temporal ideas, and the insistence with which he returned to them in his writings.[95] While Boulez acknowledges the significant impact of Proust's *À la recherche*, this is never made explicit in relation to temporality. Perhaps it may be said of Boulez, as Kristeva has said of Proust and Bergson, that he 'deemphasises "quantitative time" and favours a "qualitative time" that is experienced and felt'.[96] Just as the temporalities within Proust (involuntary memory) and Bergson (duration) are distinct and 'eminently individual', Boulezian and Deleuzian temporalities are equally idiosyncratic, and Kristeva's distinction of 'artistic concreteness and philosophical generality' is just as applicable.

Conclusion

Deleuzian/Deleuzo-Guattarian philosophy provides a theoretical focus for one understanding of difference and multiplicity in Boulez's music and thought. In Chapter 8 Boulezian difference will be considered at the level of thematicism and athematicism, while in Chapter 9 the concept of difference will be pursued in relation to the open work, accumulative development and heterophony. In Chapter 10 we will consider the binary oppositions of smooth and striated space as well as pulsed and non-pulsed time which, as we have seen, have been important for Deleuze and Guattari. Bearing in mind the previous chapters of this study, which focused on a number of competing philosophical strains within Boulez's work, Deleuze's idiosyncratic view will be considered along with alternative dialectical insights.

---

[94] Deleuze 2006, 298 (translation modified by the author).
[95] Interview with the author, 28 August 1998.   [96] Kristeva 1996, 313–14, 194.

8 Boulez, difference and repetition

Twentieth-century music, difference and repetition

According to Boulez, the entire history of the Western world is caught up in a 'dilemma' involving repetition, variation, recognition and the unknown. Indeed he believes that a profound interest in repetition and difference is found, directly or indirectly, in most musicians, and certainly in the work of contemporary composers, since the formal articulation of music is always dependent upon their dialectical relationship.[1] For Boulez, a dialectic of analogy and difference underlies the articulation of musical form,[2] and a considerable amount of space within his Collège de France lectures is spent in discussion of questions of difference and repetition, in the context of twentieth-century thematicism and athematicism. The three chapters gathered together under the title *L'Enjeu thématique* form a record of the lecture courses on the subject which he gave between 1983 and 1985, with many additional references elsewhere. While he considers thematicism within the music of Debussy, Bartók, Varèse and others, the sections which are of most relevance to his own practice are those which refer to what Schoenberg, Berg, Webern, and latterly Stravinsky, did with the notion of the theme.

The importance attributed by Boulez to questions of difference and repetition in post-war music is rooted primarily in the theoretical and practical innovations of the Second Viennese School. Multiple manifestations of the principles of variation and non-repetition are identified within their work, in avoiding 'doubling the components within an object, non-repetition of objects, no literal return of ideas, no literal reprise of formal elements'. Nevertheless, beyond the aesthetic diversity and complexity of their individual approaches, he finds 'a single principle', namely that of variation or non-repetition.[3]

In 'New Music: My Music' (c.1930), Schoenberg explains that he repeats 'little or nothing' and that repetition is almost completely replaced by variation. Something already given is altered to produce something new, with 'an apparently low degree of resemblance to its prototype, so that one finds difficulty in identifying the prototypes within the variation'.[4] It is not clear

---

[1] Boulez 2005b, 156.   [2] Boulez 2005b, 239.   [3] Boulez 2005b, 356–7.
[4] Schoenberg 1975, 102–3.

to what extent Schoenberg's terminology, such as his use of the word repetition, is self-consistent. Compare, for example, the quotation above with a
passage from 'For a Treatise on Composition' (1931) where he states that:

> the motive – can manifest its presence only through repetition . . . even
> today it is impossible to mould a form with plasticity, and in an easily
> comprehensible way, unless one uses repetition . . . it is a justifiable thesis
> that repetition is the initial stage in music's formal technique, and variation
> and development its higher developmental stages.[5]

John Cage recalls Schoenberg teaching that 'the principle of variation represented only the repetitions of something identical',[6] and that variation
was in fact 'an extreme case of repetition'.[7] Whatever the complexities of
his evolving relationship with repetition, many commentators agree that
the truly revolutionary step taken by Schoenberg was 'the renunciation of
thematic form', which was first accomplished with the early monodrama
Erwartung in 1909.[8] The decisive nature of this move stemmed from the
fact that hitherto, the repetition of themes and the intelligible treatment
of motifs had provided the clearest means of articulating musical form.
Boulez, likewise, pinpoints *Erwartung*, with its almost complete 'absence
of themes based on the determining *return* of privileged figures', as 'the
extreme point of thematic atomisation' within Schoenberg's development
and, together with *Die glückliche Hand* (1910–13), it is commended as his
most enterprising work from a thematic viewpoint.[9] In *Erwartung* Boulez
finds 'invention in a perpetual state of becoming',[10] and even in the article
'Schoenberg is dead' (1952), which contains his harshest judgements, he
takes time to mention the 'perpetual variation, or non-repetition' of the
Three Piano Pieces, Op. 11 and *Pierrot Lunaire* as 'remarkable features'.[11] By
the time of the Collège de France lectures of the 1980s, Boulez continues
to identify 'the tendency to variation, to non-literal repetition, to the evolution of forms towards a state of constant mobility' as perhaps the most
significant elements within Schoenberg's development.[12]

Even so, writers such as H. H. Stuckenschmidt and Oliver Neighbour
have rejected the term *athematic* as properly descriptive of *Erwartung* since
they perceive, albeit at a very basic level, some kind of motivic development

---

[5] Schoenberg 1975, 265.   [6] Cage 1981, 45.   [7] Cage 1981, 75, 78–9.
[8] Rosen 1976, 47. Schoenberg states in a letter to Josef Rufer in 1950 that while he supported the
notion of athematicism for a while, he later rejected it on the grounds that 'coherence in music
can be founded on nothing other than motives and their transformation and development'
(Auner 2003, 343–4).
[9] Boulez 2005b, 210–11.   [10] Boulez 1991, 283.   [11] Boulez 1991, 210.
[12] Boulez 2005b, 298.

within it.[13] Rosen and Burkholder, in contrast, whose readings concur with that of Boulez, stress that whatever motivic elements can be heard or discovered through analysis no longer possess the similarity or continuity which informs previous music, and which normally enables the listener to appreciate a motif through a principle of identity.[14]

Boulez is primarily interested in those works in which Schoenberg dispensed, for a time, with thematicism. Nevertheless, despite the anti-thematic revolution within his atonal music, Boulez believes that Schoenberg's use of certain contrapuntal techniques, especially that of strict canon, was inconsistent with, and indeed undermined, his desire for variation, since it resulted in consequents which were exact copies of antecedents, in terms of both pitch and rhythm.[15] Further, with the advent of the twelve-tone system and the traditional forms, which Schoenberg duly adopted in order to make larger structures once again possible, thematic repetition of a sort reappeared with the restatement of the series. Boulez takes issue with Schoenberg's use of the twelve-tone system for what he calls its 'confusion between theme and series', its 'ultra-thematicisation', which Boulez believes to be an inherent flaw within his system and its inevitable consequence.[16] In the third of the Op. 23 piano pieces, for example, transpositions and inversions of a five-note segment are used to produce all of the harmonic and melodic material, while the fifth piece uses a twelve-note row in such a way that the order of the pitches almost never changes throughout.[17]

Berg, in contrast, never rejected repetition with the radical purpose of Schoenberg's *Erwartung*. According to Rosen, of the three main Second Viennese composers, only Webern 'made a profound exploration of athematic forms'.[18] Boulez describes how, within Webern's early works, thematicism is intimately related to intervallic structure through the privileging of particular intervals. This process led to a consequent weakening, if not the outright annihilation, of all distinctions between what had formerly been perceived as 'principal figures' and 'secondary figures'.[19] In the Op. 9 *Bagatelles* (1911–13), we are faced with the paradox of a thematicism which, from one point of view, is no longer apparent in any accepted sense of the term while, from a different perspective, it is equally capable of being perceived as thematically all-pervasive. Boulez considers it to be Webern's 'most radical work in terms of non-repetition' since, for example, in the

---

[13] Stuckenschmidt 1959, 54; Neighbour 1983, 42.
[14] Rosen 1976, 47–50; Burkholder 1999, 175.
[15] Boulez 1991, 210. Boulez is exaggerating here since there is no case in Schoenberg's work where the consequent is an exact copy of the antecedent.
[16] Boulez 1991, 212.   [17] Boulez 1991, 290.   [18] Rosen 1976, 112.
[19] Boulez 2005b, 218–19, 224.

fifth bagatelle Webern imposes non-repetition strictly and allows nothing
to return in exactly the same way. For Boulez, at this point of Webern's
development, 'maximum coherence equals maximum perceptual insecu-
rity', a situation which is perhaps not dissimilar to that later encountered
in his own *Structures I.* It was this loss of perceptible coherence caused by
strict non-repetition, within works such as the *Bagatelles*, which persuaded
Webern to reintroduce repetition at the centre of his work.

In his two lecture series, *The Path to Twelve-Note Composition* (1932) and
The Path to the New Music (1933), Webern provides his own account of these
events. He recalls that his works of the free atonal period were informed
by the conviction that repetition should be avoided and that music should
constantly present something new. He tells of how he came to reject this view,
becoming convinced that continual novelty and the avoidance of repetition
destroyed comprehensibility and problematised the possibility of extending
musical form.[20] With the advent of the twelve-tone system, he returned to
the principle of repetition as the 'easiest way to ensure comprehensibility'
through the constant return of the given sequence of twelve notes.[21] Boulez
recognises this return to repetition in Webern's exploitation of intervallic
invariance, in the repetition of cells, and in the exact repetition of his late
canonic forms.[22]

Webern, in the early 1930s, defines a musical motive, along with Schoenberg, as 'the smallest independent particle in a musical idea', and such
motives are said to be recognisable simply through their repetition.[23] At
this stage of his career, he views Western music as the development of repetition with 'ever-increasing freedom', so that variation is to be seen as a
kind of freer form of repetition.[24] He believes that the twelve-tone system,
with its practice of not repeating any note until all twelve have sounded,
provides a new thematic technique with the advantage of even greater freedom. As he says, 'unity is completely ensured by the underlying series. It's
always the same; only its manifestations are different.'[25] Webern bases this
fundamental conviction upon Goethe's image of the 'primeval plant; the
root is in fact no different from the stalk, the stalk no different from the leaf,
and the leaf no different from the flower: variations of the same idea'.[26] For
Webern, Goethe's idea is applicable to everything, including music; hence
his assessment that variation form is somehow 'the primeval form, which is

---

[20] Webern 1963, 55.   [21] Webern 1963, 22.   [22] Boulez 2005b, 220, 223–4, 379–82.
[23] Webern 1963, 25–6. Schoenberg's writings contain several different definitions of the term
'motive'. In writings from 1917, 1934 and 1943 it is defined as 'a unit which contains one or
more features of interval and rhythm [whose] presence is manifested in constant use throughout
a piece' (Neff 1999, 59).
[24] Webern 1963, 31.   [25] Webern 1963, 40.   [26] Webern 1963, 53.

at the bottom of everything. Something that seems quite different is really the same.' Just as 'an ash tray, seen from all sides, is always the same, and yet different. So an idea should be presented in the most multifarious way possible.'

In this return to repetition, Webern does not, however, use literal repetition, but rather seeks to deduce all of his material from 'a single Idea', which exists at the precompositional level.[27] Boulez notes the paradoxical, and possibly contradictory, nature of this aspect of Webern's aesthetic, whereby he aspires to present absolute unity and constant variation simultaneously within his material. It is Webern's attempt to integrate these seemingly mutually exclusive ideas which results in what Boulez estimates to be Webern's greatest achievement.

For Boulez, 'Webern's principal contribution remains . . . in having overturned the notion of the theme from the real to the virtual'.[28] In his Op. 27 *Variations for Piano*, for example, we no longer find a set of variations beginning in the traditional way from a recognisable theme, such as Schoenberg provides in his Op. 31 *Variations for Orchestra*, but instead variations based on what Boulez terms a virtual theme. In the first movement of the Op. 27 *Variations*, the 'images' which Webern engenders from his materials are not linked uniformly to a primordial idea, as with traditional variations. They are, rather, diverse occurrences of an idea which never itself becomes perceptible, and which is only ever perceived in its multifarious manifestations.[29] The Idea is therefore said to be virtual, meaning that it pre-exists all themes and acts as the condition for 'the definition of real images and their developments'.[30]

There can be little doubt that Leibowitz's reading of Webern influenced Boulez's view. Leibowitz, who judges that Webern has 'virtually made variation into an exact science',[31] states that from Op. 17 we find 'the complete abandonment of traditional thematic principles',[32] a not too surprising observation given that his work 'from its very beginnings, is directed towards the conquest of a language dominated by the idea of perpetual variation'.[33] In the second movement of the Op. 21 Symphony, the variations which follow the 'clearly defined theme' are 'not so much variations of the theme proper as elaborations of its various structural elements', a process which 'is carried even further in Op. 27'.[34] The Op. 27 *Variations for Piano* is '*the first piece of music in which a composer has approached the concept of pure variation*' since no '*thematic* aspect of the "theme"' is reproduced within it.

---

[27] Boulez 2005b, 223–5.   [28] Boulez 2005b, 225.   [29] Boulez 2005b, 385–6.
[30] Boulez 2005b, 150.   [31] Leibowitz 1949a, 196.   [32] Leibowitz 1949a, 205.
[33] Leibowitz 1949a, 209.   [34] Leibowitz 1949a, 228.

Everything, in other words, '*is variation*, or, to put it another way, *everything is theme*', an observation which Leibowitz takes to be particularly true of the third movement.[35]

It is difficult to state unambiguously the extent to which the concept of the virtual theme is an authentic Webernian one, and the vagaries of repetition and non-repetition in the work of Schoenberg and Webern show that the question is far from transparent. The thinking and practice of both composers was not static and changed considerably in the course of their development. In surveying their output, Boulez makes definite and limiting choices, and the issue is not so much one of establishing the authenticity of his reading of Webern, as of tracing the link which he believes connects Webern's aesthetic with his own.

Whatever its source, Webern's athematicism or virtual theme implied for Boulez and his generation a renewed variation principle in which thematic elements are separated, given autonomy and recombined in variation. According to this new principle, no particular version of a thematic idea, such as the initial aggregate or the first heard phrase, is favoured over any other. Even so, certain elements may have a 'primordial' but not 'definitive' place, as the musical language no longer begins with standard recognisable objects, but rather with basic elements which continually recombine to create objects related through their similarity and difference.[36]

Webern's statements in his lectures from the 1930s clearly place him in the identity camp, since he resolutely gives sameness priority over difference. Nattiez believes Boulez's intention and practice to be similarly organicist, and he suggests that Bach, Webern and Boulez share a preoccupation with deriving multiplicity from the unitary.[37] As Webern remarked on Bach's *Art of Fugue*, 'to develop everything else from *one* principal idea . . . [provides] the strongest unity';[38] Boulez similarly praises the work for its 'inexhaustible variation of a single theme'.[39] Nevertheless, Boulez pinpoints an inherent ambiguity in Webern's espousal of both a central idea, informing all of the

---

[35] Leibowitz 1949a, 240–1. Kathryn Bailey says of Webern's serial variations that none of them 'has a theme that functions in the usual way'. Op. 27/iii, however, is the only one in which 'subsequent "variations" are not based in any way on material introduced at the beginning' (Bailey 1991, 195–7). In Boulez's Collège de France lectures, there are five references to Webern's *Variations for Piano*, normally in connection with the idea of virtuality (2005b, 150, 225, 248, 385, 403). Only in one passage (p. 385) is the location identified as the first movement. Bailey, who insists that only the third movement really involves a set of variations, blames Leibowitz for attempting to explain the first and second movements in terms of variation (Bailey 1991, 190). Dohl, however, interprets 'each of the fourteen phrases in the [first] movement as a variation of the prime/retrograde idea – each a slightly different manifestation of horizontal symmetry' (Bailey 1991, 191).

[36] Boulez 2005b, 298.   [37] Nattiez 1993b, 188.   [38] Webern 1963, 35.

[39] Nattiez 1993b, 188.

aspects of a work, and the desirability of constant variation. Furthermore, in Webern's *Variations for Piano*, perhaps in the first and third movements in different ways, he draws attention to an aspect of Webern's practice which Webern himself does not seem to have chronicled. While the main motivic idea of the first movement is fairly pervasive in the first and third sections of the movement, to what exactly can we refer each manifestation of the motive since no one example can be given originary status? Similarly, in the third movement there is no initial thematic utterance to be varied. It is precisely in this lack of an original with which to compare all other versions that we move from the province of identity to that of difference, whether it is eventually understood to be an accurate reading of Webern or, in fact, a misprision.

Athematicism: the virtual theme

The ideas of athematicism and the virtual theme, which Boulez first found in Webern's scores, had a profound influence on him, and prompted him to reflect upon his own compositional practice in terms of repetition, difference, thematicism and athematicism. In the 1980s Collège de France lectures, he applies this Webernian concept of athematicism to his own *Sonatine* for flute and piano (1946), which was also his first serial composition. It is important to bear in mind that there is a thirty-five to forty-year gap between the composition of the *Sonatine* in 1946 and his reflections upon it in the 1980s. It should not be imagined that Boulez was able to define concepts such as athematicism[40] or the virtual theme,[41] in the mid-1940s, with the kind of clarity which forty years of subsequent theory and practice later facilitated. Nevertheless, the fact that he presents the structural development within the *Sonatine* as the contrast between thematic and athematic developments, in conversation with Goléa in 1958, provides some support for the fidelity of his later reading.[42]

In the Collège de France lectures Boulez describes his initial efforts to confront thematicism and athematicism as naive,[43] and he seems, to some extent, to have stumbled towards athematicism, since he admits to not having been absolutely certain of the precise meaning of the term. In retrospect, he recognised that it consisted

---

[40] Boulez has spoken of athematicism in his music as a reaction against Schoenberg's thematic method and as a response to the ambiguity of theme and structure in Beethoven (interview with the author, 28 August 1998).

[41] Boulez was unsure of the origin of his use of the term 'virtuality', but he presumed that it came from his early scientific studies (interview with the author, 28 August 1998).

[42] Goléa 1982, 38–49.   [43] Boulez 2005b, 292.

in rejecting an *absolute* form of a theme, in order to end up with a notion of a virtual theme, (1) where the elements are not fixed at the beginning in a totally defined form, (2) where priority is not given above all to the intervals as the source of musical development, but where the other elements, duration in particular, can play a more important role to which the pitches are subordinated.[44]

Athematicism is an important element in the *Sonatine* where the material, which is referred to as athematic, is deduced from 'an abstract network of possibilities which defines the circumstances of this or that appearance'.[45] Despite this, the *Sonatine* does not in fact mark a definitive break with thematicism since it contrasts 'general thematicism, the theme reduced to a single cell, athematicism based on the neutrality of the constituent elements and on the force of the envelope, and precompositional athematicism'.[46]

The theme is said to no longer exist within itself, but rather as a developmental function in the articulation of form.[47] Consequently, it can be explicit, amorphous or anywhere between the two.[48] Like its formal model, Schoenberg's first Chamber Symphony, Boulez's *Sonatine* contains, within a continuous composition, four distinct movements, each of which has its own 'principal theme', deduced from the 'initial theme' which is enunciated in the first movement. In this sense, each of the four movements is defined by the particularity of its thematic material. Athematicism, on the other hand, is used as a means of transition, linking the four movements within the continuous thread of the piece. These transitions are of '"vague" character', 'do not have a precise thematic profile', and produce the formal opposition of athematic transitions and thematic movements. The boundary separating thematicism and athematicism is breached when the threshold of perceptibility has been crossed. Boulez tells us that he produces athematicism in the *Sonatine* through 'privileging' one of the parameters in relation to the others, and through employing 'sufficiently neutral' material. In the transitions, he makes rhythm the single organisational factor, and repeats a single rhythmic cell which has been abstracted from the 'principal theme'. Removed from its context, it assumes a 'totally neutral character'. Secondly, he neutralises the pitch material, leaving the 'choice of pitches to the application of a rhythmic grid', which is used in a totally 'undifferentiated' way. Coherence in the longest transitions is provided by their distinctive envelopes of density and register.

It is important at this stage to consider some musical examples from the *Sonatine* and from succeeding works to help illustrate the various degrees

---

[44] Boulez 2005b, 223.   [45] Boulez 2005b, 150.   [46] Boulez 2005b, 296.
[47] Boulez 2005b, 242.   [48] Boulez 2005b, 291–6.

Table 8.1. *Pierre Boulez,* Sonatine *for flute and piano, serial table*

	P												
I	0	1	2	3	4	5	6	7	8	9	10	11	
0	C	B	G	C♯	G♯	E	E♭	A	D	B♭	F	F♯	11
1	C♯	C	A♭	D	A	F	E	B♭	E♭	B	F♯	G	10
2	F	E	C	F♯	C♯	A	A♭	D	G	E♭	B♭	B	9
3	B	B♭	F♯	C	G	E♭	D	G♯	C♯	A	E	F	8
4	E	E♭	B	F	C	A♭	G	C♯	F♯	D	A	B♭	7
5	G♯	G	E♭	A	E	C	B	F	B♭	F♯	C♯	D	6
6	A	A♭	E	B♭	F	C♯	C	F♯	B	G	D	E♭	5
7	E♭	D	B♭	E	B	G	F♯	C	F	C♯	A♭	A	4
8	B♭	A	F	B	F♯	D	C♯	G	C	A♭	E♭	E	3
9	D	C♯	A	E♭	B♭	F♯	F	B	E	C	G	A♭	2
10	G	F♯	D	A♭	E♭	B	B♭	E	A	F	C	C♯	1
11	F♯	F	C♯	G	D	B♭	A	E♭	A♭	E	B	C	0
	11	10	9	8	7	6	5	4	3	2	1	0	RI
												R	

of thematicism and athematicism which would lead Boulez to progressively theorise and actualise the idea of a virtual theme. Consequently, in what follows, musical analytical comments will be provided purely in illustration of the concepts which are discussed.

In the *Rapide* first movement of the *Sonatine* (bb. 32–96), it can be seen that Boulez, at times, uses the series (Table 8.1) as a resource to provide an ordinary recognisable theme, a phenomenon he refers to as general thematicism.[49] While this short movement does feature retrograde and inverted retrograde serial fragments, what could be called the main thematic occurrences of the series involve mainly inverted and prime forms, which can be seen in Table 8.2. Despite marked differences in duration, all of the serial forms in Table 8.2 are instances of conventional general thematicism in their melodic fidelity to the basic series, and Bradshaw goes so far as to describe the complete statement of series form I (10) on the flute, with which the movement begins (bb. 33–40), as 'a true first-subject theme'.[50]

In addition to general thematicism, which involves the unfolding of entire serial forms, Boulez also employs smaller motives, which are derived from the row, and which he refers to as thematic cells or 'the theme reduced to a

[49] The pitch series of the *Sonatine* was revealed by Goléa (1982, 44). Carol Baron uses it to account for most of the pitches in the introduction (bb. 1–31) (1975, 87–95).
[50] Bradshaw 1986, 141.

Table 8.2. *Prime and inversions of the row in bb. 32–96*

Bar	Row form	Pitches	Instrument
32	I (8)	0–6	piano
33–40	I (10)	complete	flute
41–7	I (2)	complete	flute
54–5	I (8)	0–4	piano
71–3	I (4)	0–6	flute and piano
47–50	P (9)	0–9	flute
61–4	P (8)	complete (except 6), divided	piano
67–9	P (8)	0–4	piano
70	P (0)	2, 3, 4 and 6	piano
82–4	P (3)	complete	piano and flute
93–6	P (9)	complete	flute and piano

single cell'.[51] Among the clearest examples of this is the trichord (G, C♯, A♭) which opens and closes the introduction on piano (bb. 1–2; bb. 29–31), and which appears again in the coda (bb. 507–9). Occurrences of this trichord can be seen in Example 8.1. The presence of such trichords may well point to the influence of the similar trichords in the first movement of Webern's *Variations for Piano*.

The *Rapide* first movement is characterised by several occurrences of a rhythmic motive (Example 8.2) which appears in the flute part in bb. 33–5, bb. 41–3, bb. 51–2, and in the piano part at bb. 56–7 and bb. 67–9.

Thematicism operates at several levels simultaneously in the *Très modéré, presque lent* second movement. The backbone of the entire movement (bb. 97–138) is formed by one cantus firmus statement of series form I (2) in long trilled notes. Apart from this long-range statement of the theme, Boulez uses a variety of additional motives or thematic cells. There is a demisemi-quaver arpeggiated motive which varies in number of notes from six to nine. The main rhythmic thematic cell/motive from the *Rapide* section features again in bb. 116–18; bb. 126–8; bb. 131–3 and b. 134. The main melodic motive (Example 8.3), which opens this movement on the flute in bb. 98–100, returns to varying degrees in bb. 112–13; bb. 135–6; b. 137; bb. 148–9; b. 198 and bb. 201–2 which takes it into the third movement.

The movement features one more motive (Example 8.4) which is first heard at bb. 105–6 and which occurs again to varying degrees and in different

---

[51] Boulez 2005b, 296.

Example 8.1.
(a) Pierre Boulez, *Sonatine*, bb. 1–2

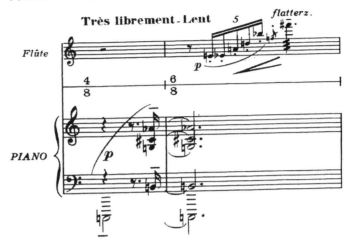

(b) Pierre Boulez, *Sonatine*, bb. 29–31

(c) Pierre Boulez, *Sonatine*, bb. 507–9

Example 8.2. Pierre Boulez, *Sonatine*, bb. 33–5

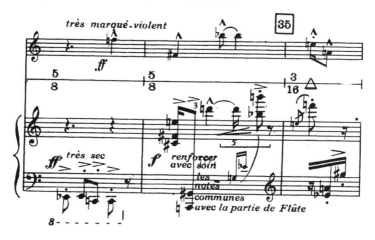

Example 8.3. Pierre Boulez, *Sonatine*, bb. 97–100

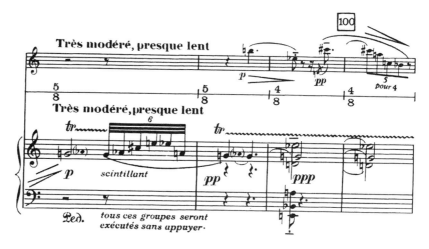

Example 8.4. Pierre Boulez, *Sonatine*, bb. 105–6

transpositions in the following places: bb. 142–3; bb. 146–7; bb. 151–2; b. 153; b. 170; bb. 195–6; bb. 196–7; bb. 199–200; bb. 205–6; bb. 413–14 and bb. 507–8.

The third movement *Tempo Scherzando* (bb. 151–295) is dominated by a three-note motive, based upon the intervals of the trichord (G, C♯, A♭), which is first heard in b. 1 of the piece. It is heard around forty times in bb. 151–200, and it completely saturates bb. 222–95, with the exception of the brief interlude at bb. 252–6. The fourth movement (bb. 342–495) restores a number of features of the first movement, including its *rapide* tempo, piano textures and melodic serial fragments in the flute part.

Having confirmed the existence of generalised themes and thematic cells, it remains to demonstrate the presence of athematicism. Jameux has noticed the similarity between bb. 85–92 of Boulez's *Sonatine* (Example 8.5) and the first movement of Webern's *Variations for Piano* (Example 8.6) which, as has been noted, is a key work for Boulez.[52] As in the Webern *Variations*, bb. 85–92 of the *Sonatine* are played on the piano alone, share similar phrasing, and involve a series of interlocking single notes and dyads made up of the same sparse intervals, such as perfect and augmented fourths, and minor ninths, which feature in the first and third sections of the Webern movement. While the pitches in bb. 85–92 of the *Sonatine* are mostly reducible to about five serial statements, all thematic traces, in a traditional sense, have been dissolved, and we are left with only characteristic intervals and rhythms, with athematicism.

The transition between the second and third movements (approximately bb. 140–50) shares something of the intervallic character and phrasing of the first transition. Nevertheless, it is difficult to hear this transition as completely athematic, since the motive, which we have already identified in bb. 105–6, sounds clearly in bb. 142–3 and more obliquely in bb. 146–7. The transition between the third and fourth movements (bb. 296–341) is conveniently identified by Boulez in *Proposals* (1948) as 'an athematic passage where the development proceeds without the support of characteristic contrapuntal cells'.[53] As Baron notes, its rhythmic cells are 'unrelated to any melodic cells', and its pitch content is made up of a number of dyads which are discontinuously culled from the series, and which overlap with one another, for example, F–F♯; G–G♯,[54] in a way which is once again reminiscent of the Webern *Variations for Piano*, encountered in transitions one and two.

For Gerald Bennett, the coexistence of thematicism and athematicism within one piece signals a certain 'stylistic inconsistency' and a lack of

[52] Jameux 1991, 231.   [53] Boulez 1991, 51–2.   [54] Baron 1975, 92.

Example 8.5. Pierre Boulez, *Sonatine*, bb. 85–92

homogeneity, which he believes to be the reason for Boulez's more decisive break with thematic writing in the compositions immediately following the *Sonatine*.[55] Despite Boulez's claim that he had changed only about ten bars of the piece between its composition in 1946 and its publication in 1954,[56] recent research shows that this was not the case. Susanne Gärtner reveals that a first version was produced in a few weeks at the beginning

[55] Bennett 1986, 61.   [56] Goléa 1982, 38.

Example 8.6. Anton Webern, *Variations for Piano*, Op. 27, bb. 1–18

Universal Edition   UE 10881

of 1946, and Boulez, according to Souris, made changes after the first performance in Brussels in 1947.[57] While these changes were made in April 1949, the piece was still not published until 1954,[58] and Gärtner's comparison of the 1946 version with the revised copy from 1949 shows that he, in fact, 'deleted or completely revised' about one hundred of the original 332 bars, particularly in the *Rapide* section. The existence of 'Messiaen-like harmony and a Jolivet-like character' in the early version leads her to conclude that Messiaen's mark on Boulez was more enduring than has generally been realised.[59] Comparing the 1946 flute part and the 1949 fair copy, Chang notes that Boulez's revisions, which pertain primarily to 'the introduction and the first part', were made in order to excise 'superfluous repetition'.[60]

While repetition and thematicism in its various forms clearly maintain an important unifying function in the published version of the *Sonatine*, the First Sonata for piano (1946) makes a much more emphatic move away from the identity-based repetition of traditional thematicism. For Boulez, the sonata, like the *Sonatine*, features 'groups of intervals organised in thematic cells, in opposition to freely chosen intervals within a totally defined chromatic'.[61] The total definition of the pitch material is provided by fairly rigorous adherence to the initial pitch series, which can be seen in Table 8.3 (a) and (b) in its prime and inverted formations.[62]

Franck Jedrzejewski (1987) analyses the First Sonata in terms of two thematic cells or motives, termed motives A and B, which together form a complete statement of the basic series. Study of the score confirms that these two thematic cells between them constitute the pitch material of the work. In his analysis of the first movement, Jedrzejewski shows that cell A (Example 8.7a) appears ninety-one times while cell B (Example 8.7b) features sixty-one times. In the second movement, cell A features eighty-five times and cell B eighty-four times.[63]

Restricting our examination of Boulez's motivic procedures to his treatment of cell A within the first movement, it can be seen that bb. 1–12 are composed of sixteen successive appearances of the cell. The entire movement proceeds in this way with many statements of cells A and B intersecting through shared common notes and various other devices. While the pitch collections are determined largely by the contents of the two cells, the surface

---

[57] Souris 2000, 181–2. [58] Gärtner 2002, 55–6. [59] Gärtner 2002, 58.
[60] Chang 1998, 227–8. [61] Boulez 2005b, 297.
[62] The format for the serial tables was given to me by Robert Piencikowski on the basis of a manuscript containing Boulez's original row tables, which is now held by a private owner.
[63] Jedrzejewski 1987, 75.

Table 8.3a. *Pierre Boulez, First Sonata for piano, serial table (prime)*

P												R
0	F♯	D	F	E♭	E	B	C	G	C♯	A	B♭	A♭	0
1	G	E♭	F♯	E	F	C	C♯	A♭	D	B♭	B	A	1
2	A♭	E	G	F	F♯	C♯	D	A	E♭	B	C	B♭	2
3	A	F	A♭	F♯	G	D	E♭	B♭	E	C	C♯	B	3
4	B♭	F♯	A	G	A♭	E♭	E	B	F	C♯	D	C	4
5	B	G	B♭	A♭	A	E	F	C	F♯	D	E♭	C♯	5
6	C	A♭	B	A	B♭	F	F♯	C♯	G	E♭	E	D	6
7	C♯	A	C	B♭	B	F♯	G	D	A♭	E	F	E♭	7
8	D	B♭	C♯	B	C	G	A♭	E♭	A	F	F♯	E	8
9	E♭	B	D	C	C♯	A♭	A	E	B♭	F♯	G	F	9
10	E	C	E♭	C♯	D	A	B♭	F	B	G	A♭	F♯	10
11	F	C♯	E	D	E♭	B♭	B	F♯	C	A♭	A	G	11

Table 8.3b. *Serial table (inversion)*

I												RI
0	F♯	B♭	G	A	A♭	C♯	C	F	B	E♭	D	E	0
1	G	B	A♭	B♭	A	D	C♯	F♯	C	E	E♭	F	1
2	A♭	C	A	B	B♭	E♭	D	G	C♯	F	E	F♯	2
3	A	C♯	B♭	C	B	E	E♭	A♭	D	F♯	F	G	3
4	B♭	D	B	C♯	C	F	E	A	E♭	G	F♯	A♭	4
5	B	E♭	C	D	C♯	F♯	F	B♭	E	A♭	G	A	5
6	C	E	C♯	E♭	D	G	F♯	B	F	A	A♭	B♭	6
7	C♯	F	D	E	E♭	A♭	G	C	F♯	B♭	A	B	7
8	D	F♯	E♭	F	E	A	A♭	C♯	G	B	B♭	C	8
9	E♭	G	E	F♯	F	B♭	A	D	A♭	C	B	C♯	9
10	E	A♭	F	G	F♯	B	B♭	E♭	A	C♯	C	D	10
11	F	A	F♯	A♭	G	C	B	E	B♭	D	C♯	E♭	11

result is not the pervasive repetition of a theme, but rather, an athematicism where the intervals within the cell are combined freely in such an assortment of ways that any sense of return or association of each cell appearance with a primordial identity is avoided.

Alongside this pervasive athematicism, Boulez continues to retain a place for repetition in the First Sonata. Indeed, the three rhythmic motives of the first bar, 'the triplet, appoggiatura and the quintuplet', form 'the

Example 8.7.

(a) Pierre Boulez, First Sonata for piano, bb. 1–2

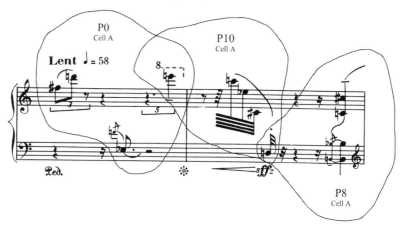

(b) Pierre Boulez, First Sonata for piano, bb. 13–14

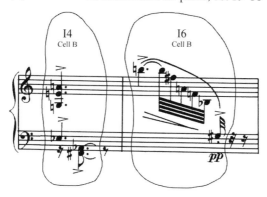

quasi-immutable referential unity' of the entire work.[64] Table 8.4 charts those places where the triplet, the appoggiatura and the quintuplet figures (referred to here as a, b and c) appear together, as they do in the first bar of the movement. With the exception of bars 25–6 which feature cell B, all other manifestations of the three rhythmic motives are based on cell A.

As can be seen from Table 8.4, when these three figures appear together, they often have characteristic interval forms. The triplet figure most often spans the interval of a minor sixth, while the appoggiatura spans either a major ninth (or higher registral version) or a minor seventh. In certain

---

[64] Jedrzejewski 1987, 74.

Table 8.4. *Intervallic breakdown of segments a,
b and c from cell A*

Bar	Cell segment	Interval	Series
1	a b c	a min 6th b maj 9th c	P (0)
11	a b c	a min 6th b maj 9th c	P (8)
23	a b c	a min 6th b maj 9th c	P (6)
25–6	a b c	a min 6th b maj 7th c	P (6)
68	a b c	a min 6th b maj 17th c	I (9)
70	a b c	a min 6th b maj 9th c	I (1)
74	c a b	c a maj 6th b min 9th	P (9)
98	a b c	a min 6th b min 7th c	I (9)
101	a b c	a min 6th b maj 9th c	P (2)
103	a b c	a min 6th b min 7th c	I (5)
107	a b	a min 6th b min 7th	I (11)

other instances, where they appear alone, Boulez is freer in varying their intervallic content.

It is clear that cells A and B do not provide the kind of general thematicism which is found in certain places within the *Sonatine*, and which was illustrated above. The thematic or athematic function of the cells should perhaps be read in the light of the following remarks made by Gerald Bennett, for whom

> the beginning of the first movement does take on something of the function of a first theme . . . However, these first bars are not a theme in the sense of a fixed, clearly-recognizable bit of music; they are a collection of intervals which usually appear in somewhat the same rhythmic garb, though never exactly the same . . . One can no longer speak of a theme here; this is a group of closely-related structures with no hierarchy between original and derived versions. Whereas traditional forms typically move from clarity of theme to relative obscurity and back to clarity, here no form is clearer or more obscure than another.[65]

What Bennett is describing is what we have come to call a virtual theme (or virtual thematic cell), the realisation of which Boulez was progressively moving towards in successive compositions. While the First Sonata has been shown to feature brief fragments of repetition, where the three rhythmic figures at times occur together with identical or similar intervals, this kind of direct repetition is much less the case than in the *Sonatine*. In the First Sonata, the two thematic cells are treated as virtual objects having initial, but not primordial, forms. The initial occurrence of cell A in the first bar of the first movement is only a singular manifestation of the virtual cell and not the cell itself. It is not a privileged identity from which all difference is to be measured but simply one formulation from among the many which Boulez chose to use or could have used within the piece. Even within those multiple examples where figures a, b and c appear together with identical or similar intervallic content, difference is maintained through the number of transpositions and serial forms used, in addition to the variety of registral positions, by means of which each manifestation is clearly related to all others but yet different.

While the First Sonata was begun in 1946, it was not published until 1951, and Peter O'Hagan's comparison of the published score with an earlier manuscript version indicates that Boulez's development was not quite as immediate and smooth as his Collège de France account suggests.[66] In the first movement, for example, while there are only a small number of differences in the *Beaucoup plus allant* sections, important changes have been made to the *Lent* passages. The manuscript version of this section is seventy-six bars long compared with forty-five bars in the final version. Furthermore, Boulez opens the draft version with 'a chromatic ostinato consisting of the three lowest notes on the piano', the recurrences of which

---

[65] Bennett 1986, 63.   [66] O'Hagan 1997, 27–32; 2006, 307–8.

were designed to provide unity.[67] The almost complete excision of all trace of this cluster from the published version changes the movement decisively, since the regular pulse the ostinato patterns would have provided is now absent. The reiteration of these pitches would, in addition, have served as 'reference points', a device which Boulez had come to reject by 1951.

O'Hagan notes that some of the passages which are omitted from the published score feature writing which is 'comparatively conservative and melodically conceived', and the serial origin of some sections in the draft version is immediately apparent in a way which is not the case in either the final version or in subsequent works. He appreciates the irony whereby the Sonata 'has evolved from precisely the kind of traditional references which Boulez is praised for having eliminated',[68] and he shows how the composer made similar changes to the second movement. The instruction 'faire entendu la thème en *sfz*', which appears in the draft score, is excised from the published version, and only traces of the 'melodic origins', found in the draft, appear 'in permutated form' in the completed version.[69]

Boulez makes no explicit mention of the Second Sonata for piano (1946–8) in his Collège de France account of the development of athematicism and the virtual theme.[70] Nevertheless, in conversation with Deliège, he speaks of the work as having an 'explosive, disintegrating and dispersive character', since each of the four movements aims to destroy its own historical formal model. The first movement, for example, attempts 'to destroy the first-movement sonata form', and Boulez tells us that he was working on 'a contrast between a style based on thematic motifs and an athematic one'.[71] As Peter McCallum observes, disintegration is achieved, in the first movement, firstly through dismantling the basic motives into their elemental intervals so that 'structural events lose their identity', and secondly through superimposing detail to the point that no specific contours are perceptible.[72] Boulez tells us that 'the very strong, sharply-outlined thematic structures of the opening gradually dissolve in a development that is completely amorphous from this point of view, until they gradually return. The whole of the first movement is made up of this contrast between very precise motifs and their dissolution into imprecise intervals.'[73]

Despite these remarks, McCallum notes that what Boulez considers to be 'very precise motifs are still, in many ways, analytical objects rather than perceptual objects', since what can be seen in the score is often imperceptible to the listener. In fact, Boulez has succeeded so well in destroying sonata

---

[67] O'Hagan 1997, 28.   [68] O'Hagan 1997, 29.   [69] O'Hagan 1997, 30–1.
[70] O'Hagan notes that the Second Sonata is not as radical in some ways as the final version of the First Sonata (2006, 308).
[71] Boulez 1976, 40–2.   [72] McCallum 1992, 63.   [73] Boulez 1976, 40.

Example 8.8. Pierre Boulez, Second Sonata for piano, bb. 1–2

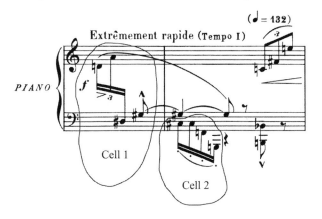

form that it is impossible actually to hear the recurrence of the motives.[74]
Thomas Bösche identifies two intervallic motives, which are prominent in
the movement, a four-note cell which occurs forty-one times and a three-
note cell which appears forty-eight times.[75] The first of these motives (D, A,
D♯, G♯), which opens the movement, is structurally significant because of
the leading role it mostly assumes within the movement's contrapuntal passages, in various presentations and transpositions. Furthermore, its initial
version (D, A, D♯, G♯), serves to act as 'a kind of structural pillar, occurring
at moments of structural importance' in a quasi-tonal way (Example 8.8).[76]
While its reappearance at the close of the exposition (b. 68) is very clear in
the score it, nevertheless, seems to lie beyond the range of our perceptual
capacities, a point for which the supposed recapitulation of the movement
provides an even more extreme case.[77] Consequently, it may be that much of
the motivic play exists primarily at the level of analysis and beyond perception in time, except in the most general way. As the movement progresses,
the cells increasingly interlink with one another until rhythmic density
mostly incapacitates aural comprehension of the pitch structure.[78] Like the
First Sonata, Boulez does, in fact, privilege a particular manifestation of the
main motive, but presents it in such a variety of ways that, while it can be
recognised as an initial identity on paper, this is almost impossible for the
listener to perceive.

The play of thematicism and athematicism, of identity and difference,
that is still to be found in the first two piano sonatas, is finally extinguished
in *Structures Ia* (1951) which, in Rosen's words, 'erases the last traces of

[74] McCallum 1992, 63.   [75] Bösche 1999, 77, 81.   [76] McCallum 1992, 66.
[77] McCallum 1992, 71–2.   [78] Bösche 1999, 82–3.

thematic form'.[79] Dissatisfied with the imbalance in the work of Schoen-berg, Webern and Berg, in which the organisation of pitch is much more developed than that of the other elements, Boulez had set out, in his early pieces, to find ways of organising the parameters more equitably. In *Structures Ia*, following on from Messiaen's *Modes de valeurs et d'intensités*, he found the means necessary to accomplish such an objective. He took his series of twelve pitches from the first of the pitch modes (3×12) used by Messiaen in *Mode de valeurs*, and used an analogous duration scale of twelve values, beginning from the value of a demisemiquaver and increasing incrementally by this duration. To this he added a dynamic series of twelve degrees and a series of twelve attacks. *Structures Ia* is a radical experiment in variation where Boulez, having defined series for all of the parameters, and systems with which to employ them, then left these to their own mechanistic unfolding without further compositional interference. The composer's role was simply one of writing out what the systems dictated to him, since all free compositional decision-making had taken place at the pre-compositional stage of planning. The result is constant variation.

Boulez speaks of his musical evolution to this point as the passage 'from a real theme to a virtual theme', since the automatic processes at the root of *Structures Ia* amount to the complete absence of return.[80] Experiencing the monotony of the result, however, he saw that the manipulation of such basic systems alone was insufficient for composition. The procedures he had used to produce a virtual theme did not take into account the very real limitations inherent within perception, and had created problems for the listener through their overabundance of detail and number of superim-posed elements. The result was too undifferentiated, lacked clearly defin-able characteristics, was beyond the capacities of human perception and, in the end, demonstrated that absence of variation is very similar to total variation. Consequently, he began to recognise the need to provide more perceptible landmarks for the listener to facilitate improved perception and comprehension.

After the degree zero, absolute determinism of *Structures Ia*, Boulez loos-ened the total systemic control of integral serialism, and progressively began to reintroduce elements of freedom into composition. To escape from the continual unfolding of linear serial statements, such as he had used in *Structures Ia*, he developed a new way of working with the series, in which the twelve pitches are divided into cells of unequal density, which we can abstractly term a, b, c, d and e. The pitches in each cell are then placed vertically as chords (frequency groups), and the intervals of one group are

---

79 Rosen 1986, 94.   80 Boulez 2005b, 306–8.

Table 8.5. *The multiplied cells form groups and fields within a domain*

aa	ab	ac	ad	ae
ba	bb	bc	bd	be
ca	cb	cc	cd	ce
da	db	dc	dd	de
ea	eb	ec	ed	ee

used to multiply the intervals of the others, thus producing a very large amount of intervallically related pitch material (Table 8.5). By changing the division of the original series, and then repeating the multiplication process, he produced five domains (matrixes of twenty-five groups), each with five fields (lines), each of which in turn have five groups. Pitch multiplication, as the process is called, is described in some detail in Boulez's Darmstadt and Collège de France lectures, and is fully demonstrated by Koblyakov (1990) in his analysis of *Le Marteau sans maître*, where he painstakingly explores the selection of harmonic relations which Boulez made from all the material which he had generated.[81]

Of 'l'artisanat furieux', which is the third movement of *Le Marteau*, but the first completed composition to feature pitch multiplication, Boulez says that its thematicism is 'diffuse' and not 'visibly present' anywhere in the score. Indeed, while there are no obvious harmonic entities (chords) and no 'literal thematicism', there are certain similarities within the sound objects, in the form of harmonic, intervallic and motivic relations.[82] The pitches in 'l'artisanat furieux' are taken almost entirely from the unfolding of the B and D fields from each of the five domains, as Boulez works his way systematically through the B fields of domains I–V in bars 1–26, and the D fields of domains V–I in bars 27–46. Example 8.9 presents fields B and D in each of the five domains, extracted from Boulez's multiplication table.[83]

Difference operates, at one level, as a product of the harmonic material, in which a number of isomorphic relationships entail that either complete identity, partial identity or similarity exist between groups within the same domain. Taking domain V as an example, and focusing only on fields B and D, in other words, those which Boulez used in this movement, we can see that groups bb and dd, as well as bd and db, are identical. In all the other

---

[81] Boulez first developed the principle of pitch multiplication in the unpublished work *Oubli signal lapidé* (1952) and he described it to some extent in the essay 'Possibly ...' (1952) (O'Hagan 2006, 310).

[82] Boulez 2005b, 310–11.   [83] See Koblyakov 1990, 3–33; Decroupet and Leleu 2006, 177–215.

Example 8.9. Fields B and D in domains I–V (extracted from Boulez's multiplication table as presented in Decroupet and Leleu 2006, 191)

fields, groups bd and db are also identical. More generally, as Koblyakov has remarked, the groups within a field usually have greater similarity to one another, in terms of structure, than groups in the other fields of the same domain. Looking to field D of domain II, he notes that:

> dc and dd are augmented triads; db and de consist of two augmented triads at a semitone distance (these groups have the same sounds); the groups dc and dd taken together create the groups db and de; finally, da consists of three augmented triads, as if being the sum of groups db and dc . . . or dd and de, or db and dd, or dc and de. Therefore a musical fragment based on this field has a high degree of harmonic unity.[84]

The pitch material which Boulez selected for use in 'l'artisanat furieux' is marked by the privileging of certain intervals such as major seconds, minor thirds, major thirds and tritones. Indeed, groups bb, bd, db and dd from domain V all have two minor thirds at the distance of a tritone.[85] A particularly notable motivic correspondence occurs at b. 25, where group bd (F♯–C–E♭) is sung by the alto, only to be followed shortly afterwards by group db (E♭–C–F♯) on the flute in b. 28 (Example 8.10). This recurrence is so noticeably the case here because it is the point in the movement at which Boulez, having worked through all of the B groups in domains I–V, now turns back through the D groups of the five domains in reverse order (V–I). Consequently, bd is one of the last B fields and one of the first D fields to be played. While groups bb and dd are also identical in domain V (F♯–A–C), their identity is not manifest in the score (b. 23 and bb. 29–30) since Boulez changes the F♯ to a G♯ in b. 30.

Those other correspondences which link groups bd and db are more remote since they are separated further in time. In terms of domain I, groups bd (b. 4) and db (b. 46) are used very differently, and the passing harmonic quality, which they share, is most likely not sufficient to create a perceptible link over the duration of the piece. While bd unfolds melodically in flute alone, db is divided between voice and flute. As for domain II, the fact that both bd (b. 8) and db (b. 39) unfold in a linear way reduces their perceptible harmonic potential. In domain III, groups bd (b. 11) and db (b. 35) are dyads (A–F♯) with limited potential for perceptual impact. The domain IV groups, bd (bb. 20–1) and db (b. 31), create very similar contours in terms of both the voice and flute, and perhaps offer greater potential for perceptibility.

There is also a degree of repetition in Boulez's use of palindrome. In bars 10–15, in which the pitches are taken from domain III, field B, voice

[84] Koblyakov 1990, 22.   [85] Decroupet and Leleu 2006, 189.

Example 8.10. Pierre Boulez, 'l'artisanat furieux' from *Le Marteau sans maître*

III

«l'artisanat furieux»

Example 8.10. (*cont.*)

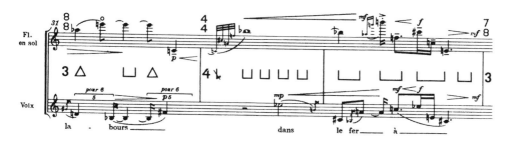

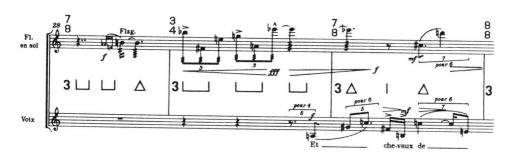

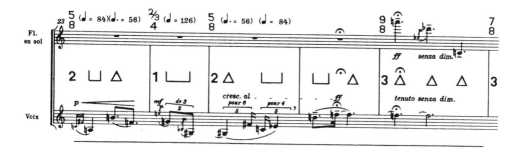

Example 8.10. (*cont.*)

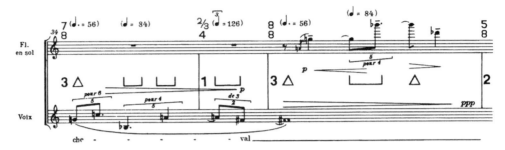

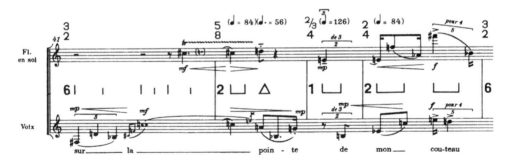

Table 8.6. *l'artisanat furieux*, the palindromic distribution of groups in bb. 10–15

Bars	10	11	12	13	14	15
Flute (groups)	be	bd	bc	bb	ba /	/
Voice (groups	/	/	ba	bb bc	bc bd	be

Table 8.7. *l'artisanat furieux*, the palindromic distribution of pitches in bb. 10–15

Bars	10	11	12	13	14	15
Flute (pitches)	D♯ C♯ E F	A F♯	B♭ G G♯	B	D C	
Voice (pitches)			C	D B G♯ G	B♭ F♯ A	E♭ E C♯ F

and flute play mostly the same line. The voice has the prime version, the flute the retrograde, and the parts intersect on B natural in b. 13.[86] The succession of groups can be seen in Table 8.6 and the succession of pitches in Table 8.7.

Other palindromic elements are perhaps less evident, for example in bb. 40–1 where the triad B–E♭–G is followed by the pitches F♯–D–B♭, an exact intervallic retrograde transposed down a minor ninth.[87] In terms of non-palindromic motives, the movement ends in bb. 46–8 with the pitch collection E♭–B–B♭–G–A, which is the transposed retrograde (a tritone lower) of a motive played on the flute in bb. 10–11.[88]

As with *Structures I*, Boulez affirms that the thematicism of *Le Marteau* is 'multiple and virtual',[89] but while similarity is established through the manipulation of intervallic correspondences and ornamental figures, amongst other means, what we are dealing with is 'not real but virtual identity', identity from a similarly derived family of musical objects. The parametric components, which are no longer extracted from a completed theme, are now found in the form of 'principles' that can only be perceived in their numerous materialisations, as the same which is always different.

To complete this consideration of the virtual theme, which has focused on the first decade of Boulez's creative development, we turn now to some of Boulez's later compositions. While *Originel* from ... *explosante-fixe* ... was begun in 1971, it was finally completed in chamber music form as *Memoriale*

---

[86] Decroupet and Leleu 2006, 180–1.   [87] Decroupet and Leleu 2006, 198.
[88] Decroupet and Leleu 2006, 210.   [89] Boulez 2005b, 311.

in 1985 and for (MIDI) flute solo and ensemble in 1991/3. Boulez's later music features a somewhat simpler harmonic style which is much more readily perceptible and comprehensible. In fact, the obvious coherence, which informs the melodic and harmonic aspects of *Originel*, may convey the mistaken impression that Boulez has resorted to the straightforward repetition of musical themes or thematic cells. Analysis of the work shows, however, that the main musical ideas are virtual ones in terms of both pitch and duration, and that virtuality and difference are manifest in a variety of ways.

One of the most distinctive and perceptible features of *Originel* is the relationship between the six cadences which conclude each of its six sections (Example 8.11). These grow progressively in length with the following numbers of pitches (2, 2, 4, 5, 6, 7). The sixth and last is a seven-note row in which no pitches are repeated. While they all conclude on the polar Eb, the central pitch of the entire piece, they are all different from one another. The leading note of each cadence is always either Aᅪ or Bb but, apart from this, the pitch order of each cadence is varied while still maintaining a clearly recognisable quality. Boulez thus creates what can be termed the virtual cadence since it has no privileged primordial manifestation.

A second virtual feature of *Originel* involves Boulez's treatment of duration. Of the 117 bars of the piece, the principal flute plays for 112 of them. Discounting three bars of held notes, of the remaining 109 bars, 75 bars have different durational compounds, 60 of which are heard only once. The durations of the remaining 15 bars (of the 75) recur from two to eight times in the course of the work, but not in any recognisable succession. It is possible to group many of these durations into families or groups to see how Boulez has created variation through the constant proliferation of very simple durational means.

The pitch dimension is no less varied than that of duration. In the course of *Originel* we become familiar with certain characteristic rhythmic shapes, the pitches and intervals of which are always different. The four phrases in Example 8.12 (a–d) are all different from one another yet clearly related to the phrase with which the solo flute part begins. It is impossible to say that any one of these figures has precedence over any other except in the order of their temporal unfolding. They are simply manifestations of a virtual theme or figure. There are no repeated pitch themes in *Originel*, but there are several places where the solo flute line features repeated intervals, permutated intervals and sometimes even brief palindromes. What *Originel* seems to show is a concept of the virtual theme that has remained at the heart of Boulez's musical practice right up to the present.

Example 8.11.

(a) Pierre Boulez, *Originel*, fig. 3

(b) Pierre Boulez, *Originel*, fig. 6

(c) Pierre Boulez, *Originel*, fig. 10

(d) Pierre Boulez, *Originel*, fig. 14

(e) Pierre Boulez, *Originel*, fig. 18

(f) Pierre Boulez, *Originel*, fig. 29

Example 8.12. (a)
Virtual thematicism in *Originel*:
(a) Pierre Boulez, *Originel*, fig. 1 − 1–fig. 1 + 1

(b) Pierre Boulez, *Originel*, fig. 7–fig. 7 + 2

(c) Pierre Boulez, *Originel*, fig. 15–fig. 15 + 3

(d) Pierre Boulez, *Originel*, fig. 19–fig. 19 + 2

Like *Originel*, *Anthèmes 1* (1992) for solo violin features several figures which, while always different from one another, are clearly related without being derived from any one primary enunciation. The piece, which has its origins in 'part of the original violin line from … *explosante-fixe* …',[90] opens with a seven-note figure (Example 8.13), which reappears many times throughout the piece but each time differently (b. 1; b. 3; b. 7; b. 9; b. 10; b. 12; b. 90; b. 96). The intervallic content of the figure is changed with every occurrence so that, while the figure is always recognisably perceptible, it does not have a primordial manifestation, and it can therefore be said to be a virtual figure.

Another characteristic figure within *Anthèmes 1* involves the use of a repeated note above a glissando in which the lower point of arrival within

---

[90] Boulez and Fink 2000, 8.

Example 8.13.

(a) Pierre Boulez, *Anthèmes 1*, b. 3

(b) Pierre Boulez, *Anthèmes 1*, b. 7

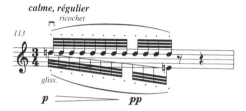

Example 8.14.

(a) Pierre Boulez, *Anthèmes 1*, b. 113

(b) Pierre Boulez, *Anthèmes 1*, b. 117

the glissando is normally varied from case to case (Example 8.14). Examples of this figure occur as follows (b. 1; b. 113; b. 117; b. 125; b. 129; b. 133; b. 135; b. 137; b. 139; b. 141; b. 143). The figure appears twelve times in the course of the piece, most often in a varied form, but there are also three exact repetitions (b. 117 and b. 139; b. 125 and b. 141; b. 129 and b. 137).

A third frequently occurring figure within *Anthèmes 1* features a sequence of trilled notes (Example 8.15). This does not include the many isolated trills within the piece but rather a particular, characteristic figure, which occurs always differently in the following places (bb. 4–6; bb. 58–60; bb. 67–71; bb. 80–8; bb. 94–6). In addition to these explicit occurrences of the figure, much of the material between b. 98 and b. 112 may also be related to it.

Example 8.15.

(a) Pierre Boulez, *Anthèmes 1*, bb. 4–6

(b) Pierre Boulez, *Anthèmes 1*, bb. 58–60

Again, while each manifestation is different, the figure is clearly recognisable and perceptible.

Boulez among his peers

Having considered the Deleuzian/Bergsonian philosophies of difference, repetition, the virtual and the actual in Chapter 7, and having followed through the working out of the virtual theme in a number of Boulez's compositions, this chapter will close with a short exposition of Boulez's early thinking on virtuality and difference in the context of his peers, namely Stockhausen and Pousseur.

Many of the key moments in the development of serial composition are, generally speaking, common to the serial generation, albeit achieved in distinctively personal ways by each composer. In terms of the rejection of thematicism, Stockhausen wrote in 1952/3:

> no repetition, no development, no contrast. Those devices all assume the existence of *Gestalten* – themes, motives, objects – that are repeated, varied, developed, contrasted; dissected, elaborated, expanded, contracted, modulated, transposed, inverted or turned back to front. All that has been given up since the first purely pointillistic works ... One never hears the same thing twice.[91]

Boulez's letters to Stockhausen from 1953 to 1954 contain some interesting remarks with regard to issues of identity, difference and repetition, and

---

[91] Cited in Maconie 1976, 35.

he writes of 'variation principles' as 'generative principles', in which 'the materials are renewed, reappear and combine in always different ways'.[92] When sounds or intervals are repeated in the same register in *Structures I*, the impression of repetition is blamed on the performer's failure to convey the individuality of the intensities, since each recurrence should have a different intensity and attack.[93] He questions Stockhausen's use of the terms 'mutation and variation',[94] and expresses concern with his tendency to focus on musical unity. The persistent appearance of the interval of the minor third in the first fourteen pages of Stockhausen's *Klavierstück VI*, for example, is criticised as fixated, repetitive and lacking in variation.[95]

The concepts of difference and repetition are also pivotal in the reading of recent music history which Pousseur presented in the late 1950s and early 1960s. He distinguishes between thematically based composition, which draws upon categories of repetition, transposition, contrast and opposition, and parametric composition in which musical 'figures' have greater diversity and are more finely differentiated.[96] Classical music is predicated on the basis of 'an aesthetic of repetition, on the actual recognition of the same in the different',[97] and Schoenberg's dodecaphony is marked as producing 'the most radical application of the *thematic* ideal' in that it brings the horizontal and vertical dimensions into a relationship of identity.[98] With Webern, in contrast, 'nothing is ever exactly the same' and even straightforward repetition produces difference in temporal terms.[99] The new parametric music of the post-Webernians produces 'multiple degrees of resemblance', '*continuously* varied phenomena' and, even when figures are alike, difference is more evident than resemblance, thus annulling all sense of repetition.[100] Pousseur's *Exercises pour piano* (1956), for example, are juxtaposed within one single large composition which is like a suite of variations, except for the fact that none of the five pieces is primordial or acts as an initial theme.[101]

Pousseur imputes to Webern the insight, later taken up by the post-Webernian composers, that a principle of perpetual variation does not necessarily entail the complete absence of repetition, and that resort to alterity does not imply the unconditional rejection of identity. He instead places alterity and identity in 'a complementary relation, a relation of mutual implication'.[102] In late Webern 'a new thematicism (a *multi*-thematicism)' is found in which identity serves variation, thus allowing him 'to control the *relations* of alterity and identity (which are no longer opposed to one

---

[92] Letter dated 'beginning of May 1953' (PSS).   [93] Letter dated 9 June 1954 (PSS).
[94] Letter dated 18 November 1954 (PSS).
[95] Estimated date of letter, the end of December 1954 (PSS).   [96] Pousseur 2004, 232–3.
[97] Pousseur 2004, 73.   [98] Pousseur 2004, 53.   [99] Pousseur 2004, 106.
[100] Pousseur 2004, 232–3.   [101] Pousseur 2004, 241.   [102] Pousseur 1972, 56–7.

another) to the maximum'.[103] Pousseur makes clear that none of Webern's series can be said to have an original form, and that the series includes 'the *group* of all its metamorphoses'.[104] The written work is no longer 'identified with any of its particular actualisations',[105] and 'the real, perceptible variability of the different structures in the work' is contrasted with its '*virtual variability*'.[106]

The term 'virtuality' appears already in the text of Stravinsky's *Poetics* where, distinguishing between imagination and invention, the composer notes that 'what we imagine does not necessarily take concrete form and can remain in a virtual state'.[107] Again, the myriad possibilities confronting the composer are described as an 'abyss of freedom' and as 'the virtuality of this infinity'.[108] While it is not possible to make a definitive judgement on the source of the term as it appears in the *Poetics*, it is important to acknowledge the well-known affinity between aspects of Stravinsky's *Poetics* and Paul Valéry's *Poetics*, which may extend to the concept of virtuality.[109]

The term appears also in Schloezer, who stated in 1947 that a musical work has 'no objective reality', and that 'its text is only a "virtuality"'.[110] He writes of an 'athematic work',[111] and applies to the musical work some words from Maurice de Gandillac's *La Philosophie de Nicolas de Cues*, which form part of a discussion of God as the absolute, and as the coincidence of opposites. Transposed into a musical context, Schloezer inflects Gandillac's text to say that the realisation of a work 'always signifies for us the putting in actual form of a virtual pre-existing reality, be it even the *Nihil* of Tradition'.[112] Again, he compares the work to a plant which 'grows from a germ and, strictly speaking, it is this germ which is a virtuality, the potential thing'.[113]

Interestingly, Gandillac was the supervisor of Deleuze's doctoral thesis, which was later published as *Difference and Repetition*,[114] and while there

[103] Pousseur 1972, 73.   [104] Pousseur 1972, 100.   [105] Pousseur 1972, 102.

[106] Pousseur 2004, 243–4.   [107] Stravinsky 2000, 97–8.   [108] Stravinsky 2000, 105.

[109] It was Valéry who revived the name 'Poetics' in French intellectual culture, and he gave his own courses on Poetics at the Collège de France. Soumagnac writes of the 'reciprocal admiration' shared by Stravinsky and Valéry (Stravinsky 2000, 42–3).

[110] Schloezer 1947, 19. In an article from 1928, Schloezer attributes the view that 'a musical (or poetic) work does not exist outside of its performance, that its text is only a virtuality' to Paul Valéry Lionel Landry and others (Schloezer 1928a, 221, 223). While Mallarmé is undoubtedly a significant source for Valéry's virtuality, Suzanne Guerlac may be correct in positing that his work is pervaded by an unacknowledged 'Bergsonian subtext' (Guerlac 1997, 113).

[111] Schloezer 1947, 215.

[112] Schloezer 1947, 290–1. Schloezer's citation from Maurice de Gandillac's *La Philosophie de Nicolas de Cues* is modified slightly and is attributed wrongly to M. de Gantillon (see Gandillac 1941, 364).

[113] Schloezer 1947, 302.

[114] Deleuze was in his final year at school when he first met Gandillac in 1943. He followed his courses at the Sorbonne, and the two men were later charged with overseeing a complete edition of Nietzsche's works (Dosse 2007, 115–17, 122, 148, 160).

are no references there to his former mentor, Deleuze later commended *La Philosophie de Nicolas de Cues* as his greatest book, in that it chronicles the birth of a number of concepts which went on to play an important role in the unfolding of modern philosophy.[115] More specifically, Deleuze refers to Cusa and to his concept of *Possest* in a number of places between 1980 and 1986.[116] While it is not the principal topic of discussion in the passage which Schloezer cites,[117] Cusa's neologism, which fuses the Latin words *posse* and *est* into a single name for God, and which has been translated as 'Actualised-possibility', is far from unrelated to the Deleuzian dualism of the virtual and the actual. For Cusa, 'because what exists exists actually: the possibility-to-be exists insofar as the possibility-to-be is actual. Suppose we call this *possest* [i.e. *Actualized-possibility*].'[118]

While Gandillac discusses *Possest* in terms of what he calls virtuality, and as emerging out of the prior concept of the coincidence of opposites,[119] this Cusan virtuality cannot be identified completely with Deleuze's more closely defined usage. Indeed, the fate of the concept of the virtual in its passage through French thought in the period between Bergson and Deleuze is rather mysterious and so far mostly uncharted. Nevertheless, the provisional judgement may be made that Bergson is for the most part behind this almost proto-Deleuzian use of the term in Schloezer, Gandillac and Valéry, which, while not the object of a fully worked out philosophy, is undoubtedly consonant with both Deleuze's project and a number of aspects of Boulez's music.

It may be that Schloezer and Pousseur have been important figures for Boulez in the formulation of the concept of virtuality, which comes into its own in the Collège de France lectures. Consideration of his writings shows that the idea, if not the term, appears as early as the articles 'Proposals' (1948)[120] and 'Possibly ...' (1952), where he stresses the importance of 'variation and constant renewal', and where the universe of the work is defined as 'a network of possibilities'.[121] While the term 'virtual' is not used, the concept seems to be in place in '... Near and Far' (1954), when he writes of the work as being based upon 'a working potential', and in which

---

[115] Deleuze 2006, 262.

[116] See Deleuze's 1980 course on Spinoza (http://www.webdeleuze.com/php/texte.php?cle=20&groupe=Spinoza&langue=2); his 1985 tribute to Gandillac (Deleuze 2006, 262); a 1986 seminar on Foucault (Astier 2006, 159) and his book on Foucault from the same year (Deleuze 1988, 112, 114), albeit the cardinal is unacknowledged in the latter text.

[117] The passage appears in the context of discussion of Cusa's concept of 'Not Other' (*Non Aliud*) and the Jewish notion of creation out of nothing (*ex nihilo*). The term virtuality is also used elsewhere by Gandillac in the context of discussion of *Possest* (1941, 296–7, 301; 2001, 49).

[118] See Jasper Hopkins's translation of Cusa's *De Possest* at http://cla.umn.edu/sites/jhopkins/DePossest12-2000.pdf, 921. Accessed 6 July 2008.

[119] Gandillac 2001, 110.   [120] Boulez 1991, 54.   [121] Boulez 1991, 116–17.

the resultant composition is merely 'one manifestation' out of thousands of possible realisations of the intersecting materials.[122] The term 'virtual' is perhaps first used in 'At the Edge of Fertile Land' (1955), where the variations in instrumental possibilities are described as already existing 'in a virtual state in the sounding body'.[123] In 'Alea' (1957) he writes of a type of form which is unfixed and evolving, which he terms 'a relative formal virtuality', and he notes the impossibility of seeing in advance the 'virtualities in the material with which one starts',[124] in other words in the 'networks of probabilities' which he sets up.[125]

In conclusion

Recalling our discussion in Chapter 7 of the virtual in Bergson, and the later appropriation of the concept by Deleuze, it may be that the older man is the chief source of the concept in post-war French philosophy. It may be that Schloezer has taken the concept from Bergson, and that Boulez and Pousseur, in turn, found it in Schloezer. There are striking parallels between Pousseur's use of the term with reference to Webern, and Boulez's later Collège de France reading. While the early use of the term, by both Boulez and Pousseur, makes it difficult to attribute it exclusively to either composer, it may be that Pousseur's application of the term to Webern's work has influenced Boulez's later, much more elaborate, account. The existence of such potential links does not invalidate the connection with Deleuzian philosophy, which we have taken time to outline. Deleuze, like no one else, makes the philosophy of difference and the concept of the virtual explicit, and he articulates it philosophically. Nevertheless, in terms of Boulez's use of the term, a Deleuzian reading works only to a certain extent, and we should not expect one to map completely onto the other. Perhaps their greatest distinguishing feature is Deleuze's insistence that the virtual is not the same as the possible, a point which is, in fact, contradicted by some of Boulez's statements, in which the virtual is exactly that, the sum of all possibilities. Despite such differences, discussion of Boulezian athematicism and virtuality within a Deleuzian context still seems a valid strategy, given Bergson's mid-century influence and Deleuze's importance in French intellectual and cultural life at the time of Boulez's Collège de France lectures. Most importantly, it is genuinely enlightening, and provides a philosophical context for making sense of some aspects of the direction taken by Boulez and his fellow serial composers.

---

[122] Boulez 1991, 142, 157.   [123] Boulez 1991, 158, 178.   [124] Boulez 1991, 29.
[125] Boulez 1991, 32.

9 Expanding the virtual

The open work: virtual form

In the mid-1950s, interest in difference over identity, manifest at the level of the virtual theme from the *Sonatine* for flute and piano onwards, was extended by Boulez to musical form itself. He addressed the topical question of chance within music in his 1957 article 'Alea', opposing the total indeterminacy favoured by Cage, which entailed the throwing of dice, tossing of coins, use of radio tuners and multidirectional score-reading. For Boulez, chance is unacceptable since it excludes choice and 'completely denies the creative act',[1] and he posited instead what he called 'controlled chance'.[2] Controlled chance found expression in what became known as open form, which aimed to create a 'sort of multi-circuited labyrinth', offering, not the infinite chance possibilities preferred by Cage, but rather, multiple choices of equal weight and value for the performer, within a composed framework.[3]

While open form is most often seen as a reaction to Cage's ideas on total chance, Mallarmé's influence is also most apparent, and indeed, Boulez first makes reference to some kind of performer choice in the context of Mallarmé's 'Un coup de dés', in a letter to Cage in December 1950.[4] Significantly, the notes for Mallarmé's *Livre*, an unfinished mobile book, were published incomplete by Jacques Scherer in 1957. The *Livre* was to allow mobility at every level of the text, from that of individual words and phrases to complete pages, and would read in more than one direction. Boulez found its multiple routes, reversibility and variability to be a revelation, and he says that Scherer's sketches 'corroborated' his own ideas.[5]

For Boulez, the 'formal, visual, physical – and indeed decorative presentation' of Mallarmé's *Livre* or the poem 'Un coup de dés', suggested the possibility of finding musical equivalents.[6] He noted music's apparent backwardness in relation to literature, where neither Mallarmé's 'Un coup de dés' nor Joyce's great novels had any contemporary musical equivalent.

---

[1] Boulez 2005b, 324.   [2] Jameux 1991, 91.   [3] Boulez 2005b, 320.
[4] Boulez and Cage 2002, 154–5.
[5] Boulez 2005b, 167. In a letter to Stockhausen (dated approximately beginning of October 1957), Boulez has sent Stockhausen (presumably) Scherer's book on Mallarmé's *Livre*. He states that he has been 'absolutely stupefied and bowled over' by Mallarmé's conclusions which 'confirm exactly everything which [he] was in the process of researching in the 3rd Sonata' (PSS).
[6] Boulez 1986, 147.

He wrote of the expansive universe of Joyce's *Ulysses* and *Finnegans Wake*, and aspired to realise such a vision equally within music.[7] While Boulez, in retrospect, does not like to draw too close a comparison between his own project and the literary achievements of Mallarmé and Joyce, he nevertheless used them as 'reference points' in the search for a new musical poetics.[8]

An interest in open form at this time was common to Stockhausen, Pousseur, Berio and others. Stockhausen's *Klavierstück XI* (1956), for example, involves a certain degree of indeterminacy through its nineteen mobile structures, from which the performer chooses randomly, but with the help of fixed performing instructions.[9] This, like Boulez's Third Sonata for piano, results in a work with many possible versions. In 'Alea', Boulez described his intention as a search for 'an evolving form which rebels against its own repetition; in short, a relative formal virtuality'.[10] Such a conception of form was simply a further extension of the tendency within contemporary music in the mid-1950s towards variable concepts.[11] In the 1980s he attributed the development of the concept of open form and, more generally, the interest in chance cultivated by other composers and artists at this time, to an 'excess of determinism' within previous Western art music. Open form calls into question traditional Western notions such as closed form and the singular perfection of the completed masterpiece.[12]

Open form, as Boulez conceived it, is based instead upon multiple relationships which, in an effort to break with traditional 'unidirectional form', require the performer to make certain choices involving several possible routes through a score, comprising both fixed and a certain number of mobile elements.[13] In this way, Boulez accepts responsibility for composing out the various possibilities within an idea, but then leaves the task of choosing from among these possibilities to the performer. In the face of several musically interesting alternatives, he was reluctant to restrict himself to only one when he could retain multiple options. Consequently, he contrasts the possibility of 'a real, completed text', which sets out from 'fixed and privileged thematic givens', with that of 'a potential virtual text' which is in a constant state of renewal and of evolution.[14]

---

[7] Boulez 1986, 144.   [8] Boulez 1991, 18.

[9] In a letter to Stockhausen (dated approx 26/7 September 1957), Boulez writes of the Third Sonata for piano in terms of 'finding a structurally aleatoric form' combined with 'fixed forms' (PSS).

[10] Boulez 1991, 29. Peter O'Hagan, who considers the Third Sonata from the point of view of performer choice, concludes from the available evidence that it was composed before the article 'Alea' was written, and that 'this seems to be a characteristic of Boulez's practice: the seemingly abstract theorising is in fact a retrospective justification for a creative step which has already been taken' (O'Hagan 1997, 72).

[11] Boulez 1991, 35.   [12] Boulez 2005b, 192.   [13] Boulez 2005b, 199.   [14] Boulez 2005b, 325.

With a virtual or open form no one version or performance will be theoretically any more valid than any other, since each possible version of the work, which exercises certain options while bypassing others, becomes simply a 'virtual variation' of the virtual form.[15] Works by Boulez which include elements of open form are the 1962 version of *Don* from *Pli selon pli*, *Structures II*, *Éclat*, *Domaines* and *Rituel*, but it is most clearly used in the Third Sonata for piano whose multiple possibilities defy, at least in theory, any definitive ordering and, therefore, performative repetition. In the Third Sonata Boulez, like Mallarmé, attempted to provide an open form in which the performer has a certain degree of choice over the material which is used and the order in which it is played. To date, only two of the five formants (movements) have been completed, which enables them to be combined in a total of four ways, which will be increased to eight on completion of all five formants.

Ivanka Stoïanova has discussed the link between Boulez's Third Sonata and Mallarmé's *Livre* and mobile poetry in terms of Deleuzian difference and repetition.[16] Scherer reveals to us Mallarmé's desire for identity in the *Livre* at the global level and within each of its component parts, such as the page and volume, in order to ensure a certain architectural order.[17] Stoïanova views Mallarmé's quest for unity and identity in the light of the Deleuzian concept of difference, and she observes that the *Livre*'s 'permutational technique' generates 'multiple meanings from "the same equation"'. In Mallarmé's poetry, words cease to operate in conventional ways and function through a kind of mutual reflection, whereby each word no longer has its own colour. The continual realignment and 'reciprocal reflections of the syllables, words, lines, pages and volumes' results instead in the creation of a 'universe of multiple meanings'. Difference is thus charged with making the 'multidirectional' Mallarméan text operate through the plurality of meanings engendered by its 'intersecting currents of thought'.[18] Identity in the *Livre* is to be understood in the identity of the structural principles which operate within it at different levels. This constitutes a 'profound identity' within which repetition functions as a play of difference, resulting in the multidirectional possibilities which constitute the work. Stoïanova believes that Boulez's Third Sonata realises, within music, a similar 'profound identity' and play of repetition as difference.

Boulez has produced his own well-known diagrams (Figure 9.1 and Figure 9.2), which clearly illustrate the possibilities for mobility in the Third Sonata.[19] Their inclusion here plays an important part in

[15] Boulez 2005b, 407.   [16] Stoïanova 1974; 1978.   [17] Stoïanova 1974, 12–13.
[18] Stoïanova 1974, 15.   [19] Boulez 1986, 153, 150.

Table 9.1. *The eight possible orderings of the five formants in Boulez's Third Sonata*

(1)	I	II	III	IV	V
(2)	I	II	III	V	IV
(3)	V	IV	III	II	I
(4)	V	IV	III	I	II
(5)	II	I	III	IV	V
(6)	II	I	III	V	IV
(7)	IV	V	III	II	I
(8)	IV	V	III	I	II

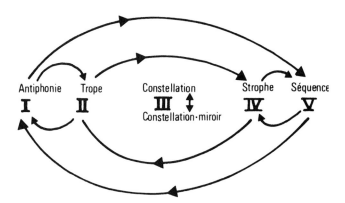

Figure 9.1. Boulez's diagram illustrating the possible ordering of formants in the Third Sonata for piano (Boulez 1986, 153)

demonstrating the practical workings of virtuality within open form. Figure 9.1 and Table 9.1 provide an overview of the entire sonata and show the eight possible ways in which the five formants may eventually be capable of being arranged.

In addition to the open nature of the global relationships linking the five formants, important aleatoric opportunities are to be found within the formants themselves. We will consider only the two formants which Boulez has so far completed. The second formant, *Trope* (Figure 9.2), is subdivided into four sections entitled *Text* (T), *Parenthesis* (P), *Commentary* (C) and *Gloss* (G). The performer can begin with any one of the four sections, which can be ordered in any one of four ways. Furthermore, the performer has to choose whether to play *Gloss* before or after *Commentary*. This results in a total of eight possible formal permutations (Table 9.2). In addition to this,

Table 9.2. *The eight possible orderings of the four sections in 'Trope'*

(1)	T	P	C	G
(2)	T	P	G	C
(3)	P	C	G	T
(4)	P	G	C	T
(5)	C	G	T	P
(6)	C	T	P	G
(7)	G	C	T	P
(8)	G	T	P	C

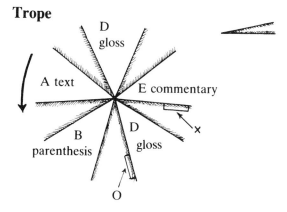

Figure 9.2. Boulez's diagram for 'Trope' (Boulez 1986, 150)

the troped material (embellishment) can be introduced into whatever form of the formant is chosen, in any of three ways which Boulez specifies.

The third formant, *Constellation (Constellation-Miroir)* always forms the structural centre of the sonata, and *Constellation-Miroir* is, in fact, the retrograde of *Constellation. Constellation* is made up of nine sizeable individual pages, which contain five basic musical structures divided into points and blocks. There are three structures of points marked out in green ink and two structures of blocks, which are distinguished from the points by their red ink. This sets up the contrast of points and blocks which is at the centre of the piece. In Jameux's words:

> The five main structures are played alternately, beginning and ending with a structure of points. They are preceded (*Constellation*) or followed (*Constellation-Miroir*) by a brief sixth structure called *mélange*, comprising three sequences of points and three of blocks (with colours reversed): . . .

Example 9.1. Pierre Boulez, Third Sonata for piano, formant 3 – *miroir*, extract

pierre boulez – troisième sonate pour piano – formant 3 – miroir

Within these five main structures the performer can to a certain extent choose his route, or at least, the means of linking the various fragmentary structures available within the large blocks or points.[20]

Example 9.1 and Figure 9.3 feature a section from Boulez's *Constellation-Miroir* and a page of Mallarmé's 'Un coup de dés', which cannot fail to make

[20] Jameux 1991, 307.

C'ÉTAIT   LE NOMBRE
issu stellaire

EXISTÂT-IL
autrement qu'hallucination éparse d'agonie

COMMENÇÂT-IL ET CESSÂT-IL
sourdant que nié et clos quand apparu
enfin
par quelque profusion répandue en rareté
SE CHIFFRÂT-IL

évidence de la somme pour peu qu'une
ILLUMINÂT-IL

CE SERAIT

pire
        non
            davantage ni moins
                    indifféremment mais autant   LE HASARD

Choit
        la plume
                rythmique suspens du sinistre
                                        s'ensevelir
                                aux écumes originelles
                naguères d'où sursauta son délire jusqu'à une cime
                                flétrie
                        par la neutralité identique du gouffre

Figure 9.3. Stéphane Mallarmé, 'Un coup de dés', extract

clear the aesthetic connection linking the two works. The typographical lay-
out itself reveals something of the openness of the texts and the possibilities
for multiple routes which they permit.

If difference or variation is employed at the level of form in *Constellation-
Miroir*, through its optional successions of events, in the second version of
Don (1960–2), the opening piece in *Pli selon pli*, aleatoricism features in
three main ways. First of all, for much of the score the orchestra is divided
into discrete ensembles with their own blocks of material, which may relate
to one another conjunctly or disjunctively and which can overlap in either
succession or superposition.[21] Secondly, at two points in the piece, the
singer has to make certain choices from a variety of options, where some
statements can be selected and others omitted.[22] Finally, from page 28 to the
end of the score, the orchestra is divided into two groups, which alternate in

[21] Bradshaw 1986, 197.   [22] Universal Edition No. 13614, fig. 33; fig. 37.

accordance with any one of six possible sequences from which the conductor can choose.

Boulez produces indeterminacy in an entirely different fashion in *Éclat* (1965) through the sixteen inserts within the piece, which include a variety of options for both conductor and performers. Apart from the variable unfolding of these inserts, the overall form of the piece is entirely fixed, with indeterminacy restricted to the local level of the individual insert. Example 9.2 features the inserts at fig. 5 and fig. 6. In some inserts (fig. 3; fig. 20) the conductor gives a sign to all of the performers to begin with one of a series of figures and to complete the cycle. These signs are to be given at irregular intervals. At fig. 5 (II) the conductor is instructed to give five signs rapidly and unequally to five instrumentalists who have one note each to play. In some inserts like fig. 5 (III) and fig. 13, the conductor can choose between possible sets of instructions. In terms of performer choice, at fig. 6 (+1) performers choose to begin with one of the figures and to complete the cycle from that point, while in the insert at fig. 16 the solo pianist can choose to play the eight short sections in whatever order is preferred. At fig. 18 (III) and fig. 19 (II) the performers choose the order in which each instrument is to sound, while the insert at fig. 20 (+1) is to be performed irregularly but allows no other options. While the overall form of *Éclat* is always the same, there are several possible variants for the unfolding of each insert.

In *Domaines* (1961–8) for clarinet solo or, alternatively, clarinet solo and six instrumental groups, the mobile form of the piece is represented in the loose-leaf format of the six *Original* cahiers and the six *Miroir* cahiers. When the piece is played in its solo format, the clarinettist is free to play the six *Original* cahiers in whatever order she/he chooses, after which the six *Miroir* cahiers are played. In the ensemble version, the clarinettist again plays the six *Original* cahiers in whatever order is preferred, but this time, at the end of the six *Originals,* the conductor chooses one of the cahiers to be played *ad lib* by the ensemble, after which the soloist plays the appropriate *Miroir* cahier. The other *Miroir* cahiers unfold likewise in this fashion. In addition to this primary formal level of aleatoricism, the clarinet soloist also has options within the unfolding of the cahiers. Each cahier is made up of six independent musical fragments which can be performed in one of two ways, either from left to right or from top to bottom. If the performer chooses to play an *Original* cahier from top to bottom, then its *Miroir* must be played from left to right, and vice versa. A third level of aleatoricism permits the performer to choose, in many places, from alternative dynamic and performance directions in which, for example in cahier A (Example 9.3), one fragment can be performed with harmonics or normally, while another can be played with flutter-tonguing or trills.

Example 9.2. Pierre Boulez, *Éclat*, figs. 5–7

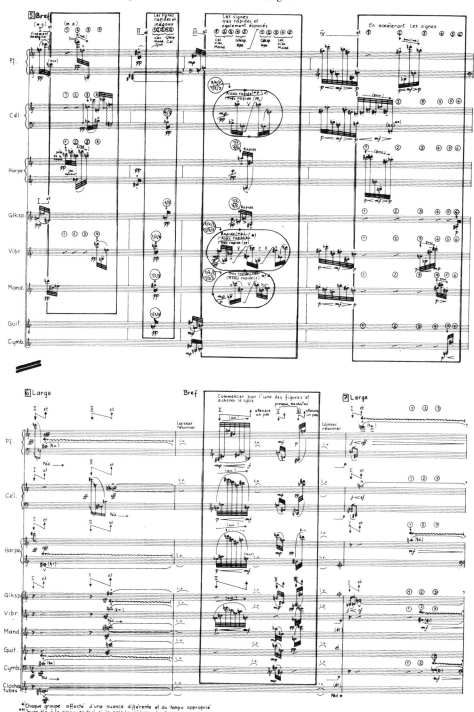

*)Chaque groupe affecté d'une nuance différente et du tempo approprié
**)Jouer ♮la à la place de ♮sol si le celesta n'a que 4 octaves

Example 9.3. Pierre Boulez, *Domaines* for solo clarinet, Cahier A

Domaines
pour clarinette avec ou sans orchestre
(1968/1969)

Pierre Boulez
(*1925)

<u>C A H I E R   A</u>

Original

As we have seen, open form enabled Boulez to envisage a composition with no definitive unfolding, but rather with virtual form. One of the problems posed by the existence of such virtual forms has been the difficulty of appreciating the real elements of formal difference within them, since only one realisation can be achieved at a time. Boulez rejects as superficial the possibility of repeating an open-form work in more than one version in the same concert. Nor is he impressed with the idea of playing certain mobile elements several times in order to display the differences between sequences in successive versions.[23] In time, he turned away altogether from the concept of the open-form work, convinced that it is problematically based upon two contradictory principles. From one point of view, the multiple choice of the open-form work is supposed to present the performer with a free choice from a variety of component possibilities of equal value. In practice, however, the performer must decide whether to leave her/his choice to the spontaneous moment of a performance or to prepare certain 'spontaneous' choices in advance. For Boulez, the first option allows the performer to make purely superficial choices, mostly from among secondary elements in the score, whilst the second option creates a curious paradox. If the performer has previously studied the score, then choice can hardly be free and spontaneous.[24] Boulez acknowledges that the material within open-form works, such as his Third Sonata, is often extremely complex and too difficult for almost any human performer to approach without prior study. Nevertheless, once the piece has been explored by a performer, it is impossible for that person to be sufficiently free from this knowledge to enable the expected freedom of choice within a performance. Despite this discrepancy, Boulez maintains that this necessary process of prior reflection leading to prepared routes between sound objects does not, in fact, weaken the concept of open form. Looking back in 1985, he said that 'spontaneity was an illusion' contrary to the complex character of the text. Instead of spontaneity of chosen route within the piece, he now suggests that personal study will lead to a better performance, which will highlight 'privileged senses' and 'stronger relations' from within the 'multiple possibilities'. Nevertheless, he acknowledges the inevitable result of study, that a few privileged pathways become established since some routes are perceived to be 'more satisfactory' than others.[25]

In time, open form came to be abandoned at the primary formal level and was reduced to the provision of more modest choices for performers concerning only 'minor categories'.[26] This decisive move away from aleatoricism, involving moment to moment performer choice, is clearly seen in the revised versions of *Improvisation III sur Mallarmé* (1983),[27] *Don* (1989),[28] and in the 1986 score of *cummings ist der dichter*, where Boulez removes choice altogether. This does not, however, mark the end of his interest in multiple outcomes. In the 1980s, he transferred the main thrust of his aleatoric interest from the momentary choice of the human performer to the newly possible, instantaneous decision-making powers of computer

---

[23] Boulez 2005b, 196–7.   [24] Boulez 2005b, 320–1.   [25] Boulez 2005b, 195–6.
[26] Boulez 2005b, 321.   [27] Boulez revised the work again in 1989 (Griffiths 2002, 7).
[28] Some aleatoric elements in *Don* were too complex for performers to follow accurately (Boulez 2003, 102).

technology, which could now respond to the human performer in the real-time of a performance.

Discussing the electronic aspects of *Répons*, he described the possibilities inherent within the real-time interaction of musicians and technology as producing compositional 'processes not completed works'. Works like *Répons* can never be complete in the form of a notated score since they require the agency of 'the machine at the moment of the performance' for their completion. In other words, the electronic part of *Répons* is, at one level, a continuation of the open-work aesthetic.[29]

Boulez has further described something of the machinic aleatoricism within ... *explosante-fixe* ... and *Anthèmes II* for violin and electronics. He speaks of the machine as having many possibilities, and of the contrasting relationship which he sets up between the 'aleatoric functions' programmed within the machine and the 'very precise functions' which the performer has. He describes how, in *Anthèmes II*, aleatoricism is inscribed within an exact field of possibilities, in which a given range of durations can occur with particular frequencies, thus enabling what he calls changes in the 'profile'. Similarly, at the beginning of *Transitoire VII* from ... *explosante-fixe* ..., the electronic rhythmic element within the accompaniment is completely aleatoric, while the notated score which the performers interpret is absolutely fixed. The key point, for Boulez, consists in the fact that the aleatoric, electronic field of options coincides with the instrumental field.[30] All this would seem to suggest that aleatoricism has become much more subtle in his music since, with the advent of the computer, he has managed to bypass the aporia of performer choice, consequently removing aleatoricism from the level of the notated score.

In addition to this new computer-generated aleatoric twist, Boulez has also expressed the view that even if open form was not ultimately successful in its original aims, it undoubtedly left its mark on subsequent music in other ways.[31] Each of the three so far completed movements of ... *explosante-fixe* ..., for example, can be played either together in the preferred order of VII–V–I or separately in a way which, at least for Boulez, seems analogous to the mobile aspects of Mallarmé's *Livre*.[32]

Another example of this relative mobility is the spiral form which Boulez associates with those of his works which, although incomplete, are suitable for performance. Spiral form allows a work to be performed at a particular stage of its development, while remaining open-ended and forever

[29] Boulez and Griffiths: BBC Radio Interview. Broadcast on 10 September 1982.
[30] Interview with the composer, 28 August 1998.   [31] Boulez 2005b, 324.
[32] Boulez and Benjamin: BBC Radio Interview, 21 February 1997.

susceptible to further development at another level of the spiral.[33] For Boulez, the idea of the spiral suggests images of 'perpetual evolution' and an expanding universe reflecting 'the complexity and infinity of relations within the system and the idea'.[34] *Répons* is an example of a spiral form which repeatedly returns to and enriches the same ideas, in a way which suggests to him the spiral architecture of the Guggenheim Museum in New York City. Employing such a notion of form enabled Boulez to perform *Répons* at various incomplete stages of its development. Going one stage further, it is possible to view Boulez's many works in progress as encompassing this same principle of openness, only at a higher level, and his entire output could be said to be open-ended and as one continuous variation. He acknowledged this aspect of his work to Deliège when he said that all of his works were 'basically different facets of one central work, of one central concept'.[35]

One of the most striking elements in Boulez's use of aleatoricism is the absence of repetition of procedure, and the great variety of means by which it is realised within each piece. *Constellation-Miroir* from the Third Sonata for piano, with its blocks, points and variable routes; the 1967 version of *Don* with its aleatoric instrumental blocks, vocal inserts and optional closing sequences for the independent instrumental blocks; *Éclat* with its inserts featuring various aleatoric devices; *Domaines* with the optional ordering of the six *Original* cahiers and six *Miroirs*, the optional performance of the six musical fragments of each cahier from left to right or top to bottom, plus the other secondary options such as dynamics. Finally, the aleatoric elements in works such as *Répons*, where the electronic modification of the soloist's music results in something different every time; the score-shadowing of ... *explosante-fixe* ... and *Anthèmes II*, where particular rhythmic options are no longer written in the score for the performer, but are instead encoded within the machine and come as a surprise to the performer as well as to the audience.

Difference as 'accumulative development'

While Boulez's interest in the possibilities of the open-form work has clearly cooled in recent years, elements of mobility continue to feature in his

---

[33] Samuel 1986, 107–8, 112. Stockhausen had composed *Spiral* for a soloist with short-wave receiver in 1968. Among the work's notational innovations is a 'spiral sign', which has the instruction 'Repeat the previous event several times, each time transposing it in all dimensions, transcending the previous limits of your skill and the known capabilities of your instrument/voice' (cited in Maconie 1976, 264). Decarsin, in the context of a discussion of Stockhausen's music, traces the notion of the spiral to Varèse (Decarsin 1998, 32).
[34] Boulez 2005b, 418–20.   [35] Boulez 1976, 50.

music, and he has remained as committed as ever to ideas of difference and multiplicity. Nevertheless, it is apparent that many of his works from the 1970s onwards exhibit a new simplification of means and clarity of form when compared with the athematicism of the integral serial works or the formal complexity of the aleatoric works. From this time onwards, Boulez permits specific harmonic areas to retain greater perceptibility. Bradshaw writes of *cummings ist der dichter* as marking 'the reintroduction of harmony as a quasi-thematic basis for development',[36] while ... *explosante-fixe* ... and *Rituel* clearly allow variation to assume a more perceptible focus. In general, the works of the 1970s and 1980s exhibit increased 'harmonic selectivity', as he focuses greater attention upon 'ever more clearly defined thematic objects, essentially neutral though they may still be'.[37] *Rituel*, for example, is based upon the same seven-note 'Originel' row at the heart of ... *explosante-fixe* ...,[38] and *Messagesquisse*, *Répons*, *Dérive 1*, *Incises* and *sur Incises* all have their origins in a six-note row E♭, A, C, B, E, D, based upon the name of Paul Sacher, to whom *Messagesquisse* is dedicated. Indeed, the pitch material of *Répons* is largely based upon the possibilities inherent within the five chords which sound at the opening of the piece.

At the level of form, Boulez's pieces begin to resemble Stravinsky's sectional forms, and in lectures from 1983 to 1985, he commends the originality of Stravinsky's discourse, which bases musical form on the permutation and return of recognisable sections. He notes, in particular, how Stravinsky succeeded, in *Les Noces* and the *Symphonies of Wind Instruments*, in transforming the ancient forms of the litany and the verse response couplet into an entirely new concept, in which formal development is paradoxically produced through formal return, in a thematicism which is based upon modified repetition.[39] Indeed, 'Stravinsky's conception of melodic development is based on psalmody and litany where deviation is minute in relation to the original model, but where the intervening extensions, contractions, displacement of accents ... finds its profound force in accumulation'.[40]

In his *Poetics of Music*, Stravinsky discusses his views on difference and variation in terms of similarity and contrast. He says that he prefers to aim for similarity rather than contrast, which he perceives to be a seductive but weaker option, and he justifies this predilection in the divisive effects which he believes variation to have on our attention. Drawing upon the philosophical maxim that 'the One precedes the Many', he concludes that 'variety is valid only as a means of attaining similarity'.[41]

---

[36] Bradshaw 1986, 206.   [37] Bradshaw 1986, 219–23.

[38] The *Originel* row appears in Boulez's sketch in *Tempo* 98 (1972), 22–3. The first *modéré* section of *Rituel* (section 2) features exactly the same pitches, but in a different order. See Goldman 2006, 150, 161.

[39] Boulez 2005b, 232, 276.   [40] Boulez 2005b, 235.   [41] Stravinsky 1942, 31–2.

Stravinsky's sectional forms operate through the alternation of blocks of familiar material whose varied reoccurrence constitutes the formal development.[42] Van den Toorn writes of *Les Noces* as possessing 'a form or architecture constructed with relatively heterogeneous blocks of material, which exhibit, upon successive (near) repeats, an unusual degree of distinction and insulation in instrumental, dynamic, rhythmic-metric, and referential character'.[43] On the *Symphonies of Wind Instruments*, he writes again of 'a highly incisive form of abrupt block juxtaposition' and '(near) repeats',[44] while Taruskin highlights 'its fascinating mosaic structure, in which discrete sections ("blocks") in varying but strictly coordinated tempi are juxtaposed without conventional transitions'.[45]

Perhaps thinking more of his own forms, Boulez prefers to describe Stravinsky's sectional forms as constituting 'accumulative development', thus avoiding any sense of repetition and, perhaps also, Stravinsky's identity-based aesthetic.[46] He speaks of 'a kaleidoscopic form where the alternation of accumulative thematic developments creates the form'.[47] Again, he professes his growing attraction for a formal conception which gives equal status to 'return and variation'.[48] In practical terms he invokes the musico-historical concepts of antiphony, response and sequence, which he believes can be re-employed and reinterpreted more liberally to meet present needs, since they are not inextricably bound to any historical definition or previous use, referring to 'allusion' rather than to literal return.

The kind of sectional alternation which becomes such an important feature from *Rituel* (1974–5) onwards is to some extent foreshadowed between figs. 3–14 of *Éclat*, in its alternation of inserts, trills, unisons and *rapide* passages. Each event is, however, very short-winded so that if this really is an embryonic example of accumulative development, it is on a decidedly small scale.

Perhaps the simplest form of accumulative development is the verse–response form of a piece such as *Rituel*, which is made up of fifteen sections, in which the even-numbered are verses and the odd-numbered are responses. In *Originel* from ... *explosante-fixe* ... Boulez simply alternates two kinds of music, this time a series of six poetic, improvisatory sections, each time punctuated with a cadence. *Transitoire VII* from ... *explosante-fixe* ... is clearly sectional in form, but in a much more elaborate way than the two pieces already mentioned. It has ten distinct ideas, which occur variously from one to six times in the course of the movement. Table 9.3 outlines the

---

[42] Boulez 2005b, 235–6.   [43] Van den Toorn 1983, 177.   [44] Van den Toorn 1983, 339.
[45] Taruskin 1996, 1486.   [46] Boulez 2005b, 236.
[47] Schoenberg also writes of the '"kaleidoscopic" shifting of "an initial formulation"' (Neff 1999, 75).
[48] Boulez 2005b, 318–19.

Table 9.3. *The sequence of sections in* Transitoire VII *from* ... explosante-fixe ...

Figure no	Section	A	B	C	D	E	F	G	H	I	J
1	Vif	1									
2	Très vif		1								
3	Rapide			1							
4	Très vif		2								
5	Rapide			2							
6	Modéré				1						
7	Très vif		3								
8	Même temps										
9	Même temps										
10	Rapide			3							
11	Modéré				2						
12	Lent					1					
13	Assez lent, flexible						1				
14	Assez rapide							1			
15	Rapide			4							
16	Modéré				3						
17	Lent					2					
18	Rapide			5							
19	Modéré				4						
20	Très modéré								1		
21	Très lent									1	
22	Extrêmement vif										1
23	Assez rapide							2			
24	Modéré				5						
25	Lent					3					
26	Modéré				6						
27	Même temps										
28	Lent					4					
29	Assez lent, flexible						2				
30	Assez rapide							3			
31	Lent					5					
32	Extrêmement vif										2
33	Assez lent, flexible						3				
34	Assez rapide							4			
35	Extrêmement vif										3
36	Assez lent, flexible						4				
37	Assez rapide							5			
38	Extrêmement vif										4
39	Allant										
40	Assez rapide							6			

succession of the ten sections (marked A–J) as they interlock in a kind of musical chain.

Each of the sections in *Transitoire VII* has its own distinctive character. The *Lent* sections, for example, are reminiscent of Stravinsky's *Rite of Spring*. The *Assez rapide* sections have a notated *rit*, the *Assez lent flexible* sections are more poetic and free, and the *Très vif* sections are heterophonous. As Boulez has confirmed in discussion with George Benjamin, the succession of the sections is discontinuous and does not follow any 'permutational scheme'.[49] *Transitoire V*, the only other so far completed part of ... *explosante-fixe* ..., has a similarly sectional, accumulative developmental form, and Boulez refers to both pieces as having a 'puzzle form'.[50]

Heterophony: the virtual line

The final manifestation of difference to be considered in this study is Boulez's heterophony, which consists of the production of virtual melodic lines, analogous to his virtual themes, virtual forms and accumulative developments. While the original meaning of the term heterophony is now uncertain, it is commonly used today, particularly by ethnomusicologists, to describe the 'simultaneous variation, accidental or deliberate, of what is identified as the same melody'.[51] It is fundamental to many non-European musical traditions, including the gamelan music of south-east Asia and the instrumental music for the Japanese Gagaku. In the chanting of Bornean head-hunters to instrumental accompaniment, in Tuareg love songs and in Mongolian folk singing, instrumental parts often consist of embellished versions of the vocal part,[52] and it is also produced in Scotland in the Hebridean tradition of metrical psalm singing.[53]

André Schaeffner, who was the first French musicologist to draw public attention to the existence of polyphony outside Europe, writes of heterophony in his *Origine des instruments de musique* (1936),[54] and it also features prominently in the continuum of harmonic possibilities presented by Schloezer in his *Introduction à J.-S. Bach*.[55] Both of these books, as well as their authors, were important for Boulez, and it is likely that his interest in heterophony was furthered by their influence, and perhaps even finds its origin in them.

---

[49] Boulez and Benjamin: BBC Radio Interview, 21 February 1997.   [50] Boulez 2003, 112, 119.
[51] Cooke 1980, 537; Malm 1977, 194.   [52] Malm 1977, 33, 59–60, 143.   [53] Cooke 1980, 537–8.
[54] Zemp, 1982, 275–6. Zemp shows how Schaeffner took up the topic several times in his writings and conferences (1936, 1951, 1961 and 1966).
[55] Schloezer 1947, 189, 195–6, 203, 205, 210.

In the article 'Variations sur deux mots: polyphonie, hétérophonie' (1966), Schaeffner presents a very scholarly genealogy of these terms, noting that Boulez 'enlarges' the concept into 'a heterophony of heterophonies', but also that he refers himself to the music of the Far East, in which 'of two lines which are superimposed, one is close to the replica of the other and only differs from it in purely ornamental variation'.[56] We also know from their correspondence that Boulez had read Schaeffner's article, expressing a desire to discuss it further with him.[57]

Heterophony was not something new for Boulez. He defined it as part of his creative wherewithal in *Boulez on Music Today*,[58] and spoke of the need to broaden and generalise its use. He tells us:

> Heterophony can be defined, generally speaking, as the superposition on a primary structure of a modified *aspect* of the same structure; . . . In heterophony, several aspects of a fundamental formulation coincide (examples are found above all in the music of the Far East, where a very ornate instrumental melody is heterophonous with a much more basic vocal line); its density will consist of various strata, rather as if several sheets of glass were to be superposed, each one bearing a variation of the same pattern.[59]

He provides a comprehensive classification in which a heterophony can be 'convergent or divergent', depending upon 'its degree of differentiation from the antecedent'.[60] In terms of its nature it can be ornamental or structural, in terms of existence it can be obligatory or optional, in terms of number it can be single, double, triple and so on, while in terms of dependence it can either be '*attached*, that is to say fixed to the antecedent, at an unchangeable determined point', or '*floating*, when its departure or arrival takes place at a given interval of time'. He explores the possibilities for heterophony in terms of the fixed or mobile transposition or multiplication of the antecedent, as well as the alteration of register and variation in size of register.

In the lecture 'Pensée européenne/Non européenne?' (1984),[61] Boulez states that heterophony 'is a way of affirming the identity of the group while acknowledging variants, even individual "deviances" '.[62] Such 'plurivalent expression', which has been more familiar in African and Asiatic cultures, has been less acceptable to Western civilisation, which has had difficulty accepting as logical 'that two enunciations of the same thought' could simultaneously concur and contradict one another. That Boulez should

---

[56] Schaeffner 1998, 171. He is referring to Boulez 1971a, 117–18.
[57] Boulez and Schaeffner 1998, 92–6. The relevant letters date from 1968. In a surviving draft of a letter to Souris, Schaeffner writes of African heterophony, and of heterophony and 'simultaneous variations' in Javanese gamelan music (dated 5 February 1967, PSS).
[58] Boulez 1971a, 117–29.   [59] Boulez 1971a, 117–18.   [60] Boulez 1971a, 121–2.
[61] The lecture was delivered in 1980.   [62] Boulez 2005a, 601.

choose to discuss heterophony in terms of multilinear logic, in the manner of Leibnizian incompossibility, is striking and brings to mind Deleuze's text on 'the fold' (1988), which we have already discussed. It shows the extent to which the virtual, as it manifests itself, for example in heterophony, is much more than a technical construct, and is for Boulez an idea with resonances well beyond the musical domain.

Examples of heterophony can be found in many of Boulez's compositions, including *Le Visage nuptial*, *Don* from *Pli selon pli*, *Figures – Doubles – Prismes*, *cummings ist der dichter* and *Rituel*. Nevertheless, it becomes a more prominent feature within certain compositions from the 1970s onwards, and Boulez has acknowledged the connection linking the development of his own heterophonous lines with the visual experiments, drawings and paintings of the artist Paul Klee. He recalls the powerful impression which Klee's Bauhaus lectures made upon him, as he recognised a certain 'coincidence of ideas'. In Klee, he found corroboration of his own ideas and a 'specifically visual approach', which, he believes, led him to 'extensions and consequences' which had previously escaped him.[63]

Boulez was interested in Klee's ideas on multiple perspective, his insights into the way 'an object, a scene, can be viewed from different simultaneous perspectives, and how the object, the scene, can be the *source* of these diverse perspectives'. In *Le Pays fertile* (1989), he acknowledges Klee's influence in demonstrating the proliferating, multiple possibilities which can be deduced from any given starting point, and he shares his concern that to be content with only one solution or point of view in a work of art or music is unsatisfactory.[64] Paradoxically, Klee's development of multi-perspectivism within the visual arts resulted, in part, from his envious awareness of polyphonic music and its capacity to express several linear dimensions simultaneously.[65] Klee's drawings and paintings are consequently conceived with the explicit intention of providing for the eye the multiplicity which he perceived to be available for the ear in traditional musical polyphony.[66]

For Boulez, the important principle to be learned from Klee, in terms of heterophony, is the simple notion of an original line being surrounded by a number of secondary lines, and the geometric organisation of such secondary lines relative to the original line (Figure 9.4).[67] Klee explains this possibility in the *Pedagogical Sketchbook* and in his Bauhaus lectures, where he envisages a curved line, first of all on its own, secondly, decorated by complementary lines, and thirdly, 'circumscribing itself'. In the final stage

---

[63] Boulez 2005b, 167. Peter O'Hagan notes a number of parallels linking Klee's theoretical writings and Boulez's Third Sonata (2006, 315–16).
[64] Boulez 1989, 10–11.   [65] Klee 1961, 86.   [66] Boulez 1989, 166.   [67] Boulez 1989, 53.

An **active** line on a walk, moving freely, without goal. A walk for a walk's sake. The mobility agent is a point, shifting its position forward (Fig. 1):

Fig. 1

The same line, accompanied by complementary forms (Figs. 2 and 3):

Fig. 2

Fig. 3

The same line, circumscribing itself (Fig. 4):

Fig 4

Two secondary lines, moving around an imaginary main line (Fig. 5):

Fig. 5

Figure 9.4. Paul Klee, *Pedagogical Sketchbook* (1953, 16–17)

of this reflection, he has 'two secondary lines moving around an imaginary main line',[68] and he illustrates the point humorously with the image of a walking man whose dog is also walking freely at his side.[69] Klee's own illustrations of the concept, which appear in Boulez's *Le Pays fertile*, are excellent visualisations, and indeed anticipations, of the renewed musical principle of heterophony which Boulez spoke of in his Darmstadt lectures, and which comes into its own in works such as *Rituel*, *Répons*, and *... explosante-fixe ....*

Klee's multiple, ornamented lines suggest to Boulez 'the faithful transcription of a melodic line', and that 'a melodic line is the equivalent of a drawn line'.[70] As before, in the case of Mallarmé, Boulez is solicitous that any parallel between the visual or literary arts and music should not be interpreted in a simplistic way. Nevertheless, the parallel between Klee's drawings and musical heterophony is striking. For Boulez, a heterophony is 'the aura of a melodic line', 'curls' which are traced freely around a 'principal line', thus providing a number of varied perspectives.[71] With heterophony, the 'fundamental structure' of the line is retained,[72] and the other lines are generated from the original line, whose succession is key for the appreciation of similarities. The 'different horizontal elements' are 'only variations of a primordial horizontal element', and by virtue of 'a principle of identity, of identification', each component pertains 'to the same model'.[73]

Linda Doeser, describing how Klee uses 'secondary lines to enhance, complement and counterbalance a primary line', highlights what would seem, from the point of view of the present study, to be the essential issue when she writes that Klee's primary line 'was not, in fact, drawn and existed as only a concept'.[74] In other words, if Klee has a primary line, it does not appear in the frame of the picture since it is a virtual line. This does not deny the fact that the artist must draw one line before he draws the others; it is to say, rather, that once the initial line is joined with its variants, priority is no longer the issue. Likewise, Boulez's heterophonies, in which simultaneous manifestations of a melodic line appear in superposition, are equally different manifestations of a virtual melodic line. This virtual line cannot be simplistically reduced to any one favoured version of the line, and will certainly not be found in the score, since all the drawn melodic lines are particular manifestations of the virtual line.

Susan Bradshaw has drawn attention to an anticipation of Boulezian heterophony in an early version of *Le Visage nuptial* (1946–89), where two

---

[68]   Klee 1953, 16–17; 1961, 105–7.   [69]   Boulez 1989, 55.   [70]   Boulez 1989, 52.
[71]   Boulez 2005b, 401.   [72]   Boulez 2005b, 582–4.   [73]   Boulez 2005b, 586.
[74]   Doeser 1995, 44.

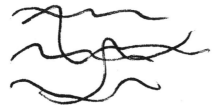

Figure 9.5. Sketch for *Don* (Paul Sacher Stiftung: microfilm 137, p. 58, extract)

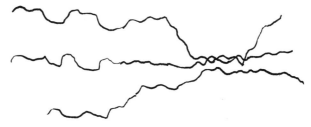

Figure 9.6. Sketch for *cummings ist der dichter* (Paul Sacher Stiftung: microfilm 136, p. 603, extract)

quarter-tone scales are used canonically in such a way that they produce a single musical line accompanied by another distorted version of itself. According to Bradshaw, it was this experiment in 'setting a melodic line on a polyphonic tracing of its outline', which later suggested to Boulez the renewed concept of heterophony as 'simultaneous variation'.[75] Sketches for *Don* from *Pli selon pli* (Figure 9.5) and *cummings ist der dichter* (Figure 9.6), feature two drawings which suggest heterophonies, and which are very similar to Klee's 'man walking the dog' sketch. Boulez's sketch for *Don* has five lines instead of Klee's three, while the sketch for *cummings ist der dichter* images the passage from disjunct intervals to conjunct intervals and back again.

In a preface to the score, Boulez describes *Rituel* as 'recurrent patterns, changing in profile and perspective'.[76] The *Modéré* sections of the piece (sections IV, VI, VIII, X, XII, and XIV) are noticeably freer than the *Très lent* sections and produce what Stoïanova refers to as 'linear multiplicity'.[77] Although the music for each of the eight instrumental ensembles is notated homophonically, the aleatoric entries of each ensemble, defined by the

---

[75] Bradshaw 1986, 150–1. Boulez has spoken of 'acoustical derivative lines, which are distorted projections of a principal melodic line' in both *Le Visage nuptial* and *Notations* (Boulez 2003, 121).

[76] *Rituel in Memoriam Bruno Maderna* für Orchester in acht Gruppen (1974–5). UE 15941.

[77] Stoïanova 1976, 21–4.

conductor, disrupts the homophony and creates a sense of heterophonic ensembles playing around one another. Conductor choice alters the phasing of the ensembles from performance to performance, and results in unpredictable consequences, as they meet vertically in ever new ways.

Dal Molin, who has explored the construction of heterophony in the Verset or *Modéré* sections of *Rituel*, shows that the piece demonstrates several of the different types of heterophony which Boulez had enumerated in the Darmstadt lectures, and which were listed above. He identifies them as structural in nature, obligatory in terms of existence, and variably as double in section IV, triple in section VI, simple in section VIII, as well as floating.[78] He shows that Boulez has generated his homophony from a number of 'originary monodies'. In section VI, for example, the originary monodic lines, played by each instrumental group, are thickened with parallel lines, which are variably transposed versions of the original lines at the intervals of the major second, the tritone and the fourth.[79] In section VIII, which is for oboe and two clarinets, the 'structure première', that is the original monody, is given to the second clarinet, and this line is then thickened, by the addition of another variably transposed clarinet line, as in section VI. The oboe presents a rhythmic variation of the clarinet line in that the durations of the held notes, as well as the number of notes in each anacrusis, are modified.[80]

In *Répons*, the section between figs. 55 and 70 is composed largely of the alternation of reiterated pitches and cascading streams of demisemiquavers played as a very fast *perpetuum mobile*. This creates an extremely exciting roller-coaster-like effect. The individual shapes of the tumbling figures are constantly varied as is their length in terms of number of notes. As a result, homophony is avoided, a smoother time is created, and a type of heterophony composed of variously conjunct, disjunct and intersecting scalar lines is produced.

Boulez's most impressive and sustained use of heterophony is perhaps to be found in the 1991–3 version of *... explosante-fixe ...*, where it is present in all three completed movements.[81] In these finally accomplished sections, a solo midi-flute is 'heterophonically shadowed by two subsidiary flutes' to create heterophony of real complexity.[82] Bradshaw writes of 'the heterophonic orchestral counterpoints' which 'generate a comparable vertical density that of itself conveys a textural frenzy sufficient to need no

[78] Dal Molin 2006, 249.   [79] Dal Molin 2006, 224.
[80] Dal Molin 2004, 30; Goldman 2006, 165.
[81] The principal flute part in *... explosante-fixe ...* was completed first and everything else was then organised around it (Boulez 1976, 106).
[82] Bradshaw 1996, 11–12.

elaboration', and she describes 'the shifting heterophonic alignment between groups of instruments' which 'begins more and more to occupy the musical foreground' as the flute part (of the 1973 chamber music version) 'has in turn become the matrix for a vast network of heterophonic possibilities'. In *Transitoire VII*, which Boulez tells us is the most difficult piece of the set, while the heterophony is pervasive, each musical section is clearly differentiated from the others in character.

Deleuzian difference and Adornian non-identity

While Boulezian athematicism, the virtual theme, virtual form, accumulative development and heterophony have been discussed in Chapters 8 and 9, primarily in the context of Deleuzian virtuality, it is important to note that Adorno also has much to say on the question of variation, repetition, sameness and difference. He writes, however, within the polar framework of Hegelian identity and non-identity thinking.[83] While the identity of thematic material is clearly established in music after Beethoven, its meaning is revealed as non-identity, in that 'holding it fast means at the same time transforming it'. It has no definitive existence in itself but only with regard to 'the possibility of the whole'.[84] While atonal works are without themes,[85] in twelve-tone composition the thematic work is part of the pre-compositional labour, and variation is so ubiquitous as to be practically imperceptible, in that 'everything and nothing is variation'.[86]

Conceptualising Schoenberg's development from his Second String Quartet onwards as an oscillation 'between the extremes of the totally thematic and the athematic',[87] Adorno judges that the principles of similarity and contrast, as well as their interconnection, 'are too abstract to create meaning on their own'.[88] In order to produce difference, an element of similarity must be retained in the form of 'shared, distinguishing characteristics'.[89] Paradoxically, non-identity can only be achieved in relation to moments of identity, without which there would be the monotonous chaos of the 'ever-same'. In an athematic, twelve-tone or serial context, he acknowledges that the inclusion of something as simple as the vaguely similar recurrence of tone colour can be sufficient to provide this necessary moment of similarity.[90] However, even 'the slightest remnant of nonidentity' will prevent the establishment of total identity.[91] Despite Adorno's much-reiterated commitment to non-identity, for example in

---

[83] Paddison 1993, 177.   [84] Adorno 2006, 46.   [85] Adorno 2006, 49.
[86] Adorno 2006, 50.   [87] Adorno 1998, 278.   [88] Adorno 1999, 160.
[89] Adorno 1997, 141.   [90] Adorno 1997, 159.   [91] Adorno 1973, 22.

his endorsement of the fragment in the critique of 'totalising systems', Paddison finds within his work 'an allegiance to totality and organic unity which derives from German Idealist philosophy and from the emphasis on motivic-thematic integration in the tradition of Austro-German instrumental music'.[92]

Alastair Williams suggests that Boulez operates within a dialectical approach to identity and non-identity thinking,[93] favouring identity, while freeing non-identity sufficiently to allow it to play a 'local and contingent' part. For Williams, Boulez's principal mode of working is analogous to the dominant thinking of instrumental reason, a thinking which subjects musical material to the identity of systems, and *Structures Ia* is predictably cited as the most obvious manifestation of this 'all-embracing rationality'.[94] To the degree that Boulez allows freedom from system within his music he is said to feature non-identity.

In the Collège de France lectures, Boulez links analogy and difference in a 'dialectical relation',[95] and variation form is spoken of as a play on 'the *identity* of the theme'.[96] No matter how the theme is varied 'the immediate reference is always linked to *identity*, to the fundamental structure, to the formal distribution. The entire play is based upon *identity* and the *identification* of a unique musical being which has been isolated from the start as a given.' Similarly, with difference, there must be sufficiently repetitive elements to enable perception and memory to recognise the idea in its different manifestations.[97]

At the level of the score, Boulez produces manifestations of difference in various ways, which have already been discussed. Identity, nevertheless, is indisputably present at one level of his activity, namely that of precomposition. It is here that he begins, with the identity of the basic series. Such is his practice, however, that after the early works, where the series is at times used in an outright thematic way, it is no longer employed as a surface phenomenon, but, rather, retreats beneath the surface of the score to the level of pre-composition. It becomes instead the generating force from which he creates virtual objects, and no longer relates through identity to the material which has been abstracted from it. The basic series or pitch collection has become a source of qualities, which Boulez abstracts from it and combines in multifarious ways, but not in any one privileged configuration.

That Boulez is concerned with identity in the context of athematicism and variation is understandable. The path from the *Sonatine* for flute and piano

---

[92] Paddison 1993, 264.   [93] Williams 1994, 199–200.   [94] Williams 1997, 47–8.
[95] Boulez 2005b, 239.   [96] Boulez 2005b, 245.   [97] Boulez 2005b, 400.

to *Structures I* had resulted in musical ideas which were at times no longer sufficiently differentiated or readily perceptible and the restoration of perceptibility, through the recurrence of the familiar, assumed capital importance. I interpret identity to mean, for Boulez, from the time of the first book of *Structures* onwards, the provision of material which gives the listener the opportunity for recognition, through its more obvious connection with what has gone before. While there are moments of outright repetition in some scores, this is not generally the case. What is more frequently encountered is the return of the same, which is always different, and which cannot be reduced to any originary identity in the score. Difference is not sacrificed to identity, since something is created which, within the context of the piece, is familiar yet always different.

Boulez's reintroduction of recognisable objects, subsequent to *Structures Ia*, is not based upon the postulate of originary identities, but rather is centred upon multiple valid manifestations of virtual themes, sections and lines. It may be that Boulez's project can be theorised in terms of either Adornian identity/non-identity or Deleuzian difference/repetition, and he uses both dialectical language and Deleuzian references in describing the development of thematicism and athematicism. Andrew Bowie notes how discussion of identity thinking is often reduced to the stark alternative of either Hegel or Nietzsche, to 'the *Aufhebung* of difference at the end of the dialectic' or one 'that refuses to resolve difference into identity'.[98] Žižek, for whom Deleuze's *Difference and Repetition* and *The Logic of Sense* are more akin to Hegel than are the Deleuzo-Guattarian writings,[99] contests Deleuze's rejection of Hegel, suggesting that the Hegelian Absolute may be translated into Deleuzian terms as 'the virtuality of the eternal process of its own actualisation'.[100] It is in this spirit that the present study leaves the theoretical question of Boulezian difference, in the conviction that the seemingly divergent impulses in the composer's work reflect two cultural movements, one French, one German, which were present within the wider philosophical culture and which are also made sonorous in his music.

---

[98] Bowie 1993, 67–8.   [99] Žižek 2004, p. xi, 20.   [100] Žižek 2004, 52, 58.

10   Continuity and discontinuity of space and time

In the previous chapters of this study, a number of binary oppositions have been identified in relation to dialectical, structuralist and post-structuralist currents of thought. While it would be desirable to consider the practical working out of a range of oppositions in Boulez's compositions, the present chapter restricts itself to just two oppositions of special importance for the composer, in both theoretical and compositional terms. Both are aspects of the global dialectic of continuity and discontinuity, which seems to have first concerned him around 1954. In a letter from that year, he informed Stockhausen of his desire to write an article on the relationship between musician and 'sound "continuum"', and of the seeming obligation upon composers 'to create a discontinuous space' for all of the sound components.[1] In line with this, and in contrast with Stockhausen's notion of some kind of 'unity within homogeneous time', he posits the possibility of '*non-homogeneous* developmental time', suggesting along the way, in the manner of the surrealists, that music needs to pulverise unitary time.

This interest in continuity and discontinuity found more formal expression in the article 'At the Edge of Fertile Land' (1955) and, in a further letter to Stockhausen, Boulez defined its 'true subject' as the continua pertaining to all of the domains, noting, in particular, problems relating to structure, tempo and the space continuum.[2] In the Darmstadt lectures he fleshed out these notions in relation to all of the musical parameters, forging, in the process, the opposition of smooth and striated space as well as that of smooth and striated time. These are concepts which have retained a pivotal place in his vocabulary, and which demonstrate the ongoing significance of the dialectic of the continuous and the discontinuous in his theoretical thinking and compositional practice.[3]

Defining musical space

Before looking to the place of musical spatiality in Boulez's work, it is perhaps necessary to clarify the meaning of this rather ambiguous term,

---

[1]   Date of letter estimated by Robert Piencikowski as the end of December 1954 (PSS).
[2]   Date of letter estimated by Robert Piencikowski as mid-January 1955 (PSS).
[3]   See for example Boulez 2005b, 696.

and to provide a context for its use. In the 1930s, the German music critic Albert Welleck spoke of the confused state of thinking on musical spatiality,[4] while in the mid-1990s, Emmanuel Nunes still felt the need to remark upon the imprecise use of terms such as musical, registral and acoustic space.[5] To be clear, Boulez's music exhibits spatiality in two discrete senses, which we can characterise as (1) interior spatiality (the pitch space continuum), and (2) exterior spatiality (the arena in which a musical performance occurs). The present study restricts itself to that aspect of Boulez's notion of interior pitch space which conceives of it as some kind of continuous or discontinuous spectrum of sounds.

The concept of musical space, in the sense of pitch space, is a fundamental one for many writers, albeit understood in a number of ways. To take only some representative examples; while Ernst Kurth conceives its organisation as analogous to that of lived space,[6] Zuckerkandl and Scruton explain it as a metaphorical phenomenon, which is unique to aural perception,[7] and the latter posits that it constitutes 'a continuum, but not . . . a dimension'.[8]

From a spatial perspective, tonal music can be thought of as tracing paths through pitch space by means of the system of keys and their modulation to distinct but related regions. Analogous with this, dodecaphonic music, as theorised and practised by Schoenberg, Webern and Berg, traces alternative paths through pitch space, by means of the twelve-tone series with its twelve transposed forms, retrogrades, inversions and inverted retrogrades. These can be manipulated whole or 'ultrathematically' (Boulez's term), as in Schoenberg, or motivically, as in Webern, whose series exploit particular intervallic characteristics in order to enable the generation of entire pieces.

Regina Busch, who has explored the place of interior spatiality in the writings of the Second Viennese composers, acknowledges it as one of a number of terms which are used innovatively in their work. While Schoenberg, Webern, Berg, Spinner, Stein and Rufer all make mention of pitch space, it is never defined clearly, and Busch suggests that it would be problematic to presume that Schoenberg always used the term in the same way.[9] In the 1934 version of the essay 'Composition with Twelve Tones', for example, he writes of 'the law concerning the unity of musical space', and in the 1941/50

---

[4] Bayer 1981, 9–10. In *La Musique et l'Ineffable* (1961), Vladimir Jankélévitch attacked the 'dubious metaphors' produced by 'the spatial mirage' (Solomos 1998, 215).
[5] Nunes 1994, 122.   [6] Scruton 1997, 51.
[7] Zuckerkandl 1956, 85–6. For Scruton, the concept of pitch space is a musical metaphor which 'exactly parallels the physical order' (1997, 21, 75). For Natalie Depraz, who compares the two masters of phenomenology, Husserl's concept of sound space is analogical, while Merleau-Ponty's is 'more metaphorical and literary' (Depraz 1998, 10–11).
[8] Scruton 1997, 14–15, 20–1.   [9] Busch 1985, 4–6.

version, he distinguishes the properties of this musical space from those of the physical world.[10] Schoenberg's notion of a unified musical space was important also for Webern who, in turn, developed his own metaphorical spatial understanding, which he discusses in his lectures.

The centrality of the concept of pitch space within Boulez's musical poetic stems in part from his study of Webern, and he drew attention in the early 1950s to a new spatial dimension in his aesthetic, which transcends the traditional axes of the harmonic (vertical) and the monodic (horizontal).[11] Webern's idiosyncratic manipulation of the series is identified as a means 'of giving structure – or, so to speak, *texture* – to musical space'.[12] By 1958, this new dimension has come to be identified as a 'diagonal', as 'a kind of distribution of points, blocks, or figures' within the sound space,[13] which is also now perhaps the most important element in Boulez's early conception of pitch space, as he focuses upon the distinctive intervallic qualities of series.[14] The freer and more deliberate control of pitch space, together with the new compositional resources which he began to employ in *Le Marteau sans maître*, is revealed later in the Darmstadt lectures, in which he can only envisage the musical 'sound-space continuum' in terms of 'limited fields', which are defined as the series is formed.[15] He creates privileged regions of sound space, where several series may share one or more figures with an original series, from which they derive.[16] Alternatively, he is able to deduce 'partial structures' from them, for example creating limited series, which use only some parts, while defective series apply 'a mechanical procedure' to the series, perhaps 'changing the module or "filtering" the frequencies'.[17] In general, such procedures enabled him to avoid continuous use of the 'chosen sound-spectrum' in its entirety.

Smooth and striated space

It seems that Wyschnegradsky is responsible for the introduction of the concepts of musical space, of simultaneity, and the notion of a continuum of sounds, into the musical sphere, certainly in a French context.[18] In the article 'Musique et pansonorité' (1927), an early formulation of his views,

---

[10] Busch 1985, 8.   [11] Boulez 1991, 8.   [12] Boulez 1991, 114.
[13] Boulez 1991, 297.   [14] Boulez 1971a, 27–8, 119.   [15] Boulez 1971a, 41.
[16] Boulez 1971a, 45.   [17] Boulez 1971a, 80–1.
[18] Criton 1996, 18–20. The problem of the continuous and the discontinuous is found in a number of writers from the German romantics (Novalis to Schelling) to Nietzsche, Bergson and Deleuze, as well as in Russian philosophical and mystical thought (Criton 1996, 52; Wyschnegradsky 2005, 62). Pearson, following Deleuze, identifies Bergson's use of the distinction of the discrete and the continuous in *Time and Free Will* as a reworking of this opposition, which the mathematician G. B. Riemann had first used in his *Habilitationsschrift* in 1854 (Deleuze 1991, 39–40; Pearson 2002, 15–16).

he declares that 'the principal problem in music' is '*the antithesis of the continuous and the discontinuous*, an antithesis which is manifested nowhere (except perhaps in higher mathematics) with greater clarity and relief than in musical art'.[19] More specifically, it is interesting to view the taxonomy of pitch spaces, which Boulez set out in his Darmstadt lectures, in the light of the codification of spatial types produced earlier by Wyschnegradsky. In the 1953 version of his study of pansonority, the Russian composer distinguishes between total and partial spaces, where partial space is further divided into regular (or uniform) spaces and irregular spaces, and where this last category also includes semi-regular spaces. There are also periodic and composed spaces,[20] and he defines the three essential properties of musical space as 'uniformity, infinity and continuity'.[21] While, unlike Boulez, he does not propose a curved space, he nevertheless posits the existence of a certain curved quality in pitch space, where the intervals of the seventh or the ninth are used.[22] In the earlier 1936 version of his study, continua can be 'disjunct, conjunct and intertwined'.[23] Finally, Wyschnegradsky thinks also of the rhythmic dimension in terms of the continuous and the discontinuous,[24] and the final version of his thesis includes two substantial chapters on musical space and musical time.

Wyschnegradsky is Boulez's most explicit predecessor in presenting a morphology of musical spaces, and there was no shortage of avenues whereby he would have become familiar with the older man's ideas. A number of his writings were available in periodicals such as *La Revue Musicale, La Revue d'Esthétique* and Souris's *Polyphonie*. Schloezer had presented his works in Paris in 1924, and it seems that Wyschnegradsky sent him a copy of the 1936 version of his book.[25] More directly, Boulez performed as one of four pianists in concerts of his works in 1945 and 1951, remarking in a letter to Cage that the music was 'very bad' and that the sounds were 'heavy'.[26]

It is interesting to note in passing that Deleuze was also aware of Wyschnegradsky's work through the auspices of Pascale Criton, who became involved with the philosopher's seminar quite by chance in 1975. While Deleuze drew on her musical knowledge for his seminar,[27] Criton also met and studied with Wyschnegradsky from 1976. In the early 1990s, Deleuze read several

---

[19] Wyschnegradsky 1927, 144.   [20] Wyschnegradsky 1996, 159, 189.
[21] Wyschnegradsky 1996, 118.   [22] Wyschnegradsky 1996, 172.
[23] Wyschnegradsky 2005, 146.   [24] Wyschnegradsky 1996, 212.   [25] Criton 1996, 45.
[26] Letter received 'after 28 November 1959' (Boulez and Cage 2002, 199). The concerts took place on 11 November 1945 and 28 November 1951 (Piencikowski 2002, 329). Boulez played in a performance of Wyschnegradsky's *Second Symphonic Fragment*, Op. 24 in the 1951 concert (http://eamusic.dartmouth.edu/~franck/iw/bio-en.htm).
[27] Dosse 2007, 526. E-mail from Pascale Criton to the author, 25 May 2008.

drafts of the essay which she later published in 1996 as her introduction to *La Loi de la pansonorité*, and which she dedicated to the philosopher.[28]

In the Darmstadt lectures, which are undoubtedly the most systematic formulation of his ideas, Boulez identifies 'the conception and realisation of a *relativity* of the various musical spaces in use' as an urgent objective.[29] He calls for the exploration of musical pitch space, and says that the musical space-continuum 'is *manifested* by the possibility of *partitioning* space according to certain laws'.[30] He acknowledges two main pitch space states, which he terms striated space and smooth space. Striated space is marked by a standard, regular measure, which creates clear perceptual landmarks for the ear to orient itself, whereas smooth space is free, irregular and dispenses with all points of reference. While Western music, including serialism, has mostly retained the traditional twelve semitonal striations of tempered space, any number of alternative ways of striating pitch space could theoretically be adopted, allowing for the limitations of human perception, and the restrictions imposed by the state of conventional instruments, which were designed with traditional tempered space in mind. Boulez envisages any number of possible striations being enacted upon untempered sound space, and he acknowledges the possibility that the pitch series, as he has expounded it, can be used in 'any tempered space, according to any temperament, and to any non-tempered space, according to any module, whether it be the octave or some other interval'.[31] Series could thus be formed of intervals which no longer conform to any homogeneous measure, such as the semitone, and could include any number of intervals.

The possibility of structuring music on the basis of alternative intervals and temperaments was of course not original to Boulez. In non-Western music, for example Indian music, the minute subdivision of pitch space and the notion of an unpartitioned continuum are commonly accepted, while in Western music the minute subdivision of pitch space and the possibility of a seamless continuum was taken up not only by Wyschnegradsky, but also by Ives, Carrillo, Bartók, Hába, Varèse and Partch, and stimulated their microtonal explorations. More open to the new microtonal possibilities in his early years, Boulez spoke in 1949 of Cage's desire 'to organize a world of sounds of indefinite pitch',[32] writing to the American composer the following year that he planned to implement some of his ideas, and that he intended to employ 'a grid of quarter-tones placed across the series'.[33] Later that year, he wrote of 'widening the principle to extreme conclusions',

---

[28] Dosse 2007, 525.   [29] Boulez 1971a, 83.   [30] Boulez 1971a, 85.
[31] Boulez 1971a, 83; 1991, 117–18.   [32] Boulez and Cage 1993, 28.
[33] Boulez and Cage 1993, 43.

telling Cage that he is aiming at developing quarter-tones so that 'in two or three years, they will be 1/12 and 1/24 tones... Moreover, I have also found a graphic formula to cover absolutely the whole scale of sounds with 1/4 and 1/3 tones'.[34] By 1955, however, while he acknowledges the experiments which other composers have conducted with intervals as small as a third, a quarter or a sixth of a tone, he is unimpressed by the compositional results, since 'a micro-interval can only be perceived clearly within a narrow tessitura', which restricts its wider use.[35] While Boulez used quarter-tones in the 1946 and 1951–2 versions of the *Gravité* and *Post-Scriptum* movements of *Le Visage nuptial*, they did not become a permanent part of his compositional means and were removed from the 1994 score.[36] He explains, in retrospect, that he came to recognise their approximate nature, when performed, for example, by an orchestral section of violins, particularly in the upper register.[37] Consequently, they were replaced with 'a dense polyphony of small intervals' and 'the multiplication of voices overlapping each other, but in semitones'.

In the Darmstadt lectures, having elaborated the principle of striated space, Boulez next lays out a taxonomy of possible striated spaces, such as straight spaces, where an 'unvarying module reproduces the basic frequencies over the whole range of audible sounds... *curved spaces*... which depend on a regularly or irregularly variable module... *regular spaces*... which always adopt the same temperament whatever the module', and *irregular spaces* which do the reverse.[38] While he theorises the possibility of such variably striated spaces, it is not known whether these ideas have ever been actualised in compositional terms, and it may be that they have remained within the realm of speculative theory. For the moment, the relationship between spatial theorising and compositional practice remains obscure, since it has not yet been the focus of sustained analysis. Furthermore, not enough is widely known of the details of the computer-assisted procedures employed in works such as *Répons*, *Dialogue de l'ombre double*, ... *explosante-fixe* ... and *Anthèmes II*, where it is perfectly possible that he has realised aspects of such long-theorised possibilities.

Smooth space, in contrast, 'can only be classified in a more general fashion... by the statistical distribution of the frequencies found within it'. The smaller the partitions or the micro-intervals within a striated space, the closer it will be to being conceived of as an unbroken smooth continuum. Boulez was realistic in acknowledging, at the time of writing in

---

[34] Boulez and Cage 1993, 86–7.   [35] Boulez 1991, 162.
[36] Boulez first used quarter-tones in his unpublished *Quatuor pour Ondes Martenot* (1945–6) (O'Hagan 2006, 308).
[37] Boulez 2003, 116–17.   [38] Boulez 1971a, 86–7.

the early 1960s, the practical difficulties involved in attempting to produce such smooth musical spaces, given a situation where musical theory was in advance of instrumental technology. He looked admiringly, at least in 1952, to Cage's experiments in producing non-tempered sound spaces with already existing instruments, courtesy of his prepared piano with its eccentric appendages. Likewise, Pierre Schaeffer's *musique concrète* appealed at first to him, on the basis that it would allow him to work with non-tempered sound spaces, and he went so far as to compose two short *musique concrète Études* (1951–2).[39] Beyond the studio, however, there simply were no instruments at that time capable of transferring ideas of smooth space and various types of striations (pitch divisions) from the realm of theory to that of live performance practice.

In 'At the Edge of Fertile Land' (1955), he imagined a synthesis of electronic and instrumental sources, which would enable movement from temperament to non-temperament,[40] and he looked forward to 'the construction of instruments whose temperament could be precisely varied according to prepared and ordered combinations'.[41] In the interim, however, he had to be satisfied with exploiting the distinctive qualities of percussion instruments, such as the xylophone or tubular bells, instruments that have complex sound spectra, which could at least go some of the way towards providing the expanded spatiality of sound that he desired. The distinctive sonorities of the unpitched percussion in *Le Marteau sans maître*, for example, produced an innovative sound world, which was later recreated by many other composers. Again, in *Improvisation II* from *Pli selon pli*, he deliberately contrasted 'three different kinds of sounds – fixed pitch, partially pitched, and unpitched ("noise")'.[42] While aware that smooth spaces and all kinds of non-tempered striated spaces would become more easily attainable through electro-acoustic and computer-assisted means, he did not want 'to abandon "the realm of music" to mechanical electro-acoustic media alone'.[43] Indeed, the commitment to live performance and acoustic instruments, which underpins this position, has remained with him throughout his career.

It is interesting to note that, despite such logical and consistent theorising, most of Boulez's compositions are in fact restricted to the exploration of striated space and, at that, the traditional striations of equal temperament. Bayer interprets this as signalling Boulez's preference for an aesthetic of spatial discontinuity instead of the continuity favoured by composers such as Cowell, Penderecki, Xenakis and Ligeti, who have all, at one time or

[39] Boulez 1991, 134–8.   [40] Boulez 1991, 161–4.   [41] Boulez 1971a, 89–90.
[42] Boulez 1986, 157.   [43] Boulez 1971a, 91.

another, used clusters and glissandi. For Bayer, smooth space is found in Boulez only as a limit case.[44]

Boulez wrote of the difficulties in perceiving minute intervals in 1955, accepting that composers would consequently need to settle for something less than the utopian vision of a complete sound continuum.[45] While he criticised what he considered to be the 'elementary' and caricatured nature of clusters and glissandi, as they appear within the music of the late 1950s and early 1960s, it is presumptuous of Bayer to equate distaste for such technical means and the sparing practical compositional evidence of smooth space with a preference for striated space. Boulez's comments, though fragmentary, seem to offer a more likely explanation. Having theorised the possibility of smooth spaces, he found they were at first impossible to achieve in practice except in the most limited ways. When more sophisticated instrumental means later facilitated their possible use, this did not always cohere with his strict performance ideals for the use of machines, where the machine must interact in real time with the performers. This, as well as the growing need for greater local perceptibility, perhaps explains why he does not seem to have developed smooth space as far in practice as in theory.

Despite the practical difficulties in developing striated and smooth spaces equal in sophistication to the theory, Boulez has nevertheless been able to use such pitch spaces as a means of articulating form. *Répons*, where the pitches of the solo instruments are transformed electronically, perhaps comes closest to achieving a smooth pitch space, or at least a more flexibly striated one. The exactly notated music for the instrumental ensemble, which is completely untransformed, is placed in direct contrast with the transformed sounds of the six soloists. While the instruments within the main ensemble are not at all resonant, the solo instruments, namely two pianos, harp, cimbalom, xylophone (doubling glockenspiel) and vibraphone are all particularly resonant. Striated space is clearly marked out through the conventional use of tempered instruments, while smooth space is suggested in a number of ways, through the complex simultaneities produced by the resonant tuned percussion, through the dense abundance of trills, and lastly through the electronic transformation of pitch.

He recalls that his first ideas for *Répons* involved the use of two pianos, which he considered tuning unconventionally, as he had done previously with the harp in *Pli selon pli*. After further consideration, however, he decided that he could achieve better results by exploring the partnership linking the piano with the newly available electronic technology. This

---

[44] Bayer 1981, 133–4.   [45] Boulez 1991, 163.

would enable the definition of a musical pitch space without the limitation entailed by the standard piano tuning, or by any other peculiar tuning of his own, involving quarter-tones or a similarly consistent division. While this option would have increased the pool of available pitches, it would still have restricted him to 'the same scale all the time', an outcome which he rejected.[46]

Retaining the conventional pitch tuning, he made precise calculations for the computer in order to transform the pitches played by the piano in a great number of ways, and in 'real time', thus producing much greater pitch proliferation than would have been provided by simply adopting an alternative tuning system. While the pianist plays as normal, her/his customary fingerings produce pitches and scales which are completely different and non-tempered, which cannot be notated traditionally, and which can only be identified according to their pitch frequency in terms of hertz. This process does not involve division of the tempered octave, but rather entails calculations which, to some extent, recall the pitch multiplication which he began to use in the early 1950s. He says:

> at the beginning of *Répons* I calculate the intervals of the chord the piano plays, or the vibraphone plays, and I augment that by another scale, and then everything is multiplied, and every pitch is multiplied six, eight or nine times. So you have an arpeggio of pitches and an arpeggio of arpeggios.[47]

Andrew Gerzso cites a chord played by piano no. 1, just after fig. 21, as an example of this practice, and he explains that 'there are five frequency shifters', each of which has 'two important parameters: the direction of the transposition or shift and the amount thereof expressed as a frequency'. Examining just one note, the low B flat from the arpeggiated chord, Gerzso shows how it is simultaneously transformed by the five frequency shifters which alter it by the following parameters: 'shift up 233.0 Hz, shift down 987.0 Hz, shift up 783.0 Hz, shift up 987.0 Hz, and shift down 233.0 Hz'.[48] To provide for such an expanded pitch space, in addition to the considerable instrumental score for *Répons*, there is an electronic score encoded within the computer which guarantees that, while the timing of pitch transformations may be aleatoric, none of the newly available pitches is the product of chance, since they are all the result of careful calculation.

---

[46] Interview with the author, 28 August 1998. Wyschnegradsky calculated that he could realise 'quarter-tones with two pianos, sixths of a tone with three pianos, twelfths of a tone with six pianos', and he had written some pieces for two pianos tuned a quarter-tone apart (Wyschnegradsky 1996, 129; 2005, 114). Hába, in contrast, favoured the use of a specially designed keyboard (Wyschnegradsky 1937, 30–1; Hába 1937, 92).
[47] Interview with the author, 28 August 1998.   [48] Gerzso 1984, 33.

Pitch is similarly transformed in *Dialogue de l'ombre double* (1985) and
... *explosante-fixe* ... .[49] Where the transformation of sound in *Répons* was
coordinated manually 'through following the score and the orchestral conductor in order to start up the appropriate programme at the correct
moment', the subsequent technological development of the score-follower
at IRCAM meant that, in works such as ... *explosante-fixe* ..., coordination
of transformations became completely automated. With the score-follower,
the computer now tracks what the soloist is playing, and compares this with
a score which is stored in its memory, and in which moments are defined
for the activation of particular sound modifications.[50]

The innovative pitch space possibilities opened up by this new technology
constitute an area which has not received sufficient attention to date. Only
with improved information will we be in a position to determine the extent
to which Boulez has managed to realise his early theoretical ideas of variably
smooth and striated pitch spaces.

Modernism and time

While Einstein's theory of relativity overturned the previously paradigmatic
Newtonian view of the universe, in which time was conceived of as absolute,
objective and universal, the questioning of temporality, that is the human
perception of time, and the propagation of a wide range of idiosyncratic
temporalities, was similarly accomplished by a number of twentieth-century
novelists, philosophers, social scientists and musicians, who recognised that
'individuals create as many different times as there are life styles, reference
systems, and social forms'.[51] It is one of the most interesting accomplish-
ments of Modernist aesthetics.[52]

Having previously noted Boulez's opposition of smooth and striated
time in relation to Deleuze and Proust, albeit briefly in Chapter 7, we must
now attempt to place his temporal reflections in the context of that wider
discussion of musical time, which was initiated in French intellectual life
by Bergson's concept of duration. In opposition to the reduction of time
into the individual moments of clock time, a view which he rejected as a
spatialised misrepresentation, Bergson (1889) posited a concept of time as
duration, as an indivisible and continuous experiential flux. In doing so, he
pointed to musical melody as exemplifying the continuity within temporal

[49] Boulez and Benjamin. BBC Radio Interview, 21 February 1997.
[50] Szendy 1998, 5.   [51] Kern 1983, 15.
[52] Kern 1983, 16–18. Proust, Woolf, Joyce, Conrad, Fitzgerald, Faulkner, Forster and William James
      all created personal temporalities which stood over and against the 'uniform public time' of the
      clock.

duration, in that to appreciate a melody, memory must somehow grasp all of its notes as a unity, as an instant.[53]

In 1925, Gabriel Marcel argued convincingly that Bergsonian duration does not accurately encapsulate musical experience. Bergson had not set out to develop a theory of musical time or duration, and he used the example of melody only metaphorically.[54] Marcel, who appreciates that Bergson's account of musical experience is entirely passive, rejects it in favour of a more participative hypothesis, in which the listener exercises 'a kind of mastery' in apperceptively grasping the internal coherence of a musical phrase or composition.[55] It is interesting to note the commonality between Marcel's hypothesis and the account of musical experience which Schloezer formulated in his early articles in the 1920s, and which finds its fullest formulation in his *Introduction à J.-S. Bach.*[56] Indeed, Marcel defined his view of the musical work in explicit relation to Schloezer on a number of occasions.[57] Schloezer further qualifies Bergson's account of melodic duration in stressing that music has an 'immanent sense' and that its existence is independent of our apprehension, our mental states, and of whatever physiological and psychological processes it may elicit within us.[58]

Further criticism was forthcoming in Charles Koechlin's article 'Le Temps et la musique' (1926), which distinguishes musical time from the quantitative time of physics and mathematics, from psychological time and from Bergson's qualitative duration. Musical time has its own character, which he relates to the flow of sounds and to the unfolding of melody.[59] Gaston Bachelard (1936), who supported Bergson in most respects, disagreed with him in holding that melody also contains elements of discontinuity, and that its continuity is in fact metaphorical, an illusory and 'sentimental reconstruction' which the mind of the listener has learned to perform.[60]

Closer to Boulez, Souvtchinsky wrote in 1932 of an aesthetic conjunction linking Bergson, Proust and Debussy, honouring the composer as the first to extend the musical instant in terms of sound duration.[61] The principal ideas within his later, more influential article 'La Notion du temps et

---

[53] Bergson 1910, 100 ff. Bergson's early understanding of duration underwent a number of modifications in his various writings from 1889, 1896, 1907 and 1911 (Émery 1998, 488–500).

[54] Marcel 2005, 86, 88–9; Brelet 1949, 47–8; Émery 1998, 490–1.   [55] Marcel 2005, 90.

[56] While both men wrote for *La Nouvelle Revue Française*, Schloezer as its principal writer on music, the extent and nature of their personal connection is unknown (Kohler 2003, 279–80, 246).

[57] Despite sharing Schloezer's interest in musical phenomenology, Marcel disagreed with Schloezer's contention that the content of the musical work is intellectual rather than emotional, and his Cartesian credo that 'nothing exists in sensibility which has not previously existed in the intelligence' is rejected as leading to a 'disastrous intellectualism' (Marcel 2005, 98–101).

[58] Schloezer 1947, 30–1.   [59] Émery 1998, 491–2.

[60] Bachelard 2001, 116; Brelet 1949, 49; Emery 1998, 492–3.   [61] Souvtchinsky 1990, 248.

la musique' (1939), not unsurprisingly, made their way into Stravinsky's Harvard lectures, as discussed already in Chapter 2. Distinguishing between 'psychological time' and 'ontological' or 'real time', in which the multifarious manifestations of the former are rooted ontologically in the latter, it is suggested that music provides 'one of the most pure forms of the ontological sensation of time'.[62] While individual composers present their idiosyncratic experiences of musical time, the spectrum of temporal possibilities is typified generally by the alternative of the chronometric (ontological), characterised by a sense of 'dynamic calm', and the chrono-ametric (psychological), which relates to the 'secondary notation of primary emotive impulses'. Stravinsky and Wagner are identified as respectively exemplifying each tendency. While Boulez does not draw upon Souvtchinsky's opposition, it is clear that he is united, in terms of compositional intent, with the author and with Stravinsky, in favouring music which is without psychologising motivation or programme.

Structured time and duration in Messiaen

The creation of alternative temporalities has been a concern for a number of twentieth-century composers, and one of the most interesting aspects of their work is the prominence given to new static temporalities which create the effect of suspending time, arresting all feeling of forward movement. Non-developmental, static temporality is an important element in the music of Debussy and Messiaen, to whom Boulez attributes his own particular interest in musical time and rhythm.[63] While Messiaen had shown himself to be a rhythmic innovator in his compositions in the 1930s and 1940s, and he had given an account of his procedures in the treatise *Technique de mon langage musical* (1944), his concerns at this stage were not explicitly philosophical. It was only when the title of the class which he ran at the Paris Conservatoire was changed in 1954 to a class in the Philosophy of Music that he felt the need to draw more directly on philosophical sources. He tells us: 'I was not at all a philosopher, but I tried to respond to the title that had been given to me. I brought to the class some of [Henri] Bergson's reflections on time, some of Louis de Broglie's reflections on time and duration.'[64]

In the seven-volume *Traité de rythme, de couleur, et d'ornithologie*, which he worked on from 1949 until his death in 1992, we see the result of this change. Messiaen is explicit in detailing the temporalities within his music.

---

[62] Souvtchinsky 2004, 241–3. Langlois relates Souvtchinsky's reflections on time to Groethuysen's article 'De quelques aspects du temps' (1935–6) (Langlois 2004, 63–4).
[63] Boulez 1986, 412.   [64] Boivin 1995, 134.

He considers the phenomenon from a great variety of musical and non-musical perspectives, drawing upon static and progressive temporalities from within the frameworks of both Christian cosmology and Japanese culture. His twin conceptions of time, the progressive and the static, express the contrast of time and eternity. He considers the contrary concepts of structured time and duration,[65] which are broadly similar to Boulez's smooth and striated time in that both composers set up an opposition between non-pulsed and pulsed times. While Boulez's account remains mostly at the level of musical technique, Messiaen, albeit as the result of external pressure, attempts to provide a more explicit philosophical basis for the temporalities underlying his rhythmic practice.[66] Quoting extensively from Bergson's statements on duration, he presents a framework comprising two distinct conceptions of time which he terms lived duration *(durée vécue)* and abstract or structured time *(temps structuré)*. In doing so he draws directly upon the digest of Bergsonian and post-Bergsonian thinking which he found in Armand Cuvillier's school philosophy textbook, and which sets out the two temporal viewpoints systematically. No attempt is made by the composer to develop or to apply the two temporalities, which are simply presented, and it is not absolutely clear that he is recommending them to us as indicative of his temporal conception. Despite this provisory caution, lived duration is defined as concrete since it 'merges our successive states of consciousness' into a perceptible unity. It is heterogeneous, in that it can have fasts, slows, and every possible intermediate tempo, depending upon the number of events which merge within it. It is qualitative, which means that it is not quantifiable or measurable, and it is subjective since it is purely within us. Structured time, in contrast, is abstract, 'an empty frame in which we include the world and ourselves'. It is homogeneous, since all of its moments are identical, quantitative in that it is measurable and numbered in relative terms, and objective since as a measure it exists outside us.[67]

Boulez, tempo and duration

The main thrust of the articles which Boulez wrote between 1948 and 1953 primarily concerns generalising the serial principle for all of the musical parameters, and linking '"polyphony and rhythm" into balanced

---

[65] Messiaen 1994, 9–12.
[66] A study of the mutual influence on matters of time and temporality between Messiaen, Boulez and the other members of the post-war avant-garde remains to be written.
[67] While Messiaen consulted an earlier edition of Cuvillier's text, the relevant passage can be found as follows: Cuvillier 1972, 230–1.

organizations'.[68] At this stage in his development, he was preoccupied with providing a renewed rhythmic basis for music rather than with questions of temporality, and discussion is normally of a technical nature. In the Darmstadt lectures, he provided his most extensive theoretical consideration of the technical questions surrounding time and temporality, discussing the mechanics of tempo and duration quite separately from temporality. He defines tempo as 'quite specific to duration' and as 'the standard which will give a *chronometric* value to numerical relationships'.[69] Tempo should not be conceived purely as a fixed norm since it may be varied in precise or imprecise ways.[70] He provides a continuum of theoretical possibilities for tempo, just as he had done for pitch space, in which it is divided into either fixed or mobile tempi. Fixed tempo is the simplest case since here it remains the same throughout. There are, however, several types of mobile tempo, in which there can be transformation from one tempo to another. Mobile tempo can be further divided into directed or non-directed mobile tempo, where the former refers to the passage from one fixed tempo to another fixed tempo, resulting in either an accelerando or a ritardando. There is also the possibility of a fixed tempo becoming non-fixed and vice versa. It may be that the technical means which Boulez outlines here correspond to what he describes, later in the lectures, as striated time, since his directed tempi seem to maintain a sense of pulse throughout in order for an accelerando or ritardando to be perceptible. Finally, with non-directed mobile tempo, 'the standard of duration will have a value undefined by any precise chronometric length of time'.[71] This would seem to imply that the notated musical events could be performed at the discretion of the performer, either within a set chronometric time limit or without any chronometric boundaries whatsoever. Once again, it may be that Boulez's non-directed mobile tempo, which he refers to as 'floating', corresponds to the non-pulsed temporality of smooth time, and he suggests as much, in committing himself to further consideration of each category in terms of 'the presence or absence of an internal pulse' at a later stage.[72]

Turning from the level of tempo to that of duration, Boulez now considers a variety of procedures which enable him to produce both regular and irregular pulse. Whatever the chosen durational values, he recognises the importance of the selection of tempo for 'the perception of pulse', and he lays out a variety of means by which a series of durations can be modified.[73] He envisages three possibilities which he terms the 'fixed', the 'mobile and

[68] Piencikowski 1991, p. xviii; Boulez 1991, 115.   [69] Boulez 1971a, 50.
[70] Boulez 1971a, 50–9.   [71] Boulez 1971a, 51.   [72] Boulez 1971a, 52.
[73] Boulez 1971a, 53–4.

non-evolutionary' and the 'mobile and evolutionary' variation of duration series. With fixed modification of durations, 'the proportions of the original remain when they are multiplied or divided by a single numerical value'. With mobile and non-evolutionary modification of durations 'the proportions of the original are modified by the addition or subtraction of a fixed value'. The last possibility for modification of durations, which is both mobile and evolutionary, is where 'the proportions of the original are modified by a variable value, which is a fixed or mobile function of its (the original's) constituents, by, for example, "dotting" all the values, whether or not they are already dotted'. The durations which are produced by these means are then placed in relation to one another, and three ways of distributing the resulting durational patterns are considered: symmetrically, asymmetrically or a combination of the two,[74] and such durational procedures can equally be applied to tempo.[75] Finally, Boulez writes of time bubbles in which 'only the proportions of the macro-structures', which could be a given length of chronometric time or a set number of bars, are specified. Performers are, in this situation, free to provide a variety of rhythmic/durational outcomes within the defined time area.

Smooth and striated time in theory

As with the possibilities for pitch space, Boulez conceives musical temporality in terms of striated time and smooth time.[76] In pulsed or striated time, regular durations are associated with chronometric time as signposts, while in amorphous, non-pulsed or smooth time there are no regular pulses or landmarks. Smooth time is only connected with chronometric time in an overall way since, in such a temporality, durations (with or without precise proportions) occur within a broad 'field of time'. Speed, acceleration and deceleration are consequently only features of striated time, while only the density of events within a chronometric time limit can vary in the passage of smooth time.

For Boulez, pulsation plays a role in striated time analogous to that of temperament in striated space. As with pitch space, the regularity or irregularity of pulsation within striated time will be determined by the 'fixed or variable' nature of its divisions.[77] The most important factor concerning pulsations which are irregular and irregularly divided is the fundamental question of their realisability, which for Boulez is dependent upon their not going beyond a given degree of practical difficulty in terms of both their

[74] Boulez 1971a, 55–6.   [75] Boulez 1971a, 58.
[76] Boulez 1971a, 88–9.   [77] Boulez 1971a, 91–2.

proportions and divisions. Nevertheless, as he makes clear in the Collège de France lectures, with particular reference to electro-acoustic music, the mere fact that a musical passage is arhythmic does not necessarily guarantee the production of a slow, suspended music or smooth time, since frenetically agitated music, which is too complex for perception to unravel, may be arhythmic without producing a sense of musical stasis.[78]

Again, as with interior sound space, Boulez provides a detailed classification of musical times, which draws upon the concepts of smooth and striated time, and upon the taxonomy of tempi, which we have already discussed. His terminology is not always easy to decipher precisely or to translate into more sympathetic language. The terms 'partition' and 'module', which he uses to define various types of striated time, are a little confusing, and Susan Bradshaw maintained that their meaning was never absolutely clear to her at the time of translation, even with Boulez at hand for consultation.

This lack of clarity may be due in part to the foreign nature of Boulez's terminology, since concepts such as partition and module do not belong to any traditional musical vocabulary. Nevertheless, given the relative lack of terminological consensus in the theoretical texts of the day, it is understandable that he should have looked outside the history of music theory for suitable terminology with which to articulate the new temporal possibilities which he was exploring. Bradshaw recalls his inability to successfully explain a problematic passage from the text, responding eventually that while he could not now explain the passage, he knew what he meant at the time of writing.[79] It may then not be too surprising to note the more cautious tone which he adopted in 1978 when he acknowledged the difficulties involved in defining new concepts of musical time, 'categories' which had been experienced at first only 'partially' or in a confused way.[80]

Returning to the terminological specifics of the Darmstadt lectures, the term module could refer to whatever durational value is accepted as standard, and from which related durations can be derived. Alternatively, it could refer to whatever tempo is regarded as standard. Partition seems to denote the division of the temporal continuum within striated time. This is

---

[78] Boulez 2005b, 101.
[79] Bradshaw says that 'the explanations are so intricate and detailed; even when challenged he refused to explain them. I believe it was wilful secrecy on his part. He showed little interest in the book. He never looked at the copy of the typescript' (quoted in Peyser 1977, 150). Claude Helffer similarly recalls that when he asks Boulez 'to explain something, he says, "I don't remember"' (quoted in Peyser 1977, 153). Philippot accepts that Boulez had to employ new terminology because of the insufficiency of older vocabulary, but he does not agree that Boulez is wilfully obscure, given the problems he faced in 'adapting a thought to an appropriate terminology'. He reproaches him for a lack of 'determination or rigour', in not providing a detailed translation of the musical meaning of his borrowed terms in order to dispel ambiguity (1966, 159–60).
[80] Boulez 2005b, 109.

achieved in practice through the placing of either clearly perceptible durations or equally perceptible tempi, depending on whatever interpretation of the term is preferred. Within the classification itself, only striated time is divided into a variety of types since smooth time has 'neither partition nor module'.[81] Straight time is defined, regardless of partition, as having a 'constant module', which means that its initial values operate between two boundaries, while the values which are derived from it will be placed, accordingly, 'between the multiples of the relationship defined by these two limits'. Curved time provides the opposite possibility in that the derived values will 'depend upon a function of the relationship defined by these two limits', and Boulez provides an example in which 'all the values will... be augmented or diminished according to the direction of the time-register which is followed'. With regular time 'whatever the module... partition remains fixed', while with irregular time 'partition varies (according to a defined numerical proportion or to the tempo)'.

In 'Time, Notation and Coding' (1960), Boulez suggests that smooth and striated time are 'capable of reciprocal interaction, since time cannot be *only* smooth or *only* striated', and he states unequivocally that his treatment of time from a formal point of view is based solely on these two categories.[82] Perhaps assuming the more familiar nature of striated time for the Western listener, smooth time is defined as 'that over which the performer has no control', and the following example is given:

> suppose that a group of instruments is playing in striated time, under a conductor, and that two instruments have to play, within a global smooth time, structures whose time is partly smooth and partly striated, though differently from that of the group. By the very fact of this alternation, the two instrumentalists will lose all sense of the regular striated time which accompanies them and they are thus necessarily placed in a smooth global time.[83]

Smooth and striated time are defined, respectively, as 'filling time' and 'counting time'. Finally, Boulez introduces the concepts of homogeneous and non-homogeneous time, in which the time within a composition can be homogeneously smooth or homogeneously striated. A piece will be composed exclusively of either smooth or striated time, but not both. Alternatively, the time may be non-homogeneous, in which case striated and smooth time can be alternated or superposed upon one another, and it is this last possibility which will be of most interest to us in considering a number of scores.[84] As we will see, Boulez uses temporality as an envelope,

---

[81] Boulez 1971a, 93. [82] Boulez 1986, 87. [83] Boulez 1971a, 94. [84] Boulez 1971a, 93.

opposing the two temporalities as an effective means of articulating form, of playing with perception, and of establishing or inhibiting orientation and direction.[85]

In the 1960s, Boulez, who had been interested since the 1940s in the music of other continents, acknowledged the influence of Eastern temporality in his thinking of time, in particular in the production of smooth, non-pulsed time. He acknowledged that 'time structure, the conception of time being different' was one of the principal elements of his study of ethnic musics, and he expressed an interest in the precise 'organization of rhythmic structures' in the music of Bali and India.[86] In a later interview, he contrasts the richness of an Asian conception of time with that more utilitarian Western approach which prefers to move from A to B in a straight line. His preferred option is to combine Eastern delight in sound with 'a sense for logic and development'.[87]

The trace of Eastern music in Boulez's work goes well beyond matters of time and temporality, and it has influenced his choice and use of instruments, his love of timbre, and his sometime interest in micro-intervals. While he defined his musical goal from an early age as one of uniting the Second Viennese developments in the pitch domain with those of Stravinsky and Messiaen in the rhythmic field, his experience of Eastern music in Messiaen's classes and from Schaeffner's ethnomusicological recordings undoubtedly shaped his thinking of musical time significantly. Whatever its ultimate source, his affinity with Asian music and its static temporality provides a fascinating connection with both Debussy and Messiaen.

A sense of stasis is also found in the music of Cage and Feldman, and while Goeyvaerts described his own early compositions as 'static music',[88] it was Stockhausen who made the most sustained theoretical effort to rethink the place of time in music. In an article from 1955 he explores the connection between 'structure and experiential time',[89] while in ... *how time passes* ... (1957), processes are applied to duration in line with the twelve-tone treatment of pitch, and which correspond to the acoustical facts in the pitch domain of fundamental pitches and their harmonic spectra.[90] Without naming particular works, he is clearly describing *Gruppen* (1955–7) when he discusses the possibility of three orchestras, which on the basis of three different fundamental durations and their duration-spectra, form separate 'time-strata' which unfold independently of one another.[91] Referring no doubt to *Zeitmasse* ('Time Measures') (1955–6), he describes a process in

[85] Boulez 2005b, 419.   [86] Boulez 1986, 421–2.   [87] Gable 1985–6, 112.
[88] Maconie 1976, 7; Kurtz 1992, 35.   [89] Stockhausen 1958, 64.   [90] Stockhausen 1959, 20.
[91] Stockhausen 1959, 25, 29.

which 'a first duration-formant has a constant tempo, a second is "as fast as possible", a third speeds up and a fourth slows down, and all are to be played simultaneously; and only the fundamental duration of such a time-spectrum is exactly measured as a single value'.[92] Finally, he presents the idea of 'a serialisation of successive proper times', an idea which is accomplished in *Klavierstück XI*.[93]

With the concept of the 'moment' and 'Moment-form' Stockhausen formulated a type of musical structure in which each 'moment' has its own distinguishing features, and is perceived as a distinct 'implicit eternity' and not as a stage in a developmental process.[94] He compares Moment-form with particular aspects of Eastern cultural traditions, such as the Japanese Noh theatre or haiku verse, forms which concentrate upon the immediately present moment with 'no thought for the past or future'.[95] Moment-form, which was first used in *Carré* and *Kontakte* (both 1959–60), is responsible for the formal structure of most of his compositions from the 1960s.[96] He describes its use in *Kontakte* in terms of a 'concentration on the NOW – on every NOW – as if it were a vertical slice dominating over any horizontal conception of time and reaching into timelessness, which I call eternity: an eternity which does not begin at the end of time, but is attainable at every *moment*'.[97]

The relationship between Boulez's concepts of smooth and striated, of pulsed and non-pulsed time with Moment-form and the other aspects of Stockhausen's temporal theory is not absolutely clear. Both compositional frameworks are clearly focused upon the creative opposition of two conceptions of time, a time which is pulsed, striated, developing and progressive, and a time which is non-pulsed, smooth and static. For the purposes of the present discussion, it is enough to note the fact of their shared interest in forging such temporalities, and their centrality in the articulation of musical works.

Smooth and striated time in practice

It is clear from Boulez's scores that the two temporalities, the striated and the smooth, the pulsed and the non-pulsed, have been elements within his compositional practice from the earliest published pieces, albeit in a more elementary form.[98] Bradshaw has written of the play of regular and irregular

---

[92] Stockhausen 1959, 32; Stockhausen 1989, 49. [93] Stockhausen 1959, 36–7.
[94] Griffiths 1995, 145. [95] Stockhausen 1989, 59–60. [96] Kurtz 1992, 100.
[97] Quoted in Griffiths 1995, 144–5.
[98] Boulez tells us that the opposition of smooth and striated time was an indirect consequence of the generalised series in which pitch and duration were treated autonomously (2005b, 300).

pulses in the *Sonatine* for flute and piano,[99] while several writers, including Boulez himself, have drawn attention to the existence of pulsed and non-pulsed writing in the First Sonata for piano (1946).[100] According to Boulez, each of its two movements 'is based on a duality: rhythm without perceptible pulsation, at slow or moderate speed' and 'rhythm based completely on rapid pulsation in an irregular metre'.[101]

While the subsequently formulated distinction of smooth and striated time may already be implicit in the 'rhythmic opposition' of the First Sonata, David Gable judges that time within the sonata is exclusively striated, since he understands the concept to include not only regularly pulsed rhythms but also the marking of time with any kind of fixed point, whether it is regular or irregular.[102] Beyond the sonata, Gable identifies several practical means which Boulez uses in later works to create smooth, non-pulsed time, including rubato, fermatas, indeterminacy, heterophony, the intrinsic characteristics of certain sonorities and occasional cues to the players from the conductor. Before considering the place of smooth and striated time in several compositions, we will briefly consider these devices.

In *Le Marteau sans maître* and the compositions which immediately followed it, rubato and fermatas are employed freely to produce non-pulsed time, in what have become distinctively Boulezian gestures. Gable correctly finds evidence of rubato in all of the movements of *Le Marteau* except within the second movement, *Commentaire I* from the *Bourreaux de solitude* cycle, which has clearly perceptible pulsation. Whereas in Chopin rubato does not dispense with 'an essentially stable underlying metre', Boulez reverses the situation so that local rhythmic figures 'must be relatively strictly respected while, paradoxically, the tempo remains in constant flux'. In a similar way, fermatas, which have rarely been of particular importance in previous music, are used as a disruptive force in *Le Marteau*, shaping and controlling the sense of time. Citing *Commentaire II* from the *Bourreaux de solitude* cycle as an example, Gable notes the way in which 'acceleration and deceleration' are constantly broken up through the unusually high frequency of fermatas.[103]

In *Don, Figures – Doubles – Prismes* and *Rituel*, Gable considers a number of significant factors in the production of smooth time, including the role of heterophony in blurring all sense of pulse. Instrumental sonority is also used, as Boulez contrasts the opposition of instruments producing sustained sounds, such as woodwind, brass, and bowed strings, with instruments

[99] Bradshaw 1986, 145.
[100] Claude Helffer writes of the rhythm in the *Beaucoup plus allant* sections of the first movement as exhibiting striated time. He says that 'the other sections which concern "smooth" time often imply temporal unity irregularly divided by 2, 3, 4 or 5' (1986, 65).
[101] Boulez 2005b, 297.   [102] Gable 1990, 436–7.   [103] Gable 1990, 438.

which are struck or plucked and which have resonant sounds, like the piano, celeste, harp, glockenspiel and xylophone. The role of the conductor is also crucial, for example, in *Répons* where the strictly striated time, which the conductor beats out for the chamber orchestra, contrasts markedly with the temporal flexibility enjoyed by the six soloists. While they receive a certain number of directions from the conductor, their parts are temporally freer and are integrated much more liberally within the ensemble.[104]

The tendency towards greater perceptibility in Boulez's music is also the case with temporal organisation. In the earliest works there is no question of smooth and striated time articulating the form of a work, as later became the case. While smooth, unpulsed time is clearly perceptible in *Le Marteau*, this temporality, as we have seen, is almost uniform throughout the work, and may even be said to be rather amorphous. *Constellation-Miroir*, the central formant of the Third Sonata, provides a particularly impressive example of an extended piece which exists in homogeneously smooth time. Rosen, who believes 'the decentralized concept of time in Boulez's later work' to be 'perhaps his most radical contribution to music', describes *Constellation-Miroir* as 'the immovable, still centre' of the piece.[105] Having brought temporality to the forefront of perception, Boulez now employed the much more obvious and perceptible opposition of smooth and striated time in pieces like *Éclat* (1965), using them to articulate the form of the piece.[106]

Gable notes that temporality in *Éclat* is, to a significant degree, established through the choice of instrumentation and timbral possibilities, since Boulez opposes resonating and non-resonating instruments.[107] While the music played by the percussion instruments is smooth and non-pulsed, and results from the choices made by the conductor at the moment of the performance, the material allotted to the sextet occupies pulsed, striated time. Indeed, Bradshaw identifies an unfolding 'argument' between pulsed time, 'improvised durations, and time that is proportionately free within periods measured by surrounding pulsation'.[108] A sketch in the Paul Sacher Stiftung reveals the plan of the work (Figure 10.1).

Robert Piencikowski has produced his own structural plan, which reflects the piece in its completed form, as shown in Table 10.1.

A *résumé* of performance indications used within *Éclat* gives an idea of the degree to which Boulez plays with pulse. While there is pulsation

---

[104] Gable 1990, 440–1.   [105] Rosen 1986, 96.
[106] For Bradshaw, Boulez was unsuccessful in realising the formal opposition of smooth and striated time in his pieces from the late 1950s and early 1960s, in which smooth time predominates (1986, 225–6), and the composer acknowledged the difficulty in perceiving anything more defined than fasts or slows, regularity or irregularity (Boulez 2005b, 202).
[107] Gable 1990, 441.   [108] Bradshaw 1986, 203.

Piano cadence

> Development 1
>
> Static cycle   Presentation of the solo group and the ripieno group
>
> Development 2

1st Instrumental cadence reprise (partial piano variation)

Figure 10.1. Plan of *Éclat*, taken from Boulez's sketch (Paul Sacher Stiftung: microfilm 138, p. 24)

Table 10.1. *Plan of* Éclat *(Piencikowski 1993, 51)*

Fig. [0]	1st Cadence (piano and sextet)
Fig. 2	Development 1 (keyboards)[a]
Fig. 14	Centre (keyboards)
Fig. 20	Development 2 (keyboards)
Fig. 25	2nd Cadence (*tutti*)

[a] Piencikowski uses the term 'keyboard' in this context to denote all stringed instruments which are plucked or struck, namely piano, celeste, harp, glockenspiel, vibraphone, mandolin, guitar, cimbalom and tubular bells (1993, 51).

up to fig. 14, it is not regular. The durational indeterminacy of the initial cadenza for piano and sextet is reflected in the instructions *Librement* and *Tenir très longtemps*. In development 1, instructions include *Extrêmement flexible; Flexible; allonger les notes* and *irregulier*. The static central section beginning at fig. 14 is prefaced – *Assez lent, suspendu, comme imprévisible (avec de brusques resserrements et de brusques détentes)* and fig. 16 is marked *Vague, flottant, sans aucune orientation rythmique*. Development 2 is still *Libre, espacé* and *Tenir très longtemps*. Indeed it is only with the last section (figs. 25–30), that we encounter unambiguously pulsed music although the piece ends with the instruction *inégalement espacé*.

Boulez uses a great variety of means to create smooth, non-pulsed time in *Éclat*. The opposition of degrees of pulsed and non-pulsed time, which is fundamental to the form of the entire piece, is in a sense anticipated in the opening piano cadenza. It begins with a six-chord flourish, notated as a rhythmic glissando (Example 10.1), and is followed by nine regularly pulsed

Example 10.1. Pierre Boulez, *Éclat*, opening flourish

single notes and dyads which build a widely spaced resonating chord which is taken up by the sextet.

The time-bubble inserts in *Éclat* facilitate non-pulsed time through indeterminacy. There are eight inserts in development 1 (figs. 2–14), four in the static central section (figs. 14–20) and four in development 2 (figs. 20–5). Again, Boulez uses a variety of means in the inserts which Jameux categorises as 'optional', 'instantaneous' and 'controlled'.[109] In the insert at fig. 3 (Example 10.2), the simultaneously sounding blocks with different numbers of pitches (4, 3, 2, 1) ripple in arpeggios and blur all sense of pulse. At fig. 5 (II) (cf. Example 9.2) five instruments have one pitch each to play, as the conductor signs rapidly and at unequal intervals to the players, making the resulting pulse unpredictable and irregular.

A more comprehensive account of the inserts, from the viewpoint of their indeterminacy, is provided in the discussion of open form in Chapter 9. On the question of time bubbles, there are some interesting examples in the sketches at the Paul Sacher Stiftung. Figures 10.2 and 10.3, for example, are sketches for time bubbles, 'Bulles de temps', which Boulez made while writing *Improvisation III sur Mallarmé*.

Returning to *Éclat*, the truly unpulsed section of the piece is the central static section from figs. 14 to 20, where the establishment of rhythmic pulse is prevented through a variety of means. There are no traditional barlines, no time signatures, no conventional indications of duration, just pitch,

[109] Jameux 1991, 339.

Example 10.2. Pierre Boulez, *Éclat*, fig. 3

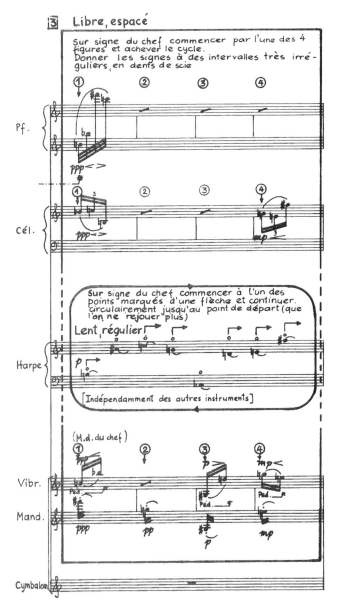

and duration is instead decided metronomically. For the entire passage, the metronomic indications are relative (fig. 14) and the conductor is given final control. In a number of places, Boulez offers a choice of two sets of alternative metronome markings to the conductor, as can be seen at fig. 15 where the options of 80 or 240 are available.

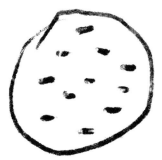

Figure 10.2. Time bubble sketch for *Improvisation III sur Mallarmé* (Paul Sacher Stiftung, microfilm 137, p. 294, extract)

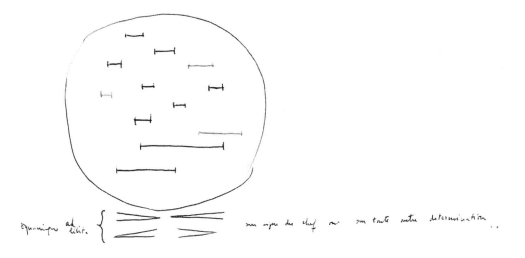

Figure 10.3. Time bubble sketch for *Improvisation III sur Mallarmé* (Paul Sacher Stiftung, microfilm 137, p. 341, extract)

At fig. 14 we are told that 'in each rhythmic sequence indicated by [ ], one [the conductor] will choose, in the case of two possibilities, either always the higher metronome mark or always the lower'. Within this choice of metronome markings, most of the static middle section is organised, in terms of notation, without traditional rhythmic values such as crotchets or quavers. Duration is instead provided through the use of a series of figures, which indicate 'the number of rhythmic units attributed to each value', and Table 10.2 shows the numbers of such units between figs. 14 and 15.

The inserts at fig. 15 (III); fig. 16; fig. 18 (III) and fig. 19 (II) all have the indication 'with no rhythmic orientation; order of the instruments

Table 10.2. *Éclat, the*
number of rhythmic
units for each value
between figs. 14 and 15

$$1 = \text{MM}60$$
$$\left[3 \qquad 1 \quad \begin{smallmatrix} 2 & 4 \\ 4 & 2 \end{smallmatrix} \quad 4 \right]$$

Example 10.3. Pierre Boulez, *Éclat*, fig. 25

ad lib'. The piano insert at fig. 16 also has the indication 'Vague, floating'. In this way, the central section of *Éclat* gradually creates an increasing sense of stasis, especially from fig. 19.

Development 2 (figs. 20–5) marks the end of both the variable metronome markings, and of the numbered rhythmic units. Instead, traditionally notated durations and conductor beats return as in development 1, although the piece is still unstable and irregular in pulsation at this point. It is only with cadence 2 (fig. 25–end) that regular pulse is introduced for the first time. Here, the initial idea from cadence 1 returns, only in reverse, since this time the sustained chord leads into the flourish which is now performed by piano and sextet, as opposed to the solo piano of the opening. At fig. 25 (Example 10.3), time signatures appear for the first time in the work and are maintained to the end of the piece except for the final system (fig. 30) where conductor indications by number are reintroduced. However, even here, pulsation is not entirely stable since it is subtly undermined by a sequence of arrows (figs. 25–6) which create a series of bar-length glissandos, analogous to the rhythmic glissando of the opening. While *Éclat* essentially contrasts the macro-states of pulsed and non-pulsed time, the result is much more subtle and involves many intermediate states.

The play of smooth and striated time features in *Répons* as one of its most prominent formal and expressive characteristics, and Boulez describes how 'the principal image unfolds in regular or irregular pulsed time, and the derived image or images unfold in a free and independent time, not pulsed or pulsed in a different way'.[110] As Nattiez has shown, the entire orchestral introduction (opening–fig. 21) is articulated around a clear succession of polar notes.[111] Despite the generally static, non-pulsed nature of the polar notes, each section of the orchestral introduction contrasts the unpulsedness of the polar notes with a variety of pulsed elements. The section from fig. 4–fig. 5, for example, which is centred around a polar B♭, has moments which are clearly striated by regularly pulsed melodic fragments, and through the regular reiteration of the polar pitch on a number of instruments. Even so, at some points, the trilled polar pitch is extended at length in unpulsed time and acts as the basic backdrop against which the pulsed entries are heard.

When the six soloists enter for the first time at fig. 21 only the attacks of the clangorous chords are indicated by the conductor, and these resonant sounds are at first amplified and then transformed electronically. From fig. 21 to fig. 31 smoothly timed passages for the six soloists alternate with temporally striated passages for the main ensemble. This brief description is a simplification of what actually happens, since the articulation of certain passages for the soloists with the use of square brackets [ ] indicates that they are not to resonate beyond their strictly notated duration. These short phrases occur within striated time and act as introductions to forceful ensemble chords, which are paradoxically extended in time. In a sense, then, Boulez plays with the natural characteristics of the two groups only then to swap them.

In the Passacaglia-like section from fig. 42 to fig. 47, the *Klangfarbenmelodie* in the ensemble, which opens the section, sounds out a clear pulse, which is at first reinforced by the soloists. Eventually, however, there is a smoothing of the pulse. Over the course of the section there is a quasi-duel between the pulsed ensemble and the heterophonic temporal smoothing of the elaborately ornamented solo parts. As the section climaxes, loud brass chords sound forcefully through the drowning density of smooth time to provide pulsed points of coherence but, in this case, within the context of a vast mesh of unpulsed heterophony. The strident pulses subside eventually and are stilled in the sea of unpulsed rhythms which conclude the section. It could, therefore, be described as the passage from pulsed to non-pulsed time, with their mutual interpenetration along the way, a process which calls to mind certain procedures in Paul Klee, where the artist effects

---

[110] Boulez 2005b, 451.   [111] Nattiez 1993b, 197–9.

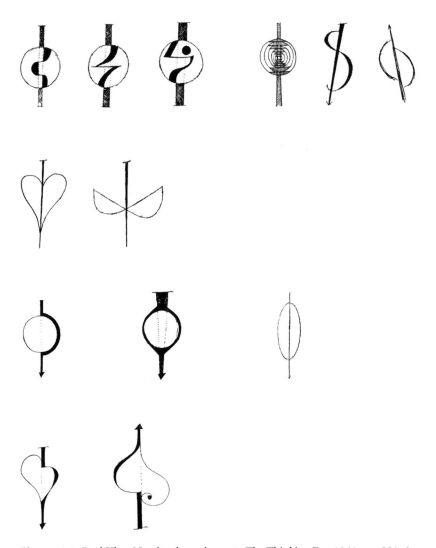

Figure 10.4. Paul Klee, Notebooks, volume 1, *The Thinking Eye*, 1961, pp. 331–2.

the interpenetration of two distinct shapes, such as a line and a circle, in order to produce a great variety of results from seemingly simple means (Figure 10.4).

At some points in *Répons*, the number of simultaneous events is enough to erase all sense of pulse. Heterophonous lines, each of which may be individually pulsed, can, when played simultaneously, create such a complex web of sound that all sense of pulse disappears. The *Rapide* section from fig. 54 to fig. 69, for example, features *martellato staccato* moments in alternation with heterophonous scalar passages. The soloists' parts are

Table 10.3. Répons, *the numbers of successive heterophonic runs within a section (quasi-bar)*

Fig.	Heterophonies	Fig.	Heterophonies
55	2	62	4
56	2	63	4
57	3	64	5
58	3	65	5
59	3	66	5
60	4	67	5
61	4	68	5

Table 10.4. Répons, *the number of notes within each heterophonic line at fig. 57*

Heterophony no.	1	2	3
Number of notes	15	13	22
	13	13	20
	15	16	20
	15	14	21
	12	16	22
		13	17
			17
			22
			17

'independent of the conductor' and 'non-synchronised' in the purely martellato sections, but are synchronised with the conductor for the duration of the roller-coaster-like heterophonies, in which synchronous demisemiquaver runs of varying lengths are superposed. Table 10.3 shows the number of successive heterophonic scalar runs within a section (a quasi-bar), while Tables 10.4 and 10.5 indicate the number of notes within each run at fig. 57 and at fig. 67. Each heterophonic run has the duration of one crotchet beat. At fig. 67, for example, these demisemiquaver heterophonies consist of up to 52 pitches which are played against lines with varying numbers of pitches, in this case, 40, 25, 37 and so on.

At fig. 55, where the heterophonies begin, Boulez intimates that while the beats and the metronome markings are all indicated, 'the internal speed of these groups can be very free in relation to the beats'. At fig. 57 he indicates

Table 10.5. Répons, *the number of notes*
within each heterophonic line at fig. 67

Heterophony no.	1	2	3	4	5
Number of notes	34	4	30	33	52
	11	9	30	33	15/22
	34	9	13	33	22/14
	34	31	30	33	12/25
	9	10	30	33	52
	34	31	15	33	40
	34	31	30	33	25
	34	31	8	33	14
		31	30	33	52
		10	30	13	9/18
		31	30	33	52
		7	30	33	37
		31	30		10/10
		31			5
					4
					52

that 'the synchronisation of the groups will become more and more approximate as they grow'. In contrast to this, the ensemble players are to follow
crotchet beats in the non-heterophonic sections. Presumably referring to
fig. 54–fig. 69, Boulez has spoken of the demisemiquavers (described here
as heterophonies), which unfold in a very quick tempo and which produce
a 'stroboscopic effect', which is so fast that it is impossible for him as the
conductor to tell whether or not the musicians are with him or operating
independently.[112]

A play of smooth and striated time features prominently in *cummings ist
der dichter*, which Boulez composed in 1970 and then reworked in 1986.
Bradshaw wrote of the 1970 version as being concerned with 'the progressive transformation of pulse into the eventual "polyphony" of variously
characterized time measurements'.[113] One of the most interesting contrasts
between the two versions of the piece arises from the differences in their
notation. While the 1970 version is notated with many of the conventions
which Boulez had established in compositions like *Éclat*, including performer cues, irregular pulses, non-fixed durations, sections without time
signatures and indeterminacy, the 1986 version is much more traditional in

---

[112] Interview with the author, 28 August 1998.   [113] Bradshaw 1986, 209.

Table 10.6. *Sectional plan of* cummings ist der dichter
(1986), from fig. 15 to the end

fig. 15 (+1) to fig. 15 (+8)	2/1 Très lent, suspendu, régulier
fig. 16 to fig. 16 (+10)	Rapide, incisif
fig. 17 to fig. 17 (+5)	2/1 Très lent, suspendu
fig. 17 (+6) to fig. 17 (+9)	Rapide, incisif
fig. 18 to fig. 18 (+3)	2/1 Très lent, suspendu
fig. 18 (+4) to fig. 18 (+9)	Rapide, incisif
fig. 19 to fig. 19 (+3)	2/1 Très lent, suspendu
fig. 19 (+4) to fig. 19 (+13)	Rapide, incisif
fig. 20 to fig. 20 (+7)	2/1 Très lent, suspendu
fig. 20 (+8) to fig. 20 (+15)	Rapide, incisif
fig. 21 to fig. 21 (+3)	2/1 Très lent, suspendu
fig. 21 (+4) to fig. 21 (+8)	Très modéré
fig. 22 to fig. 22 (+4)	2/1 Très lent, suspendu
fig. 23 to fig. 28 (+11)	[Mostly] Très modéré
fig. 29 to fig. 29 (+3)	2/1 Très lent, suspendu

notation in that everything is subject to metronome markings and full durational indications, and indeterminacy is dropped. In the 1986 version, the
first section (up to fig. 15) is marked mostly *modéré* or *très modéré*. From
fig. 15, which is at the halfway stage in the 1986 score, the static and previously unpulsed sections are now marked *Très lent, suspendu, régulier* with
the time signature 2/1, and they now alternate with several pulsed sections.
The form of the piece, from fig. 15 to the end, can be seen in Table 10.6.

All of Boulez's later pieces feature the alternation of smooth and striated time. *Dérive 1* (1984, 1986) for ensemble begins with the instruction
Très lent, immuable, and bb. 1–27 form a static section made up almost
completely of ornamental demisemiquaver flourishes and long held trills.
This is followed in bb. 27–33 by a contrasting section which is pulsed in
regular time, although a faint trill hanging over from the first section always
remains present. In bb. 33–46 the trills begin to reassert themselves, and
simple ornamentation returns as the texture builds once again until the
static close of the piece at bb. 46–54, which is marked 'Rester dans le Tempo
initial'.

The form of *Dérive 1*, with its rather static opening and close, contrasts
with that of *Transitoire VII* (1991/3), from … *explosante fixe* …, which has
pulsed outer sections and a still centre. At fig. 20 (*Très modéré*) there are
five bars of descending demisemiquaver runs, which drop down to the
Très lent centre of the piece at fig. 21. This eight-bar section, the still core

of the composition, defines the form, at the most basic level, as pulsed–
non-pulsed–pulsed, although pulse varies constantly throughout with the
continuous succession of its sections. *sur Incises* (1996, 1998) contrasts the
pulsed time of the toccata sections with the non-pulsed time of the resonant
sections.

A philosophical postscript

While Deleuze welcomed Boulez's concepts of the smooth and the striated, transforming them and integrating them idiosyncratically within his
philosophy, the temporal experiments of the post-Webern generation were
received less warmly by Adorno. In the *Philosophy of New Music*, he had
already rejected the static suspension of musical time in the passage from
Debussy to Stravinsky, which he imputes to a 'spatialisation of music', that
is 'a pseudomorphism of music on painting'.[114] In 'On the Contemporary Relationship of Philosophy and Music' (1953), the usefulness of the
observation that musical space and musical time are not 'absolutely distinct
from empirical space and empirical time' is questioned on account of its
vagueness, while he notes that the 'temporal consciousness' of music from
Palestrina to Webern 'is endlessly different'. The expression 'static music',
which he finds in neo-classicism, is dismissed as a 'superficial analogy' at
odds with music's truly immanent time, which is inherently historical.[115]
In 'Criteria of New Music' (1957), static music is termed an 'illusion', on
account of the facile opposition it mounts to the developmental principle,
and the intolerable temporal 'indifference' it suggests in the face of music's
material dynamism. Stravinsky is charged with fostering this illusion of
temporal simultaneity to the detriment of 'temporal dialectic'.[116]

Concepts of time are central to Adorno's problems with the music of
Boulez's generation. In 'The Ageing of the New Music', he takes issue with
the lack of genuine motion at the heart of serialism, which he believes is at
odds with music's necessarily dynamic nature, and with the play of identity
and non-identity which its temporal unfolding makes possible.[117] In 'Vers
une musique informelle', he registers a certain strangeness in his engagement with Stockhausen's 'theory of a static music' a propos of *Zeitmasse*.[118]
The unity of pitch and duration, which Stockhausen proposes on the basis
of their common origins in vibration, is rejected as a premature confusion

---

[114] Adorno 2006, 141.   [115] Adorno 2002, 142–4.
[116] Adorno 1999, 190–1. See also 'Stravinsky: A Dialectical Portrait' (1998, 152).
[117] Adorno 1988, 103.   [118] Adorno 1998, 271.

of objective and experiential time.[119] Indeed, certain unnamed controversialists are taken to task for failing to adopt Bergson's distinction of *temps espace* (spatial time) and *temps durée* (experiential time), applying both indiscriminately to the new musical temporality.

The absoluteness of Adorno's early rejection of static temporality is moderated in his later writings where, despite describing Bergson's twin opposition as a 'crass dichotomy', he recognises it in his *Negative Dialectics* as an unconsciously dialectical attempt to 'reconstruct the living experience of time' in the face of abstract philosophical and natural scientific conceptions.[120] While the attempt is ultimately unsuccessful in reaching the dialectical concept, since it makes an absolute of the dynamic moment in response to the 'reification of consciousness', he concedes that it captures something of the historic dichotomy between 'living experience and the objectified and repetitive labor process'. Static time may now be acceptable, but only in relation to its dynamic other, and certainly not in any immediate Bergsonian way. In the *Aesthetic Theory*, he accepts that contemporary composers can employ a wide range of solutions in their handling of musical time. While still maintaining that time is inescapably 'invariant', he now allows that 'once this invariant is an object of reflection it becomes an element of composition and no longer an a priori'.[121] Following Bergson, artworks are now 'only completely perceptible in *temps durée*',[122] 'objectivation makes the artwork into an instant', into 'something momentary',[123] and musical time is now unambiguously 'remote from empirical time'.[124]

It is not possible to provide a detailed critique of Adorno's understanding of musical time within the present study but, given the significance of his engagement with Boulez and his Darmstadt colleagues, it has been important at least to note the development of his thinking on the issue. His later position, in which he to some extent acknowledges the legitimacy of a dialectical opposition between the static and the dynamic, provides a possible point of contact with Boulez and Deleuze, both of whom go much further than Adorno or even Bergson in imagining the possibility of many intermediate temporalities between the homogeneously smooth and the homogeneously striated. Ultimately, the temporal multiplicity of Deleuze's conceptual philosophy comes closer to the subtle variability of the smooth and the striated as they appear in Boulez's compositions. The dialectic of temporal opposites which Adorno includes in his later philosophy and musical writing is rather stark and it seems that while his attitude towards the static softened to some extent, one senses a certain anxiety for the

---

[119] Adorno 1998, 312.   [120] Adorno 1973, 333–4.   [121] Adorno 1997, 23.
[122] Adorno 1997, 69.   [123] Adorno 1997, 84.   [124] Adorno 1997, 137.

progressive, the historical and the dialectical. In a sense the debate returns to the structure/process dichotomy which was discussed in Chapter 6, and it seems clear that Adorno interprets music that embodies static temporality as a denial of history and its movement. This is not a problem for Boulez whose music embodies the aporia to the extent that it becomes an important generator of musical form.

In conclusion

If the complexity of working with multiple philosophical perspectives was indicated in the introduction, a number of similarly fundamental musical problems are equally worthy of note. The schema of Boulez's compositional trajectory which was presented in Chapter 8 draws directly on the composer's own retrospective account of his development, and consequently raises some rather significant questions. Woven into the text of his Collège de France lectures, this basically linear narrative, which successfully illustrates the development of specific and limited aesthetic and compositional values, also has the effect of obscuring the intricacies of his compositional journey in its historical unfolding. Boulez's account, which is not an attempt to retrace the micro-stages of his journey, gives the impression of a certain inevitability in compositional development, which belies the effort, the trial and error, the false starts, as well as the revised, lost or suppressed works which contributed in essential ways to his progress. Indeed, many of his musical sketches, early drafts of completed works and incomplete compositions have now been studied by scholars, who have carefully considered how they contribute to and nuance our understanding of the composer's development.[1]

Questions concerning the early gestation of compositional materials and techniques, which have been noted at a number of points in this study, have nevertheless not been the primary focus of attention, and discussion in the later chapters has proceeded generally in relation to completed works and scores. The investigation of the composer's workshop and the gestation of his ideas is clearly of great interest and value but it does not negate the validity of dealing with that body of completed and published works which the composer has seen fit to release into the world. Having said this, in focusing on the composer's published oeuvre there is the danger that the musicologist only engages partially with the composer's work, with the part that reflects what the composer perceives to be his own successes. Alternatively, studies that emanate from a legitimate interest in sketch study can run the risk of blurring the distinction between sketches and completed works, and scholars will vary in the degree of importance which they give

---

[1] Scholars working on Boulez's sketches and other documentary source material include Robert Piencikowski, Pascal Decroupet, Peter O'Hagan, Werner Strinz and Paolo dal Molin.

to sketches, incomplete works and those completed compositions which a composer chooses not to acknowledge through performance or publication. In Boulez's case, to take some of the now best-known examples, material which was originally intended for the unpublished *Oubli signal lapidé* was used in the composition of *Le Marteau sans maître*, *Don* and *Tombeau* from *Pli selon pli* and *cummings ist der dichter*,[2] while *Pli selon pli* and *Éclat* both have their origins in material which was generated for Jean-Louis Barrault's staged production of *Orestie* in 1955.[3] In contrast to the growing body of work which is being produced on the micro-gestation of Boulez's compositional technique, such questions have arisen in the present study only in relation to particular examples from specific completed works such as the *Sonatine* and the First Sonata. The principal focus throughout has been to consider composition and musical theory in relation to primarily philosophical ideas, and to discuss certain relationships and corollaries in musical and philosophical thinking.

A related problem which complicates matters further is the fact that Boulez has reworked a number of his compositions, some of them several times, and some pieces exist in more than one published version. In the course of discussion a number of examples have been noted where changes to a score indicate a significant theoretical shift. The fact of rewriting and publishing more than one version of some scores also raises the question of the chronology of Boulez's works. While these are issues which have not been dealt with to any significant degree here, insights from scholars working intensively on more restricted portions of Boulez's output have been called upon to provide greater historical detail.[4] In more philosophical terms, it raises the question of the general and the particular and the extent to which it is legitimate to theorise beyond the micrological level of the specific example, integrating individual insights within a more extended and global narrative.

Despite the remarkable coherence and consistency in Boulez's approach to composition, there have also been important shifts in his musical perspective, and there is no doubt that *sur Incises*, for example, is a very different composition from *Le Marteau sans maître* from a number of points of view. Without expecting the same kind of highly theorised and practical consistency in the domain of philosophical ideas, the range of philosophical engagements which Boulez has been implicated in throughout his career

---

[2] O'Hagan 2006, 310–12.   [3] O'Hagan 2006, 317, 324–5.

[4] To take only a few examples, Piencikowski, Kobylakov, Decroupet, Strinz, O'Hagan and Gärtner have concentrated mostly on Boulez's earlier works (up to the mid-1960s); Dal Molin has worked on the works of the 1970s and Goldman has focused on a number of mostly shorter works from the mid-1970s to the present.

does not ultimately result in a heterogeneous, self-contradictory or inconsistent musical world-view. There is a coherence and consistency to his thought which endures throughout his career and which is not seriously compromised by the presence of terminological and conceptual borrowings from competing philosophies, which are not always compatible with one another. While the conclusions to several chapters endeavour to make some of these links and points of consistency more explicit, the composer's efforts do not amount to an overt or fully worked-out philosophy of music. When André Boucourechliev wrote of serialism in 1982 in terms of three 'fundamental' and 'successive' criteria which may be summarised as (1) a negational musical system, (2) 'a new general grammar' and (3) 'a new philosophy of music ... based on concepts and working-principles of discontinuity, relativity and plurality', he could almost have had Boulez's trajectory in mind,[5] since his three principles provide a dialectical moment of negation, the development of structures and a philosophy of multiplicity.

That Boulez is not a philosopher was set out clearly in the course of the introduction and at various points throughout the text. The validity of the musical/philosophical conjunctions which have been established do not depend upon whatever philosophical credentials Boulez may or may not have. Nor has there been any attempt to apply philosophical ideas to music. In each of the chapters we have considered how Boulez uses a number of key terms which pertain to the philosophical domain, although he almost never does so in the context of philosophical discussion. The primary thesis throughout has been that Boulez's music and theory provide a kind of philosophy in action, philosophy in music. Negation is enacted for example in the brief moments of the generalised series, deduction is practised in numerous compositions and difference is embodied in the multiplicitous presentations of his virtual themes, his experiments with variable and kaleidoscopic forms and heterophonies. In this sense, the intention has been to reflect a relationship of reciprocity in which music and ideas are mutually illuminating, and the integration of aesthetics and analysis which has been attempted within the framework of intellectual history is ultimately concerned with arriving at a better understanding of Boulez's music.

To this end dialectics, axiomatic deductivism, structuralism and poststructuralism have been considered in turn along with a number of figures of importance in Boulez's ideational development. In attempting to place Boulez within a broader modernist framework a significant amount of attention has been given to his early mentors, Souvtchinsky, Schloezer, Schaeffner and Souris, as well as to a great number of figures of variable designation

---

[5] Boucourechliev 1987, 22.

such as Messiaen, Leibowitz, Stockhausen, Pousseur and Adorno. Time has been spent along the way in considering the connections which each of these figures had with one another as well as their relationships with Boulez. This part of the study was based largely on the writings and correspondence of each of the protagonists, and in the process we considered Boulez's relationship to the surrealism and phenomenology which were prominent in the intellectual and aesthetic milieu of his youth.

Later chapters attempted to trace the development of a number of key ideas throughout Boulez's work and in relation to other significant composers and philosophers/thinkers. While making explicit connections between Boulez's theoretical statements and practical developments and the ideas of a range of significant thinkers, for example the eighteenth- and early nineteenth-century German Idealists, there is no implication that Boulez was doing philosophy. The range of binary oppositions which were noted and discussed in Chapter 3 have great potential for directing analysis, as Jonathan Goldman has shown in his work on the construction of Boulez's musical forms.[6] Genealogical studies of notions such as Boulez's binary oppositions or of the nature of his dialectic raise the question of the origins of these ideas, and pragmatic decisions have had to be made as to where and when to halt a particular line of enquiry. It is not claimed, for example, that no one theorised in terms of binary oppositions before Kant formulated his antinomies, but rather that a clear argument can be made that Boulez has been influenced by a strain of thinking which reached a significant stage in its development in the era of German Idealism. To fail to draw such lines would lead to an untenable and prolonged regress of ever more remote sources and references.[7]

While deduction was looked at from a theoretical standpoint in Chapter 5, it seems that the best place to grasp the intricacies of the actual deductions which Boulez has made in practice is in those analytical studies which trace the gestation of his resources from the Idea, from the selection/construction of basic material through a number of prismatic stages to its eventual deployment on the surface of the score.

If anything, the consideration of serialism and structuralism which was undertaken in Chapter 6 serves to reinforce the conviction of a number of previous writers that despite certain parallels between them, these movements did not ultimately share any deep commonality. Stronger links were discovered with the post-structuralism which followed, and Chapters 7–10

---

[6] Goldman 2006.

[7] Nor does the study claim to account for all the philosophical resonances in Boulez's work or for all the citations which can be found in the writings of philosophers. The brief references to Boulez in Alain Badiou's recent *Logic of Worlds* (2009), for example, are not discussed.

showed how Deleuzian post-structuralism with its focus on the multiple and its affinity to modernism in music and the other arts brings it close in a number of ways to the later articulation of Boulez's thought. Even here though, it has been important to remain open to competing philosophical views, and in these later chapters the attempt was made to avoid the imposition of a Deleuzian reading as if Boulez's music could only be discussed in such terms. While Adorno's relationship with Boulez's music and ideas is not straightforward, aspects of his thinking on identity, non-identity, musical time and temporality cannot be ignored and they offer a fascinating and productive alternative view to that of Deleuze.

In attempting to reflect Boulez's seeming ambivalence in the face of competing philosophical schools of thought, the present study has refrained from presenting a fundamentally dialectical, deductivist, structuralist or post-structuralist line. In giving each movement its place within the composer's work, no fundamental epistemological or methodological questions have been resolved, and no indication is offered as to whatever might be the most preferable or productive philosophical approach to musical composition. While the over sixty years of Boulez's compositional and theoretical endeavours have given rise to moments which have been variably determinable in dialectical, deductivist, structuralist and post-structuralist language, his music, like all music, should not be reduced to the history of philosophy. Nevertheless, contemporary art music has too often been interpreted in isolation from the wider intellectual and aesthetic culture in which it has developed. In presenting Boulez's music and ideas in relation to the philosophical currents of his time, the aim has been to reconnect music and ideas and to show some of the ways in which they may be implicated with one another in the work of one of the most original and influential composers to have been at work in the second half of the twentieth century.

References

Adorno, Theodor W. 1956. 'Modern Music is Growing Old', *The Score* 18: 18–29.

Adorno, Theodor W. 1966. 'Form', *Darmstädter Beiträge zur Neuen Musik* 10: 9–21.

Adorno, Theodor W. 1972. *Dissonanzen: Musik in der verwalten Welt*. Göttingen: Vandenhoeck & Ruprecht.

Adorno, Theodor W. 1973. *Negative Dialectics*. Trans. E. B. Ashton. London: Routledge.

Adorno, Theodor W. 1976. *Introduction to the Sociology of Music*. Trans. E. B. Ashton. New York: The Seabury Press.

Adorno, Theodor W. 1983. *Prisms*. Trans. Samuel and Shierry Weber. Cambridge, MA: MIT Press.

Adorno, Theodor W. 1984. *Gesammelte Schriften* 18, Frankfurt am Main: Suhrkamp.

Adorno, Theodor W. 1988. 'The Aging of the New Music', trans. and ed. Robert Hullot-Kentor and Frederic Will. *Telos* 77: 95–116.

Adorno, Theodor W. 1993. *Hegel: Three Studies*. Trans. Shierry Weber Nicholsen. Cambridge, MA: MIT Press.

Adorno, Theodor W. 1997. *Aesthetic Theory*. Ed. Gretel Adorno and Rolf Tiedemann, trans. Robert Hullot-Kentor. London: Athlone.

Adorno, Theodor W. 1998. *Quasi una Fantasia: Essays on Modern Music*. Trans. Rodney Livingstone. London: Verso.

Adorno, Theodor W. 1999. *Sound Figures*. Trans. Rodney Livingstone. Stanford: Stanford University Press.

Adorno, Theodor W. 2002. *Essays on Music*. Selected, with introduction, commentary and notes by Richard Leppert, trans. Susan H. Gillespie *et al.* Berkeley: University of California Press.

Adorno, Theodor W. 2003. *Adorno: Eine Bildmonographie*. Herausgegeben vom Theodor W. Adorno Archiv. Frankfurt am Main: Suhrkamp.

Adorno, Theodor W. 2006. *Philosophy of New Music*. Trans. and ed. Robert Hullot-Kentor. Minneapolis: University of Minnesota Press.

Adorno, Theodor W., and Alban Berg. 2005. *Correspondence 1925–1935*. Ed. Henri Lonitz, trans. Wieland Hoban. Cambridge: Polity.

Adorno, Theodor W., and Pierre Boulez. 2001. 'Gespräche über den Pierrot Lunaire', in *Schönberg und der Sprechgesang, Musik-Konzepte* 112/13, ed. Heinz-Klaus Metzger and Rainer Riehn, 73–94.

Aguila, Jésus. 1992. *Le Domaine Musical: Pierre Boulez et vingt ans de création contemporaine*. Paris: Fayard.

Albèra, Philippe. 2003. '... L'éruptif multiple sursautement de la clarté ...', in *Pli selon pli de Pierre Boulez*, Geneva: Contrechamps, 59–82.

Artaud, Antonin. 2005. *Le Théâtre et son double*. Paris: Gallimard.

Astier, Frédéric. 2006. *Les Cours enregistrés de Gilles Deleuze 1979–1987*. Mons: Éditions Sils Maria.

Aubin, David. 1997. 'The Withering Immortality of Nicolas Bourbaki: A Cultural Connector at the Confluence of Mathematics, Structuralism and the Oulipo in France', *Science in Context* 10/2: 297–342.

Auner, Joseph. 2003. *A Schoenberg Reader: Documents of a Life*. New Haven: Yale University Press.

Bachelard, Gaston. 2001. *La Dialectique de la durée*. Paris: Quadrige/PUF.

Bailey, Kathryn. 1991. *The Twelve-Note Music of Anton Webern*. Cambridge: Cambridge University Press.

Barnes, Jonathan. 2000. *Aristotle: A Very Short Introduction*. Oxford: Oxford University Press.

Baron, Carol K. 1975. 'An Analysis of the Pitch Organization in Boulez's "Sonatine" for Flute and Piano', *Current Musicology* 20: 87–95.

Barraqué, Jean. 2001. *Écrits*. Réunis, présentés et annotés par Laurent Feneyrou. Paris: Sorbonne.

Bayer, Francis. 1981. *De Schönberg à Cage: Essai sur la notion d'espace sonore dans la musique contemporaine*. Paris: Klincksieck.

Beiser, Frederick. 2005. *Hegel*. New York and London: Routledge.

Bennett. Gerald. 1986. 'The Early Works', in *Pierre Boulez: A Symposium*, ed. William Glock. London: Eulenburg, 41–84.

Berdyaev, Nicolas. 1933. *The End of our Time: Together with an Essay on the General Line of Soviet Philosophy*. Trans. Donald Atwater. London: Sheed & Ward.

Berdyaev, Nicolas. 1938. *Solitude and Society*. Trans. George Reavey. London: Geoffrey Bles.

Berdyaev, Nicolas. 1950. *Dream and Reality: An Essay in Autobiography*. Trans. Katharine Lampert. London: Geoffrey Bles.

Bergson, Henri. 1910. *Time and Free Will*. Trans. F. L. Pogson. London: George Allen & Unwin.

Bergson, Henri. 2004. *Matter and Memory*. Trans. Nancy Margaret Paul and W. Scott Palmer. Mineola, New York: Dover.

Bernstein, David W. 2002. 'Cage and High Modernism', in *The Cambridge Companion to John Cage*. Cambridge: Cambridge University Press, 186–213.

Bogue, Ronald. 1989. *Deleuze and Guattari*. London and New York: Routledge.

Boissière, Anne. 1999. *La Vérité de la musique moderne*. Villeneuve d'Ascq: Septentrion Presses Universitaires.

Boivin, Jean. 1995. *La Classe de Messiaen*. Paris: Christian Bourgois.

Borio, Gianmario, and Hermann Danuser (eds.). 1997. *Im Zenit der Moderne: Die Internationalen Ferienkurse für Neue Musik, Darmstadt, 1946–1966*. 4 vols. Freiburg im Breisgau: Rombach Verlag.

Bösche, Thomas. 1999. 'Auf der Suche nach dem Unbekannten oder Zur Deuxième Sonate (1946–1948) von Pierre Boulez und der Frage nach der seriellen Musik', in *Die Anfänge der seriellen Musik*. Berlin: Wolke, 37–96.

Boucourechliev, André. 1981. 'André Boucourechliev/Boris de Schloezer', in *Boris de Schloezer, Cahiers pour un Temps*. Paris: Centre Georges Pompidou/Pandora Editions, 17–24.

Boucourechliev, André. 1987. *Stravinsky*. Trans. Martin Cooper. London: Victor Gollancz.

Boulez, Pierre. 1963. *Penser la musique aujourd'hui*. Paris: Éd. Gonthier (Gallimard).

Boulez, Pierre. 1971a. *Boulez on Music Today*. Trans. Susan Bradshaw and Richard Rodney Bennett. London: Faber & Faber.

Boulez, Pierre. 1971b. 'Pierre Boulez interrogé . . .', *Les Cahiers canadiens de musique* (Spring–Summer): 31–48.

Boulez, Pierre. 1976. *Conversations with Célestin Deliège*. London: Eulenburg.

Boulez, Pierre. 1986. *Orientations: Collected Writings*. Ed. Jean-Jacques Nattiez, trans. Martin Cooper. London: Faber & Faber.

Boulez, Pierre. 1987. 'Timbre and Composition – Timbre and Language', *Contemporary Music Review* 2/1: 161–71.

Boulez, Pierre. 1989. *Le Pays fertile: Paul Klee*. Texte préparé et présenté par Paule Thévenin. Paris: Gallimard.

Boulez, Pierre. 1991. *Stocktakings from an Apprenticeship*. Collected and presented by Paule Thévenin, trans. Stephen Walsh. Oxford: Clarendon Press.

Boulez, Pierre. 1995. *Points de repère I. Imaginer*. Textes réunis par Jean-Jacques Nattiez et Sophie Galaise. Paris: Christian Bourgois.

Boulez, Pierre. 2003. *Boulez on Conducting. Conversations with Cécile Gilly*. Trans. Richard Stokes. London: Faber & Faber.

Boulez, Pierre. 2005a. *Regards sur autrui (Points de repère II)*. Textes réunis et présentés par Jean-Jacques Nattiez and Sophie Galaise. Paris: Christian Bourgois.

Boulez, Pierre 2005b. *Leçons de musique (Points de repère III)*. Textes réunis et établis par Jean-Jacques Nattiez. Paris: Christian Bourgois.

Boulez, Pierre, and John Cage. 1993. *The Boulez–Cage Correspondence*. Documents collected, ed. and intro. Jean-Jacques Nattiez, trans. and ed. Robert Samuels. Cambridge: Cambridge University Press.

Boulez, Pierre, and John Cage. 2002. *Correspondance et documents*. Nouvelle édition. Mainz: Schott Music International.

Boulez, Pierre, and Jonathan Cott. 1985. 'Sur l'état de la musique aujourd'hui', *Débat* 33: 140–51.

Boulez, Pierre, and Wolfgang Fink. 2000. 'Wolfgang Fink in Conversation with Pierre Boulez', in CD booklet, DG 463 475–2, Hamburg.

Boulez, Pierre, and André Schaeffner. 1998. *Correspondance 1954–1970*. Présentée et annotée par Rosângela Pereira de Tugny. Paris: Fayard.

Bowie, Andrew. 1993. *Schelling and Modern European Philosophy*. London and New York: Routledge.

Bradshaw, Susan. 1986. 'The Instrumental and Vocal Music', in *Pierre Boulez: A Symposium*, ed. William Glock. London: Eulenburg, 127–229.

Bradshaw, Susan. 1996. 'Composer or Recomposer?', *Musical Times* 137 (October): 5–12.

Breatnach, Mary. 1996. *Boulez and Mallarmé: A Study in Poetic Influence*. Aldershot: Scolar Press.

Brelet, Gisèle. 1949. *Le Temps musical*. Paris: Presses Universitaires de France.

Breton, André. 1963. *Manifestes du surréalisme*. Paris: Gallimard.

Breton, André. 1969. *Entretiens*. Paris: Gallimard.

Breton, André. 1987. *Mad Love*. Trans. Mary Ann Caws. Lincoln and London: University of Nebraska Press.

Brillouin, Léon. 1961. 'Science et imagination', *La Nouvelle Revue Française* 9/101 (Mai): 835–47.

Burde, Wolfgang. 1993. *György Ligeti: Eine Monographie*. Zurich: Atlantis Musikbuch.

Burkholder, J. Peter. 1999. 'Schoenberg the Reactionary', in *Schoenberg and his World*, ed. Walter Frisch, Princeton: Princeton University Press, 162–91.

Busch, Regina. 1985. 'On the Horizontal and Vertical Presentation of Musical Ideas and on Musical Space (1)', *Tempo* 154: 2–10.

Butor, Michel. 1964. 'Mallarmé selon Boulez', in *Essais sur les modernes*. Paris: Gallimard, 95–109.

Cage, John. 1981. *For the Birds: In Conversation with Daniel Charles*. London: Marion Boyars.

Carroll, Mark. 2003. *Music and Ideology in Cold War Europe*. Cambridge: Cambridge University Press.

Caws, Peter. 1992. 'Sartrean Structuralism?', in *The Cambridge Companion to Sartre*, ed. Christina Howells. Cambridge: Cambridge University Press, 293–317.

Chang, Sangtae. 1998. 'Boulez's Sonatine and the Genesis of his Twelve-Tone Practice'. Ph.D. diss., University of North Texas.

Charbonnier, Georges. 1961. *Entretiens avec Claude Lévi-Strauss*. Paris: Union Générale d'Éditions.

Charles, Daniel. 1965. 'Entr'acte: "Formal" or "Informal" Music?', *Musical Quarterly* 51 (January): 144–65.

Clifford, James. 1982. 'Ethnographie polyphonie collage', *Revue de Musicologie*, 68/1–2: 42–56.

Cooke, Peter. 1980. 'Heterophony', in *The New Grove Dictionary of Music and Musicians*, ed. Stanley Sadie. London: Macmillan, vol. 8, pp. 537–8.

Coplestone, Frederick C. 1990. *A History of Medieval Philosophy*. Notre Dame, IN, and London: University of Notre Dame Press.

Court, Raymond. 1971. 'Langage verbal et langages esthétiques', *Musique en jeu* 2: 16–29.

Craft, Robert. 1972. *Stravinsky: The Chronicle of a Friendship 1948–1971*. London: Victor Gollancz.

Craft, Robert. 1992. *Stravinsky: Glimpses of a Life*. London: Lime Tree.

Criton, Pascale. 1996. 'Wyschnegradsky, théoreticien et philosophe', in Ivan Wyschnegradsky, *La Loi de la pansonorité*. Texte établi et annoté par Franck

Jedrzejewski avec la collaboration de Pascale Criton. Geneva: Contrechamps, 9–54.

Cuvillier, Armand. 1972. *Nouveau précis de philosophie: La connaissance*, 8th edn, Paris: Armand Colin.

Dahlhaus, Carl. 1983. *Foundations of Music History*. Trans. J. B. Robinson. Cambridge: Cambridge University Press.

Dahlhaus, Carl. 1987. *Schoenberg and the New Music*. Trans. Derrick Puffett and Alfred Clayton. Cambridge: Cambridge University Press.

Dal Molin, Paulo. 2004. 'À propos des versets de Rituel in memoriam Bruno Maderna', *Mitteilungen der Paul Sacher Stiftung* 17: 29–34.

Dal Molin, Paulo. 2006. '. . . "Sans cause extérieure apparente, ni affluents, ni glaciers, ni orages" . . . La construction de l'hétérophonie dans les versets de *Rituel*', in *Pierre Boulez: Techniques d'écriture et enjeux esthétiques*, ed. Jean-Louis Leleu and Pascal Decroupet. Geneva: Contrechamps, 217–54.

Dastur, Françoise. 2000. *Telling Time*. London and New Brunswick, NJ: Athlone.

Decarsin, François. 1998. 'Metamorphoses of Invention', *Perspectives of New Music* 36/2: 13–39.

Decroupet, Pascal. 2003. 'Comment Boulez pense sa musique au début des années soixante', in *Pli selon pli de Pierre Boulez: Entretien et études*. Geneva: Contrechamps, 49–57.

Decroupet, Pascal, and Jean-Louis Leleu. 2006. '"Penser sensiblement" la musique: production et description du matériau harmonique dans le troisième mouvement du *Marteau sans maître*', in *Pierre Boulez: Techniques d'écriture et enjeux esthétiques*, ed. Jean-Louis Leleu and Pascal Decroupet. Geneva: Contrechamps, 177–215.

Delaere, Mark (ed.). 1994. 'Karel Goeyvaerts: Paris-Darmstadt 1947–1955. Excerpt from the Autobiographical Portrait', *Revue belge de Musicologie* 48: 35–54.

Deleuze, Gilles. 1983. *Nietzsche and Philosophy*. Trans. Hugh Tomlinson. London: Athlone.

Deleuze, Gilles. 1986. 'Boulez, Proust et Le Temps: "Occuper sans compter"', in *Éclats/Boulez*, ed. Claude Samuel. Paris: Éditions du Centre Pompidou, 98–100.

Deleuze, Gilles. 1988. *Foucault*. Trans. and ed. Seán Hand. London: Athlone.

Deleuze, Gilles. 1990. *The Logic of Sense*. Trans. Mark Lester with Charles Stivale, ed. Constantin V. Boundas. New York: Columbia University Press.

Deleuze, Gilles. 1991. *Bergsonism*. Trans. Hugh Tomlinson and Barbara Habberjam. New York: Zone.

Deleuze, Gilles. 1993. *The Fold: Leibniz and the Baroque*. Trans. Tom Conley. London: Athlone.

Deleuze, Gilles. 1994. *Difference and Repetition*. Trans. Paul Patton. London: Athlone.

Deleuze, Gilles. 1995. *Negotiations*. Trans. Martin Joughin. New York: Columbia University Press.

Deleuze, Gilles. 2004. *Desert Islands and Other Texts: 1953–1974.* Ed. David Lapoujade, trans. Michael Taormina. Los Angeles: Semiotext(e).

Deleuze, Gilles. 2006. *Two Regimes of Madness: Texts and Interviews 1975–1995.* Ed. David Lapoujade, trans. Ames Hodges and Mike Taormina. Boston: MIT Press, Semiotext(e).

Deleuze, Gilles, and Félix Guattari. 1988. *A Thousand Plateaus: Capitalism and Schizophrenia.* Trans. Brian Massumi. London: Athlone.

Deleuze, Gilles, and Félix Guattari. 1994. *What is Philosophy?* Trans. Graham Burchell and Hugh Tomlinson. London: Verso.

Deleuze, Gilles, and Claire Parnet. 1987. *Dialogues.* Trans. Hugh Tomlinson and Barbara Habberjam. London: Athlone.

Deliège, Célestin. 1967. 'La Musicologie devant le structuralisme', *L'Arc* 26: 50–9.

Deliège, Célestin. 1988. 'Moment de Pierre Boulez: sur l'introduction orchestrale de *Répons*', *InHarmoniques* 4: 181–202.

Deliège, Célestin. 1992. 'Musiques militantes dans un siècle de crises', in *Mélanges offerts à Nicolas Ruwet*, ed. L. Tasmowski and A. Zribi-Hertz, Paris, 6–23, www.entretemps.asso.fr/Deliege/Celestin/Textes/MusiquesMilitantes.html (viewed online 27 April 2009).

Deliège, Célestin. 1995. 'En exil d'un jardin d'Eden', *Revue de Musicologie* 81/1: 87–119, www.entretemps.asso.fr/Deliege/Celestin/Textes/Eden.html (viewed online 27 April 2009).

Deliège, Célestin. 2001. 'Le Temps affronté: les années post-weberniennes', in *Musique contemporaine: Perspectives théoriques et philosophiques.* Mardaga, 191–216.

Depraz, Natalie. 1998. 'Registres phénoménologiques du sonore', in *L'Espace: musique/philosophie*, Textes réunis et présentés par Jean-Marc Chouvel et Makis Solomos. Paris: L'Harmattan, 3–15.

Descombes, Vincent. 1980. *Modern French Philosophy.* Trans. L. Scott-Fox and J. M. Harding. Cambridge: Cambridge University Press.

Di Pietro, Rocco. 2001. *Dialogues with Boulez.* Lanham, MD, and London: The Scarecrow Press.

Doeser, Linda. 1995. *The Life and Works of Klee.* Bristol: Parragon.

Dosse, François. 1997. *History of Structuralism*, 2 vols. Trans. Deborah Glassman, Minneapolis: University of Minnesota Press.

Dosse, François. 2007. *Gilles Deleuze et Félix Guattari: Biographie croisée.* Paris: La Découverte.

Dufour, Valérie. 2003. 'La *Poétique musicale* de Stravinsky: Un manuscrit inédit de Souvtchinsky', *Revue de Musicologie* 89/2: 373–92.

Dufour, Valérie. 2004. 'Strawinsky vers Souvtchinsky: Thème et variations sur la *Poétique musicale*', *Mitteilungen der Paul Sacher Stiftung* 17: 17–23.

Dufour, Valérie. 2006. *Stravinski et ses exégètes (1910–1940).* Éditions de L'Université de Bruxelles.

Dufourt, Hugues. 1991. *Musique, pouvoir, écriture.* Paris: Christian Bourgois.

Dufourt, Hugues. 1993. '*Oeuvre* and History', *Contemporary Music Review* 8/1: 71–94.

Dupouy, Christine. 1987. *René Char*. Paris: Belfond.

Eagleton, Terry. 1996. *Literary Theory: An Introduction*. Minneapolis: University of Minnesota Press.

Eco, Umberto. 1971. 'Pensée structurale et pensée sérielle', *Musique en jeu* 5: 45–56.

Eco, Umberto. 1976. *A Theory of Semiotics*. Bloomington: Indiana University Press.

Eco, Umberto. 1984. *Semiotics and the Philosophy of Language*. London: Macmillan.

Eco, Umberto, 1989. *The Open Work*. Trans. Anna Cancogni. Cambridge, MA: Harvard University Press.

Émery, Éric. 1998. *Temps et musique*. Lausanne: L'Age d'Homme.

Engel, Pascal. 2006. 'Vies parallèles: Rougier et Cavaillès', *Philosophiae Scientiae* 10/2: 1–30.

Eribon, Didier. 1991. *Michel Foucault*. Trans. Betsy Wing. London: Faber & Faber.

Ffrench, Patrick. 1995. *The Time of Theory: A History of Tel Quel (1960–1983)*. Oxford: Clarendon Press.

Forster, Michael. 1993. 'Hegel's Dialectical Method', in *The Cambridge Companion to Hegel*, ed. Frederick C. Beiser. Cambridge: Cambridge University Press, 130–70.

Foucault, Michel. 1977. 'Theatrum Philosophicum', in *Language, Counter-Memory, Practice*, ed. Donald F. Bouchard, trans. Donald F. Bouchard and Sherry Simon. Ithaca, NY: Cornell University Press, 165–96.

Foucault, Michel. 1998. 'Pierre Boulez, Passing through the Screen', in *Michel Foucault: Aesthetics. Essential Works of Foucault 1954–1984*, vol. 2, trans. Robert Hurley. London: Penguin, 241–4.

Foucault, Michel, and Pierre Boulez. 1985. 'Contemporary Music and the Public', *Perspectives of New Music* 24/1: 6–12.

Gable, David. 1985–6. 'Ramifying Connections: An Interview with Pierre Boulez', *Journal of Musicology* 4/1: 105–13.

Gable, David. 1990. 'Boulez's Two Cultures: The Post-War European Synthesis and Tradition', *Journal of the American Musicological Society* 43/3: 426–56.

Gandillac, Maurice de. 1941. *La Philosophie de Nicolas de Cues*. Paris: Aubier, Éditions Montaigne.

Gandillac, Maurice de. 2001. *Nicolas de Cues*. Paris: Ellipses.

Gärtner, Susanne. 2002. 'Pierre Boulez' "Sonatine für Flöte und Klavier" und ihre neu aufgetauchte Frühfassung', *Die Musikforschung* 55/1: 51–9.

Gerzso, Andrew. 1984. 'Reflections on Répons', *Contemporary Music Review* 1/1: 23–34.

Glebov, Sergey. 2006. 'Le Frémissement du temps: Petr Suvchinsky, l'eurasisme et l'esthétique de la modernité', in *Pierre Souvtchinski, cahiers d'étude*, sous la direction d'Éric Humbertclaude. Paris: L'Harmattan, 163–223.

Glock, William (ed.). 1986. *Pierre Boulez: A Symposium*. London: Eulenburg.

Goldbeck, Frederick. 1950. 'Current Chronicle: France', *Musical Quarterly* 36/2: 291–5.

Goldman, Jonathan. 2001. '*Understanding Pierre Boulez's Anthèmes [1991]: "Creating a Labyrinth out of another Labyrinth"*'. diss., Université de Montréal, www.andante.com/reference/academy/thesis/anthemsthesis.pdf

Goldman, Jonathan. 2006. '*Exploding/Fixed: Form as Opposition in the Writings and Later Works of Pierre Boulez*'. Ph.D. diss., Université de Montréal.

Goléa, Antoine. 1982. *Rencontres avec Pierre Boulez*. Paris and Geneva: Slatkine.

Grant, M. J. 2001. *Serial Music, Serial Aesthetics: Compositional Theory in Post-War Europe*. Cambridge: Cambridge University Press.

Griffiths, Paul. 1995. *Modern Music and After: Directions Since 1945*. Oxford: Oxford University Press.

Griffiths, Paul. 2002. 'Pierre Boulez: "Pli selon pli"', in CD booklet, DG 471 344–2, Hamburg, 4–7.

Guerlac, Suzanne. 1997. *Literary Polemics. Bataille, Sartre, Valéry, Breton*. Stanford: Stanford University Press.

Guillaume, Paul. 1979. *La Psychologie de la forme*. Paris: Flammarion.

Hába, Alois. 1937. 'Quelques réflexions sur l'interprétation et sur les bases théoriques de la musique à quarts et à sixièmes de ton', *La Revue Musicale* (Juin–Juillet): 92–5.

Hanslick, Eduard. 1986. *On the Musically Beautiful*. Trans. and ed. Geoffrey Payzant. Indianapolis, IN: Hackett.

Hegel, G. W. F. 1975. *Hegel's Logic: Being Part One of the 'Encyclopaedia of the Philosophical Sciences'* (1830), 3rd edn. Trans. William Wallace. Oxford: Clarendon Press.

Hegel, G. W. F. 1977. *Phenomenology of Spirit*. Trans. A. V. Millar. Oxford: Oxford University Press.

Helffer, Claude. 1986. 'Analyse musicale, pédagogie et interprétation', *Analyse musicale* 2: 62–7.

Herzen, Alexander. 1956. *Selected Philosophical Works*. Trans. L. Navrozov. Moscow: Foreign Languages Publishing House.

Hirsbrunner, Theo. 1985. *Pierre Boulez und sein Werk*, Laaber: Laaber-Verlag.

Honderich, Ted (ed.). 1995. *The Oxford Companion to Philosophy*. Oxford: Oxford University Press.

Hopkins, Jasper. 2002. 'Nicholas of Cusa (1401–1464): First Modern Philosopher?' www.cla.umn.edu/jhopkins/CUSA-midweststudies.pdf, accessed 13 May 2008.

Humbertclaude, Éric (directeur). 2006. *Pierre Souvtchinski, cahiers d'étude*. Paris: L'Harmattan.

Jakobson, Roman 1988. 'Linguistics and Poetics', in *Modern Criticism and Theory: A Reader*, ed. David Lodge. London and New York: Longman, 32–57.

Jameux, Dominique. 1991. *Pierre Boulez*. Trans. Susan Bradshaw. London: Faber & Faber.

Jedrzejewski, Franck. 1987. 'La Mise en œuvre du principe dodécaphonique dans la 1re Sonate de Pierre Boulez', *Analyse musicale* 7: 69–76.

Jedrzejewski, Franck. 2005. 'Avant-propos', in Ivan Wyschnegradsky, *Une philosophie dialectique de l'art musical*. Paris: L'Harmattan, 7–9.

Kant, Immanuel. 1929. *Critique of Pure Reason*. Trans. Norman Kemp Smith. London: Macmillan.

Kern, Stephen. 1983. *The Culture of Time and Space 1880–1918*. Cambridge, MA: Harvard University Press.

Klee, Paul. 1953. *Pedagogical Sketchbook*. Trans. and intro. Sibyl Moholy-Nagy. London: Faber & Faber.

Klee, Paul. 1961. *The Thinking Eye*. Ed. Jürg Spiller, trans. Ralph Manheim with assistance from Charlotte Weidler and Joyce Wittenborn. London: Lund Humphries.

Koblyakov, Lev. 1990. *Pierre Boulez: A World of Harmony*. Chur: Harwood.

Kohler, Gun-Britt. 2003. *Boris de Schloezer (1881–1969). Wege aus der russischen Emigration*. Cologne: Böhlau Verlag.

Kojève, Alexandre. 1980. *Introduction to the Reading of Hegel: Lectures on the Phenomenology of Spirit*. Assembled by Raymond Queneau, ed. Allan Bloom, trans. James H. Nichols, Jr. Ithaca, NY, and London: Cornell University Press.

Kristeva, Julia. 1996. *Time and Sense: Proust and the Experience of Literature*. Trans. Ross Guberman. New York: Columbia University Press.

Kuhn, Thomas. 1962. *The Structure of Scientific Revolutions*. Chicago: University of Chicago Press.

Kurtz, Michael. 1992. *Stockhausen: A Biography*. Trans. Richard Toop. London: Faber & Faber.

Langlois, Frank. 2004. 'Introduction', in *Un siècle de musique russe (1830–1930)*. Arles: Actes Sud/Association Pierre Souvtchinsky, 13–95.

Leach, Edmund. 1970. *Lévi-Strauss*. London: Fontana.

Lee, Jonathan Scott. 1996. 'Mimêsis and Beyond: Mallarmé, Boulez, and Cage (1986–87)', in *Writings about John Cage*, ed. Richard Kostelanetz. Ann Arbor: University of Michigan Press, 180–212.

Leibowitz, René. 1949a. *Schoenberg and his School: The Contemporary Stage of the Language of Music*. Trans. Dika Newlin. New York: Philosophical Library.

Leibowitz, René. 1949b. *Introduction à la musique de douze sons*. Paris: L'Arche.

Lerdahl, Fred. 1992. 'Cognitive Constraints on Compositional Systems', *Contemporary Music Review* 6/2: 97–121.

Lévi-Strauss, Claude. 1970. *The Raw and the Cooked: Introduction to a Science of Mythology: I*. Trans. John and Doreen Weightman. London: Jonathan Cape.

Lévi-Strauss, Claude. 1973. *Anthropologie structurale deux*. Paris: Plon.

Lévi-Strauss, Claude, and Didier Eribon. 1991. *Conversations with Claude Lévi-Strauss*. Trans. Paula Wissing. Chicago and London: The University of Chicago Press.

Ligeti, György. 2001. *Neuf essais sur la musique*. Trans. (from German) Catherine Fourcassié. Geneva: Contrechamps.

Lippman, Edward. 1992. *A History of Western Musical Aesthetics*. Lincoln and London: University of Nebraska Press.

Lyotard, Jean-François. 1972. 'Plusieurs silences', *Musique en jeu* 9: 64–76.

Lyotard, Jean-François. 1986. 'La Réflexion créatrice', in *Éclats/Boulez*, ed. Claude Samuel. Paris: Éditions du Centre Pompidou, 14–17.

Lyotard, Jean-François. 1991. *The Inhuman: Reflections on Time*. Trans. Geoffrey Bennington and Rachel Bowlby. Cambridge: Polity.

Lyotard, Jean-François. 1997. *Postmodern Fables*. Trans. Georges Van Den Abbeele. Minneapolis: University of Minnesota Press.

Lyotard, Jean-François. 2004. *Libidinal Economy*. Trans. Iain Hamilton Grant. London: Continuum.

McCallum, Peter. 1992. 'Deuxième sonate – que me veux-tu?: Sonata Form in the First Movement of Boulez's Second Piano Sonata', *Studies in Music* 26: 62–84.

Macey, David. 1993. *The Lives of Michel Foucault*. London: Vintage.

Maconie, Robin. 1976. *The Works of Karlheinz Stockhausen*. London: Oxford University Press.

Malabou, Catherine. 1996. 'Who's Afraid of Hegelian Wolves?', in *Deleuze: A Critical Reader*, ed. Paul Patton. Oxford: Blackwell, 114–38.

Mallarmé, Stéphane. 1994. *Collected Poems*. Trans. Henry Weinfield. Berkeley: University of California Press.

Malm, William P. 1977. *Music Cultures of the Pacific, the Near East and Asia*. 2nd edn. New Jersey: Prentice-Hall.

Marcel, Gabriel. 2005. *Music and Philosophy*. Trans. Stephen Maddux and Robert E. Wood. Milwaukee, WI: Marquette University Press.

Meine, Sabine. 2000. *Ein Zwölftöner in Paris: Studien zu Biographie und Wirkung von René Leibowitz (1913–1972)*. Augsburg: Wissner Verlag.

Menger, Pierre-Michel. 1990. 'From the Domaine Musical to IRCAM: Pierre Boulez in conversation with Pierre-Michel Menger', trans. Jonathan W. Bernard, *Perspectives of New Music* 28/1: 6–18.

Messiaen, Olivier. 1994. *Traité de rythme, de couleur, et d'ornithologie*, vol. 1. Paris: Alphonse Leduc.

Metzger, Heinz-Klaus. 1960. 'Just Who is Growing Old?', trans. Leo Black, *die Reihe* 4: 63–80.

Metzger, Heinz-Klaus. 1961. 'Abortive Concepts in the Theory and Criticism of Music', trans. Leo Black, *die Reihe* 5, 21–9.

Metzger, Heinz-Klaus. 1980. *Musik Wozu: Literaturen zu Noten*. Frankfurt am Main: Suhrkamp.

Mosch, Ulrich. 2004. *Musikalisches Hören serieller Musik: Untersuchungen am Beispiel von Pierre Boulez' Le Marteau sans maître*. Saarbrücken: Pfau.

Mueller, Gustav E. 1996. 'The Hegel Legend of "Thesis-Antithesis-Synthesis"', in *The Hegel Myths and Legends*, ed. Jon Stewart. Evanston, IL: Northwestern University Press, 301–5.

Nattiez, Jean-Jacques. 1973a. 'Rencontre avec Lévi-Strauss: le plaisir et la structure', *Musique en jeu* 12: 3–10.

Nattiez, Jean-Jacques. 1973b. 'Analyse musicale et sémiologie: le structuralisme de Lévi-Strauss', *Musique en jeu* 12: 59–79.

Nattiez, Jean-Jacques. 1986. 'On Reading Boulez', in Pierre Boulez, *Orientations*. London: Faber & Faber, 11–28.

Nattiez, Jean-Jacques. 1993a. 'Cage and Boulez: A Chapter of Music History', in *The Boulez–Cage Correspondence*. Trans. Robert Samuels. Cambridge: Cambridge University Press, 3–24.

Nattiez, Jean-Jacques. 1993b. *Le Combat de Chronos et d'Orphée*. Paris: Christian Bourgois.

Nattiez, Jean-Jacques. 2005a. 'Pierre Boulez Professeur', in Pierre Boulez, *Leçons de musique*. Paris: Christian Bourgois, 11–16.

Nattiez, Jean-Jacques (ed.). 2005b. 'Document. Darmstädter Internationale Ferienkurse für Neue Musik. Transcriptions des journées des 16, 18 et 23 Juillet 1963'. 'Table Ronde avec Luciano Berio, Pierre Boulez et Henri Pousseur', *Circuit* 15/3: 23–52.

Nattiez, Jean-Jacques. 2008. *Lévi-Strauss musicien: essai sur la tentation homologique*. Actes Sud.

Neff, Severine. 1994. 'Introduction', in Arnold Schoenberg, *Coherence, Counterpoint, Instrumentation, Instruction in Form*. Lincoln and London: University of Nebraska Press, pp. xxiii–lxix.

Neff, Severine. 1999. 'Schoenberg as Theorist: Three Forms of Presentation', in *Schoenberg and his World*, ed. Walter Frisch. Princeton: Princeton University Press, 55–84.

Neighbour, Oliver. 1983. 'Arnold Schoenberg', in *The New Grove Second Viennese School*. London: Macmillan, 1–85.

Nicolas, François. 2005 'De l'intellectualité de Boulez (1): Ses références à la pensée scientifique', www.entretemps.asso.fr/Nicolas/IM/, accessed 12 March 2008.

Nunes, Emmanuel. 1994. 'Temps et spatialité', in *Espaces*, Les Cahiers de L'IRCAM 5: 121–41.

O'Hagan, Peter. 1997. 'Pierre Boulez. Sonate "Que me veux-tu?" An Investigation of the Manuscript Sources in Relation to the Third Sonata and the Issue of Performer Choice'. Ph.D. diss., University of Surrey.

O'Hagan, Peter. 2006. 'Pierre Boulez and the Foundation of IRCAM', in *French Music since Berlioz*, ed. Richard Langham Smith and Caroline Potter. Aldershot: Ashgate, 303–30.

Olivier, Philippe. 2005. *Le Maître et son marteau*. Paris: Hermann.

Paddison, Max. 1993. *Adorno's Aesthetics of Music*. Cambridge: Cambridge University Press.

Patton, Paul. 1994. 'Anti-Platonism and Art', in *Gilles Deleuze and the Theater of Philosophy*, ed. Constantin V. Boundas, and Dorothea Olkowski. New York and London: Routledge, 141–56.

Paulme-Schaeffner, Denise. 1982. 'André Schaeffner 1895–1980', *Revue de Musicologie* 68/1–2: 363–5.

Paulme-Schaeffner, Denise. 1998. 'André Schaeffner (1895–1980)', in *Pierre Boulez, André Schaeffner: Correspondance 1954–1970*. Paris: Fayard, 11–13.

Pearson, Keith Ansell. 2002. *Philosophy and the Adventure of the Virtual: Bergson and the Time of Life*. London: Routledge.

Peyser, Joan. 1977. *Boulez: Composer, Conductor, Enigma*. London: Cassell.

Philippot, Michel. 1954. 'Liberté sous conditions', *Domaine Musical* 1, Grasset: 24–37.

Philippot, Michel. 1966. 'Pierre Boulez Today', *Perspectives of New Music* 5/1: 153–60.

Piaget, Jean. 1953. *Logic and Psychology*. Manchester: Manchester University Press.

Piaget, Jean. 1971. *Structuralism*. London: Routledge & Kegan Paul.

Picon, Gaëtan. 1981. 'Les Formes et l'esprit (la pensée de Boris de Schloezer)', in *Boris de Schloezer*, Cahiers pour un Temps. Paris: Centre Georges Pompidou/Pandora Editions, 61–6.

Piencikowski, Robert. 1991. 'Introduction', in Pierre Boulez, *Stocktakings from an Apprenticeship*. Oxford: Clarendon Press, pp. xiii–xxix.

Piencikowski, Robert. 1993. '"Assez lent, suspendu, comme imprévisible". Quelques aperçus sur les travaux d'approche d'*Éclat*', *Genesis* 4: 51–67.

Piencikowski, Robert. 1998. 'Introduction', in *André Schaeffner: Variations sur la Musique*. Paris: Fayard, 11–17.

Piencikowski, Robert. 2002. '. . . iacta est', in *Pierre Boulez/John Cage: Correspondance et Documents*, new edn. Mainz: Schott, 41–60.

Popper, Karl. 1957. *The Poverty of Historicism*. London: Routledge & Kegan Pual.

Pousseur, Henri. 1954. 'L'Impossible Objet', *Domaine Musical* 1, Grasset: 109–14.

Pousseur, Henri. 1964. 'Music, Form and Practice (an Attempt to Reconcile Some Contradictions)'. Trans. Margaret Shenfield, *die Reihe* 6: 77–93.

Pousseur, Henri. 1970. *Fragments théoriques I sur la musique expérimentale*. Brussels: Université Libre de Bruxelles.

Pousseur, Henri. 1972. *Musique, sémantique, société*. Paris-Tournai: Casterman/Poche.

Pousseur, Henri. 1997. *Musiques croisées*. Paris: L'Harmattan.

Pousseur, Henri. 2004. *Écrits théoriques 1954–1967*. Choisis et présentés par Pascal Decroupet. Sprimont: Mardaga.

Rey, Anne. 1993. 'The Musical Press in France', *Contemporary Music Review* 8/1: 45–50.

Rosen, Charles. 1976. *Schoenberg*. Glasgow: Fontana/Collins.

Rosen, Charles. 1986. 'The Piano Music', in *Pierre Boulez: A Symposium*, ed. William Glock. London: Eulenburg, 85–97.

Rougemont, Denis de. 1954. 'There is no "Modern Music"', *Encounter* 3/2 (August): 50–1.

Rouget, Gilbert, and François Lesure. 1982. 'Qui étiez-vous André Schaeffner?', *Revue de Musicologie* 68/1–2: 3–15.

Rougier, Louis. 1920. *Les Paralogismes du rationalisme*. Paris: Félix Alcan.

Rougier, Louis. 1921. *La Structure des théories déductives*. Paris: Félix Alcan.

Rougier, Louis. 1955. *Traité de la connaissance*. Paris: Gauthier-Villars.

Rougier, Louis. 1956. 'La Nouvelle Théorie de la connaissance', *La Nouvelle Revue Française* 4/42 (Juin): 999–1015.

Ruwet, Nicolas. 1972. *Langage, musique, poésie*. Paris: Seuil.

Sadie, Stanley (ed.). 1980. *The New Grove Dictionary of Music and Musicians*. London: Macmillan.

Sadie, Stanley, and John Tyrrell (eds.) 2001. *The New Grove Dictionary of Music and Musicians*. 2nd edn, London: Macmillan.

Samuel, Claude (ed.). 1986. *Éclats/Boulez*. Paris: Éditions du Centre Pompidou.

Samuel, Claude. 1976. *Conversations with Olivier Messiaen*. Trans. Felix Apra-hamian. London: Stainer & Bell.

Samuel, Claude. 2006. 'Interview with Pierre Boulez', in CD booklet, *Pierre Boulez: Le Domaine Musical*, vol. 1, Accord 476 9209.

Savage, Roger W. H. 1989. *Structure and Sorcery: The Aesthetics of Post-War Serial Composition and Indeterminacy*. New York: Garland.

Schaeffner, André. 1998. *Variations sur la musique*. Paris: Fayard.

Schelling, F. W. J. 1978. *System of Transcendental Idealism (1800)*. Trans. Peter Heath, intro. Michael Vater. Charlottesville: University Press of Virginia.

Schelling, F. W. J. 1984. *Bruno, or, On the Natural and the Divine Principle of Things*. Ed., trans. and intro. Michael G. Vater. Albany: State University of New York Press.

Schelling, F. W. J. 1989. *The Philosophy of Art*. Ed., trans. and intro. Douglas W. Stott, foreword David Simpson. Minneapolis: University of Minnesota Press.

Schiffer, Daniel Salvatore. 1998. *Umberto Eco: Le Labyrinthe du monde*. Paris: Ramsay.

Schiller, Friedrich. 1967. *On the Aesthetic Education of Man*. Ed., trans. with intro., commentary and glossary Elizabeth M. Wilkinson and L. A. Willoughby. Oxford: Clarendon Press.

Schloezer, Boris de. 1928a. 'À la recherche de la réalité musicale', *La Revue Musicale* 9/3 (Janvier): 214–28.

Schloezer, Boris de. 1928b. 'À la recherche de la réalité musicale', *La Revue Musicale* 9/4 (Février): 48–52.

Schloezer, Boris de. 1928c. 'À la recherche de la réalité musicale', *La Revue Musicale* 9/6 (Avril): 244–9.

Schloezer, Boris de. 1947. *Introduction à J.-S. Bach. Essai d'esthétique musicale*. Paris: Gallimard (Bibliothèque des idées).

Schloezer, Boris de. 1954a. 'Musique et histoire', in *La Musique et ses problèmes contemporains. Cahiers Renaud-Barrault* 2/3: 116–20.

Schloezer, Boris de. 1954b. 'Musique contemporaine, musique moderne', *La Nouvelle Revue Française* 2/15 (Mars): 513–16.

Schloezer, Boris de. 1955. 'Retour à Descartes', *La Nouvelle Revue Française* 3/30 (Juin): 1084–8.

Schloezer, Boris de. 1956. 'À propos des concerts du Domaine Musical', *La Nouvelle Revue Française* 4/41 (Mai): 930–2.

Schloezer, Boris de. 1963. 'Présence du passé', in *La Musique et ses problèmes con-temporains, Cahiers Renaud-Barrault* 41 (Décembre): 244–52.

Schloezer, Boris de, and Marina Scriabine. 1959. *Problèmes de la musique moderne.* Paris: Minuit.

Schoenberg, Arnold. 1975. *Style and Idea.* Ed. Leonard Stein, trans. Leo Black. London: Faber & Faber.

Schoenberg, Arnold. 1994. *Coherence, Counterpoint, Instrumentation, Instruction in Form.* Trans. Charlotte M. Cross and Severine Neff, ed. and intro. Severine Neff. Lincoln and London: University of Nebraska Press.

Scruton, Roger. 1997. *The Aesthetics of Music.* Oxford: Clarendon Press.

Solomos, Makis. 1998. 'L'Espace-Son', in *L'Espace: Musique/Philosophie*, textes réunis et présentés par Jean-Marc Chouvel and Makis Solomos. Paris: L'Harmattan, 211–24.

Souris, André. 2000. *La Lyre à Double Tranchant: Écrits sur la musique et le surréalisme*, présentés et commentés par Robert Wangermée. Sprimont: Mardaga.

Souvtchinsky, Pierre. 1946. 'Igor Strawinsky', *Contrepoints* 2 (Février), 19–31.

Souvtchinsky, Pierre. 1954. 'À propos d'un retard', in *La Musique et ses problèmes contemporains, Cahiers Renaud-Barrault* 2/3: 121–7.

Souvtchinsky, Pierre. 1956. 'Le Mot-Fantôme', *La Nouvelle Revue Française* 4/42 (Juin): 1107–9.

Souvtchinsky, Pierre. 1982. 'Un homme à découvert', *Revue de Musicologie* 68/1–2: 389–90.

Souvtchinsky, Pierre. 1990. *(Re) Lire Souvtchinski.* Textes choisis par Éric Hubert-claude. La Bresse.

Souvtchinsky, Pierre. 2004. *Un siècle de musique russe (1830–1930).* Réalisée et présentée par Frank Langlois. Arles: Actes Sud/Association Pierre Souvtchinsky.

Stacey, Peter F. 1987. *Boulez and the Modern Concept.* Aldershot: Scolar Press.

Stanley, Glenn. 2001. 'Historiography', *The New Grove Dictionary of Music and Musicians*, 2nd edn, ed. Stanley Sadie and John Tyrrell. London: Macmillan, vol. 11, pp. 546–61.

Stockhausen, Karlheinz. 1954. 'Situation actuelle du métier de compositeur', *Domaine Musical* 1, Grasset: 126–41.

Stockhausen, Karlheinz. 1958. 'Structure and Experiential Time', trans. Leo Black, *die Reihe* 2: 64–74.

Stockhausen, Karlheinz. 1959. '... how time passes ...', trans. Cornelius Cardew, *die Reihe* 3: 10–40.

Stockhausen, Karlheinz. 1963a. *Texte zur elektronischen und instrumentalen Musik* 1. Cologne: DuMont Schauberg.

Stockhausen, Karlheinz. 1963b. 'Invention et découverte', in *La Musique et ses problèmes contemporains, Cahiers Renaud-Barrault* 41 (Décembre): 147–68.

Stockhausen, Karlheinz. 1988. 'Musique dans l'espace', trans. from German Christian Meyer, *Contrechamps* 9: 78–100.

Stockhausen, Karlheinz. 1989. *Stockhausen on Music: Lectures and Interviews*. Comp. ed. Robin Maconie. London: Marion Boyars.

Stoïanova, Ivanka. 1974. 'La *Troisième Sonate* de Boulez et le projet mallarméen du livre', *Musique en jeu* 16: 9–28.

Stoïanova, Ivanka. 1976. 'Narrativisme, téléologie et invariance dans l'œuvre musicale: à propos de *Rituel* de Pierre Boulez', *Musique en jeu* 25: 15–31.

Stoïanova, Ivanka. 1978. *Geste – texte – musique*. Paris: Union Générale d'Éditions.

Stravinsky, Igor. 1942. *Poetics of Music in the Form of Six Lessons*. Trans. Arthur Knodel and Ingolf Dahl. Cambridge, MA: Harvard University Press.

Stravinsky, Igor. 1972. *Themes and Conclusions*. London: Faber & Faber.

Stravinsky, Igor. 2000. *Poétique musicale sous forme de six leçons*. Édition établie, présentée et annotée par Myriam Soumagnac. Paris: Flammarion.

Stuckenschmidt, H. H.. 1959. *Arnold Schoenberg*. Trans. Edith Temple Roberts and Humphrey Searle. London: John Calder.

Sweeney-Turner, Steve. 1994. '*The Sonorous Body: Music, Enlightenment and Deconstruction*'. Ph.D. diss., University of Edinburgh.

Szendy, Peter. 1998. 'Musique, temps réel', *Résonance* 14: 5–9.

Taruskin, Richard. 1996. *Stravinsky and the Russian Traditions: A Biography of the Works through Mavra*. 2 vols. Oxford: Oxford University Press.

Thomson, Virgil. 1946. 'Les Comptes d'Orphée', *Contrepoints* 5 (Décembre): 17–45.

Tiedemann, Rolf. 1996. 'Nur ein Gast in der Tafelrunde', in *Von Kranichstein zur Gegenwart: 50 Jahre Darmstädter Ferienkurse*. Stuttgart: Daco Verlag, 149–55.

Tugny, Rosângela Pereira de (ed.). 1998. *Pierre Boulez, André Schaeffner: Correspondance 1954–1970*. Paris: Fayard.

Van den Toorn, Pieter C. 1983. *The Music of Igor Stravinsky*. New Haven and London: Yale University Press.

Volta, Ornella. 1989. *Satie: Seen through his Letters*. Trans. Michael Bullock. London and New York: Marion Boyars.

Walsh, Stephen. 2006. *Stravinsky: The Second Exile: France and America, 1934–1971*. London: Jonathan Cape.

Walterskirchen, Konrad. 2006. 'Pëtr Suvčinskij (1882–1985)', in *Pierre Souvtchinski, cahiers d'étude*, sous la direction d'Éric Humbertclaude. Paris: L'Harmattan, 1–125.

Wangermée, Robert. 1995. *André Souris et le complexe d'Orphée*. Liège: Mardaga.

Wangermée, Robert. 2000. 'Avant-propos', in André Souris, *La Lyre à Double Tranchant: Écrits sur la musique et le surréalisme*. Sprimont: Mardaga.

Webern, Anton. 1963. *The Path to the New Music*. Ed. Willi Reich, trans. Leo Black. Bryn Mawr, PA: Theodore Presser Co.

Wiggershaus, Rolf. 1994. *The Frankfurt School. Its History, Theories and Political Significance*. Trans. Michael Robertson. Cambridge: Polity.

Williams, Alastair. 1994. '"Répons": Phantasmagoria or the Articulation of Space?', in *Theory, Analysis and Meaning in Music*, ed. Anthony Pople. Cambridge: Cambridge University Press, 195–210.

Williams, Alastair. 1997. *New Music and the Claims of Modernity*. Aldershot: Ashgate.

Williams, James. 2003. *Gilles Deleuze's Difference and Repetition: A Critical Introduction and Guide.* Edinburgh: Edinburgh University Press.

Worton, Michael. 1992. 'Introduction', in René Char, *The Dawn Breakers.* Newcastle upon Tyne: Bloodaxe Books, 11–45.

Worton, Michael. 1996 '"Between" Poetry and Philosophy: René Char and Martin Heidegger', in *Reconceptions: Reading Modern French Poetry*, ed. Russell King and Bernard McGuirk. University of Nottingham, 137–57.

Wyschnegradsky, Ivan. 1927. 'Musique et pansonorité', *La Revue Musicale* 9 (Décembre): 143–52.

Wyschnegradsky, Ivan. 1937. 'La Musique à quarts de ton et sa réalisation', *La Revue Musicale* 171 (Janvier): 26–33.

Wyschnegradsky, Ivan. 1996. *La Loi de la pansonorité.* Texte établi et annoté par Franck Jedrzejewski avec la collaboration de Pascale Criton. Geneva: Contrechamps.

Wyschnegradsky, Ivan. 2005. *Une philosophie dialectique de l'art musical.* Édité et annoté par Franck Jedrzejewski. Paris: L'Harmattan.

Zemp, Hugo. 1982. 'Deux à huit voix: Polyphonies de flûtes de Pan chez les Kwaio (Iles Salomon)', *Revue de Musicologie* 68/1–2: 275–309.

Žižek, Slavoj. 2004. *Organs without Bodies: Deleuze and Consequences.* New York and London: Routledge.

Zuckerkandl, Victor. 1956. *Sound and Symbol: Music and the External World.* Trans. Willard R. Trask. London: Routledge & Kegan Paul.

Recorded interviews

Boulez, Pierre and George Benjamin. BBC Radio 3 Interview on *... explosante-fixe* .... Broadcast 21 February 1997.

Boulez, Pierre and Paul Griffiths. BBC Radio 3 Interview on *Répons.* Broadcast on 10 September 1982.

Campbell, Edward. Unpublished Interview with Pierre Boulez. 28 August 1998.

Index